THE MARINE CORPS' SEARCH
FOR A MISSION, 1880–1898

THE MARINE CORPS' SEARCH FOR A MISSION, 1880–1898

Jack Shulimson

UNIVERSITY PRESS OF KANSAS

© 1993 by the University Press of Kansas
All rights reserved

Published by the University Press of Kansas (Lawrence, Kansas 66049), which was
organized by the Kansas Board of Regents and is operated and funded by Emporia
State University, Fort Hays State University, Kansas State University, Pittsburg
State University, the University of Kansas, and Wichita State University

Library of Congress Cataloging-in-Publication Data

Shulimson, Jack.
    The Marine Corps' search for a mission, 1880–1898 / Jack
Shulimson.
        p.   cm.—(Modern war studies)
    Includes bibliographical references and index.
    ISBN 0-7006-0608-4
    1. United States. Marine Corps—History. I. Title. II. Series.
VE23.S52   1993
359.9′6′0973—dc20   93-7181

British Library Cataloguing in Publication Data is available.

Printed in the United States of America
10 9 8 7 6 5 4 3 2 1

I wish to dedicate this book
to the memories of my parents,
Samuel William Shulimson and Sylvia Silverman Shulimson,
and to my father-in-law and mother-in-law,
Alexander Wittman and Fanny Cooper Wittman

CONTENTS

ILLUSTRATIONS

PREFACE

As a historian for the Marine Corps, it was natural for me to select a Marine topic for study, but there were other reasons for my focus on the Corps as well. In a sense, while still part of society, the scholar is always somewhat the outsider as he or she attempts to be an aloof, detached observer. This alienation is especially true for the historian, who, while molded by the past, can never recapture and always remains outside of it. As a civilian and historian for the Marine Corps, I am intimately connected with the Marine Corps in a way, but I still am not really a part of it, always the outsider looking in. In some respects, as a historian, this situation has advantages, because one asks questions that would never occur to those on the inside. More important, I discovered that I have something in common with the Marine Corps. Although serving with the Navy, the Corps has always remained somewhere on the fringes of naval service, not quite accepted and also on the outside looking in.

Although I originally thought I would concentrate on the early twentieth-century Marine Corps, I became intrigued by the fact that from 1883 until 1898, all newly commissioned Marine officers were graduates of the Naval Academy. The question of the Marine officer corps and its professional development interested me, and I soon became engrossed in studying the Marine officer corps and its relationship to developments in both the Navy and the Marine Corps—and to general trends in the United States as well. Using the concept of jurisdictional links as developed by sociologist Andrew Abbott in 1985, which ties together a profession, the work it does, and its relationship to other professions, I was able to establish connections not only between the Marine Corps and Navy, but also to the larger American society. In the final analysis, this book is a study of connections. In one sense, we may all be outsiders looking in, but on the other, there are the connecting links that bring us all into the human family.

Like any student, researcher, and writer, I was dependent upon the special expertise of several colleagues, associates, and archivists who were willing to share their knowledge or time. First, Professor Keith Olson of the History Department at the University of Maryland, my "unofficial" adviser, patiently read all my chapter drafts and made comments and provided insights that always improved the manuscript. Professor Allan Millett of Ohio State University read the manuscript and asked some probing questions that required a rethinking of my conclusions and a sharpening of my presentation. Professor Carol Reardon also provided special insight, Dr. Timothy K. Nenninger of the National Archives was always helpful in my search of Marine Corps and Navy records, and Maryellen Trautman of the National Archives Library guided me deftly through the maze of published government documents relating to the Marine Corps. A former colleague, Dr. Graham Cosmas, now of the U.S. Army Center of Military History, provided me with an expert reading of my Spanish-American War chapter, and another former colleague, Dr. V. Keith Fleming, served as an excellent sounding board for my developing ideas. Dr. Edgar F. Raines of the Center of Military History gave me the benefit of his research in Army records on the movement of Army artillery officers to form a coast defense artillery "marine corps" under the Navy. Lieutenant Colonel Merrill L. "Skip" Bartlett, USMC (Ret.), formerly on the history faculty of the U.S. Naval Academy, generously shared research notes and manuscript pages while working on his biography of Marine Commandant Major General John A. Lejeune.

Both Mr. Charles Anthony Wood and his successor J. Michael Miller at the Marine Corps Historical Center made the rich resources of their collections available for my perusal, and Mr. Richard Long provided me access to his unique set of files relating to nineteenth-century Marine Corps personalities. Evie Englander and the Marine Corps Library staff were always helpful as were Danny Crawford and the reference staff of the Marine Corps Historical Center, especially Mrs. Ann Ferrante and Mrs. Regina Struthers. I also benefited from the advice of Mr. John ("Jack") T. Dyer, Jr., the art curator of the center, in the selection of illustrations. Mr. Robert Struder of the editorial staff provided judicious advice, and Henry ("Bud") I. Shaw, Jr., and his successor as chief historian, Benis M. Frank, were most unselfish in sharing their extensive knowledge of Marine Corps history and lore. Colonel John E. Greenwood, Jr., USMC (Ret.), former deputy director of Marine Corps history and now editor of the *Marine Corps Gazette*, was a source of constant backing and encouragement. Brigadier General Edwin H. Simmons, USMC (Ret.), director of Marine Corps history and museums, supported and encouraged my educational and outside professional activities.

Mike Briggs of the University Press of Kansas always provided an encouraging word through the various reiterations of the draft manuscript, and Meredith Hartley expertly formatted my draft and carefully and skillfully inserted my revisions. Despite all this assistance, I alone am responsible for judgments and any factual errors. In no way do the opinions expressed in this book represent the views of the U.S. Marine Corps or the U.S. government.

I need also to mention the love and support of my immediate family. First, the three boys who loved to play with daddy's funny note cards: Mark, the eldest, who used to meet me on weekday evenings in the reading rooms of the Library of Congress; Kenneth, who occasionally could be persuaded to sit in the Archives and make lists of seemingly meaningless names; and Daniel, the youngest, who loved to ride the elevators but also helped to arrange the research cards in chronological order. The next generation begins with Samuel Aaron Shulimson, the new son of Mark and my attractive and talented daughter-in-law, Jody Pollack Shulimson. Finally, there is Corinne, still my lovely bride, who refused to type one page of manuscript but made everything else possible.

1. INTRODUCTION: PROFESSIONALISM AND REFORM

In December 1880, Marine Capt. Henry Clay Cochrane, recently promoted after eighteen years of military service, caustically entered in his diary, "a great year in the M.C. [Marine Corps]." He then recorded a litany of misfortunes that had befallen the officer corps: one lieutenant had died in a riding accident, another had been sent "home insane," and still another had been dismissed for cause. A Navy court-martial had convicted a senior Marine colonel for behavior unbecoming an officer, and the Philadelphia police had arrested a Marine major for drunkenly accosting women in the street. Reform legislation that would modestly expand the officer corps and open up promotions remained stalled in Congress, and the President's appointment of a well-connected junior lieutenant to a prime staff position over thirty of his seniors had caused much rancor. There was little, noted Cochrane, to encourage that "small band of officers" who had "battled many years" for reform of the Corps.[1]

During the days of sail, Marine sharpshooters, positioned in the fighting tops of men of war, cleared the decks of opposing ships with musket fire. When this mission receded with the coming of steam, Marines continued to assist in manning gun batteries and serving as ships' police. They also formed the nucleus of any landing party. On shore, Marines provided the security forces to protect naval installations. Occasionally, when needed, the Marine Corps formed ad hoc battalions to keep the peace or to reinforce the Army.[2]

By the late 1870s the Marine Corps was an organizational anomaly and in some disarray. Dispersed into small detachments of usually 100 men or less, the Marine Corps had no formal company, battalion, or regimental structure. In 1876, a budget conscious Congress had reduced the rank of the commandant from brigadier general to colonel, cut enlisted strength from about 3,000 to 2,000 men, and restricted further second-lieutenant appoint-

1

ments until the officer corps numbered 75. Marine reformers among the younger officers called either for a "funeral or a resuscitation" for the Corps.[3]

During the three decades following the Civil War, the Marine officer corps underwent a metamorphosis. At the beginning of the period, influence was the usual avenue of entry, older officers were apathetic, and junior and company grade officers faced long, frustrating years with little prospect for promotion. By the turn of the century, both entry into and promotion within the officer corps depended upon passing relatively stringent examinations, many officers were graduates of the Naval Academy, and some had attended advanced schools of both the Army and the Navy. The Spanish-American War and internal reform were only partly responsible for the transformation.

The Marine officer experience was only one result of the several large trends that altered all aspects of American life during this period. Among the most important of these impulses were technological change, advances in formal knowledge, an expanding industrialism, a restructuring of both private and public organizations, and a pervasive professionalization of American society. Whether called "a search for order," "the visible hand," or "the organizational revolution," the dominant feature of the entire process was an avowed emphasis upon rationality and control. The result was a general corporate organization of society and the beginning of the age of the specialist and the manager. Almost all scholars who have looked at the late nineteenth century have noted the "great divide" that differentiates that period from the twentieth century. As Thomas Haskell wrote, it was "a world full of the familiar phenomena of an urban-industrial society, but quaintly out of focus, as if seen through eyes accustomed to a different order of human existence."[4]

This basic change in the structure of American life was the result, not of violent convulsions, but "silent" and almost imperceptible revolutions in everyday life. One aspect of this "silent revolution" was the growth of large and complex organizations; another was the coming to the fore of the professions and the professional.[5]

During the latter half of the nineteenth century, the professions, like the corporation, took on their modern cast. With the industrialization and urbanization of American life, there was a virtual explosion of professional groups and organizations. The older professions like medicine and law were reborn while newer professions and professional associations emerged. In 1867, engineers established the American Society of Civil Engineers. Historians organized the American Historical Association in 1884 and the next year economists formed the American Economic Association. Of the fifty-eight professional organizations formed during the nineteenth century, thirty-seven, or over 60 percent, came into existence between the years 1870 and 1900. The new associations reflected an increasing specialization and tendency toward technology in response to the industrialization of the new machine age.[6]

The new professions that arose took shape in an increasingly institution-alized and bureaucratic context. As the professions developed, they also be-came more interdependent on one another. Within this relatively elaborate intertwining of interests, the professions worked out their relationships with each other and with society. Engineers, accountants, and even lawyers worked for large corporations. The modern university provided the institu-tional framework for many of the professionals of the newer social sciences.[7]

Although there is general agreement about the centrality of the profes-sions to the social and economic structure of modern civilization, there are wide differences of opinion in the scholarly community about the nature of professionalism. Some would restrict the discussion to such professions as the law and medicine, while others write articles about the professionaliza-tion of nearly everyone. There is even disagreement whether there is a stan-dard definition of professionalism, or whether there is even a need of such a definition. As one recent author observed, the debate has resulted in a "confusion so profound that there are even disagreements about the exis-tence of the confusion."[8]

Although much of the discussion of professionalism remains mired in dis-putation about traits, functions, and power, sociologist Andrew Abbott has suggested that scholars have left unexamined the actual work that profes-sions do.[9] For Abbott, it is not the characteristics or structure of profession-alism that is significant but rather the work the profession performs, how it controls that work, and its relationship with similar or competing profes-sions. According to Abbott, the essential element of professionalism is the link between the profession and its work. He calls this link "jurisdiction." Abbott concludes that to study professionalism, one must determine "how this link is created by work, how it is anchored by formal and informal social structure, and how the interplay of jurisdictional links between professions determines the history of the individual professions themselves."[10]

From the perspective of intersecting jurisdictions, Abbott argues, one can determine how professions develop, how they relate to one another, and what is the basis of the work they do. He insists that the professions form an interdependent "ecology." According to Abbott, professions do not stand

alone, but also are not encompassed by any overarching theory of professionalism: "They exist in a system." The system, however, is a complex one.
Changes in one area may work through the entire system of professions, but
more likely this "ripple effect" is confined to "one general task area, through
the rearrangement of jurisdictions, the strengthening of some, the weakening of others." Thus, the interaction of professions in any given instance is
usually limited to general task areas. Assuming that the profession of military officer is one such task area or system within the general system of professionalism, Abbott's construct provides a most fruitful framework.[11]

Using Abbott's construct and carrying it one step further, one can make
the case that for the military profession, jurisdiction is where the outside
forces of society, the individual military organization or service, and professionalism all come together. During the nineteenth century, the driving societal force was the new technology and industrialism which revolutionized
warfare both on land and on the sea. For the Navy officer it resulted in a
professional jurisdiction based upon organization, technology, and the strategic concept of sea power; for the Army officer, it created a jurisdiction
based upon organization, new weaponry, and the study of land warfare. In
contrast to both the Navy and Army officer, the Marine officer had no such
clear demarcation of jurisdictional responsibility. While sharing many of the
same attributes of both the Army and Navy officer, the Marine officer's jurisdiction revolved around organization and mission.[12]

By the end of the nineteenth century, both the U.S. Army and the U.S.
Navy officer corps had taken on attributes of professionalism common to all
the modern professions. Retaining its unstructured and individualistic character past the Civil War, the U.S. Army officer corps as early as the Jackso-
nian period had developed an intellectual and scientific approach to warfare. Although the U.S. military traced its beginnings to a revolutionary
struggle against monarchy, it had adopted much of the professional ethos of
the European military with an emphasis on such aristocratic values as courage, solidarity, personal fealty, and a highly developed sense of honor.[13]

Following the Napoleonic Wars, the entire concept of warfare changed.
New tactics, larger armies, and complex administrative and logistic problems required new thinking about warfare and an emphasis upon organization and planning. The officer had to be the "manager" of violence and still
remain the "heroic" leader of previous ages.[14]

Ironically, the "inner elite" of one of the "most caste-bound and privi-
leged officer corps in Europe," the Prussian, stood in the vanguard of the

new military order. Although "spiritually pre-industrial neo-feudalist warriors" in outlook, the Prussian Junkers were the first to organize themselves for modern war. Their major achievement was the Great General Staff. Originating with the reforms of Gerhard von Scharnhorst after the debacle of Jena in 1806, the General Staff emphasized military theory, doctrine, and officer education.[15]

The evolution of the German General Staff was symptomatic that the same rationalistic impulses at work in the rest of Western society also operated upon the military. Industrialism and technology brought new implications to warfare. The improvements in small arms and ammunition, the development of rifled artillery, and the appearance of the steam engine all tended to extend the battlefield or area of operations, both on land and at sea. This more fluid environment for the military demanded "continuous improvisation and initiative." With the Germans leading the way, military officers "exhibited qualities of mind common to any manager of a large-scale enterprise."[16]

U.S. military officers were well aware of the professional trends in Europe. Prior to the Civil War, French influences were dominant with an emphasis upon fortifications, artillery, engineering, and tactics. Both the U.S. Military Academy, established in 1802, and the Naval Academy, established in 1845, focused largely on the technical, with an emphasis on the engineering, aspects of military art. A few experimental post-graduate schools concentrated on specialties such as engineering and artillery. Denis Mahan, the father of the future Admiral Alfred Thayer Mahan, taught a generation of Army officers at West Point the principles of Jomini and stressed rapid movements, lines of communication, and strategic points. Mahan maintained that "military science was a specialized body of knowledge understandable only through intense study." Yet, this budding antebellum military professionalism with its narrow technical predilection neglected the Clausewitzian dictum for the decisive battle and awareness that war was a bloody, violent, and often chaotic affair. Emory Upton, then at West Point and later to become the Army's leading theorist, perhaps spoke more perspicaciously than he realized at the time when he stated on the eve of the Civil War, "Our profession differs from all others. . . . It is a profession of fate and a fatal profession."[17]

In the ordeal of the Civil War, the American military learned to raise massive armies and deploy and resupply them by rail and water. They also used weapons with increased range and faster rates of fire and ironclad ships of war. The price of military victory for the Union forces was high and was paid for in human lives: 1,095,000 casualties for both sides, 640,000 Union soldiers and sailors, and 455,000 Confederates.[18]

Despite the massive bloodletting of the Civil War, its immediate impact on the U.S. military structure was relatively small. The government quickly demobilized large wartime forces and both the U.S. Army and U.S. Navy returned to their prewar missions—the Army to fighting the Indians, and the Navy to showing the flag in less developed areas and protecting American maritime interests. One new duty was the preservation of internal law and order. Army garrisons policed the South during the Reconstruction period, and soldiers, sailors, and Marines protected the railroads during the labor unrest of 1877. It was a period of low military appropriations, slow promotion, and general demoralization. By the end of the 1870s, the U.S. regular military establishment numbered only 38,000 men, constituting only 2 percent of the total U.S. labor force, 1 percent less than the armed forces of 1860.[19]

Yet, this same rather dismal period with all of its debilitating effects on the armed forces also was one of professional growth. Working "against inertia in an atmosphere of distrust," the more forward-looking American military officers continued to keep abreast of European developments despite lack of money, men, and material. These relatively few reform-minded officers, aware of their own experience of modern combat in the Civil War and influenced by German writing and thinking, attempted to restructure and modernize their own services. With the support of certain strategically placed, high-ranking officers, such as General of the Army William T. Sherman, Vice Admiral of the Navy David D. Porter, and Rear Adm. Stephen B. Luce, the reformers were able to bring about a revival and transformation of American military professionalism to meet the demands of war in an industrial age.[20]

The first manifestation of the new professionalism lay in an expansion of officer education and associations. General Sherman and Admirals Porter and Luce were avid supporters of post-graduate training for military officers. Sherman believed that West Point was only the beginning of the education of a military officer. Admiral Porter thought that the Naval Academy was too narrow and had a "tendency to make a man a machine, confine his intellectual faculties within a certain sphere and take from him that independence of thought." Porter advocated that a naval officer should receive "a more liberal education" once he had completed the course at Annapolis and served some time at sea. Influenced by both General Sherman and Admiral Porter, Rear Admiral Luce proposed to various secretaries of the Navy the establishment of a Naval War College where naval officers could study "the science of their own profession—the science of war."[21]

The Army started its advanced officer-education program shortly after the Civil War. The Artillery School resumed its course of instruction at Fortress Monroe, Virginia, in 1868, and the Engineering School of Application at Willett's Point, New York, also opened its doors about the same time. General Sherman installed his protégé Col. Emory Upton as the superintendent of the Artillery School in 1877. Upton had just returned from a world tour during which he studied "the organization, tactics, and educational systems of foreign armies." While at the Artillery School, Upton published his *The Armies of Asia and Europe* and resumed work on *The Military Policy of the United States.* Influenced by the German military educational and staff system, Upton unsuccessfully campaigned to alter the American military structure. At the artillery school, he implemented some reforms, taught the new developments in artillery and their implications for the battlefield, and added history, strategy, and logistics to the curriculum. A few years later, General Sherman emplaced what was to be the capstone of the Army educational system for over twenty years, the School of Application for Infantry and Cavalry at Fort Leavenworth, Kansas. To the Army reformers, the purpose of this advanced education, in the words of Upton, was to "form a corps of officers who in any future contest may prove the chief reliance of the Government."[22]

The Army made the first steps in officer education immediately after the Civil War, but naval officers took the lead in the establishment of a professional organization complete with its own journal. In the fall of 1873, a number of naval officers serving in Washington and Annapolis formed the United States Naval Institute. According to one of the founders, Lt. Theodorus B. M. Mason, they modeled themselves after the Royal United Service Institute of Great Britain. Meeting on October 9, 1873, in the lecture room of the Department of Physics and Chemistry at the Naval Academy, the assembled officers became "a sort of mutual learning company." Two months later, on December 11, they adopted a formal constitution with the stated object to advance the "professional and scientific knowledge in the Navy." Membership was open to all officers of the Navy and Marine Corps and to the academic staff of the Naval Academy. At the monthly meetings, one or two officers would read a paper on some aspect of naval warfare, technology, or organization and then the floor would open to general discussion. In 1874, the Institute began publishing the papers presented at the meetings in its official journal, appropriately called the *Proceedings of the U.S. Naval Institute.* Although the Institute wanted to inculcate open debate on all issues, Lieutenant Mason observed that most of the articles in the *Proceedings* dealt with historical events because of "the diffidence of officers to launch out and express their opinions on the questions of the day." Yet, historians of the next century would agree that the Institute and its *Proceedings* served as both a "forum and clearing house" of naval professional thought and "as a progenitor and disseminator of seminal ideas."[23]

Army officers soon followed the example of their naval colleagues. In 1878, a group of Army officers living in New York City formed the Military Service Institute of the United States. Like their Navy brethren, the founders credited the Royal United Service Institute for their inspiration. Concerned about the professional isolation of Army officers scattered among the garrisons and small posts around the nation and especially in the West, they desired to provide a "beneficial interchange of views and profitable recitals of experience." Like the Naval Institute, the Military Service Institute started its own journal, *Journal of the Military Institute*. Eventually other smaller and more specialized military professional organizations came into existence, such as the Cavalry Association and the Infantry Society, each with its own professional journal. Throughout this period, there was a "flowering of professional associations and military periodical literature."[24]

American military professionals were not isolated from American society, but, in fact, were subject to the same basic influences as their counterparts in the civilian world. As the technological and organizational revolutions of the late nineteenth century transformed American life, they also had their impact on the military profession. With the termination of Reconstruction and the end of the Indian wars, the Army and Navy looked beyond the borders and across the seas to meet the new challenges of a world made smaller by the steam engine and the development of armored men of war and modern gunnery. Reflecting modern societal trends, military officers emphasized efficiency and the desire to prepare for war "scientifically." Drawing their "technical inspiration from foreign military models," American military reformers obtained their "political strength from the nation's emerging civilian professional elite." A more aggressive American foreign policy in the last two decades of the nineteenth century gave military professionals a legitimacy they had not previously possessed.[25]

Military professionalism did not evolve in a single line. Both the Navy and Army were complex multifaceted organizations. The broad rubric of military officer contained various specialties with varied interests and ambitions. Within the Navy, for example, there were line officers, engineers, surgeons, paymasters, and naval constructors, not to mention the Marines, each with his own specific skills and each competing for part of the naval budget. Large independent bureaus, mostly made up of staff officers, wielded great power within both the Army and Navy, and especially with Congress. In both services, divisive differences often existed between line and staff. This occasionally acrimonious debate between staff and line was more than a simple struggle for power, but was in actuality a struggle for recognition and the establishment of jurisdictions by conflicting military professionals. Both Navy and Army line officers interpreted military officership in the narrow sense of command on the battlefield or on board ship. They viewed other officers and the bureaus as merely support to their own activities. Although not differing with the line officers over the general functions of the Army and Navy, the bureau and staff officers wanted to retain control of their own discreet organizations. Although willing to cooperate and consult with the line, the bureaus and staffs "used all their resources at the intersects of power" within the services and with Congress "to gain acceptance as valuable soldiers of the Republic."[26]

As part of the federal government, the military could not hope to escape the political realities of the time. The president appointed his secretaries of Army and Navy for their political strengths, not because of their military expertise. Military officers were dependent upon the patronage system for their initial appointments to West Point or Annapolis or for their direct commissions into the service, and political sponsorship often assured officers career-enhancing positions and assignments. Individual congressmen and senators generally were not interested in broad questions of military policy and organization, but were very concerned with questions of patronage. As one writer observed, "Perhaps nothing caused so many irritations to so many members of the House and Senate as their failure to have their way in the thousands of small appointments that were required across the country from year to year." Military professionals, such as Emory Upton, who challenged the political system directly, often ended up defeated and frustrated. Most successful military officers became adept at bureaucratic politics. Remarking on the political adroitness of the military, one historian concluded, "Military services acted much as pressure groups, exploiting their contacts with those in positions of influence and using public-relations techniques to create general support for military reform."[27]

In the broadest sense, reform and professionalism were attempts to come to grips with the emerging modern world. The motives of the military reformers and professionals were not entirely altruistic and free from either institutional or individual self-serving. It may be an overstatement, as one naval historian has argued, to say that "career anxieties . . . not only for one's own career, but for the Service as a whole" lay behind the reform and professional impulse of the "naval aristocracy." There is, however, more than a germ of truth in this contention, but perhaps more to the point is that "the untidy use of power in a democracy was simply masked by the illusion that it was systematically and rationally organized." Another historian observed that the Navy of the late nineteenth century was a "paradise for the historian or sociologist in search of a society's response to change." If this is true for the Navy, it applies equally as well if not more so to the Marine Corps.[28]

The Marine officers of the last decades of the nineteenth century accommodated slowly and with difficulty to the sudden challenges in organization and mission that the modern era posed. In the decade following the Civil War, despite the appearance of a nascent reform movement, Marine officers failed to agree among themselves about their own role or that of their service.

During the 1880s, naval reformers and professionals inaugurated an intellectual ferment within the Navy that led to new thinking about naval warfare that tied the Marine Corps and its officers closer to the Navy. Curiously, most Marine reformers played only a peripheral role since they viewed progress and professionalism in narrow terms. They sought to make the Marine Corps an elite guard force for the Navy concentrating on raising officer standards, improving discipline, and cutting desertion rates. Their efforts to push reform measures through Congress, however, proved fruitless. It was only a legislative fluke that finally resulted in new Marine officers coming from the Naval Academy, the only major innovation during this period. Although the Navy professionals had no great love for the Marine Corps, they were willing to use the Marine Corps to further their own interests. Only a few Marine nonconformists sought out new directions for their Corps.

With the new steel Navy becoming a reality the United States shifted to a naval policy of control of the seas, at least in American coastal waters and in the Caribbean. These developments led to new opportunities for Marine officer professionalism as well as new hazards. A Navy board recommended the removal of Marines from naval warships, while on the other hand, the Navy's first contingency planning effort in 1890 called for Marines to be the major component of any landing force on enemy shores.

In 1891 the new Marine Commandant, Charles Heywood, influenced by the Marine reform element, introduced several measures to raise officer professionalism. These included more stringent promotion standards and the establishment of a School of Application. At the same time, the retirement of several senior officers opened promotion opportunities. Some Naval

Academy cadets sought out the Marine Corps because it actually offered faster immediate promotion than the Navy.

Heywood also attempted to identify the mission of the Marine Corps with that of the Navy. He tried to assign Marine ships' detachments under their own officers to the secondary gun batteries of the new steel armored ships. This endeavor backfired because it brought the Marines into conflict with the Navy progressives. In what amounted to a jurisdictional dispute, younger naval professionals pushed openly to remove Marine detachments from warships.

Through the years prior to the Spanish-American War, minor skirmishes continued to revolve around the secondary battery and Marine ship-detachment issues. An aborted attempt by Army artillery officers to form a Marine artillery organization under the Navy complicated the situation even further. At the same time, the Marine Corps School of Application flourished, Marine officer standards continued to be raised, and Marine officers attended the Naval War College and served on the faculty of that institution. During these years, reform merged with officer professionalism and institutional and individual self-interest. These factors combined with patronage politics in Congress and in the Navy Department to provide the background for the playing out of the Marine and Navy officer relationships during this period. At the end of 1897, the secretary of the Navy created a Navy Personnel Board, which examined the possible amalgamation of the Marine officer corps with that of the Navy. Obviously, despite the advances in the attainment of the outward professional attributes of the military officer, the Marine officer had failed to achieve a clear jurisdictional link with the Navy.

The Spanish-American War and its immediate aftermath served as a benchmark for the Marine Corps. Although prewar Navy contingency planning implied the use of a Marine Corps landing force, there was still no clear mission for the Marine Corps at the outset of the war. Nevertheless, the ad hoc Marine battalion mobilized in April 1898 provided an advanced base for the fleet blockading Santiago de Cuba. Moreover, disputes between the Army and Navy commanders over the conduct of the Santiago campaign convinced naval professionals that they could not depend upon the Army to secure bases for fleet purposes. In 1900, the Navy General Board's assignment of the advance base mission to the Marine Corps finally gave the Marine officer that clear connection to the Navy that had eluded him over the previous two decades.

The interaction between Navy and Marine officers depended upon two strains of professionalism: the first was distinguished by the outward characteristics or attributes of the military officer, and the second was based upon the jurisdictional links between the two officer groups. Influenced by the increasing demands of new ship technology, the new Navy professionals questioned the very relevance of the Marine officer and even the existence of his Corps. This phenomena occurred simultaneously with a growing reform movement within the Marine officer corps itself and demands for improving the recruitment of Marine officers and increasing standards of performance. These appurtenances of professionalism appeared at the very same time as the Marine officer professional jurisdiction entered a state of flux. The resulting dynamics created a tension that influenced both the professionalization of the Marine officer corps and the institutional survival of the Marine Corps itself.

2. THE OLD CORPS: A FEW TENTATIVE STEPS, 1865–1880

In the years following the Civil War, the Marine Corps experienced much of the same "doldrums" as the other military services. It was a period of austere budgets, fewer personnel, and reduced expectations. Marine officers feared amalgamation with the Army or the simple abolishment of their Corps. A brooding institutional "anxiety" would dominate the history of the Marine Corps for the next few decades, and Marine officer reform and professionalism would be haphazard, at best.

Much of the torpor within the Corps rested with the quality of its officers. The war had brought only marginal improvement in officer recruitment. To make up for defections to the Confederacy and to meet wartime requirements, the Marine Corps commissioned from 1861 to 1865 more than 75 new officers. Because of patriotic fervor and other wartime inducements, these officers probably were equal to, if not better than, those recruited prior to the war. Yet, their background more or less was the same as the older officers. They were either patronage appointments or sons of military officers and political officials. Several of the new officers had received appointments to the Naval Academy or West Point and failed to complete the course of instruction for one reason or another. One Marine officer observed: "There are lots of ex-naval students in the service. Looking down the register I see no less than eight who graduated at the back door." Marine Lt. Henry Clay Cochrane remembered that in July 1861, when Congress created 30 new vacancies in the Corps, he estimated there were about 500 to 2,000 applicants. He remarked: "It took about as much influence to get . . . [a Marine Corps commission] as to get any other government appointment three times as valuable. . . ."[1]

Following the Civil War, the same pattern of patronage selection continued. One newspaper notice announced that a Marine Corps examining board was to interview prospective officer candidates. According to the an-

nouncement, there were over 500 applicants for six vacancies. The requirements for candidacy were relatively simple: applicants were to be between
the ages of twenty and twenty-five; they were to apply directly to the president of the United States through the secretary of the Navy; and "they must
pass examinations in reading, writing, spelling, arithmetic, geography, and
English grammar. . . ." The secretary of the Navy, however, determined who
would take the examinations and most often made his decision on the basis
of dispensing political favors. Admiral of the Navy David D. Porter used his
own considerable influence in the dispensation of Marine commissions. His
son, Carlisle P. Porter, a former Naval Academy midshipman who failed to
graduate and later served in the Volunteer Navy during the Civil War, received a Marine Corps commission in December 1866.[2]

During this period, Marine officers became more and more demoralized
as they realized they faced deadly routine at both sea and shore stations
with little promise of professional challenge or promotion. In 1871, Marine
Capt. Robert T. Huntington wrote home despairingly to his father, "I get
out the register and make calculations of how long it will take for me to be a
major, and I can't see so far ahead as that." He doubted he would attain that
rank in thirty years when he would be forced to retire. Still, individual officers undertook certain ventures in hopes of bringing about change.[3]

In this relative nadir of Marine fortunes and officer professionalism, Marine
Capt. James Forney, at the behest of the secretary of the Navy, visited Europe for over a year to examine foreign Marine Corps and their accommodation to the new "iron ships." Forney, the son of John Forney, a prominent
Philadelphia newspaperman active in Republican politics, entered the Marine Corps in 1861. He served with distinction during the war, breveted
three times, and breveted once again after the war in 1867 when he commanded a Marine landing party against "savages" on Formosa. Captain Forney departed the United States in July 1872. He travelled to England, Spain,
France, Italy, and Turkey and also took charge of the U.S. naval exhibit at
the Universal Exhibition in Vienna. He returned to Philadelphia in September 1873 and prepared his report for the secretary.[4]

Captain Forney submitted a 422–page account together with a 30–page
synopsis of his observations of foreign Marine Corps and his recommendations for his own Corps. He devoted over 300 pages to the British Royal Marines, describing uniforms, training, drill, composition, and organization.
The British Marines at that time contained some 14,000 men with about
half on sea duty. In contrast to the American Marines, the British were orga-

nized into companies consisting of both artillery and infantry. Forney also depicted the French, Spanish, German, and Italian Marines, although he used the Royal Marines as his standard of measurement for the U.S. Marine Corps.[5]

In his report, Forney recommended a brigade organization for the U.S. Marine Corps, with a brigadier general in command and three permanent regiments. He proposed training in both artillery and infantry and schools to teach the latest procedures and techniques. Contrasting unfavorably the professional preparation of new U.S. Marine officers to those of the Royal Marines, Forney advised against commissioning from civilian life. Instead, he suggested that all new Marine officers should be graduates of West Point. Captain Forney called for a general increase in officers and continued officer training and examination.[6]

Forney concluded, "If the Marines are so useful in England . . . they are even more so in these United States, with our very small regular force, scattered in the territories, and hardly even available in local tumults or in the hazardous service of distant seas." He foresaw more "direct communication with the Orient and a growing trade and predicted, "Our present Navy will undoubtedly increase with the increase of our commerce and possessions." Believing that "additions to our squadrons and improvements in their armaments and discipline are therefore among the reasonable certainties of the future," Forney argued, "The increase and revision of the organization of the Marine Corps will naturally follow."[7]

Despite some favorable publicity in William Conant Church's influential *Army and Navy Journal* as a sign of rejuvenation of the Marine Corps, Forney's recommendations largely fell on fallow ground in the Navy Department. Although a *Journal* article reported that the secretary of the Navy would include the synopsis in his *Annual Report*, he never did. By the end of the following year, the Marine Corps was in one of its perennial struggles for survival.[8]

In December 1874, based on speculation that the House of Representatives Committee on Appropriations would recommend either the abolishment of the Marine Corps or its transfer to the Army, several Marine officers formed a secret organization to deter any such action. Meeting at the Marine Barracks in Washington, the officers adopted several resolutions, including the formation of an executive committee and the assessment of dues to cover expenses. Among the recommendations of the meeting was a proposal to underwrite the publication of material that would show the Marine Corps in a favorable light.[9]

Apparently the Marine officer association participated to some extent in the fairly strenuous public relations campaign that followed. Two publications appeared in 1875. The first was the republication—in an enlarged edition of the pamphlet first published in 1864—of statements of support for the Marine Corps by prominent naval officers. The thrust of the revised pamphlet was that the Marine Corps was a vital part of the Navy, needed to keep discipline on board ship, to guard the Navy yards, and to make up part of a naval landing brigade. Most of the old letters were reprinted along with more contemporary ones. Navy Capt. Stephen Luce argued cogently against any move to abolish the Corps and did not wish to see the "Marine Corps interfered with except for improving it." He suggested that Marine officers be "admitted to the military school at West Point for a four years' course." Navy Capt. John Walker stressed the importance of the Marines and recommended the formation of both Marine infantry and artillery with the latter garrisoning seaboard forts and the appointment of new officers from the Naval Academy.[10]

At about the same time as the publication of the pamphlet, the first history of the Marine Corps appeared, compiled by Marine Capt. Richard S. Collum. Although one of the number of "bilged" midshipmen from the Naval Academy who received a Marine commission during the Civil War, Collum was well versed in military history and literature and had worked on the history for over two years. He provided the draft of the manuscript, and a professional journalist, Almy M. Aldrich, edited the volume and took author credit.[11]

The history itself was rather undistinguished, consisting largely of a description of Marine battle exploits and large excerpts from the annual reports of the secretary of the Navy and the commandant of the Marine Corps. Unhappy with Aldrich's alterations of his original draft, Collum vowed to revise the book at a later date "without the aid of a journalist." The Marine captain claimed that he received no money from the sale of the volume and that his only motive was to place "the service of our Corps before the public in a true light." There is no proof of any specific relationship between the Marine officers association and the history, but it would not be surprising if the association provided part of the subsidization for the book's printing.[12]

The most remarkable feature of the Aldrich history was an introductory essay by Captain Luce in which Luce traced the use of Marines back to the ancient Phoenicians and Greeks. Although there is no direct evidence that

Luce had access to the Forney report, he made many of the same observations and comparisons. He noted that most leading naval powers such as Great Britain and Germany found the need for a Marine Corps, and like Forney, he compared the professional preparation of officers of the United States Marine Corps with that of the Royal Marines and found it wanting. Luce, too, recommended that new Marine officers attend West Point and that the Marine Corps adopt a permanent brigade organization. He viewed the mission of the Marine Corps for the most part in the traditional manner as "sharpshooters" and guard detachments on board ship. Yet, Luce used phrases such as the Marines should provide "the necessary military element of our sea-forces," and quoted Lord Nelson approvingly that "every fleet should have a perfect battalion of Marines, and, commanded by experienced officers, they would be prepared to make a serious impression on the enemy's coast."[13]

In October 1875, Lt. Henry Clay Cochrane, who had earlier worked on a draft of legislation affecting the Marine Corps, decided to issue a clarion call for reform. In a confidential pamphlet that he circulated among the officer corps, Cochrane opened with the blunt statement: "That there is a deep seated and wide spread antipathy toward the Marine Corps only the blind and imbecile can doubt." Cochrane claimed that the Marine Corps was "Neither Respected Nor Respectable" and stated that the purpose of his pamphlet was "to arouse every officer to the necessity of some action that will make us respectable and useful." Cochrane then presented several recommendations to rehabilitate the Corps. He demanded mandatory retirement at age sixty-two, examinations for promotion, officer vacancies to be filled by Naval Academy or West Point graduates, a brigade organization with permanent regiments, and the fleet Marine officer to hold the rank of major. Cochrane also referred to the possibility of redesignating the Marine Corps as the United States Naval Artillery. In his concluding argument, he observed, "I feel that at present we have no . . . special incentive to anything beyond the mere mechanical performance of a monotonous routine and the idle gratification of social instincts; that we lack inducement and encouragement more than capacity or inclination; and that with something to work for . . . we can make a far different showing."[14]

In his pamphlet, Cochrane advocated that the Marine officers take their case directly to Congress and support his proposed bill that contained the reform measures that he had laid out. He noted that in the past, Marine officers contented themselves " 'with keeping quiet,' clandestinely prowling around the Capitol in citizens' clothes to avoid observation, and repeating the old, old story of gathering certificates of character from naval officers . . .

with which we beg, cap in hand, our annual appropriation—with only partial success." He pointed out that the chairman of the House Naval Affairs Committee had called for the abolishment of the Marine Corps stating in effect that the Corps was "a parasite on the body of the Government . . . and a barnacle on the hull of the Navy." Cochrane remarked that only fortuitous circumstances prevented Congress from acting against the Marine Corps during the previous session. According to Cochrane, only sweeping new legislation would suffice to turn things around and permit the Marine Corps to reform itself and survive.[15]

Cochrane was not alone in his efforts. Prior to and after the publication of his pamphlet, letters appeared in the Washington newspapers and especially in the *Army and Navy Journal* calling for a "grand reform" of the Marine Corps. The *Journal* itself in September referred to a special meeting of concerned officers and in an editorial cited the need for a "transfusion of new blood" into the Corps. This movement among the officers differed from that of the previous year, seeming to be confined to the more junior and "progressive" officers. Somehow, a Washington newspaper, *The Chronicle*, obtained a copy of one of the confidential letters and published it. The author, Marine Capt. Robert Huntington, admitted that he was addressing only the younger and "progressive officers in the Corps." According to Huntington, the Marine Corps consisted of two elements, the progressive and the conservative, largely divided by age and seniority: "To the one, the present is the best moment; the other looks to the future. It is the irrepressible conflict between conservatism and progress." Most of the advocates of reform wanted a mandatory retirement age of sixty-two which would mean that the then commandant, Brig. Gen. Jacob Zeilin, would have to step down. Huntington counseled that junior officers should organize to influence the enactment of legislation that would ensure the appointment of an officer to the commandancy "who will adorn that position." Huntington observed, "However just and proper our cause may be, it will not succeed unless we can influence the press and lobby."[16]

While the 1876 Naval Appropriation Act resulted in reductions of the officer and enlisted strength of the Marine Corps, the Marine lobbying effort had succeeded in keeping the losses at a minimum. The reformers continued to exchange opinions and hope for the best. Their focus, however, changed to the succession of the commandancy as General Zeilin announced his pending retirement. On October 25, in his final report, he took exception to those who recommended major changes in the Marine Corps structure. Zeilin defended the status quo, declaring, "The present organization of the

Marine Corps is the best that can be devised." Six days later he stepped down from office.[17]

With a reputation as a traditionalist and strict disciplinarian verging toward the martinet, Col. Charles G. McCawley, Zeilin's successor, was neither the first nor last choice of the reformers. Not necessarily privy to the confidences of the reform group, but sharing with its members some similar goals, McCawley desired to improve the officer corps and to make the Marine Corps a more efficient and elite military organization. Relatively conservative, however, McCawley foresaw no new mission for the Marine Corps and remained satisfied with its ad hoc organization. Thus, a McCawley commandancy promised some reform, but limited, if any, change in the traditional mission and organization of the Corps.[18]

With the 1876 legislation that suspended officer appointments until the number of officers reached 75 either through dismissal, retirement, or resignation, McCawley attempted to cleanse the service of several of its chief mischiefmakers. Wanting to make an example for others, the commandant pressed court-martial charges against the worst offenders. In March 1877, Colonel McCawley recommended charges against 2d Lt. Julius C. Shailer, who not only borrowed money without paying from his fellow officers, but also from enlisted men. Within a month, Lieutenant Shailer proffered his resignation. McCawley also forced the resignation of 1st Lt. Edward T. Bradford, whom the commandant observed "has been reported more frequently [than any other officer] for not paying his debts." A first lieutenant, Andrew Stevenson, described by a fellow officer as "a liar with the lowest instincts" and "unfit to associate with gentlemen," escaped the commandant's dragnet, however, by first offering his resignation and then withdrawing it once charges against him were dropped. Nevertheless, the *Army and Navy Journal* assessed McCawley's first year in the commandancy as one that contributed to a marked improvement in the morale of the Marine Corps and observed that in the officer corps, "Three old offenders will not appear in next year's registers."[19]

Despite his modest success in winnowing out the chaff among the officers, Colonel McCawley quickly learned the limitations of his power relative to officer assignment. In early 1877, soon after becoming commandant, he attempted to appoint Col. M. R. Kintzing, the Corps' most senior officer, to the much-sought-after command of the Brooklyn Navy Yard Marine Barracks. Maj. John L. Broome, who had held this prized position for over ten years, was not about to give up his post voluntarily. He quickly appealed to

Col. Charles G. McCawley, eighth commandant of the U.S. Marine Corps (1876–1891). He was neither the first nor the last choice of the Marine officer reform group. (Marine Corps Historical Center Collection)

politically influential patrons to take his case to the secretary of the Navy. In April 1877, the leading Democratic member of the Senate Naval Affairs Committee, Senator James McPherson of New Jersey, wrote to the secretary asking that Broome be retained at Brooklyn, arguing that Broome "had the esteem of the most prominent men of Brooklyn of both political parties." Despite the vehement protest of Colonel Kintzing, the navy secretary over-ruled McCawley and kept Major Broome at Brooklyn. The secretary denied that his action reflected negatively on Kintzing's reputation as an officer and a gentleman, but merely the desire "not to disturb the present arrangements at Brooklyn."[20]

Political considerations were even more important when it came to staff appointments, which congressmen often viewed as personal favors to be dis-tributed as they saw fit. The death of Marine Corps Paymaster John Cash in March 1877 led to a scramble for the vacant post. As one naval officer ob-served, "The position will be given to an officer of the Corps and probably the one who has the most influence." Admiral Porter wrote personally to the new president, Rutherford B. Hayes, in favor of the candidacy of his son, Marine Lt. Carlisle P. Porter. The leading applicant, however, was 1st Lt. Green Clay Goodloe, a member of a prominent Kentucky political fam-ily. Goodloe's uncle, Green Clay Smith, was a Union general and former ambassador to Russia. More important, Goodloe's fiancée was the daughter of Senator Beck, a powerful figure in Kentucky political circles. Lieutenant Goodloe had served on his uncle's staff during the Civil War and then se-cured an appointment to West Point, but failed to graduate. He entered the Marine Corps as a second lieutenant in 1869. The following year, he se-verely injured his leg fighting a fire in the Brooklyn Navy Yard, which left him "maimed for life." On March 22, 1877, Goodloe accepted his appoint-ment as paymaster of the Marine Corps with the rank of major, selected over many candidates senior to him. Faced with the workings of the political spoils system, the impetus for reform remained muted.[21]

During the summer of 1877, questions of political influence and reform of the Marine Corps receded from the foreground as labor unrest arose across the nation. After the Baltimore and Ohio Railroad announced a 10 percent cut in wages, a series of wildcat strikes broke out along the line. On July 17, the governor of West Virginia, Henry W. Matthews, called for federal assis-tance to keep the peace. President Hayes reluctantly agreed to the governor's request and immediately directed the secretary of war to provide the neces-sary forces. With the labor violence spreading spontaneously to Maryland,

Pennsylvania, Indiana, Illinois, and Missouri, the governors and local officials of those states also looked to the federal government for help. As part of the federal force, the Marine Corps organized two ad hoc battalions to put down the civilian disturbances.[22]

The military had not sought out the strike mission which the president had thrust upon them. Gen. William T. Sherman expressed the opinion of many officers when he stated that strike duty was "beneath a soldier's vocation." However, military officers came largely from the upper- and upper-middle-class strata of society and shared the same prejudices and perspectives about worker solidarity as their civilian counterparts. Fearing the results of social upheaval, the military were natural allies of corporate America in wanting to maintain the established order. One Marine officer warned a friend that the recent labor upheavals were the result of the "pernicious teachings of Communism and Internationalism." Despite their rhetoric and their dislike of social disorder, the military largely viewed the riot control mission as an argument for obtaining popular support and an increase in appropriations during a time of reduced budgets.[23]

The Marine Corps reaction to its peacekeeping role during the summer unrest, like the rest of the military services, was largely rhetorical and symbolic. In the immediate aftermath of the crisis, the Marines paraded before Washington dignitaries and basked in the public accolades. In a burst of initial enthusiasm, the secretary of the Navy assured Colonel McCawley of the Department's willingness "to cooperate in the adoption of any measure necessary to their [the Marines'] comfort and an increase of their efficiency." The commandant issued a general order in which he quoted complimentary phrases of Army commanders about the Marines and then ended with a grandiloquent flourish: "Such conduct cannot fail to impress upon the whole country the fact that the Marine Corps now, as in the past, well sustains its old reputation of 'ever faithful.'" By November, however, these words were largely forgotten and Colonel McCawley, himself, made only passing reference in his annual report to the Marine participation in breaking the strikes.[24]

Despite the relatively small mention that McCawley made of the strike experience in his annual report, Marine Corps publicists used their peacekeeping role as an example to demonstrate the necessary existence, even during peacetime, of a Marine Corps and a professional military. Lt. Henry Clay Cochrane, in a two-part article published in 1879 in the *United Service*, pointed to the inability of the police and local militia to control the mobs while the Army regulars and Marines with "a modicum of men" were able to restore order. Ten years later, Captain Forney wrote in the same publication that one of the missions of the Marine Corps was the preservation of "civil order." Capt. Richard S. Collum, in his revised history of the Marine Corps published in 1890, devoted two chapters to the Marine role in the 1877 labor upheavals. Perhaps Captain Forney made the most original suggestions in a report to the commandant in September 1877 concerning the activities of the battalion he commanded. Forney recommended the formation of a separate artillery force to be called the "U.S. Marine Light Artillery" which would have its own commanding officer, but remain part of the Marine Corps. The Marine artillery force would not go to sea, but would be stationed at "large seaport towns and cities for their defence in case of foreign war or local disturbances." Thus Forney, in his report, used the Marine role in the labor strikes to advocate changes in Marine Corps organization that he and other reformers had long supported.[25]

Given the paucity of promotion and advancement opportunities, Marine officers struck out in different professional directions to enhance their careers. One of the obvious avenues was to seek out some form of advanced schooling. A few attempted to keep abreast of military knowledge through an extensive reading program. In October 1877, Lt. Richard Collum wrote, "I find it absolutely necessary to study hard two hours every day in order to make myself a passable officer." He mentioned that recently he had completed works by Jomini, Vauban, and [Denis] Mahan, "and with all that I feel that I am just beginning to *crawl*." Most Marine officers, however, neither had the inclination, ability, nor the discipline to embark on their own self-improvement course of instruction, although several sought more formal means of professional education such as the Army Artillery School at Fort Monroe or the Navy Torpedo School at Newport, Rhode Island. As one Marine applicant to the Artillery School maintained: "Marine officers while attached to ships of the Navy are required to instruct and drill their Guards in great Gun exercise, and no better opportunity can be offered for instructing Marine officers at no extra expense whatever than the Artillery School at Fort Monroe presents." He further observed that the curriculum at the school which included fortifications, surveying, telegraphy, and the art of war provided skills which "will of all times be of great use to a Marine officer yet we have no [Marine] school where this knowledge can be obtained."[26]

From 1875 to 1880, despite a number of Marine officer applicants, only three attended the Army Artillery School. Second Lt. Julius C. Shailer, appointed in April 1875, was the first Marine to be assigned. He graduated the following year, but failed to receive any benefit from his instruction, and his inability to keep out of debt forced his early resignation from the Marine Corps. First Lt. Daniel Pratt Mannix, who followed Shailer and completed an expanded two-year course of instruction in 1878, particularly distinguished himself. The son of an Irish immigrant, he enlisted in the Navy during the Civil War, changing his middle name from Patrick to Pratt after an admiral who had befriended him, and then received a Marine Corps commission in 1865. In the forefront of the reform movement, Mannix had compiled rules and regulations relating to the duties of Marine guards and codified the accounting procedures for Marine uniforms and equipment while on special assignment at Headquarters Marine Corps just prior to his appointment to Fort Monroe. At the Artillery School, he wrote a treatise called "Extent and Value of the Cooperation of the Navy During our Late Civil War" and made excellent scores on the artillery range. During the final firing exercises in 1878, Mannix made a ricochet shot "remarkable for its accuracy." After Mannix, 1st Lt. William S. Muse also attended a two-year term at the Artillery School, finishing in May 1880.[27]

During this same period, a few officers also attended the much shorter three-month course at the Newport Navy Torpedo School which specialized in the teaching of mine warfare and experimented with the newly developed underwater self-propelled missiles. After Lieutenant Mannix graduated from the Artillery School, he reported to the Torpedo School on June 1, 1878. Captain Forney received permission to attend the course the following year, and Capt. F. H. Corrie applied in June 1880. With its relatively brief term, the Torpedo School demanded a concerted effort upon the part of its students. One student officer at the school observed that from Monday through Thursday, his time was spent in the lecture room for four hours a day and then studying in his room. Friday was for "practical torpedo exercise," and Saturday was reserved for study. The faculty included experts on electricity "when the subject was in its infancy, relatively a new thing, particularly for torpedo work."[28]

Colonel McCawley viewed the opportunity for professional and technical education for his officers with mixed emotions. He favored better trained officers and continually recommended in his annual reports for all new Marine officers to come from the naval or military academies. Yet, he suspected, and probably with good cause, the motivations of many of the Marine officers who applied for the artillery and torpedo schools. He believed that most were interested only in escaping their turn at sea duty or some other onerous duty rather than honing their military skills. Moreover, he pointed out in October 1879 "that with the limited number of officers now in the Corps," he could not approve any of the applications for the Artillery

School. By the following May, he told the secretary of the Navy that the continuing shortage of officers would not allow him to recommend any officer for additional schooling "or any special duty."[29]

Certain Marine officers, nevertheless, carved out personal little niches for themselves, which had no, or only a tangential, relationship to the Marine Corps. Capt. William F. Remey, Jr., parlayed his talent to interpret the maze of Navy regulations and a degree in law to becoming the chief legal officer of the Navy. A member of a prominent Iowa Republican family, Remey and two of his brothers became career military officers. Through the influence of the senior U.S. senator from Iowa, Remey received his commission as a Marine second lieutenant at the age of nineteen in November 1861. He served on board one of the Navy's blockading ships during most of the Civil War and then had a brief shore tour at the Norfolk Navy Yard until the war ended. After a stint at sea in the Pacific, Remey returned to various assignments on the east coast. In 1870, he became the acting judge advocate of the Marine Corps. At the same time, he attended law school in Washington and was "found competent to practice at the bar."[30]

After three years as acting judge advocate, Remey became the subject of some controversy. At least one Marine officer complained to the secretary of the Navy that Remey had not been to sea since 1867 and wondered why, despite his qualifications for the position, Remey should not share, "some of the disagreeable details of the Service." Although the secretary of the Navy answered that "the Department must be the judge of the use to which it puts its officers," Remey two months later received orders to take command of the Marine guard of the *Colorado* at Key West. While at Key West, Remey's legal skills and experience still caused him to be detailed to court-martial duty whenever he was available. After only eight months, the secretary of the Navy in July 1874 ordered Remey to resume his duties as acting judge advocate of the Marine Corps. Internal political machinations, however, soon resulted in another transfer. According to Remey's brother, another Marine officer used influence to detail Remey to sea duty in order to "get him out of the way." After two years on board the *Richmond* in the Pacific and another brief stay at Norfolk, Remey arrived back in Washington to serve on the Navy Board of Inspection under Admiral Porter.[31]

In May 1878, the naval solicitor, John A. Bolles, a civilian and former Massachusetts secretary of state, died in office. Congress then abolished the office, which had been in the Department of Justice, and, at the end of June, the secretary of the Navy designated Captain Remey to act as naval solicitor for the Navy Department. Remey was responsible for advising the secretary of the Navy on naval regulations, courts-martial, and special examining and retiring boards. In February 1879, the secretary wrote Remey that since the latter was "discharging the duties formerly assigned to the Naval Solicitor and Judge Advocate General, you will hereafter be regarded as acting Judge Advocate General of the Navy Department, and will be addressed and recognized as such." During the course of the next year, friends of Remey worked to obtain legislation that would make the position permanent. The Navy secretary wrote legislators that he supported a House bill that would permit the appointment of a judge advocate of the Navy from the officers of the Navy or the Marine Corps. While serving in the position of judge advocate, the officer would have the equivalent rank of colonel in the Marine Corps or captain in the Navy. Admiral Porter lobbied openly for the bill, arguing that the post was important to discipline for the Navy and should not be politicized by appointing a civilian to the position. Porter remarked that Captain Remey would probably receive the nomination. He knew that Remey had some "opponents in the staff branches of the Navy owing to some decisions against their unreasonable demands upon the country but this is only in his favor." After perfunctory debate, both houses passed the bill in June 1880, and, as expected, President Hayes appointed Captain Remey as judge advocate general of the Navy with the rank and pay of colonel in the Marine Corps.[32]

Remey served as judge advocate general for twelve years and was quite popular in Washington. Courtly in manner and gracious to the ladies, hostesses counted upon Remey "to give brilliance and style to their entertainments." Unmarried, he lived alone in a fairly luxurious apartment across from the Metropolitan Club of which he was a member. Called either "Judge" or "General," Remey was a prominent member of Washington society and wielded some influence in the Navy Department and with certain leading politicians of both parties. He obviously was in a strategic position to be of some assistance to the Marine Corps.[33]

For most Marine officers, however, their lot was dull routine whether at sea or on shore. At the various navy yards, the Marine officer mounted guard, visited various guard posts, inspected the food, drilled the troops, served on courts-martial, took part in special ceremonies, and retained responsibility for equipment and clothing. Lt. Henry Clay Cochrane once made only one entry in his daily diary: "Killed a mosquito."[34]

Life for a Marine officer on board ship was not only dull, but also involved a struggle for status. One Marine lieutenant observed that he was outranked by all of the naval officers on board his ship, although he had been commissioned before all of them except for the captain and the executive officer. To add insult to injury, Navy regulations of 1876 assigned rooms according to rank, despite previous regulations and tradition that reserved the fourth room on the port side to the Marine officer. According to Lt. Louis E. Fagan, he not only had to give up his apartment, but was forced to make his quarters in a room outside the pantry where "the vigilant and multitudinous cockroaches file nightly upon my little toenails."[35]

Sea duty also had its more pleasant moments for both Marine and naval officers. Squadron commanders and captains of individual ships often scheduled their ports of call at the height of the local social season. As one historian observed, "Parties, dinner, and dances were looked upon as a well-earned and welcome relief after a week or two at sea." The European or Mediterranean Squadron often made its "unofficial" winter headquarters at Ville France on the Riviera. In 1877, Capt. McLane Tilton, the fleet Marine officer on board the *Trenton*, the command ship of the European Squadron, wrote that while at Ville France, he often went ashore during the afternoon and walked to Nice, two miles by one route and four miles by another. He then toured the promenade and listened "to the band which plays splendid French music." Tilton then walked back to the ship or took an omnibus, as he wished: "The scenery, the air, the sea, the sunshine, and Villas are all perfectly lovely to contemplate." He noted that he had not attended any parties or dinners except for those held on board the *Trenton* since "I don't care for such things."[36]

The routine on board the ship was often not too onerous for the Marine officer. Tilton told his wife that although he heard the reveille gun at five o'clock in the morning, he catnapped in his room until eight. At that time, his boy, a young Jamaican, brought him his coffee or tea and half a gallon of hot water. Tilton then made his toilet and "leisurely put on . . . [his] clothes." He then sauntered out on deck about nine o'clock and exchanged pleasantries with the other officers: "If anyone asks me how are you old fellow, I reply, 'I don't feel very well; no gentleman is ever well in the morning.'" The Marine captain then returned to his room, buckled on his sword "with difficulty buttoning . . . [his] coat which has grown too small for . . . [him] around the stomach, and go[es] on deck where the guard is paraded for 'quarters.'" After a prayer by the chaplain, Tilton then drilled his troops in the manual of arms. Occasionally, Tilton recalled, the "old man sends for some of us, and gives us a blowup, for some imaginary thing done or undone, after which we laugh chew and smoke until 11:00 breakfast." Unless there was a scheduled afternoon drill, the Marine captain had the rest of his day free.[37]

Shore duty for the Marine officer also had its advantages. Several of the naval installations were located in the larger cities of the eastern seaboard, including Boston, Philadelphia, New York, and, of course, Washington. Marine officers often met and socialized with many of the more prominent individuals of their community. It was, however, in the capital city that the Marine officer was in the heart of the social swirl. The young wife of Colonel McCawley entertained often and well, opening the commandant's house at the Washington Barracks Mondays and Thursdays for dancing and receptions. Young Marine lieutenants rode and raced their thoroughbred horses at local race courses. On Pennsylvania Avenue, more senior Marine officers hobnobbed with congressmen, government officials, and other military officers at the famous Ebbitt House.[38]

The social activity among his officers was not entirely pleasing to Colonel McCawley. Too often, he discovered the number of officers visiting Washington nearly equalled those assigned to the city. He often found that many of these visitors attempted to use their influential contacts to countermand his orders relative to undesirable or unpopular assignments or duties. The Marine commandant in September 1879 asked the secretary of the Navy for permission to issue a general order that would limit the number of officers allowed to visit Washington without the permission of the Navy Department. He remarked: "This order is urgently called for by the numerous cases which have taken place latterly whereby the Hon. secretary of the Navy has been greatly annoyed and incensed." By this time, McCawley had succeeded in obtaining the authority to rotate the commanders of the Marine barracks at New York, Norfolk, Philadelphia, and Boston every five years and the commanders of the other barracks as he saw fit.[39]

Still under the legislative dictum to reduce the officer corps, Colonel McCawley continued with his efforts to prune the number of officers down to 75. By 1879, forced resignations and retirements of more senior officers brought the Marine officers to the desired size. With the reduced number, McCawley complained, "the constantly decreasing number of second lieutenants will shortly render the duties of all lieutenants much more onerous, and at the same time cause more difficulty (as it already does) in making agreeable details for shore duty."[40]

In 1880, for the first time in four years, the Marine Corps commissioned seven second lieutenants. These new officers were much like those that preceded them: one was the son of a prominent Indiana politician, another had attended the Military Academy for two years, while a third was the son of a socially prominent Virginia family. The latter officer, Littleton W. T. Waller from Norfolk, had actually wanted a commission in the cavalry, but he was

too short. His father, a friend of Senator Wade Hampton from South Carolina, asked the senator to intercede for the younger Waller. According to one
account, Hampton received assurances that the Marine Corps did not have
such "foolish standards" as the Army. In response to his request, Secretary
of the Navy Richard W. Thompson replied, "Certainly Senator, we'll appoint him" and told his clerk to "make out a commission of Marines for Mr.
Waller." This story is probably somewhat apocryphal, but indicative of the
importance that political influence continued to play in Marine Corps officer appointments.[41]

The most flagrant use of political patronage, however, continued in the
selection of staff officers. In early 1880, Capt. William A. T. Maddox retired
as an assistant quartermaster in a career marked either by dishonesty or
gross incompetence, and probably a little bit of both. Many senior lieutenants with strong qualifications applied for the position, but it went to a relatively junior lieutenant, Woodhull S. Schenck, whose stepfather was active
in New York Republican politics and a good friend of Secretary of the Navy
Thompson. According to Schenck, the secretary had told him, "Wood, you
shall have it." The Senate Naval Affairs Committee recommended disap-
proval of Schenck's appointment, but was overridden by the full senate.
Supporters of Schenck had pointed out during the debate that only a few
years before Major Goodloe, the paymaster of the corps, a son-in-law of
Senator Beck of Kentucky, was promoted from a junior lieutenant to his position as paymaster under similar conditions. One disgruntled Marine officer wrote: "Where the current of promotion resembles the flow of Puerto
Rico Molasses in winter, simple humanity would dictate a cessation of advancing favorite juniors over faithful seniors." Colonel McCawley in his annual report referred to the need of legislation "to define the manner for staff
appointments."[42]

Despite the efforts of the reformers and initial steps taken by Colonel Mc-
Cawley, Marine Corps officer professionalism remained a sometime thing.
For the Marine Corps, reaction and reform continued to coexist in an uneasy and occasionally fractious relationship. Even among the reformers,
there was no clear concept of the role of the Marine officer except a dissatis-
faction with their own personal prospects and a vague desire to improve officer recruitment, education, and performance. A few such as Forney and
possibly Cochrane perceived a new structure and mission for the Marine
Corps, but they were a small minority. The transition from the "old" to the
"new" would be a tortuous and circuitous one.

3. NEW DIRECTIONS AND OLD BATTLES, 1880–1885

In the early 1880s, as the Navy undertook several new initiatives, the Marine officer corps, with a few notable exceptions, confined itself to a limited campaign of officer and administrative reform. Indeed, the basic change in Marine officer selection during this period resulted from the interface of naval progressives with influential legislators. The Marine commandant and his officers played little or no role in the process.

Clique-ridden and prone to internal feuds, the Marine officer corps proved resistant even to the relatively modest professional standards that Colonel McCawley wished to establish. The court-martial of both senior and junior officers was a common occurrence. For example, hot-tempered Capt. Robert L. Meade was often at odds with both his superiors and his contemporaries and faced charges or the threat of trial. A member of a leading Philadelphia family, Meade was the nephew of the Civil War general George Meade and the brother of a prominent naval officer. Meade, himself, had attended the Naval Academy before the Civil War and then served a short term in the Navy as an enlisted man. Commissioned as a Marine officer in June of 1862 and captured during an aborted attack on Fort Sumter the following year, he spent much of the war in a Confederate prison camp. In 1879, a Navy rear admiral reported Meade to the secretary of the Navy for using "improper language." On this occasion, McCawley defended Meade to the secretary, explaining that Meade had a quick temper and that "this one incident should not be used against him as weighed against the rest of his career."[1]

A few years later, however, Meade was in more trouble. In 1882, he and another officer at the New York Barracks, Capt. Frank D. Webster, filed charges against one another, Meade "for using profane and insulting language," and Webster for assault. The secretary of the Navy suspended both officers from duty without pay. Again because of his war record, the secretary reduced his sentence to a six-month suspension of duty. One year later, however, Meade again faced possible court-martial. Disagreeing with his commanding officer, Meade had refused to obey the latter's orders about the duties of the officer of the day. This time, the secretary of the Navy cautioned him "against the habit of insubordination which you have heretofore exhibited and a continuance of which will not be tolerated." The obvious fact, however, was that the Navy Department tolerated such actions, if one had friends in influential positions.[2]

Events such as the Meade escapades left the Marine Corps open for ridicule and a target for enterprising journalists. A Philadelphia newspaper in January 1882 devoted an article to what it called the "social Marines." The author observed that both the Army and Navy had developed aristocracies centered around West Point and Annapolis, "But the simon-pure, super-aesthetical, ultra-social concern is the Marine Corps." According to the reporter, the qualifications for appointment to the Marine Corps depended upon an aspirant's "1. social connections. 2. birth. 3. figure. 4. ability as a dancer. 5. evidence that he has never served in the ranks or performed other labors of a degrading sort." After completing this catalog of Marine virtues, the article then listed the names of several officers who were the "sons and nephews of army and navy officials and of Senators and of high officials." The account also called attention to the number of officers who had attended either the Military Academy or Naval Academy and failed to graduate and then "are run into the Marine Corps, where 'inflooence' is available." Thus, whether deserved or not, the Marine officer corps had a Captain Jenks popular image to overcome.[3]

While the Marine officer corps remained at a low ebb, several factors working for change in American naval policy merged and would eventually affect the development of the Marine Corps. This combination included a new favorable political climate caused by both foreign and domestic developments. An increasing surplus in the U.S. Treasury permitted more spending on the Navy. The growing European naval rivalry and construction raised fears among both naval officers and politicians about U.S. vulnerability. In South America, the War of the Pacific (1879–1883) with Bolivia and Peru against Chile resulted in the eventual victory of the latter and created the "Chilean myth." Congressmen favorable to a larger Navy and a more aggressive foreign policy in Latin America pointed to three British-built modern armored ships in the Chilean Navy and the threat they posed to American cities.[4]

This shift of policy also coincided with the incumbency of a series of reform-minded secretaries of the Navy that extended through successive administrations, both Republican and Democratic. In 1881, President James Garfield appointed William H. Hunt as his secretary of the Navy. Garfield needed a southerner to balance his cabinet, and Hunt, born in Charleston, South Carolina, a former Whig, and attorney-general of Louisiana in 1876, met this political qualification. He also, however, was a man of integrity, well-respected in Washington, and had a long-abiding interest in the Navy. He also had a son in the naval service. During his short-lived tenure, he initiated the first steps in a revitalization of naval construction and the beginnings of what eventually evolved into the "New Navy."[5]

Hunt's successor as secretary of the Navy was William E. Chandler, a prominent New Hampshire politician who took over the office in 1882 and continued Hunt's policy. While not seeking to "cope on equal terms with the foremost European armaments," the new secretary insisted that the United States had to be prepared "to assert at all times our natural, justifiable, and necessary ascendancy in the affairs of the American hemisphere." The building of the New Navy occurred concurrently with the first stages of a more outward-looking American foreign policy. Indirectly, all of this would influence developments within the Marine Corps, including the makeup of its officers and their relationship to the Navy.[6]

As part of the new outward thrust, one Marine officer, 1st Lt. Daniel Pratt Mannix, took part in a unique advisory venture with the Chinese Navy. Assigned in October 1878 to command the Marine guard of the USS *Ticonderoga*, he became the secretary and aide to Commodore Robert W. Shufeldt. Using the *Ticonderoga* as his flagship, Shufeldt undertook a sensitive mission to Africa and the Orient for the departments of State and the Navy to explore commercial possibilities and to show the American flag. In hopes of opening negotiations with the Kingdom of Korea, Shufeldt met in August 1880 in Tientsin with Li Hung-chang, the powerful viceroy of Chihili Province and the Chinese minister of foreign affairs. In the course of their conversation, Li mentioned that he desired to establish a naval school and asked Shufeldt if he could recommend any American officers as instructors. In a letter to the viceroy, Shufeldt nominated Lieutenant Mannix, mentioning that the latter was a graduate of the Army artillery and Navy torpedo schools. The American commodore described Mannix as "cool and deliberate in judgement . . . and [having] a knowledge of seacoast and field defense, strategy, grand tactics, and the operations of modern war."[7]

On September 21, 1880, Li Hung-chang had his secretary draft letters to both Commodore Shufeldt and Lieutenant Mannix. Li thanked Schufeldt for his military advice and for bringing Lieutenant Mannix to his attention. The Chinese viceroy stated that he was offering the torpedo position to Mannix and requested that the commodore urge the latter to accept. In his letter to the Marine lieutenant, Li provided the terms of the proposal. Mannix would receive a liberal salary paid in Mexican dollars, a rank of major in the Chinese Navy, a house, and additional funds for "medical and coal expenses," as well as first-class accommodations for his passage to and from China. The Chinese asked that Mannix arrive as soon as possible and that any further details would be worked out in Tientsin.[8]

On February 23, 1881, the Chinese Legation in Washington officially requested the Department of State to grant Lieutenant Mannix a three-year leave of absence to take the position of instructor at the Tientsin naval college. When asked his opinion, Colonel McCawley wrote that he had no objection to Lieutenant Mannix accepting the Chinese invitation and "regard[ed] it as a high compliment to the Marine Corps." McCawley, nevertheless, also had reservations. He referred the secretary of the Navy to the shortage of officers in the Corps and closed with the statement that he could not recommend the leave of absence. Despite the hedging by the commandant, the secretary approved a one-year leave and granted Mannix the authorization "to apply for an extension of this leave from time to time, to carry out the wishes of the Chinese Government."[9]

In the interim, the *Ticonderoga* had completed its voyage and Mannix was in Washington assisting Commodore Shufeldt in the preparation of the cruise report of the ship. In March, an American diplomat in China, Charles L. Fisher, wrote to Shufeldt stating that the viceroy inquired "of you and major [Mannix] and is wondering why he does not hear from you—and also why major does not telegraph at the viceroy's expense when he will leave for China." Fisher then told Shufeldt that Li had received a favorable reply from the Koreans and that they were willing to negotiate.[10]

Both Shufeldt and Mannix made their preparations to return to China. Just before Mannix departed in April 1881, he spoke to newsmen in St. Louis and San Francisco, observing that China had taken several progressive steps and that former President Ulysses S. Grant's recent trip there evoked interest in the U.S. military system. Mannix remarked that he had received a three-year leave of absence to teach at the Tientsin naval school, but confessed that he knew "very little of the school as yet, except that English is now being taught as a preparatory step." The curriculum itself, he noted, would include engineering and ordnance, and Mannix stated that he understood the "Chinese youth are said to be quite apt in learning and have

Pictured here as a captain, 1st Lt. Daniel Pratt Mannix took a leave of absence from the Marine Corps to serve as an instructor at the Tientsin naval school in China from 1881 to 1885. (National Archives [#127-N-526934])

a liking for military instruction." He anticipated a pleasant tour of duty in China and added that Commodore Shufeldt would join him since Secretary of State James Blaine was about to appoint Shufeldt as naval attaché to the U.S. legation there.[11]

No official connection existed between Shufeldt's assignment to the legation and Mannix's position with the navy school, but there was a clear relationship. Although he went to China to conclude negotiations with the Koreans, Shufeldt also operated under much broader orders. Secretary Blaine instructed the commodore, "Your large experience in the East and facilities which will be afforded you, render it desirable that you should report fully to this Department on military and naval organization of the Chinese Empire, and the present condition and probable extension of our commerce there." With Mannix owing his appointment to Shufeldt's influence, the American government obviously believed that the two missions complemented one another and furthered U.S. interests in China and the Far East. Shufeldt would negotiate his treaty with the Koreans, but his relations with the Chinese soon deteriorated. After the publication in a California newspaper of a letter critical of Li Hung-chang and the Chinese government, Shufeldt's stay in China was of short duration. Mannix, however, remained in China for four years.[12]

In mid-May 1881, Lieutenant Mannix, accompanied by his wife, his two small children, and a servant, arrived at Shanghai by steamer from Japan. The servant, a large African-American woman, apparently caused a sensation when she disembarked. As Mannix's son several years later reminisced: "The waterfront loafers, who had been eying us contemptuously, took one look at us and fled screaming, 'First the White Devils and now a Black Devil.'" From Shanghai, the Mannix family traveled by canal boat to Tientsin, and finally to Taku, near the mouth of the Peiho River, the site of a fort and of the proposed "School of Application." On June 28, 1881, Mannix concluded a formal contract with the Chinese. It more or less confirmed the terms that Li had offered the previous September. Mannix was to serve for three years, his salary starting from the time he left Washington on April 1. As an officer in the Chinese Navy, he was to obey all lawful orders and to continue to serve China in the event of war unless the war was with the United States or if he were recalled by his government. The Chinese and Mannix expected that the American government would routinely extend his one-year leave of absence from his regular duties.[13]

Almost immediately upon arriving, Mannix established the School of Application at Fort Taku, "modelled after our Artillery School at Fort Monroe." Based on his experience at Monroe, he adapted "an almost similar programme of instruction" for the new school at Taku. He also instituted a course in "sub-marine mines," which undoubtedly resembled the course offered at the U.S. Navy Torpedo School at Newport. At Taku, the students consisted of 200 enlisted men selected from nearby regiments. Mannix had four Chinese assistant instructors who acted as translators, although the men were still "required to familiarize themselves with the English commands and names" because all the nomenclature of artillery, torpedoes, and fortification material was in English. Mannix also recommended that the top students of a more theoretical naval school, recently established at the

Tientsin Arsenal, should be "assigned to [his] charge to form an advanced class at Taku so that their course could proceed with that of the enlisted men in practical work during the summer season." The viceroy approved this plan and provided Mannix some students who had recently returned from the United States. According to one newspaper account, the Marine officer wanted to provide the new students with muskets so that he could hold battalion drill. The Chinese authorities denied the request on the basis that the boys might shoot each other with the firearms. Mannix countered that he would use blanks, but the Chinese again refused the weapons stating that the students would stab one another with the bayonets. At that point, Mannix gave up on the Chinese supply bureaucracy and borrowed the rifles from a U.S. Navy ship then in port.[14]

On November 15, 1881, Lieutenant Mannix applied to the Navy Department for an extension of his one-year leave of absence from the Marine Corps. When the commandant received a copy of the request, Colonel McCawley this time left no doubt that he opposed such a use of one of his officers. He declared: "I have never believed that it is for the interest of the U.S. Marine Corps to grant this leave, and I cannot therefore approve it." McCawley further remarked that he was "aware that Lt Mannix proposes to remain at least three years, if not more, in China. When we have not officers enough to do the duty required I cannot approve such an application." Secretary of the Navy William Hunt nevertheless overrode McCawley's objection, stating that given all the circumstances, including the "fact that he is carrying out an agreement entered into with the Chinese Government, with the sanction of our own Government, the Department has decided to extend his leave another year."[15]

Mannix developed a three-year course of instruction for his advanced students. The first half-year through June, the curriculum consisted of "submarine mining," including electricity, telegraphy signals, and practical drills. From July through November, the instruction turned to coastal defense and military engineering with courses in trigonometry, mounted reconnaissance, and coast surveying. The first half of the second year provided more general and theoretical courses under the rubric of "Military Art and Science," incorporating strategy, "grand tactics," and military history. Then came classes in international law and the "Laws of War" and more practical work in surveying, reconnaissance, and mines and torpedoes. In the third year, the course of study required students to learn and practice artillery techniques and study the military organization of other nations. After a general review of all courses, the three-year program ended with a final examination.[16]

Li Hung-chang approved Mannix's proposed curriculum in November 1882 and issued a proclamation announcing competitive examinations for the new school. Although the school had been in existence for over a year, it had not reached its total complement of students. Li attempted to make the school attractive to young aspirants by increasing the monthly allowance and "to bestow marks of honour upon them" upon completion of their studies. Entrance requirements limited applicants to "members of respectable families," under the age of eighteen. In addition, candidates needed to provide the superintendent of the school "the names of their great grandfathers, grandfathers, and fathers" and pass a written examination. Upon completion of their course work, all graduates of the school would serve in the various branches of the naval service: "Those who stand at the head of their classes will be rewarded with commissions, and those who are lower will receive rewards in money, brevet-rank, and clothing."[17]

In writing to the commandant of the Marine Corps in November 1882, Mannix reported that the Chinese authorities appeared well satisfied with his efforts. In addition to the viceroy accepting his curriculum, a board of officers had examined his students and were impressed with the "proficiency shown by the class in the practical exercises and the readiness with which questions were answered." Afterwards, the viceroy advanced "the students in rank and pay." Royal Navy Capt. R. M. Lang, whom Li had made a vice admiral to reorganize his Navy, recommended that the students serve two more years with Mannix. He believed that at that point the Chinese students would be truly conversant "with torpedo warfare and there will be no necessity for a foreign officer." Lang told Li that "Major Mannix is really doing good work."[18]

In forwarding his report on his activities to Washington, Mannix asked for another extension of his tour of duty in China. Commandant McCawley continued to take a parochial view of the Marine lieutenant's assignment. In his endorsement on the request, Colonel McCawley wrote, "It seems to me, if he is to remain in China, he should be willing to resign from the U.S. Marine Corps." Secretary of the Navy Chandler, like Secretary Hunt before him, overrode McCawley's objections. Very succinctly, he observed: "My dear colonel: I am inclined to think that the advantages in having a U.S. officer in Chinese employment out-weigh the inconvenience to our own service from the deprivation of the services of Lt. Mannix." McCawley scrawled in pencil on Mannix' original request, "Grant him one year's extension."[19]

With his Chinese rank of major and compensatory salary, Mannix lived much better than the average lieutenant of Marines and was not subject to the long separation from his family that sea duty often required. At Taku, where Mannix maintained his house, his son remembered the family had some twenty servants and "each servant seemed to have several assistants." A fairly large number of European families also resided at Taku where the men, like Mannix, served as officers in the Chinese military or customs. Mannix's son recalled, however, that the children all spoke Chinese as it was the common language during their play. He once ran home to his mother "because the little Chinese boys laughed at him for not having a pigtail." His mother remedied the situation by "pinning a pigtail" to the inside of his cap, which bore the "insignia of a Mandarin, Third Class." The boy named his Manchurian pony after General Lo, the superintendent of the Taku forts, a huge man and special friend and patron of his father. Life for the Mannix family in Taku village progressed at a pleasant pace, occasionally broken up by a shopping excursion to Tientsin.[20]

In November 1883, Mannix once more requested an extension, this time for six months, dating from April 1 "to complete the three years course of instruction." Colonel McCawley, in what had almost become a ritual, forwarded the request to the secretary of the Navy, "disapproved." Again Secretary Chandler overruled the commandant and Mannix received his six-month extension. In April 1884, the Chinese added a new wrinkle. Probably at the request of Li Hung-chang, the Chinese minister in Washington arranged with the U.S. government for Mannix to remain another full year in China. General Lo informed Mannix, and Mannix officially applied for the additional leave of absence. In this instance, Colonel McCawley passed on the request without comment except to ask that he be notified if the secretary of the Navy granted the leave.[21]

With his extended leave of absence guaranteed, Mannix negotiated a new contract with General Lo. The one-year agreement assigned the Marine officer as torpedo or mine instructor at Port Arthur and PeiTang as well as at Taku. For his additional responsibilities, he received another $1,000 per annum. Mannix was to spend two months each at his new posts, but his family would remain at Taku. For his troubles, Mannix would receive two months extra salary upon his departure from China. Like his first contract, Mannix agreed that he would serve China in event of war except against his own country or if ordered to leave by his government.[22]

In August 1884, fighting broke out between France and China over French penetration into Tonkin. Mannix's son remembered that for several nights his father remained "at the Fort in anticipation of an attack which never came." When he heard of the outbreak of the war, Colonel McCawley took it upon himself to remind the Navy Department that Lieutenant Mannix was in the employ of the Chinese and the "officer in charge of a Torpedo School of Instruction at Tientsin China." At the time, however, the department apparently decided to ignore the commandant's warning.[23]

U.S. officials were more concerned about German influence in Tientsin. John Russell Young, the American minister to China, wrote Mannix in November 1884 wanting to know about several German officers who had arrived in that city. He asked "What is their grade, character, and what do they propose to do?" In his reply, Mannix stated that he understood that the Chinese minister in Berlin had arranged with the German government for 24 officers. Among their number were both naval and army officers. Admitting it was difficult to "learn anything authentic about these gentlemen," Mannix, nevertheless, understood that the Navy officers planned to introduce some ironclads being built in Germany. Although apparently unknown to Mannix, the Army officers were probably part of a German cadre for a military academy that Li Hung-chang opened in Tientsin in 1885.[24]

In his letter to Mannix asking about the German officers, Minister Young also wrote that in accordance with the wishes of the Chinese government he had requested another six-month extension for the Marine lieutenant. By this time, even Secretary Chandler was having some reservations about the Mannix mission, perhaps motivated in part by the French-Chinese situation. He approved the extension but warned: "There seems to be a question as to whether your continuance in the employment of the Chinese Government does not, under . . . the Constitution of the United States, endanger your commission as an Officer of the U.S. Marine Corps." By October 1885, Mannix had returned to the United States and immediately received sea orders as the Marine officer on board the USS *Brooklyn*. For his services, the Chinese awarded Mannix the Medal of the Third Class, Second Rank of the Double Dragon, but a Joint Resolution of Congress that would have permitted him to accept did not pass.[25]

The Mannix mission had several implications for the Marine Corps. For one, as even Colonel McCawley recognized, it raised the prestige of the Corps in the eyes of other military professionals. Yet, at the same time, Mannix, to prove his competency, had to pursue a career pattern that was not the norm for the average Marine officer. More important, however, his China experience pointed to new directions for the Marine Corps and in the professional training of its officers. As opposed to the traditional Marine emphasis on drill and light infantry tactics, Mannix had become an expert artillery and mining officer. Given his close relationship to Shufeldt, he no doubt shared many of the latter's views relative to the organization and structure of modern navies. In his recommendations to Li Hung-chang,

Shufeldt suggested the formation of a Marine artillery organization. It seemed natural for Mannix to believe that Marine officers should be educated in torpedoes, mines, and harbor defense. Moreover, he probably perceived such a mission for the Marine Corps as a whole.[26]

Both the Shufeldt and Mannix missions to China suggested an expanding role for the United States and its Navy in the world arena. Aware of the changing technology of war, such naval progressives as Adm. Stephen B. Luce and Commodore Shufeldt feared the vulnerability of what they considered American strategic and maritime interests to European imperial designs. Heightened, perhaps, by "career anxiety," or, at least "anxiety," for their service, the naval progressives used this so-called vulnerability to campaign for a larger and more modern Navy. Shufeldt, for example, headed a naval advisory board, whose recommendations led to the building of the first steel ships of the U.S. Navy. Yet, self-interest and even institutional self-interest were not the only factors at work. Since the Civil War, the nation had obtained a coaling station in Samoa, concluded a commercial treaty with Korea, influenced strongly the economy and government of the island monarchy of Hawaii, and in the Shufeldt and Mannix missions provided advisors to the Chinese Navy. Even in this period of American self-absorption, the United States had long-standing economic, political, and strategic interests in wide parts of the world which would impinge upon both the Navy and the Marine Corps.[27]

In Washington, however, the Marine Commandant Colonel McCawley had more mundane concerns. His conception of Marine Corps mission and structure was along much narrower lines. McCawley intrinsically linked reform of the Marine officer corps with his desire to form the entire Marine Corps into an elite guard of the Navy. One of the basic thrusts of his commandancy was the effort to standardize training and drill. He continually monitored the inspections of Marine shore barracks and insisted that Marine commanders personally conduct battalion drill and tactics.[28]

McCawley took quick umbrage at what he considered dereliction of duty on the part of senior commanders. For example, in August 1882, he scolded Lieutenant Colonel C. D. Hebb of the Boston Barracks for confining several NCOs in cells prior to their trials. After receiving an inspection report a few months later that described the Boston Barracks as "streaked with tobacco juice, and the rooms untidy," he observed to the secretary of the Navy that a change of commanding officers was in order.[29]

Part and parcel of this entire effort was McCawley's campaign to improve

In the early 1880s, in accordance with the wishes of the commandant, the Marine guard at the Pensacola Barracks in Florida practices skirmish tactics. Note the white helmets. (Henry Clay Cochrane Collection, Marine Corps Historical Center)

the lot of the Marine enlisted man and reduce the large desertion rate that had plagued the Marine Corps since its inception. He had the support of much of the reform element of the Marine officer corps, especially Capt. James Forney, but for the most part opposition from the old guard.

McCawley's predecessor, General Zeilin, had not thought it possible to bring about changes, but McCawley believed otherwise. He maintained that more selective recruiting, improved working and living conditions, more regular pay periods, more recreational facilities, and promotion by merit would have their effect on the desertion rate. The commandant blamed the sutler system, or at least the selling of beer by the sutler or post trader, for much of the evils besetting the Marine enlisted men. He pointed out that widows of former officers held most sutlerships and they hired corporals and sergeants as agents. According to McCawley, "This reduced them [the noncommissioned officers] to mere traders selling to the men and most of the business consists of selling beer." The commandant contended that if the men were paid monthly there would be no need of sutlers or post traders.[30]

By the early 1880s, McCawley had made many of the changes that he had wanted, but with relatively little impact on Marine Corps desertions. Early in his commandancy, he had established promotion standards for the noncommissioned ranks. Later, in 1878, he forbade the sale of beer "by sutlers or their agents" in Marine barracks. On June 22, 1880, he announced that enlisted men would be paid monthly rather than quarterly. Yet the number of desertions for the three-year period, 1876 to 1879, averaged 290 men annually as opposed to an annual average of 414 men for the period 1879 to 1882. This was an increase in the desertion rate from 14 percent to 20 percent in relation to total enlisted strength.[31]

Many of the older officers blamed the banning of the selling of beer in the barracks for the increase in desertion. Maj. Augustus Nicholson, the adjutant and inspector of the Marine Corps, declared that the order "forced many good soldiers to leave and to be replaced by 'drones and outlaws.'" He argued that it drove the men to "frequent the worst places." According to Nicholson, if the Corps could not "rule out an evil, it was best to license it." In April 1881, Lt. Col. C. D. Hebb, the commander of the Boston Barracks, attempted to blame the large number of desertions in his command—10 in March—on the sale of beer and the fact "that the men get paid too often." He declared that the post trader did not keep the canteen open because it did not pay and "that men who owe money leave without paying him." Lt. Col. J. L. Broome, then commander of the New York Barracks, viewed the problem as more complex. In a letter to McCawley, he declared that 36 men had deserted the post in August and September 1881. Broome believed the monthly pay periods helped to prevent desertion, but recommended the sale of ale or lager beer in that it would hinder the use of harder liquor. Broome, however, stated he did not know why the men had left "except for those recruits who do not like discipline and desert for that reason."[32]

In February 1882, Nicholson, Broome, and Hebb supported a petition by the enlisted men of the New York Barracks for the secretary of the Navy to rescind the order banning the sale of beer and light spirits. McCawley forwarded the correspondence but disagreed with Nicholson and Hebb who blamed the order for the increase of desertions. McCawley declared there were a number of reasons for the increase, "but the one more powerful . . . is that there are not enough men allowed by law to do the duty required, and that they are overworked." The commandant insisted that the demands of the service had increased "since the order was issued and for this reason, more than any other, the men desert." He argued that more emphasis should be made upon recruiting better men. Colonel McCawley then questioned the motives of the officers, especially Nicholson, in their support of the petition. He observed that the post traders needed to sell liquor in order to make a profit and noted that the secretary had just appointed Nicholson's son, Henry, as post trader at New York. McCawley claimed the issue was not liquor, because men who wanted it would "drink to excess whenever they can get it," but what was sought was "the facility of procuring credit for drink in garrison." He then asked Secretary Hunt not to revoke the order "for the benefit of those who propose to fatten upon the pay of the enlisted men." The secretary denied the petition.[33]

The issue, however, did not die. The commandant of the Boston Navy Yard, Commodore O. C. Badger, asked Lieutenant Colonel Hebb "why so much drunkenness, overstaying liberty, and so many desertions of Marines at this Navy Yard?" Hebb gave his usual stock answer: the inability to sell malt liquor and the too frequent payment of troops. Badger forwarded Hebb's reply to Colonel McCawley. McCawley then took an informal poll among Marine commanding officers as to their opinions about both pay and the selling of beer and wine on post and the relation of both to the question of desertion. Most commanders replied that they favored permitting some sort of mild drink on post, but nearly all denied that the monthly payments had any effect on the desertion rate. McCawley then sent his findings to the secretary of the Navy. The Marine Corps commandant observed that if the Navy "permits the sale of malt liquor, it should be done under proper restrictions." The secretary of the Navy, William Chandler, still refused to withdraw either order. In March 1883, he carefully outlined the conditions under which post traders could continue to function. He called for their appointment by the secretary of the Navy upon the recommendation of a council of administration approved by the Marine commanding officer and the commandant of the respective Navy yard. According to Chandler, the commandant of the Marine Corps would issue the general rules, based as much as possible on current Army Regulations, for the councils of administration. The secretary then declared that the trader "shall not be permitted to have, keep, or sell, spirituous liquors," which included beer and wine.[34]

Colonel McCawley's efforts to limit desertions were perhaps doomed from the start. The problem of desertion during this period was endemic to all of the services as is shown by the desertion rates for the Army which varied from a low of 6.9 percent in 1876 to a high of 15.8 percent in 1882. Many factors over which McCawley had no control largely determined how attractive men found the Marine Corps. Economic conditions certainly played a role. If jobs were plentiful, men were more unlikely to enlist and more likely to desert. According to one scholar, background and personal attributes of individuals had more of a correlation to desertion rates than any particular military situation. Here, McCawley had few options, because Marine recruiters operated largely in the port cities on the eastern seaboard. The only West Coast Marine recruiting office was in San Francisco. Very often the Marines found their recruits from the "sea faring class" of these cities' waterfront areas. As one experienced recruiting officer remarked, "It is impossible to make a soldier out of a sailor," and the "rabble from the large cities, make very indifferent soldiers."[35]

During his commandancy, McCawley raised the standards for Marine Corps recruits, insisting that they be literate and be able to speak English. He also experimented with expanding the manpower base that the Marine Corps drew upon. In September 1879, he ordered Capt. James Forney to open a "Recruiting Rendezvous" in Philadelphia. Forney remained in this post until September 1882. During this period, Forney took some initiatives and advertised and sent posters to all of the principal post offices in the United States. According to Forney some recruits came to Philadelphia to enlist from as far away as Maine, Georgia, and Michigan. As would be expected, however, in a breakdown of origins of the recruits Forney enlisted from September 1879 until November 1880, 200 of the 337 native-born enlistees were from Pennsylvania. Another 108 were foreign born, making up nearly a quarter of the 445 men enlisted by Forney during the year. The following year the ratio of foreign born increased, with 113 in that category, constituting nearly one-third of the 360 total recruits. Of that latter number, 206 were mechanics, 61 clerks, 78 laborers, and 15 "reenlisted soldiers." According to the physical profile of the men Forney enlisted, the average Marine recruit was twenty-six years of age, stood about five feet, nine inches tall, and weighed 150 pounds. Given the extra effort that Forney employed in obtaining recruits, including locating his office out of the waterfront area to attract a better quality of recruit, these men probably were somewhat above the average in physical characteristics and in overall skills. Despite the Forney experiment, attracting native-born, high-quality recruits into the Marine Corps remained a major problem. Throughout the rest of McCawley's term, the desertion rate hovered close to 25 percent.[36]

Despite his inability to reduce Marine Corps desertions, McCawley made some real contributions to enhance Marine Corps enlisted life. He encouraged enlisted men to seek out promotions and provided status to noncommissioned officers. More important, he insisted that Marine officers not abuse their power. As he wrote to one commanding officer: "Enlisted men have rights which officers must respect; and it will not do for an officer to talk about a soldier disobeying orders when he himself is disobedient and giving illegal orders."[37]

Obviously the efforts to improve the quality of enlisted personnel depended upon the caliber of the officer corps. McCawley often faced frustrations in making the simplest reforms. For example, he recommended in his second annual report that Marine officers take a physical examination upon promotion to a higher rank. Naval regulations required such an examination for naval officers to determine if they were still fit for sea duty, and McCawley wanted to extend the practice to the Marine Corps. In 1881, he made the recommendation administratively in the case of Capt. George P. Houston when he approved the latter's promotion to major "subject to examination." The older officers rallied around Houston, one writing to the *Army and Navy Journal* arguing that naval promotion examinations were not applicable to experienced Marine officers since "captain is the highest grade liable for duty on shipboard." The anonymous author then suggested that the examination for Captain Houston be waived since he had been unable to march for years because of "an incurable malady which affects his lower limbs." Houston, himself, carried his case to the president, who referred it to the attorney general for interpretation. The latter ruled that the regulation applied only to the Navy, and Marine officers were not subject to its provisions. Captain Houston received his promotion to major, much to the unhappiness of Captain Forney, who would have been promoted if Houston had not qualified. Forney appealed unsuccessfully to Senator J. Donald Cameron of Pennsylvania to use his influence to force Houston's retirement so that he could be promoted.[38]

Having relatively little success in making the changes he wanted on his own, Colonel McCawley looked for remedies in legislative action. Joining forces with the Marine reform element, McCawley wanted to get an "omnibus" Marine bill through Congress, "to present all our wants at once." In early 1881, he lent his support to legislation introduced by friendly congressmen and senators which would have expanded the number of Marine officers to 88, promoted the commandant to the rank of brigadier general, and provided for a fleet Marine officer who would receive the temporary rank and pay of the next highest grade while serving in that capacity. Both a House bill and a corresponding Senate bill contained stipulations that called for officer promotion examinations and placed seniority requirements on staff appointments. Furthermore, graduates of the U.S. Military and Naval academies or deserving noncommissioned officers were to fill all new vacancies in the Marine officer corps.[39]

Marine officers worked closely with their congressional allies to support these reform bills. Captain Cochrane and Col. William Remey, the Navy judge advocate general, met with Senator James McPherson of New Jersey, the chairman of the Senate Naval Affairs Committee. With his assent, they largely wrote the arguments that the committee incorporated into its report advocating passage of the legislation. On January 18, 1881, Senator McPherson made the report public. In effect, it maintained that the object of the Senate bill was to make the Marine Corps "nearly upon a equal footing with military organizations of similar strength and in professional accomplishment which is certain to result from their suitable recognition by Congress." About a month later, the House Naval Affairs Committee reported favorably its bill. The Committee, however, had made one major revision. It omitted the references to Military Academy and Naval Academy graduates and substituted the wording that new appointees to the Marine Corps would be from "civil life and preference being given to such meritorious non-commissioned officers in said corps." The committee offered no reason for the substitution. Unfortunately for the Marine Corps, neither bill reached the floor of either body of Congress before adjournment.[40]

During the next session of Congress, the Marine Corps's congressional friends tried once more. Senators and congressmen presented six bills that related to the structure, size, and promotion opportunities of the Marine officer corps. In December 1881, Senator McPherson introduced essentially the same piece of legislation that he had earlier. According to the latest version, the Navy Department would offer Marine Corps commissions in equal proportion to graduates of the Military Academy and the Naval Academy, to deserving noncommissioned officers, and to candidates from civilian life. In a letter to the secretary of the Navy in May 1882, Colonel McCawley formally lent his support to the McPherson bill then pending in both houses of Congress. Despite clearing the Senate Naval Affairs Committee, the legislation continued to encounter delays and eventually failed to reach the floor of either the House or Senate. In August 1882, Captain Cochrane wrote McCawley that the Corps "may yet have to come to my plan of getting *a little at a time*."[41]

The enemies of the Corps had also been active. A congressman from Florida entered a resolution that would have asked the president of the United States his views about the "expediency and economy of the early abolition of the Marine Corps." During the debate on the naval appropriation bill, Senator Eugene Hale, a member of the Senate Naval Affairs Committee, mentioned as an aside that Congress had not tackled the larger issues of naval reform. Among these issues, he listed "The question of the Marine Corps, . . . its proper relation to the American Navy, whether it shall be turned over bodily to the Army . . . whether it shall be reduced in part or in a less proportion." Notwithstanding these ominous voices in Congress, neither the House nor the Senate was prepared to take such draconian measures. For both McCawley and the Marine reformers, however, their efforts had appeared to come to naught.[42]

Despite the apparent dead end in the House and Senate, Congress was about to enact some of the most far-reaching legislation for both the Navy and the Marine Corps. Both Democratic Representative Washington C. Whitthorne of Tennessee and his successor as chairman of the House Naval Affairs Committee, Republican Representative Benjamin W. Harris from Massachusetts, supported additional appropriations for the Navy. Although most Democratic southern congressmen, with some notable exceptions, such as Whitthorne, largely opposed or were indifferent to the needs of the Navy, a bipartisan coalition existed in Congress that was working to finance new naval construction. The apparent glue that held the uneasy alliance together was a concern with U.S. external relations and the ability of the Navy to protect American commercial and political interests abroad.[43]

Changing internal conditions within the Navy Department itself and the budding professionalization of the Navy officer corps also served as a springboard both for reform and growth. Secretary Hunt added to this impetus with the appointment to influential positions within the department of officers advocating change. His selection of Capt. John Grimes Walker to head the Bureau of Navigation was perhaps the most significant of these appointments. Even in the early 1880s, the Bureau of Navigation was the "first among equals" of the separate bureaus within the Department. With the Office of Detail in his bureau, Walker controlled the duty assignments of all naval officers and employed this power to place reform-minded officers in key positions. In early 1882, he convinced Secretary Hunt to establish the Office of Naval Intelligence within the Bureau of Navigation and made the office not only a center for information gathering but an embryonic nucleus for a planning staff. [44]

Whether the Navy should retain its traditional coastal defense and occasional "showing the flag" role or develop a modern ocean-going fleet that could undertake offensive operations had become a moot point by this time. The existing Navy could carry out neither mission. By the 1880s, the policy of repairing older ships rather than replacing them had reached a point of diminishing returns. Out of the 140 naval ships in commission at the beginning of 1882, only 31 were seaworthy. [45]

Secretary Hunt worked closely with the congressional coalition and with the reform element in the Navy to appropriate funds for new ship construction. The Navy secretary endorsed the majority report of a specially appointed Naval advisory board headed by Rear Adm. John Rodgers, which recommended a building program of 18 unarmored steel cruisers, 20 wooden cruisers, 10 torpedo boats, and 5 rams. In February 1882, Hunt invited Representative Harris, of the House Naval Affairs Committee, and other influential legislators from both the House and Senate to meet with him and a group of naval officers to discuss the needs of the Navy. Although the House Naval Affairs Committee bill for additional construction failed to pass, the Naval Appropriation Act of August 5, 1882, authorized the building of two new steel cruisers, but failed to fund them. At the same time, Congress restricted repairs of the older wooden vessels to no more than 30 percent of the cost of a new vessel. The secretary also appointed Rear Adm. Robert Shufeldt to head a new naval advisory board to make further recommendations for the next session of Congress. [46]

Although best remembered for its authorization of steel ships and the beginning of the New Navy, the 1882 Navy appropriation act also had a tremendous influence on future Navy and Marine Corps officer commissioning and upon naval officer promotions. Since the Civil War, the naval officer corps had continued to grow, infused each year with fresh graduates of the Naval Academy. By 1882, however, the U.S. Navy had one officer for every four enlisted men. During the debate over the appropriation bill, Senator Hale pointed out that the American Navy had 1,400 commissioned officers with a fleet of 39 steam vessels as compared to the British Navy which had 2,600–2,700 line officers with over 340 steamships in its fleet. Everyone including members of Congress agreed that the officer corps needed some pruning. Representative George Robeson, a former secretary of the Navy, headed a special subcommittee to study the problem and had charge of the appropriation bill in the House. The final version of the bill approved by both houses of Congress called for a reduction of 250 Navy line officers. This would be achieved by two means: first, no promotions were to be made to a higher grade until there were two vacancies in the next rank, and second, Congress eliminated guaranteed commissions into the Navy for all Naval Academy graduates. The new law would limit the number of commissions to the actual number of vacancies. One scholar determined that it would take the death or retirement of 64 commodores or 128 rear admirals to promote one ensign.[47]

For the Marine Corps, the most important aspect of the new legislation was the provision that, in effect, limited Marine commissions to Naval Academy graduates. The impetus for this move came not from the Marine Corps, but from the Navy. Over the years several naval officers had proposed in professional journals the limitation of appointments in all corps of the Navy to actual vacancies and to Naval Academy graduates. The argument was that it would create a homogenous officer corps and end corps disputes within the Navy. Cmdr. Bowman H. McCalla remembered that Congressman Robeson brought Commodore John G. Walker, chief of the Bureau of Navigation, a rough draft of the appropriation bill. McCalla, who at the time was assigned to the Bureau, related that he recommended to Walker the language that eventually was incorporated into the bill: "And from those [naval cadets] . . . appointments shall hereafter be made as it is necessary to fill vacancies in the lower grades of the line and of the Engineer Corps of the Navy and of the Marine Corps."[48]

The Naval Appropriation Act of 1882 "tarred with the same brush" the commissioning of officers in the Marine Corps and the Navy. While having little influence on this particular legislation, the commandant and several of the Marine "progressive officers," for several years prior to 1882, had pushed for permitting the appointment of Naval Academy graduates to the Marine Corps. In fact, over the years, Colonel McCawley had corresponded with several Naval Academy cadets who had inquired about the possibility of receiving a Marine Corps commission. To one, McCawley replied that while there had not been any transfers "from the Line of the Navy to the U.S. Marine Corps," he knew "of no reason why it cannot be done if the Department thought proper." In the past, the Navy Department had denied such requests on the basis that there was "no precedent" for such transfers, but the Act of August 5, 1882, provided the precedent. Although the language of the law did not specifically rule out the commissioning of candidates from civilian life, the surfeit of Naval Academy graduates and the limited number of actual vacancies made appointments from any other source unlikely. From 1883 through 1897, all of the new Marine officers were graduates of the Naval Academy.[49]

Both the commandant and the new secretary of the Navy, William Chandler, used the passage of the 1882 act to urge Congress to increase the number of Marine officers. In a letter to Chandler in September, Colonel Mc-Cawley wrote about the need for additional officers and especially about the critical shortage of second lieutenants. Chandler, in turn, in his annual report, recommended to Congress that the Marine Corps commission 16 new second lieutenants which would bring the total to 30. Specifically mentioning the August act, he asked that new appointments come from the Naval Academy. In an exchange of correspondence with Senator Eugene Hale of the Senate Appropriation Committee in February 1883, Chandler promised that in return for 8 new second lieutenants, the "appointments would be made from those final graduates of the Navy Academy in June, . . . standing highest in their class, and not required for other branches of the Naval Service."[50]

The Appropriation Act of March 3, 1883, provided for the increase of second lieutenants for the Marine Corps. At the same time, influenced by the Shufeldt Advisory Board, the same legislation appropriated the money for building three steel-protected cruisers and a dispatch boat. This act together with the appropriation act of the previous year, by happenchance, tied together the building of the New Navy with the reform of the Marine officer corps.[51]

The most significant development for the Marine Corps during these years was the infusion of the new second lieutenants from the Naval Academy. As expected, the August 5, 1882, legislation had a debilitating effect upon morale at the Naval Academy. The law not only eliminated the distinctions between cadet midshipmen and cadet engineers and made all naval cadets responsible for the same curriculum, but it limited the number of vacancies available upon graduation. Rear Adm. Francis Ramsay, the superintendent of the Naval Academy, remarked to Secretary Chandler about the lagging discipline at the school. He declared that the "law of August 5th has made much of the trouble . . . , and Cadets do not hesitate to tell me that they do not study as there is no chance of their remaining in the service." Ramsay observed that all knew that "at least two-thirds of each class have not the least chance of getting into the Navy under the present law." Indeed, no more than 7 percent of the candidates who entered the Naval Academy in 1881 were to receive commissions six years later.[52]

The first class to feel the full impact of the new law was the class of 1881 which returned from its two-year cruise and took its final exam in June 1883. Of the 86 graduates, only 23 received commissions. Although eligible, 2 cadets turned down commissions, and a third was discovered to have secondary syphilis. The top 3 graduates became assistant naval constructors and went abroad for postgraduate work in naval architecture. Three entered the Engineer Corps, 7 became ensigns in the Navy line, and 10 were to receive commissions as Marine second lieutenants.

Because of promotions, by the end of June there were 10 vacancies, instead of 8, in the Marine Corps second lieutenant ranks. On July 2, Commodore John G. Walker of the Bureau of Navigation informed Colonel McCawley of the names and precedence of the 9 cadets who were to receive Marine Corps commissions. They were Francis E. Sutton, Lincoln Karmany, Charles A. Doyen, Charles H. Lauchheimer, William H. Stayton, Henry C. Haines, James E. Mahoney, George Barnett, and Franklin J. Moses. The tenth, Harry K. White, did not secure his commission until October because of red tape. The Navy backdated his commission to July 1, however, and he came directly after Sutton in the lineal list. All of the cadets stood relatively high in their class with Sutton, White, and Karmany ranking sixth, seventh, and eighth, respectively. Barnett and Moses brought up the bottom, placing twenty-third and twenty-fourth. Of the 10 new officers, 6 were among the top 15 of their class. According to Superintendent Ramsay, the Academy's Academic Board interfered very little in the cadet's selection of service. Only White, Haines, and Mahoney did not receive their first choice. White's second choice originally had been the Engineer Corps, but he changed his mind after calculating the chances of promotion in the various corps.[53]

In early September, after a short leave, the new officers reported to the Marine barracks under Maj. Charles Heywood at the New York Navy Yard. At Brooklyn, as one of them remembered, they received instruction in "infantry drill and of our duties on board ship." Heywood appeared satisfied by their progress, and in mid-October, he wrote to McCawley that the young lieutenants "are doing Officers of the Day's duty now, and do it very well." The lieutenants had completed company and skirmish drill, "have been thoroughly instructed in making out accounts, muster rolls, ration returns, and the Company and Post guard accounts, and have been in charge of Companies four times on Battalion drill." Heywood believed his charges were ready to assume their regular duties. Second Lt. George Barnett recalled fondly that he and his comrades threw a farewell party for themselves and at two o'clock in the morning they called upon Major Heywood, inviting him to join the festivities, "which he did. While he was there, we proposed his health as the next Commandant of the Marine Corps." According to Barnett, Heywood, ever after that, "seemed to have a soft spot in his heart for all of us." In his annual report, Colonel McCawley concluded, "The recent appointment of officers from the Naval Academy is a long desired step in advance, and is one which it is believed will have excellent results for the service at large."[54]

With 4 deaths and 1 retirement among its officers in 1883–1884, the Marine Corps commissioned 5 new second lieutenants in July 1884, all graduates of the Naval Academy. Four were members of the class of 1882, while C. Marrast Perkins of the class of 1881 transferred from the Engineer Corps into the Marine Corps. The other new officers were Jacob G. McWhorter from Augusta, Georgia; Thomas C. Prince from Canton, Ohio; Arthur H. Clarke from Newport, Rhode Island; and Joseph H. Pendleton from Rochester, Pennsylvania. In contrast to the previous year's group, however, these new officers had attained relatively modest academic records at Annapolis. Only McWhorter, who placed ninth, stood in the top 10 of his class. Perkins was the last man of the class of 1881 to receive a commission. Among the remaining Marine members of the class of 1882, Prince ranked eighteenth, Clarke twenty-first, and Pendleton twenty-third out of the 25 members who received commissions.[55]

Despite some speculation in both Congress and in the press about the creation of a Naval Academy aristocracy, the makeup of the new Marine officers varied. Two of the 15, Pendleton and Prince, came from a working-class background. Pendleton's father was a bricklayer in Rochester, Pennsylvania, while Prince's was a carpenter in Canton, Ohio. Only Haines was a son of a naval officer. McWhorter listed his father's occupation as a farmer, although he was apparently well-to-do, because the son attended private schools in Georgia. With appointments to the Naval Academy, the domain of congressmen, except for a few the president made at large, most candidates had some political connection. Young Sutton, however, the son of a Rome, New York, surgeon, won his appointment through a competitive examination in spite of the fact that his family had opposed the election of the local congressman. However, 2 of the new officers, Moses and White, had obvious political influence. White's father held a patronage position as a clerk in the Treasury Department while Moses' father, a Charleston attorney, was the Reconstruction governor of South Carolina. Both Moses, whose family converted to the Episcopal Church, and Lauchheimer had Jewish backgrounds, and Lauchheimer's father had immigrated from Germany to Baltimore where he established a thriving mercantile business.[56]

Of the remaining seven new officers, only five provided information about their fathers' occupations. Barnett's father ran a hotel in Boscobel, Wisconsin; Clarke's was a professor in Newport, Rhode Island; Doyen's was a carriage manufacturer in New Hampshire; Karmony's was a general insurance agent in Lebanon, Pennsylvania; and Stayton described his father as a "common merchant" in Clayton, Delaware. The two other officers, Mahoney and Perkins, were from Massachusetts and Georgia, respectively. Mahoney gave only the name of his mother, and Perkins's name did not appear in the same application book as the others.[57]

These Marine officers resembled but also differed from Peter Karsten's "naval aristocracy" of Naval Academy graduates. The Marine officers came, for the most part, from the middle- and upper-middle-class strata of society. Peter Karsten's sample, on the other hand, contained a higher representation of officers' sons and sons of the wealthy. Because of the congressional selection of Annapolis applicants, most naval cadets normally came from prominent families in their communities. Moreover, the candidates faced demanding entrance requirements including written examinations and a personal interview. Obviously, neither Karsten's sample nor the Marine officers represented a cross section of young American manhood, yet, taking into account the political ramifications and the required educational background, the new Marine officers more closely approximated such a cross section than did the naval officers. Indeed, the Marine Naval Academy graduates made a leavening of the Marine Corps whose "commissions . . . have heretofore been the rewards of political and official favorites."[58]

In 1884, a presidential election year, Marine Corps legislation became hostage to partisan politics and the sudden infusion of new lieutenants was to come to an end. The Democrats who were in control of the House of Representatives used every opportunity to embarrass the Republican administration under Chester A. Arthur, the former vice president who assumed the presidency after the death of Garfield. Democratic Congressman Samuel J. Randall, chairman of the House Appropriations Committee, asked why the Marine Corps was requesting funding for 93 officers when the Appropriations Act of 1876 had reduced the number of officers to 75. Colonel McCawley explained that "the Marine Corps having been reduced below that number [75], the Department held that the law had been complied with, and that no bar to appointments up to the original number of 30 second lieutenants existed." Despite the protests of McCawley and Secretary Chandler, the House in its Navy appropriation bill allowed the Marine Corps 22 second lieutenants, but would not permit any new appointments until the officer corps numbered fewer than 75. Randall insisted that additional language be inserted to read "and the whole number of officers . . . shall not exceed 75" so that the Navy Department could not void the stipulation as it had with the 1876 law.[59]

Colonel McCawley and Secretary Chandler then turned to the Senate to remove the offending restrictions upon Marine Corps appointments. In detailed memoranda to the secretary, who forwarded the material to the Senate, McCawley argued that unlike the Navy, the Marine Corps had too few officers. He pointed out that the Army had 1 officer for every 15 enlisted men while the Marine Corps had 1 officer for every 26 enlisted men. According to McCawley, "experience has shown" that 75 officers "will not suffice" and that the Corps "has labored under the disadvantage of not having enough [officers]." He questioned the feasibility of renewing the legislation when it had not worked before. Apparently convinced in part by the commandant's case, the Senate Appropriations Committee refused to incorporate the House's provisions relating to the number of Marine Corps officers. The full Senate followed the committee's lead when it passed the bill.[60]

The Marine Corps, however, lost this battle. For a time, the Senate stood firm in the initial conferences to settle the differences between the Senate and House versions of the bill. Reaching an impasse in July, the two bodies agreed to pass a temporary measure that would fund the Navy Department for six months. The Democratic-controlled House and the Republican Senate continued to play politics with the bill when Congress reconvened during the next session. As part of the "lame duck" Arthur administration, Secretary Chandler had limited power to influence the legislators. Finally at the end of January 1885, Senator Hale told the Senate that after the conferees studied the 1876 law they agreed "that the scope and intention of that act is to fix the number of officers in the Marine Corps at seventy-five." With this admission by the Senate, the House dropped the Randall provision that forbade the Marine Corps to exceed 75 officers. Still the immediate effect was to limit the Marine Corps to 75 officers and end, at least temporarily, the entry of new lieutenants from the Naval Academy or from any other source.[61]

Even as prospects for Marine officer reform and professionalism dimmed, the Navy entered a period of intellectual ferment. It reflected in part the general ascendancy of the progressive naval officers. One of the key architects of the naval reformation was Rear Admiral Luce, commander of the North Atlantic Station. Influenced by Sherman's taking of Charleston during the Civil War by cutting the lines of communication after a naval force had failed to take the city, Luce believed there was a strong correlation between naval and military strategy. He had for some time advocated the establishment of a naval postgraduate school and discussed the matter with Emory Upton who had encouraged him. After an initial rebuff in 1877, he waited until 1884 to recommend the idea once again, this time to Secretary of the Navy William Chandler. Despite objections from all of the bureau chiefs except for Commodore John G. Walker of the Bureau of Navigation, Secretary Chandler liked the concept and appointed Luce to head a three-man board to study its feasibility. Based on the board's recommendation, Secretary Chandler in October 1884 issued a general order establishing the Naval War College at Newport and made Luce its first president.[62]

The Naval War College was the first institution of its type in the world. At a time when all graduate professional education in the United States was in its infancy with the Johns Hopkins Graduate School only six years old, Luce announced that his purpose was to make the War College "a place of original research on all questions relating to war and to statesmanship connected with war." The curriculum included military science, the art of naval warfare, and marine international law. With Luce's implicit belief that military and naval strategies were just the reverse sides of the same coin, he placed a strong emphasis on historical study and the discovery of the "immutable principles of war." Even so, as Luce wrote to Admiral Porter, he wanted to make "the War College a sort of School of Application as well as a theoretical school." Although the first class consisted of only eight Navy lieutenants, most of whom believed "they had been shanghaied," the War College set about its task to teach them about their profession, "the profession of war."[63]

In the naval professional literature of the period, officers expounded on the need to prepare themselves for the challenges that they would face in a more competitive world. In one of the first publications of the new Office of Naval Intelligence, Cmdr. William Bainbridge-Hoff wrote about "Modern Naval Tactics." Taking a leaf from Admiral Luce's refrain, Bainbridge-Hoff asserted that many of the tactical precepts of armies fighting on land applied equally as well to "fleets engaging at sea." To engage the enemy on the open sea, Bainbridge-Hoff observed, a commander must counter with a "fleet at least equal to his own in number, construction, speed, and offensive power." He described the "sea-going armor-clad" as the "most formidable line-of-

battle-ship," but also believed the question still open whether the ram supported by torpedo boats might not be its equal. Although acknowledging
the shortcomings of the American Navy when compared to the Europeans,
especially the British, he argued that the necessity for a modern navy would
arise and that American officers must lay the foundations for this eventual-
ity: "Harder more precise work, a devotion to a specialty is what is required."[64]

Several other naval writers of the period concerned themselves with a renewed emphasis upon landing operations and the naval brigade. In a seminal article in the *Proceedings of the United States Naval Institute*, Lt. T. B. M.
Mason contended that the naval brigade was a component part of the fleet
and required more training and drill than an occasional ceremonial parade.
Drawing upon the lessons of the Key West demonstrations during the *Virginius* affair in 1873, he held that the brigade must be a balanced military
force of both infantry and artillery. Lt. John C. Soley, also in the *Proceedings*,
referred to historical examples to demonstrate that in past wars, especially
against an enemy without a strong navy, naval forces often deployed ashore.
During peacetime, according to Soley, naval landing parties served to protect American commercial interests in less-developed countries. In a *Proceedings* prize-winning essay, Lt. John Carlos G. Calkins stated that "no field of
military activity deserves more attention than the landing of landing parties
of seamen." He noted that the British, French, and Russians all recently had
employed a naval brigade ashore.[65]

Writing in a similar vein, Lt. Cmdr. Casper F. Goodrich described the
previous British intervention in Egypt and pointed out that the employment of naval forces ashore was "not peculiar to the British Navy alone." He
wrote that American naval forces "are frequently landed in various parts of
the world for police duty in cases of emergency, panic, or distress, and in
times of general peace their performances make up the real active history."
In the conclusion of his report published by the Office of Naval Intelligence,
Goodrich recommended more "*homogeneous landing parties* capable of self-
supporting and sustained action in the field at some little distance from the
base."[66]

Despite the emphasis upon landing operations, Bainbridge-Hoff, Mason,
and Calkins did not even mention Marines. Soley referred to the Marine
participation in the attack on Fort Fisher during the Civil War and stated
that they were not entirely to blame for the fiasco "as they only shared the
general panic." He advised, nevertheless, that the Navy land as many Marines as possible in their own boats and under their own officers. Goodrich,
on the other hand, made no recommendations relative to the use of Ameri-

can Marines. He, however, devoted five pages to the description of the British Marine infantry and artillery units in the Egyptian campaign. Naval officers, nevertheless, considered Marines an integral part of the naval brigade.[67]

As commander of the North Atlantic Station before he assumed the presidency of the War College, Admiral Luce shared the general fascination with landing operations. Dubbed by his officers "the Great North American Drill Sergeant," he included as part of the North Atlantic Squadron's 1884 summer maneuvers in August a three-day encampment on Gardiners Island off Long Island Sound. The naval brigade consisted of 660 officers and men including a Marine battalion of 99 enlisted men and 4 officers. Calling this exercise unique and "of a nature before unknown in our service," the report covering the activities of the naval brigade concluded, "Landing forces are among the most important subjects to which they [naval officers] may give their attention." The report hailed the exercise as "a fit opportunity to notice deficiencies and to draw lessons." Just as significant, the authors of the final report perceived the necessity of such landings "to protect American interests abroad and . . . to enforce the government's demands upon states or tribes which listen to no other argument than force."[68]

While naval officers studied the implications of landing operations, Marine officers remained curiously silent. Ironically, with their narrow focus on promotions, desertions, line and staff relations, and other mundane administrative concerns, both Colonel McCawley and the Marine reformers largely failed to obtain even the relative modest changes they desired. Even the legislation providing for the entry of Naval Academy graduates into the Marine officer corps was the result of the efforts of naval reformers who had no especial affection for the Marine Corps, but were willing to use the Corps to further their own ends. Only a few Marine mavericks, such as Capt. Daniel Mannix and possibly Capt. James Forney, had a broader vision for their Corps.

4. THE TRANSITIONAL YEARS, 1885–1889

During the first Cleveland administration, the nascent professionalism among Marine officers and related Marine reform movement advanced at an uneven pace. The progress that occurred was largely in the area of officer education and affected principally individuals rather than the officer corps as a whole. For the most part, it was a period of missed opportunities as the forces behind the development of the New Navy gained momentum.

Although President Grover Cleveland had little relish for foreign involvements, a revolution in the spring of 1885 on the Isthmus of Panama, then part of Colombia, resulted in the deployment of a Marine expeditionary force that foreshadowed those of a future age. Despite the president's reluctance, he could not disregard American strategic or economic interests in the Caribbean basin nor U.S. obligations to protect American citizens and to guarantee, under the 1846 treaty with Colombia, the Panama transit.[1]

Faced with a difficult decision, on the evening of April 1, 1885, the president met with Secretary of State Thomas F. Bayard, Attorney General Augustus H. Gaylord, and new Secretary of the Navy William H. Whitney, a New York financier and lawyer who had long been active in Democratic politics. Although not wanting to intervene in "a purely domestic broil," the three conferees believed they had little choice under the circumstances. Upon leaving the conference, Secretary Whitney alerted Rear Adm. James E. Jouett, the commander of the North Atlantic Station, who was embarked in his flagship, the *Tennessee*, at New Orleans. The secretary then telegraphed James B. Houston, president of the Pacific Mail Company, that the government had decided to keep the Panama transit open and asked Houston to delay the departure of one of his steamers so that it could take an armed expedition to Panama.[2]

The next morning the Navy Department was the scene of unusual activity as Whitney consulted with his advisors about the composition of the force that would go to the Isthmus. The inexperienced secretary relied heavily on his senior bureau chiefs, especially Commodore John G. Walker of the Bureau of Navigation. According to his recent biographer, Walker saw the Panama affair as a "perfect opportunity . . . to strengthen the Navy and to promote an active foreign policy." He selected one of his protégés, Cmdr. Bowman H. McCalla, to head the expedition under the overall command of Admiral Jouett.[3]

On April 3, Whitney telegraphed Rear Admiral Jouett and defined the mission of the U.S. expeditionary force. The secretary instructed Jouett to display "great discretion" and told him that his "sole duty is confined to seeing that a free and uninterrupted transit across the Isthmus is restored . . . and that the lives and property of American citizens are protected." Whitney cautioned the admiral not to interfere "with the constituted authorities," and said that he had "no part to perform in the political or social disorders of Colombia, and it will be your duty to see that no irritation or unfriendliness shall arise from your presence at the Isthmus." Two days later, the secretary directed McCalla to assume command of the entire force "subject to the orders of the admiral commanding the North Atlantic Squadron." Whitney thus established a clear chain of command and, moreover, limited the U.S. expedition to keeping the transit open and protecting American lives.[4]

Commodore Walker, in all likelihood without the concurrence of Secretary Whitney, sent McCalla a second set of instructions that altered the clear lines of command established by the first. Emphasizing the importance of the expedition and "that we should keep the country with us in the matter," Walker ordered McCalla to report directly back to Washington, in effect, bypassing Admiral Jouett. The commodore advised McCalla that the letter was confidential and said, "There will be no record of it in the Navy Department, but you may consider it as an order to be carefully carried out."[5]

The reasons behind Walker's extraordinary letter can only be a matter of conjecture. The evidence would indicate that while the administration may have been concerned with the immediate troubles on the Isthmus and the implementation of its international legal obligations to keep the transit open, part of the naval officer establishment, centered around Walker, was taking a longer view of the situation. Most naval officers agreed on the economic and strategic importance to the United States of an Isthmian canal and continued to be suspicious of the activities of the European countries in the Caribbean, especially of the French-owned Panama Canal Company on the Isthmus. One naval officer earlier had written, "On visiting the Isthmus, the first thing to attract attention is the political and strategic designs of the French regarding the future control of the canal." Indeed, one reporter quoted Admiral Jouett (although the admiral later repudiated the interview) to the effect that French interests were behind both the revolt in Panama and the difficulties at the time between Guatemala and its neighbors Nicaragua and El Salvador. Walker did not mention any French collusion in his letter, but well may have had in mind the establishment of a permanent advanced base from which the United States could project its power into Central America.[6]

The naval expedition ashore in Panama eventually consisted of a two-battalion Marine infantry brigade, under Maj. Charles Heywood, and a supporting Navy bluejacket artillery contingent totaling 796 officers and men. Including the crews of the ships lying offshore, the total force numbered well over 1,200 men, and with overwhelming military strength, the Marines and sailors quickly established order. They occupied Panama City and Colon on the western and eastern coasts respectively and opened up the railroad transit between the two cities. At the end of April, a Colombian relief force arrived in Panama City Bay. After three-way negotiations, involving Admiral Jouett, the Panamanian rebel leader, and the commander of the Colombian expedition, the Colombians took over control of the city, and by mid-May, the last American troops departed Panama.[7]

Although on the surface the American military intervention appeared to go smoothly, there was turbulence underneath, especially in the sensitive area of command relations. Major Heywood, whose troops arrived first on the scene, resented turning over command of the shore forces to Commander McCalla, an officer many years his junior in length of service. More significant, Admiral Jouett became infuriated when he received several U.S. newspapers and "was astonished to learn" that McCalla had been in direct communication with the Navy Department and that several of his dispatches were "directly contradictory to my official telegraphic reports." Jouett ordered McCalla to give him a copy of the messages that the latter had sent to Washington. At the same time, the admiral asked Major Heywood to forward a copy of all orders that the Marine commander had received from McCalla. On May 7, Jouett wrote to Whitney and repeated his complaints about McCalla's "irregularities." He stated that McCalla, by telegraphing directly to the Navy Department and bypassing the usual chain of command, "placed his whole command in a most critical position without the slightest necessity for doing so." Although remarking that McCalla violated the customs of the naval service, Jouett allowed that his subordinate had the units under him "well organized, efficient, and ready for any service." McCalla defended his conduct on the ground that he was operating under secret orders of the Navy Department to report events as he saw them and that as the commander on the scene he exercised his own judgment. Apparently Secretary Whitney never realized, notwithstanding Admiral Jouett's continuing protests, the extent of McCalla's independent actions while on the Isthmus.[8]

For the Marine Corps, the intervention revealed the fragility of its manpower resources in both officers and men. As Colonel McCawley observed to Secretary Whitney, the Atlantic Coast shore stations had been depleted of half their Marine enlisted strength, and only 11 Marine officers of all grades remained at the eastern posts. For the most part, the Marine Brigade in Panama was essentially a composite of the east coast Marine barracks guards. Major Heywood had commanded the important New York Barracks before assuming control over the Marine forces.[9]

With good cause, Colonel McCawley could boast, "It is with pride that I call the attention of the Department to the prompt and cheerful manner in which its orders were obeyed by the officers and men, and to the extraordinary dispatch with which these troops were sent to their destination at such short notice." He observed that one officer had left the bedside of his dying mother to join the Marine Panama expedition. Marine 2d Lt. Frank E. Sutton probably expressed the sentiments of most of his comrades about the expedition when he wrote, "My delight on leaving New York was more than exceeded by my joy on returning."[10]

While for a time basking in public and official approbation upon the return of the Marine battalions, the Marine Corps soon found itself under attack from an unexpected quarter. In an extended report on the Isthmus expedition to the secretary of the Navy, Commander McCalla, while describing the Corps "as highly efficient and admirably disciplined," criticized the Marines for using the tactics "of a bygone day." He suggested that Marine officers needed advanced professional schooling and training in the employment of artillery and machine guns. Moreover, McCalla argued that the Marines wasted too much time on shore in barracks and recommended summer maneuvers for the entire shore establishment in conjunction with the fleet and the Army. McCalla proposed that the Navy Department purchase its own transports to carry future naval brigades and that the fleet should practice more realistic landing operations. In effect, McCalla recommended the establishment of a naval expeditionary force, with a definable role in such an organization for the Marine Corps.[11]

Commandant McCawley angrily responded to McCalla's report. In a lengthy letter to the secretary, the commandant answered each of McCalla's criticisms. Referring to the comments on Marine tactics, McCawley replied that the Marine Corps used the same tactics as the Army, and if these were wrong, "it is singular that it is left to a naval officer to discover this." He then declared that the Marines did not waste time in barracks since they faced constant guard duty in the Navy yards. The commandant rejected the idea of a summer maneuver, stating that it was his experience after thirty-eight years of service that he "never found the least trouble in having every duty as well performed in camp as in garrison after a few day's experience." Throughout his letter to the secretary, McCawley emphasized the limited number of officers and men available to him. He defined the main missions of the Marine Corps in the traditional terms of ships' detachments and sentry duty at the Navy yards. He made no reference to any future expeditionary role for the Marines.[12]

The furor soon died. The Navy Department published McCalla's report, and Secretary Whitney released Colonel McCawley's letter to the press and there the matter ended. For both the Marine Corps and the Navy, the immediate effect was relatively slight. Despite their machinations, neither Walker nor McCalla obtained their objectives, either a forward base or a permanent landing force. The Panama venture, nevertheless, had revealed a rift between the Navy progressives and the leadership of the Marine Corps including most Marine officers on the future role of the Marine Corps in the New Navy.[13]

William C. Whitney, notwithstanding his seeming naiveté in the Panama affair, was an able secretary of the Navy and championed many of the reforms of the naval progressives. In an interview with a New York newspaper in May 1885, he declared that he intended "to introduce a new system into the Navy Department" and run the department "on business principles in the future."[14]

Whitney's major contributions, however, lay in the support he gave to the continued building of the New Navy. The secretary observed that American industry had the capacity to make the steel forgings for the heavier guns of the main batteries, the machine and rapid fire guns of the secondary batteries, and the armored plating for the new steel ships. Although Congress never appropriated the $35 million he recommended to subsidize American steel manufacturers, Whitney contracted with the Bethlehem Iron (later changed to Bethlehem Steel) Company to produce the required forgings for the new gun and ship construction. During his administration of the Navy Department, the government authorized thirty new warships, including the "first modern armored cruising ships" (later designated the second-class battleships), the *Texas* and the *Maine*.[15]

The Navy secretary owed his success in obtaining funding for the new ships, with its subsequent boost to the domestic steel industry, to a close working relationship with key congressional leaders, especially in the House of Representatives. In 1885, the Democratic-controlled House transferred from its Appropriations Committee the control of the naval appropriation bill to the more sympathetic Naval Affairs Committee. The new chairman of the committee, Representative Hilary A. Herbert from Alabama, a former Confederate Army officer, wanted the position although he had never served on the committee and admittedly knew "practically nothing of the Navy." Herbert claimed that he desired the chairmanship to break down sectionalism and as a Southerner, whose section had little interest in the Navy, he could remain objective and work for the national good. According to Herbert, Secretary Whitney later told him that he had wanted the congressman for "the committee all along."[16]

In his role as chairman, Herbert soon learned that the Navy Department spoke with many voices. Shortly upon entering his new duties, the novice chairman invited the officers in Washington to visit him, since as he later stated, "Naval officers always have views, and these they are quite ready to give to those who may be expected to have any power." According to Herbert, almost every one of them "had his own idea of the character and classes of ships . . . , of the equipment in Navy yards, [and] the value and uselessness of Marines." A few years later, Herbert complained to the press, "It is difficult to determine what is desired by naval officers or needed by the Navy. All want something different, and to ascertain what is most desirable of all the schemes submitted is akin to impossible."[17]

Despite the continued construction of the new ships, the transformation of the old Navy into the new occurred over time. Monitors and unarmored cruisers coexisted with the laying of the keels of the forerunners of the modern battleships. Officers and politicians who were progressive in one matter proved reactionary in another. Secretary Whitney and Congressman Herbert, who both generally supported naval reforms, opposed funding the Naval War College, and Alfred T. Mahan, the so-called Prophet of Seapower, whom Whitney removed as president of the War College in 1888, appeared a conservative when it came to the new technology. In contrast, younger officers looked to the new technology, managerial reorganization, and efficiency to build the new Navy. The years of the Whitney stewardship were a period of flux in which the old and new blended together creating a renewed emphasis on naval policy and strategy as well as on ship design and weaponry.[18]

Simultaneous with the activity in ship construction occurred a renewed concern about coastal defense. In 1885, Congress authorized the formation of a joint Army-Navy board, headed by President Cleveland's secretary of war, William C. Endicott, to study the state of the nation's harbor defenses and to propose necessary improvements in light of the recent rapid developments in both coastal and naval artillery. The Endicott Board made its report the following year, recommending a massive outlay of money, $127 million, to fortify twenty-eight harbor sites. This extensive fortification effort involved the purchase of 677 high-powered breech-loaded rifled guns and 824 rifled mortars, supported by floating batteries, submarine mines, torpedo boats, rapid-firing guns, and searchlights. Although providing no funds, Congress in 1888 established under the War Department a Board of Ordnance and Fortifications headed by Army Maj. Gen. John M. Schofield to test weapons and to recommend measures to implement the Endicott Board harbor-fortification program.[19]

With the Army largely responsible for coastal defense, both Army and Navy officers agreed that the Navy was the primary "*aggressive* arm of the national military power." Navy captains William T. Sampson and Charles F. Goodrich, both members of the Endicott Board, insisted that the new armored ships were to "act offensively and not be confined to the defense of ports." In a speech in support of the continued buildup of the Navy, Congressman Herbert said that it was not the administration's policy to have the largest Navy, but "to have a navy respectable in size, with ships equal to any that float, demonstrating at the same time to the world our ability to increase that navy to any extent that may be required."[20]

Congressman Herbert voiced the sentiments of a growing bipartisan coalition of congressmen and politicians from both political parties as well as naval officers. They believed that a close relationship existed between naval and national power and that the expansion of American interests abroad justified the parallel growth of the American Navy to protect these same interests. The new European imperialism combined with the developments in ship and weapon technology stirred concern among U.S. officials that the European powers had designs of obtaining new footholds in both South and Central America and in the West Indies. Their chief apprehension was the possibility of a foreign-dominated canal between the two Americas. One naval officer observed in 1886 that the American military was prepared only for "another Civil War, or one of those wretched little wars peculiar to colonizing nations." He feared that the chances of war with a major European naval power were very real. This anxiety dominated much of the thinking of the naval officer corps who transmitted their concerns to the responsible civilian authorities. As Bradley Fiske, one of the young reformers, later wrote: "Nobody was the father of the new navy. The new navy was the child of public opinion created by Navy officers." According to Fiske, the secretaries of the Navy "were only instrumentalities for influencing Congress and the President to do what naval officers like Luce, Walker . . . , and others urged them to do."[21]

The push toward a modern offensive Navy had obvious significance for the Marine Corps mission and officer professionalism. Naval officers in their professional literature continued to emphasize landing operations and speculated about their influence upon both services. In the 1886 *Naval Institute Proceedings*, Navy Lt. Carlos G. Calkins in his prize-winning article with the long and prosaic but descriptive title, "What Changes in Organization and Drill Are Necessary to Sail and Fight Effectively Our War Ships of the Latest Type," recommended a reorganization of the Corps and its relationship to the New Navy. Calkins stated that the Marine Corps as a police force was "invaluable and justifies its continuance in spite of the want of adaptability of its system of training to nautical conditions and modern weapons." He suggested limiting the number of Marines on board warships to only those needed for guard and police duty and wanted to reduce the number of Marine officers to two per squadron. Although recognizing the specialized "nautical" skills acquired by the younger Marine officers at the Naval Academy, Calkins believed it impractical to employ their talents on board ship. Calkins's major proposal was the establishment of Marine battalions at two or three central bases to provide "for advanced military instruction and . . . an organized force for detached service." These battalions would also furnish guards for separate ship detachments and the Navy yards.[22]

The Calkins article brought an immediate reaction from naval and Marine officers. In the most extreme statement, Navy Ens. William L. Rogers, in the same issue of the *Proceedings*, questioned even the existence of the Marine Corps. He perceived little need for a police force in the Navy and declared that sailors could take the part of Marines in landing operations. And, although rejecting Calkins's suggestions reducing the number of Marines on board ships, two Marine correspondents saw merit in his central idea. Maj. James Forney, a longtime advocate of a more structured Marine Corps, proposed a regimental organization, with three large depots located at Mare Island on the West Coast and Philadelphia and Norfolk on the East Coast. Another Marine officer, 1st Lt. Littleton W. T. Waller, was of the opinion that one central depot would suffice and it should "be made a School of Instruction for officers and men." Both Forney and Waller wanted Marines trained in gunnery and automatic weapons, and Waller even recommended that Marine landing forces consist of both infantry and light artillery. Except for brief mention of strike duty and the Panama experience, however, neither Waller nor Forney, nor for that matter any of the naval officers explored the implications of an "organized Marine force for detached service" and its possible relationship to landing operations.[23]

Landing operations, nevertheless, provided a constant theme for naval writers. The *Naval Institute* prize-winning article for the following year dealt with the naval brigade. Its author, Lt. C. T. Hutchins, observed that modern navies still required the ability to deploy rapidly armed forces ashore. He pointed to the recent examples of the British in Egypt, the French in China, and the U.S. expedition in Panama. Hutchins wrote that the naval brigade might not be equal to regular troops but was more than adequate against others. He wanted more regularity in organization and training of the brigade and fewer ceremonial formations. He thought the brigade should consist of 20 infantry companies, totaling 1,000 men, supported by an artillery of 10 guns and 230 men. The personnel of the brigade would be the sailors and Marines of the fleet, and the ships themselves would serve as the supply depots for the brigade. Hutchins believed the Marines of the fleet should form a separate battalion, about 220 men and their officers, to serve under the brigade commander who was usually a Navy officer. Although he defined a clear role for Marines in the naval brigade, he repeated many of the same criticisms that McCalla had made in his report following the Panama expedition. Lieutenant Hutchins particularly emphasized the need for the Marines to change their tactics, train with automatic weapons, and receive regular instruction in target practice. In Hutchins's mind, nevertheless, the naval brigade remained largely a Navy, rather than a Marine, organization.[24]

In the 1888 *Proceedings*, Ensign Rogers returned to the discussion of the naval brigade with some revised observations. He had changed his mind about the role of the Marines on board ship, believing they could take over the secondary batteries. Even more important, he agreed with Hutchins that the Marines should form a separate battalion as part of the naval brigade. Rogers wanted the establishment of guidelines for brigade commanders and the development of infantry tactics for the brigade once it was ashore, looking to German and French armies for examples rather than the U.S. Army's Upton's *Tactics*. The Navy ensign recommended that the fleet's guns should cover any landing force and that companies should land together in the same boats. He concluded that "naval officers should look

upon duty ashore as an integral, though secondary, part of their profession."
As one modern historian has noted, the discussion of landing operations in
the *Naval Institute* during this period "established the amphibious operation
as a special branch of naval tactics, and underscored its importance in modern war."[25]

For the Marine Corps, notwithstanding the articles in the professional journals, the four years of the first Cleveland administration were mainly a period of circumspection. Colonel McCawley, by this time, was not looking
for new initiatives. His main concerns remained preserving the traditional
missions and increasing both the enlisted and officer strength of the Marine
Corps. With the prohibition of new officer appointments by law until the
total number of officers numbered fewer than 75, the Marine Corps by 1887
was down to 15 second lieutenants. In December 1887, McCawley, in what
had become an annual refrain, observed to Secretary Whitney that this
number of lieutenants "was totally inadequate to perform the sea duty." He
remarked that the flag ships were down to 1 officer and said, "At none of the
Shore Stations are there enough men to carry on duty." Throughout all of
his appeals for redress of the situation, the only reference that McCawley
made to the New Navy was that the newer ships would require larger Marine guard detachments.[26]

   Even in his limited aims to make the Marine Corps the elite guard force of
the Navy, many of the Marine officer reformers and their allies believed that
Colonel McCawley had become too sanguine about the desertion and discipline problems plaguing the Corps and too ready to blame the lack of personnel for all of his problems. The *Army and Navy Journal*, which hitherto
seldom took the Marine Corps to task, published an editorial in 1887 entitled "Reckless Recruiting." The editorial applauded Colonel McCawley for
his "conscientious efforts" to increase the "usefulness and efficiency" of the
Corps, but said that its recruiting practices were counterproductive. The
Journal claimed that the Corps, especially in the large cities, haphazardly selected recruits, "oftentimes from the scum of the earth." According to the
editorial, many of the new Marine recruits were deserters from either the
Army or the Navy and in turn deserted from the Marine Corps. It also
noted that the Corps lost nearly a quarter of its strength annually to desertion. Observing that recruiting in New York and Philadelphia was left to a
sergeant, the *Journal* recommended that the commandant appoint a senior
officer to head the recruiting service and select only the best men.[27]

   Colonel McCawley personally answered the *Journal*'s editorial with a letter to the editor. He denied that noncommissioned officers were in charge of the recruiting effort in the large cities and said that the commanding officer of each barracks swore in all recruits and was ultimately responsible for them. The commandant admitted, however, that the Marines were not obtaining the best men: "Every officer knows that if written testimonials of good character were demanded from recruits, that it would be impossible to enlist men to carry on duty." He observed that "men enlisted in the large cities have always been of an inferior class" and that the Marine Corps did not have funds to send officers into the rural areas where better men could be obtained. McCawley asserted the Marine Corps was no worse than either the Army or the Navy, both of which had much the same problems relative to desertion.[28]

In its next issue, the *Journal* replied to McCawley. The article, perhaps authored by Marine Capt. Henry Clay Cochrane, rejected out of hand each of McCawley's explanations. According to the article, the commanding officer could not personally attend to recruiting together with all of his other responsibilities. However, McCawley, if he took his case to Congress and the administration, could receive a special appropriation for recruiting since it would result eventually in the saving of money. The *Journal* found it incredulous that the Navy Department could spend millions on new ships that would be "manned by men of 'an inferior class.'" Recognizing that the Marines had a shortage of officers, the author maintained that at least one experienced captain or major could be spared for recruiting duty. The *Journal* concluded that the "Marine Corps has now and has always had our own best wishes and support. We would be pleased to see it in the van, but men of an 'inferior class' will never get it there." Colonel McCawley noted in his 1888 report 415 desertions for the year, equaling 22 percent of the Marine enlisted strength.[29]

Many of the old discipline problems that inhibited professionalism in the officer corps also haunted the McCawley commandancy during the later years. During the last three months of 1885, three Marine officers received official reprimands, and in October 1885, Secretary Whitney admonished 2d Lt. T. Glover Fillette about the latter's perennial indebtedness since entering the Marine Corps in 1880. Obviously nettled, Whitney wrote Fillette that the "Department is not disposed to be subjected to further annoyance concerning your pecuniary transactions." The following month, Maj. George F. Collier informed McCawley that he had suspended one of his first lieutenants, S. W. Quackenbush, for ten days for being absent without leave. In December, Colonel McCawley reported 1st Lt. William P. Biddle to Secretary Whitney for "disrespectful and insubordinate conduct." According to McCawley, Biddle appeared before the commandant and "proceeded to argue with me about the propriety of his orders." Lieutenant Biddle demanded permission to see the secretary, which McCawley refused to give. Biddle then "persisted in an insolent manner, and left my office." The secretary ordered Biddle to explain his actions in writing.[30]

This rash of officer malfeasance continued during the next three years. In 1886, the major scandal involved Capt. John H. Higbee, who had commanded one of the battalions in the Panama intervention. At Norfolk, a Marine junior officer accused Captain Higbee of being intoxicated during a formal parade. According to 1st Lt. Robert G. Benson, Higbee "was so drunk that he did not appear to know where he was or what he was doing." Benson declared that he "never witnessed such disgraceful conduct on the part of an officer in the presence of a battalion and spectators." A court-martial sentenced Higbee to half pay and suspension from rank and duty for a period of three years. The court recommended clemency, and Secretary Whitney reduced the suspension to a period of eighteen months.[31]

McCawley also had problems with Maj. James Forney, who had been in the forefront of the Marine reform movement. In February 1887 the Marine commandant reprimanded Forney for irregular financial procedures. Major Forney was commanding officer of the Norfolk Barracks, and the post treasurer, and he was also in charge of the company fund established to provide for some of the creature comforts of the Marine enlisted men. He deposited $249 of the money into his own personal account at the Exchange National Bank of Norfolk rather than opening up a separate trust. Unfortunately for Forney, the bank failed and he lost the money. At McCawley's behest, the Navy Department ordered Forney to make good on the funds out of his own pocket. Forney then accused McCawley of harassment, and the Marine commandant denied the charge. He wrote to Secretary Whitney that Forney made "more errors" than any other commanding officer and McCawley believed it his responsibility "to call to account any officer who is derelict in his own duties."[32]

McCawley's relationship with other senior commanders also proved vexatious. He refused to assign Col. Thomas Field to recruiting duty in Philadelphia and appealed to the secretary of the Navy to assign the colonel to the Norfolk Barracks. As McCawley explained to Whitney, "It is not for the interest of the Marine Corps to place the highest officer in it (next to the Commandant) upon purely nominal duty." The commandant then stated that if Field found it inconvenient to leave Pennsylvania, he could retire and permit the promotion of an officer "who will be obliged to do his duty." Secretary Whitney ordered Field to Norfolk. In the case of Lt. Col. C. D. Hebb, who commanded the barracks at Portsmouth, New Hampshire, McCawley asked for an investigation in the loss of $639 worth of uniforms. According to McCawley, the disappearance of such a large quantity of government property indicated "gross negligence" on Hebb's part.[33]

Serious incidents involving Marine officers continued to embarrass the Corps. In December 1887, the captain of the Navy steamer *Nipsic* sent 1st Lt. H. C. Fisher back to the New York Navy Yard under arrest. The following year, Rear Adm. James A. Greer, the commander of the European Squadron, court-martialed 1st Lt. Otway G. Berryman for being drunk on duty. The resulting court-martial found Berryman, who had a history of alcohol-related offenses, guilty and directed that he be suspended from duty for two years at half pay. Secretary Whitney approved the sentence of the court.[34]

Although Marine officers' conduct often fell far short of expected standards of behavior, legislative efforts to raise professional qualifications again failed for various reasons, not the least one being divisions among the Marine officer corps. Although individual congressmen and senators supported various maneuvers to benefit Marine officers in succeeding sessions, it was not until the spring of 1888 that a serious push was made. In April of that year, the Senate Naval Affairs Committee, headed by Democratic Senator James McPherson of New Jersey, favorably reported a bill that would substantially enlarge the officer corps and provide promotions for both the staff and senior line officers. According to its provisions, the Marine Corps would total 93 officers: 88 line and 5 staff officers. In addition, the bill would provide for a brigadier general commandant and for a fleet Marine officer with the temporary rank and pay of major while serving in that capacity. Regular majors would become commanders of minor posts ashore and assistant commanders of the larger Marine barracks, and none would serve on board ship. Observing that there would be a "surplus" of Naval Academy graduates for the next three years, the committee also recommended an increase of 12 second lieutenants for the Marine Corps. The secretary of the Navy would fill these new billets over a three-year period with equal increments from each of the Naval Academy classes completing their course of instruction during these years.[35]

As early as February, several Marine officers had formed a committee to lobby for this bill. They sent out letters to other Marine officers attempting to obtain their support, both moral and financial. Not all officers, however, approved of the campaign. Capt. Henry Clay Cochrane, who had led earlier attempts for similar legislation and who was one of the leading Marine re-formers, opposed the bill. He believed it was designed to benefit certain offi-cers and especially the staff. Cochrane observed that Major Goodloe, the paymaster, "Senator Beck's son-in-law, who has already gained two grades, forty-five numbers, and at least twenty-five years over his brother officers" would be one of the chief beneficiaries. Cochrane, claiming to speak for the interests of the younger officers, wrote to the secretary of the informal Ma-rine lobbying committee: "We need lieutenants more than we need colonels and we need majors on the large foreign squadrons more than [at] a one company shore station."[36]

Cochrane's motivations were actually much less altruistic than they ap-peared on the surface. The bill added three more colonels, not including the commandant, and two more lieutenant colonels, while the Marine Corps retained the same number of majors. If Congress enacted the legislation, Cochrane feared that several senior officers, who were about to retire, might be induced by the additional rank to remain on active duty, thus limiting the promotional opportunities for their juniors, and his own. In any event, he knew that the bill provided for promotions for five captains to major and that with his placement on the lineal list he would not be one of them. Moreover, under the provisions of the bill, once the new captains became majors, they were not subject to sea duty. As Cochrane wrote to one of his fellow captains, Louis E. Fagan, the others "will be *per terram* officers and you and I *per mare*."[37]

In his letter to Fagan, Captain Cochrane divulged his frustrations and his unhappiness with the course of the Marine Corps and with its efforts to in-fluence legislation. He noted that twelve years previously he had written ad-vocating the provisions contained in the bill about the fleet Marine officer, "but today I am a gray-headed, bald-headed father of a family and no such temporizing, relapsing, and conditional 'rot' suits me." Cochrane exclaimed, "If I have to go to sea, I want to go as a real major." He declared that he was unwilling to "serve twenty-five years as a captain (at sea when required) for the sake of being a major on shore for a few years commanding a two-cent post." According to Cochrane, the Marine Corps required 10 "at least real, sure enough, come-to-stay majors who will take their sea duty" on the ships of the New Navy and "let the captains take the second rates."[38]

Even without dissension among the officers, the Senate bill probably stood little chance of passage in a presidential election year as Congress hur-ried to adjourn. As the bill was about to come to the floor of the Senate for a vote on May 17, 1888, Democratic Senator Francis M. Cockrell of Mis-souri objected and stated "Let that go over." The presiding officer agreed that the "bill will be passed over, but retain its place on the calendar." Neither the Senate or the House ever voted on the bill.[39]

The struggle to pass the McPherson bill revealed the remaining deep rifts among the Marine officer corps. Although Captain Cochrane's viewpoints obviously paralleled his self-interest, he voiced many of the sentiments of the other reformers when he claimed, "We stand well before men, and always seem to have a full hand which we do not know how to play." According to Cochrane, "The Navy is undergoing a complete revolution, but the Marine Corps slumbers." Cochrane and the reform group wanted to tie any Marine legislation into the New Navy. During the first Cleveland administration, they witnessed the intellectual ferment among their naval colleagues, but failed to see any corresponding movement among Marine officers or any encouragement for such activity from Colonel McCawley and the Marine Corps establishment.[40]

Although the Marine Corps during the second half of the 1880s suffered from a general lassitude, individual Marine officers participated in the general rise of professionalism throughout the naval service. From 1885 through 1888, nine officers engaged in some form of advanced schooling. All nine attended the Navy Torpedo School at Newport, and four stayed to attend the War College. Much of this impetus came from the Navy Department, especially from the Bureau of Navigation, rather than from the Marine Corps. In his Panama report published by the Bureau of Navigation, Commander McCalla called for Marine officers to attend both the Navy Torpedo School and the Army's artillery school at Fort Monroe. In reply, Colonel McCawley pointed to the demands upon his officer corps but insisted that "such few officers as can be spared have been and will continue to be given such [educational] opportunities."[41]

In January 1885, 2d Lt. Harry K. White, while enrolled at the Navy Torpedo School, also served on two specialized boards: one to develop a new system of spar torpedo fittings, and the other to determine the best means of ship defense against torpedo boat attacks. After White completed the course at the end of April, the secretary of the Navy ordered 2d Lt. Francis E. Sutton and 1st Lt. George F. Elliott to Newport. Sutton and Elliott finished their three-month term at the Torpedo School in September. The following year, Colonel McCawley, at the insistence of Secretary Whitney, selected two more officers for the school, 1st Lt. Howard K. Gilman and Capt. William S. Muse.[42]

Up to that time, although the Naval War College had opened its doors in the summer of 1885, no Marine officers had attended the college. Admiral Luce, its first president, even had offered "every facility to any Marine officer who will come here and deliver a lecture (or read a paper) on any subject connected with military or naval operations, or in any way related to the science and Art of War." On August 20, 1886, just before Gilman and Muse were about to graduate from the Torpedo School, Commodore John G. Walker of the Bureau of Navigation, looking for likely candidates for the War College, wrote McCawley that the Department wanted the two Marine officers "to report to Captain A. T. Mahan" [Luce's successor] at the college for an additional two months. The Marine Corps protested and asked the secretary to revoke the orders, at least for Captain Muse, on the basis that there was already an acute shortage of Marine officers both on shore and at sea. Replying for the secretary of the Navy, Walker denied the request, stating that the term would be brief and that the department wanted the two Marines to receive its benefits.[43]

The following year, two more Marine officers, 1st Lt. Samuel Mercer and 2d Lt. Charles H. Lauchheimer attended both the Torpedo School and the War College. Lieutenant Lauchheimer found the War College worthwhile, writing to his classmates from the Naval Academy that he was "absorbing most valuable information on the art of war as viewed both from a Military and Naval standpoint." While restrained in his enthusiasm, he believed "it to be a very good institution, and one which will eventually be 'ripe' with much good to the profession."[44]

Despite Lauchheimer's praise, he and Mercer were the last Marine officers to complete the War College's course of instruction during Secretary Whitney's tenure in office. Although the secretary ordered Colonel McCawley in April 1888 to send two officers to the Navy's Torpedo School, he placed no requirement upon the Marine Corps to send the two on to the War College. This decision probably reflected Whitney's disillusionment with both Luce and Mahan at the War College, rather than any desire to cut Marine officer training. Whether at the War College or the Torpedo School, most of the Marine officers who attended either institution believed that they benefited from the advanced instruction that they received. Second Lt. George Barnett, who completed the Torpedo School curriculum in the spring and summer of 1888, wrote his Naval Academy classmates that "he was much pleased" with his brief stay at the school.[45]

One Marine officer, 1st Lt. Howard K. Gilman, who graduated from both the Torpedo School and the War College, had followed another avenue in his professional pursuits. A year prior to his going to school, Gilman authored a *Marines' Manual*, especially designed for use by Marine enlisted men. It consisted of a "nuts and bolts" description of the basic duties of the enlisted Marine: saluting, marching, standing guard, and duties on both ship and shore. The small book contained a compendium of Navy Department orders and Marine Corps circulars that outlined the major responsibilities of the individual Marine. It even included conversion tables of foreign currencies into American dollars. Colonel McCawley recommended to the secretary of the Navy that he distribute the book throughout the Marine Corps as it filled "a want long felt." The Navy Department purchased 2,000 copies "for the use, free of expense, of the non-commissioned officers and enlisted men of the U.S. Marine Corps." A few years later, a Marine officer observed that Marine officers trained enlisted men, "by the book," and the book was Gilman's *Manual*.[46]

Gilman followed this volume in 1886 with another publication entitled *Naval Brigade and Operations Ashore*. Like the manual, his work on the naval brigade was a handbook rather than an analytical study of landing operations. It broke no new ground, but rather offered practical advice on such matters as establishing field kitchens, ship-to-shore movement of troops and supplies, and brigade organization. It outlined the duties of the brigade commander, adjutant, and company officers. Gilman made references to what today would be called combat loading, stating that supplies "should be placed on board in such a manner that they may be easily reached in the order in which they are required for service." He, nevertheless, perceived the naval brigade in traditional nineteenth-century terms and foresaw only a limited role for the Marines as skirmishers or as part of the main line. Yet, whether by chance or by design, Gilman, a Marine officer, had written the only official Navy Department publication on the subject.[47]

While Colonel McCawley offered encouragement to Lieutenant Gilman's efforts to provide some structure for Marine enlisted men and guidance for the naval brigade ashore, the commandant's contributions at best were modest. Although not actively opposing additional Marine Corps officer training and professional education, here too McCawley took very few initiatives.

The graduates of the Naval Academy that entered the Marine Corps after 1883 brought at least a common education and tradition which eventually resulted in a more positive self-image among Marine Corps officers. Although possessing a certain professional accreditation, academy graduates for the most part proved neither better nor worse officers than their predecessors.

Some officers, such as 2d Lt. Harry K. White, had atypical early tours of duty. In June 1885, White, who had already spent one year at the Navy Torpedo School and had ambitions to become a naval constructor, requested permission from the secretary to attend the British Navy Royal College of Naval Architecture at Greenwich, England. In his endorsement to the request, Colonel McCawley observed that White had "done very little duty in the Marine Corps," and had shown "no aptitude whatever as a soldier." He believed that White proposed to use the Marine Corps "only as a stepping stone . . . while others do his duty." McCawley recommended to the secretary of the Navy that the latter transfer White to another branch of the naval service and that the Marine Corps receive an officer in return. If this were not feasible, the commandant wanted to assign White to the European squadron to take charge of a Marine ship's detachment. White received neither the appointment to Greenwich nor a transfer to another naval corps. He avoided sea duty for a time, but by 1888 he had served on board the *Lancaster* with the European squadron. Colonel McCawley continued to view Marine officer assignments from a traditional perspective and opposed most deviations from this tradition.[48]

From 1884 to 1887, nevertheless, 2d Lt. George Barnett, who was also a member of the Naval Academy class of 1881, had a unique tour of duty in Alaska with an uncommon amount of responsibility for someone of his rank and age. Assigned to the Navy ship *Pinta*, Barnett commanded the ship's guard and was in charge of the U.S. Naval Guard House at Sitka. Ostensibly under the command of the captain of the *Pinta*, he had a free hand at Sitka while the ship remained at Juneau or visited other Alaskan ports. With large parts of the territory under Navy administration, Lieutenant Barnett had under his authority about 2,000 Indians native to the Sitka region. Barnett recalled that he administered the law and even held court, having jurisdiction over most civil and criminal matters except murder, which cases went to a U.S. district court in Oregon. Barnett learned the local language and found the natives "peaceful and provident for indians." Despite his innate racism, Barnett had an appreciation for the Indian culture, remarking "The status of the individual families was well defined by their customs and traditions and they had a certain pride of descent that made for character."[49]

Barnett slowly adjusted to his new environment. In October 1885, he wrote to his Naval Academy classmates that his duty was not too arduous, but fairly unpleasant "on account of being so thoroughly cut off from all social enjoyment." His correspondence with the captain of the *Pinta* concerned relatively mundane matters: the forwarding of muster rolls, requisitioning supplies, and submitting prisoner reports. With the establishment of U.S. territorial civil government in Sitka during the middle of his tour, he lost some of his official duties, but enjoyed more off-duty amenities. In October 1886, Barnett wrote to his classmates that Sitka "compares more favorably with other places in a social way." He mentioned that there were more families with "several pretty girls." The local community formed a theatrical company that helped to occupy the long winter hours. Despite the improvement in the social life of Sitka, Barnett cheerfully departed in June 1888 and looked forward to his new assignment at the Washington Navy Yard as a most welcome change. Yet, as Barnett later acknowledged, the Sitka assignment provided him with a most valuable experience in independent command.[50]

Most of Barnett's fellow Naval Academy graduates had more conventional first tours of duty, either at the Marine barracks in the various Navy yards or at sea on board ship. Colonel McCawley jealously protected his new officers from what he considered abuse of their services. Some naval commanders wanted to use the new Marine lieutenants with their special naval training as "watch officers" when assigned to their ships. In one such case involving 2d Lt. William H. Stayton, Colonel McCawley vigorously protested to the secretary of the Navy: "If officers of the Marine Corps can be detailed as watch officers of the Navy, it would seem to follow that officers of the Navy can be detailed to perform the duties of the Marine Corps."[51]

Most of the new second lieutenants found life both on board ship and on shore relatively routine and dull. Second Lt. Charles A. Doyen at the New York Barracks wrote that he "was at present engaged in perusing the pensive sentinel around the boundaries of the New York Navy Yard." His classmate, 2d Lt. Francis E. Sutton, after a brief stint at the Torpedo School, received orders to the Portsmouth Navy Yard in New Hampshire. Sutton humorously complained that at Portsmouth he was "gradually degenerating into a vegetable. Those who have been here in the fall or winter can understand the charms of this place." He even compared his position with that of Barnett in Alaska and remarked that the latter had "a far more enviable station." The lot of many of his classmates at sea was hardly much better. Second Lt. C. Marrast Perkins on board the USS *Tennessee* related that much of the period he suffered from seasickness and the "remaining time has hardly been worth the mention." Perkins told his classmates that he had "concluded that the life of a Marine officer is not an exciting one." Another Marine lieutenant classmate commented "that the status of Marine officers and men on board ship is 'damned peculiar.'"[52]

Many of the young officers, nevertheless, discovered a certain sense of adventure in the sea duty with its foreign travel and occasional demonstrations of force. Second Lt. H. C. Haines joined his ship at Lisbon, Portugal. From Lisbon, the *Lancaster* made its way into the South Atlantic via England, the Mediterranean, and the Congo. While in the South Atlantic station, the ship visited Capetown, Zanzibar, and Madagascar. In the Orient, Lt. James E. Mahoney served on board the USS *Marion* which anchored for a time in a Korean port. Although he found Seoul "dirty and filthy, the city and its people are very interesting to a foreigner." Second Lt. Charles Lauchheimer's visit to Seoul was not as a tourist. Assigned to the *Ossippe*, Lauchheimer marched the ship's guard to Seoul "to protect the legation. The mere show of force had the desired effect and after three days spent at the legation, we returned, leaving the poor Coreans trembling with fright and promising never to do so again."[53]

Of the Marine second lieutenants from the Naval Academy, two were dead by the end of the decade. Second Lt. Arthur H. Clarke, while serving on board the *Iroquois* in May 1888, inexplicably committed suicide. The second death occurred during the naval confrontation with Germany in Samoan waters. In the March 1899 hurricane, which destroyed the small American fleet there, one of the casualties was 2d Lt. Francis E. Sutton. A large wave broke across the deck of Sutton's ship, the *Vandalia*, and swept him into the sea. His shipmates never recovered his body. Of all his classmates, the popular Sutton had shown the most promise as a Marine officer.[54]

Like the Panama crisis at the beginning of the Cleveland administration, the Samoan situation, near its end, strengthened the American perception that European imperialistic designs conflicted with American interests. In 1887 and 1888, German sailors and marines intervened forcibly to remove undesirable native Samoan rulers. American-initiated negotiations failed to resolve the situation, and another Samoan chief led a revolt against the German puppet king. In December 1888, the Samoan rebels defeated a German landing force. In response, the Germans bombarded the Samoan capital of Apia and seized several American citizens, whom they later released. At that point, Secretary Whitney sent three ships of the Pacific Squadron to Samoa, and in January 1889 President Cleveland placed the matter before Congress with the warning that the Germans threatened the independence of the islands.[55]

Despite speculation in the American press, neither Germany nor the United States wanted war. Secretary Whitney told reporters, "It is a serious business to declare war with Germany or any power. . . . I do not care to assume that responsibility." He then deferred to Congress, stating that "whatever Congress directs we will execute to the best of our ability." Congress appropriated $500,000 for the protection of American property and lives in Samoa. However, the German "Iron" chancellor, Prince Otto von Bismarck, had by that time defused the crisis by calling for a conference at Berlin where British, German, and American representatives eventually resolved the dispute. In March, the hurricane that sank three American ships and three German ships in Apia harbor blew aside the warlike ardor on both sides. Only the relatively modern British warship, the *Calliope*, survived the storm.[56]

Despite the early end of the crisis, the Samoan situation spurred the continued growth of the Navy and played on U.S. suspicions of German intentions, not only in the Pacific, but also in the Caribbean. As some historians suggest, the Cleveland administration strongly upheld the American position in Samoa so as not to reveal any weakness and to dissuade an aggressive Germany from any adventures in the Caribbean basin. With a growing awareness of American vulnerability abroad, naval officers and American policy makers concluded that a "modern fleet was essentially an offensive weapon—an extension of a nation's power and prestige outward."[57]

Although the Whitney administration of the Navy Department may have "laid out the route to the battleship navy," the portents of this trend were less clear for the Marine officer corps. Although naval professionals wrote about projection of force ashore from the sea, Marine officers with one or two exceptions took almost no part in the discussion. Individual officers attended the Naval War College and Torpedo School at Newport, but this was usually at the insistence of Navy Department officials and often over the objections of the Marine Corps commandant. Colonel McCawley's enthusiasm at the beginning of his commandancy to improve the quality of the officers and enlisted men for the Marine Corps had also waned over the years. The officer corps remained badly divided and unable to unite over legislation to expand it. Even though the younger officers from the Naval Academy may have brought more professional preparation to their positions, their careers followed much the same pattern as other Marine officers. Neither the Panama expedition at the beginning of the Cleveland administration nor the Samoan crisis at the end provided any clear direction for the Marine Corps. As a result, Marine Corps officer professionalism remained iconoclastic and individualistic.

5. MARINE PROFESSIONALISM AND THE NEW NAVY, 1889–1891

In 1889, the newly inaugurated Benjamin Harrison, the grandson of a previous president, promoted a more outward-looking foreign policy, especially in the Caribbean, South America, and the Pacific. He supported increased American trade in these areas and an expansive interpretation of the Monroe Doctrine based on American naval power. In the first years of his administration, the New Navy became a reality. With the waning of the McCawley commandancy, the developments in the Navy offered new opportunities for reform and professionalism for the Marine officer corps as well as new dangers.[1]

With an obvious expanding role for the Navy, President Harrison wanted the secretary of that cabinet position filled by a man of marked ability. Upon the recommendation of Elihu Root, a prominent New York lawyer, Harrison chose Benjamin Franklin Tracy for the post. A person of "solid rather than brilliant parts," Tracy was a loyal member of the Thomas Platt faction of the New York Republican party and served a term as chief justice of the New York State Court of Appeals. During the Civil War, he commanded a New York volunteer regiment during the Wilderness Campaign and attained both the brevet rank of brigadier general and the congressional Medal of Honor. According to a contemporary journalist, the fifty-nine-year-old secretary was "tall, strong, vigorous, dignified, graceful in manner without suggesting a particle of weakness for 'soft' manners."[2]

Secretary Tracy brought good judgement and a talent for management to his office. He opened channels of communications with both the officer corps and members of Congress. Tracy continued to foster the bipartisan coalition that supported the Navy and maintained friendly relations with his predecessor, William Whitney. As one of his first steps, he issued a general order in June 1889 that streamlined the coordination between the bureaus and increased the power of the Bureau of Navigation.[3]

Despite the strengthened authority of his position, Rear Adm. John G. Walker, chief of the Bureau of Navigation, had other concerns. Walker had already served two terms, and his chances for reappointment were slim. With the completion of the three ABC ships, the *Atlanta*, the *Boston*, and the *Chicago*, and the placement of them into service, Walker saw a new opportunity for himself. He convinced Secretary of the Navy Tracy to form the three ships together with the gunboat, the *Yorktown*, into a "Squadron of Evolution" to test and develop fleet tactics. Tracy then placed Walker in command of the new squadron after the completion of his tour in the Bureau of Navigation. Walker perceived the Squadron of Evolution as the vanguard of a new battle fleet.[4]

The establishment of the Squadron of Evolution was part of a growing consensus within the Navy about the battle fleet. In July 1889, Rear Adm. Stephen B. Luce published an article, "Our Future Navy" in the *North American Review*, later reprinted in the *United States Naval Institute Proceedings*. Luce compared the fleet to a military ground force, calling it a "sea army." He observed that the basis of any land army was the infantry of the line, which the rest of the combat arms served as adjuncts. Similarly, argued Luce, the ship of the line was the basis of any fleet, the rest being auxiliaries. The admiral then suggested that the new ship of the line was the battleship. He wrote that the United States, by concentrating on cruising ships, was "pretending to build up a Navy without the constituents of a line of battle." In the discussion of the article in the *Proceedings*, all of the correspondents, including Capt. Alfred Thayer Mahan and Lt. Richard Wainwright, voiced their agreement with Luce's emphasis upon the battleship.[5]

In his 1889 *Annual Report*, Secretary Tracy took up this refrain. He contrasted the strength and makeup of the European navies with that of the American. Compared to eleven European fleets, he observed that even with completion of the current U.S. ship-building program, the American Navy lagged behind. It would have fourteen fewer ships, including one fewer armored vessel, than the Austrian Navy, ranked last among the European powers. Although noting the U.S. naval reforms and progress since 1881, Tracy concluded that "the fleet has still only a nominal existence."[6]

The secretary declared that the United States with its extensive two-ocean coastlines and with twenty large coastal population centers lay at the mercy of the more modern European navies. He referred to U.S. interests in the Gulf of Mexico and the Pacific as "too important to be left unprotected." The American unarmored cruisers were fine for commerce raiding, but the nation "absolutely requires the creation of a fighting fleet." To Tracy, this meant an oceangoing battleship Navy to break blockades, to repulse an attacking fleet, and finally to carry the war to the enemy's own shores. Specifically, Secretary Tracy recommended a fifteen-year construction program that would involve the building of twenty battleships, divided between two fleets, twelve for the Atlantic and eight for the Pacific. Thus, in actuality, Tracy advocated moving U.S. Navy strategy away from defense and commerce raiding to "the larger doctrine of control of the seas."[7]

Prior to his annual message, the secretary of the Navy had carefully prepared the way for this policy departure. Within the Navy Department, he had established a series of special boards to study specific improvements within the Navy. Two of the most important were a Policy Board, under Commodore J. P. McCann, the commandant of the Boston Navy Yard, and a Board of Organization, Tactics, and Drill, under Commodore James A. Greer, the former commander of the European Squadron. The McCann Board was to report to Tracy on the number and type of ships that the American Navy required while the Greer Board was to examine ship organization, fleet tactics, and landing operations. Much to Tracy's chagrin, however, the findings of both boards led to controversy and discord rather than to smooth waters for the New Navy.[8]

Tracy's annual message, however, struck a responsive chord with most naval and Marine officers. In what was probably a typical response, reflecting the views of most of the officers advocating change, Marine 2d Lt. Harry K. White wrote in December 1889 that the Navy secretary had "struck the nail on the head in his report. . . . What we want most is ironclads, battleships. He shows what the Navy really needs to be worthy of our great country."[9]

Changes were also occurring within the Marine Corps. The Navy appropriation bill of March 1889 increased the enlisted strength of the Marine Corps by 100 men, but also, unexpectedly, permitted the infusion of younger blood into the officer corps. Like the Act of 1882, which provided for appointments to the Marine Corps from graduates of the Naval Academy, the initiative came from within the Navy Department rather than from the Marines. Concerned about morale among the cadets at the Naval Academy, the superintendent and the Academy's Board of Visitors recommended more specialized training and the guarantee of commissions for graduates. Despite some questions on motives and one Congressman joking that the purpose was "to make up in officers what we lack in ships," Congress incorporated in the appropriation bill several of the recommendations. It mandated that at least 15 members of every Naval Academy graduating class receive officer appointments each year, 12 to the Navy line, 2 to the Navy engineer corps, and 1 to the Marine Corps, irrespective of vacancies in each branch. On July 1, 1889, Navy Cadet Albert L. Draper, ranked twenty-seventh out of the 28 members of his class who were commissioned, became a second lieutenant in the Marine Corps, the first new officer in five years.[10]

With the retirements of Lt. Col. John L. Broome and Col. Thomas Y. Field in 1888 and 1889 respectively, the numbers of the "old guard" among the officers began to diminish. This "changing of the guard" allowed for the promotion of several of the younger officers and the appearance of new faces at the Washington headquarters. Commandant McCawley brought in newly promoted Lt. Col. Charles Heywood to command the Washington Barracks. In 1889, as Colonel McCawley's health began to fail, Heywood and Capt. Daniel P. Mannix, who joined the Washington staff in February, began to take over more of the administrative details of running the Marine Corps.[11]

Captain Mannix had completed his tour of sea duty after four years in China and was obviously back in Colonel McCawley's good graces. On September 14, 1889, in a long, gossipy letter to Capt. Henry Clay Cochrane, Mannix wrote about the need for change in the Marine Corps. In the main body of his letter, Mannix enthusiastically explained his idea for a Marine officer board, similar to the Navy's Greer Board. This Marine board, Mannix proposed, would examine the demands that the new ABC protected vessels would make on Marine organization, arms, drill, equipment, and even uniforms. He declared that the board should stir the Corps to do "something besides hanging on to the skirts of the Army or Navy." Mannix had already discussed with members of the Greer Board, apparently with the concurrence of the commandant, the possibility of Marines manning the machine guns and secondary batteries on the new ships, "leaving the sailors for the great guns." The Marine captain suggested that the board should study the establishment of an apprentice system to maintain Marine enlisted strength and form a "practical school of application" that would embrace training in electricity, torpedoes, gunnery, and drill for both officers and men. He concluded with the warning that if the Marine Corps did not plan for itself, "the Greer Board will do it for us and perhaps not altogether to our liking."[12]

On October 1, in a letter to the secretary of the Navy, which Mannix either drafted or influenced, Colonel McCawley asked for 400 more Marines "to supply the demands of the new ships." He then recommended that the secretary direct the Greer Board "to consider the Marine Corps in connection with the New Navy, and that its duties on board ship be well defined." The commandant proposed that the Board might want to examine the role of Marines as sharpshooters, manning the secondary batteries and receiving instruction at the "great guns." He offered to provide the secretary "a board of officers of the Marine Corps . . . to furnish suggestions as to its needs."[13]

Secretary Tracy turned the commandant's letter over to the Greer Board for its comments. Commodore Greer in his reply wrote that the Board was of the "opinion, but upon imperfect information that the number of enlisted men in the Marine Corps should be increased." Greer requested that the commandant of the Marine Corps provide detailed memoranda to the Board and that a Marine officer appear before it "and state in full the views of the Colonel Commandant." The Board president declared that before he and his colleagues recommended an increase in the number of Marines afloat, the board needed "to see their [the Marines'] duties in ships more specifically defined." He then added, "The fighting duties of the Marines in ships should undoubtedly be extended, and should be more clearly defined." In his endorsement to Greer's letter on October 14, 1889, the Navy secretary ordered McCawley to comply with the Board's desire for more data and to send a Marine officer to represent the Corps before the Board.[14]

On October 18, Colonel McCawley provided the "Board of Organization" a series of memoranda outlining his recommendations relative to the duties of Marines on board ship and the formation of a school of application at the Washington Barracks. These corresponded closely to the ideas that Captain Mannix had outlined earlier to Henry Clay Cochrane. Marines would man the secondary batteries under their own officers on board ship; Marine officers on board ship would command the guns of the secondary battery, serve as signal officers, and teach infantry tactics to both sailors and Marines; and, finally, Marine instructors at the proposed School of Application would serve to teach "officers and men . . . in all the duties required of them on shore and afloat." The school would consist of a battalion of 200 men and "while under drill and preparation for sea service, would also be in readiness at the shortest notice for any temporary emergency which might arise." The Marine commandant informed Commodore Greer that he had appointed Captain Mannix to represent the Marine Corps before the board, assuring Greer that "Captain Mannix is a most intelligent officer of large experience, and can fully explain to the Board my views on the whole subject."[15]

The deliberations of the Greer Board on Marine-related subjects hardly went the way the Marine Corps wanted. Earlier, Cmdr. Henry Glass, a member of the Board, had presented a six-page memorandum in which he argued that the Navy had to put itself "in harmony with existing conditions, and to make the most efficient use of modern ships." Glass would "cut off every individual not actually essential to the effective working of the vessel." According to Captain Cochrane, Glass three years later told him during a game of whist, that he (Glass) proposed to the board that they "move to dispense with Marines afloat." He would grant the Marine Corps an increase to 2,500 men and recommend that it "be held in readiness for emergencies." In any event, Captain Mannix reported back to Colonel McCawley that when he appeared before the Greer Board, he received a most unfriendly reception. One Navy lieutenant, probably William F. Fullam, "violently opposed" the Marine Corps recommendations and "argued at length to that effect."[16]

Unsubstantiated rumors soon reached Colonel McCawley that the Greer Board had recommended to the secretary of the Navy the removal of Marine guard detachments from Navy warships. On November 13, 1889, the *New York Times* carried a story to that effect. Two weeks later, the *Army and Navy Journal* referred to the *Times* story, claiming that the "Marine Corps is credited with being a reliable body of men, but it has been asleep for the past 50 years." The *Journal* concluded that "the clattering of the hammers in the construction of the new Navy has brought it [the Marine Corps] back to life." According to the periodical, every Marine officer knew that something had to be done: "It remains for the Greer Board to recommend and for the Marine officers to push the matter to a conclusion."[17]

On December 18, in a personal letter to Rear Admiral Luce, Colonel McCawley complained that he learned "with the greatest chagrin" from the newspapers that the Board had made its recommendation to the secretary of the Navy. He declared, "At this moment I have yet no official information on the subject, and am waiting the pleasure of the Department to communicate it to me." Privately, he knew that the published reports were accurate, but "of course until the Dep't takes some action by referring the matter to me for reply, or by filing it, (which would be better) nothing can be done." Secretary of the Navy Tracy decided against accepting the Board's recommendation, and much to McCawley's relief, Marine guards remained assigned to Navy ships. Yet this issue colored all Marine-Navy relations for the near future.[18]

As typified by the proceedings of the Greer Board, the reform element now dominated the Navy line. With allies among several of the more progressive older officers, the so-called Young Turks were in the ascendancy. Frustrated by years of slow promotion, the now not-so-young "Turks" strove for a complete revamping of the naval service from ships to personnel. Thanks to

Commodore Walker and his Bureau of Navigation, many were now in strategic positions, if not holding commensurate rank, to influence developments.[19]

Impressed by new business and managerial techniques, these naval professionals attempted to rationalize and organize the New Navy to meet the challenges of advancing technology and what they perceived as a more dangerous world. Navy Lt. Richard Wainwright observed that all professions required "study and application . . . but in no profession is this more so than in that of the naval officer." According to Wainwright, the one constant was change both in "methods and instruments" that the officer had to master "or the advances in his pursuit will leave him behind."[20]

Whether resulting from personal "career anxiety," "institutional anxiety," or merely reflecting the temper of their times and the nature of their profession, the progressive naval officers viewed the outside world through a Social Darwinian lens. This was especially true in their perspective of American foreign relations and the defense needs of the United States. They saw the United States surrounded by prospective enemies and especially vulnerable to naval attack. Many feared that the United States military could not even accomplish their secondary war missions, let alone defeat the enemy. With the U.S. growing interests in the Caribbean and the Pacific, they believed the chances existed for a great-power war to pull in the United States. However, it would take nearly a decade to modernize American fortifications and to create a truly modern Navy.[21]

The new naval outlook determined the conclusions of the McCann Policy Board. After reviewing the strength of potential enemies, the proximity of possible coaling stations, and the probable conflict areas, the board called for a Navy second in size only to that of Great Britain. Although asking for tactically offensive battleships, the board believed that the U.S. would be involved in "a strategically defensive conflict." Its Navy would largely command the contested waters since it would be operating close to its bases in contrast to any probable European foe. The board recommended to Secretary Tracy the building of about 200 warships of all types, including 10 "offensive battleships" supported by 25 "defensive" capital ships. The new construction would cost the government nearly $300 million, an almost unthinkable sum at the time. In January 1890, like the Greer Board's recommendations earlier, the policy board's report leaked to the press and caused an instant furor in Congress and the public at large. Although sympathetic with many of the board's findings, Secretary Tracy publicly repudiated the report as did most legislators.[22]

Although both the Greer and McCann boards ended in controversy,

Rear Admiral Walker's experiment with the Squadron of Evolution proved more constructive. By February 1890, Walker began a series of ship maneuvers and landings in European waters to test and develop fleet tactics. He had carefully selected both the officers and sailors of his command. At a time when over half the enlisted force of the U.S. Navy was foreign born, nearly 75 percent of the crews of his squadron were American-born. The small American naval force practiced amphibious operations near Nice nearly every day during a two-week period in February and March. Ships' battalions at first drilled independently and then consolidated into a naval brigade. At the end of the two weeks, the forces ashore consisted of over 700 sailors and Marines supported by eight pieces of artillery.[23]

From Malta in April, Walker wrote Secretary Tracy, expressing his satisfaction: "I look upon the visit of the Squadron here as an education to those officers who are taking advantage of the opportunity." He then observed that the "winter's work . . . has been excellent. . . . Much has been seen, much has been learned." Although Walker remarked on some of the disadvantages of the foreign cruise—"temptations to shore going and the necessity for social entertainments"—he, nonetheless, believed the advantages far outweighed the inconveniences. The squadron commander concluded that "we have made a beginning in the matter of a Squadron for drill and instruction which will, I am sure, when the prejudices of the conservative Navy have been overcome, be considered as one of the most important and creditable things inaugurated during your administration of naval affairs."[24]

While the Squadron of Evolution demonstrated the need for a balanced fleet and provided a test vehicle for the New Navy, both Tracy and Walker had more mundane reasons for its deployment overseas. For one, they saw it as an opportunity to obtain firsthand information about the European fleets and to learn about new developments in naval technology. Second, they wanted to impress the Europeans with the advances the U.S. Navy had made. And finally, they viewed the squadron as a public relations ploy to pressure Congress for the continued funding of the Navy's new ship construction program.[25]

Despite the damage caused by the premature publication of the McCann Board, Secretary Tracy still had enough remaining political capital to push the administration's naval policy through Congress. Recuperating in the White House as a guest of the president after a devastating fire in February 1890 had destroyed his house, killed his wife and a daughter, and left him badly burned, the Navy secretary continued to monitor the progress of the Navy bill. Faced with opposition from such formidable personages as Senator William E. Chandler, the former secretary of the Navy, who argued that battleships could "not get in and out of harbors," Tracy allied the administration with a bipartisan congressional coalition of Navy supporters. These included the powerful Republican speaker of the House of Representatives, Thomas B. Reed; the chairman of the House Naval Affairs Committee, Charles A. Boutelle; the senior Democratic member of the committee, Hilary A. Herbert; Senator Eugene Hale, the dominant figure on the Senate Naval Affairs and Appropriations committees; and the influential Democratic representative, William G. McAdoo of New Jersey. Knowing when to compromise and when to exert pressure, these congressional leaders skillfully maneuvered the naval bill through both houses. On June 30, 1890, President Harrison signed the bill into law.[26]

The new law appropriated $18 million for the building of three "sea-going, coastline battleships." Although a compromise from the eight that Secretary Tracy called for in his annual report, the bill was still a departure in naval legislation. It called for "creating a fighting fleet to seize command of the open sea," even if, as in this case, the open sea was limited to about 1,000 miles off the United States coast.[27]

Allowing that the naval bill was a milestone in the creation of the battleship Navy, Senator Henry Cabot Lodge described it during the Senate debate as a continuation of the actions set in motion by the previous two administrations. Several decades later, military historian Walter Millis observed that "the new battleships were less a bid for 'sea power' than a response to the remorseless advance of technology." In order to move the legislation through Congress, Secretary Tracy and the congressional leadership had to define the mission of the new ships in terms of coast defense.[28]

Even the Navy progressives still found a secondary role for the Navy in the old coast-defense mission. Only the previous year, Navy Capt. William T. Sampson had proposed a reserve fleet of torpedo boats, rams, and coastal monitors to supplement the Army coastal fortifications. Sampson, however, left the manning of his reserve fleet to naval reservists. According to Sampson, while the Army and the reserve fleet defended the coastal waters, the regular Navy was to destroy the commerce of the enemy, attack the enemy coastal waters, and "to meet and defeat the enemy's main fleet."[29]

In the spring of 1890, Little, Brown and Company published a new book, *The Influence of Seapower upon History, 1660–1783*, that in its own right influenced the course of the debate upon the nature of the new Navy. The book, by U.S. Navy Capt. Alfred Thayer Mahan, was compiled of the lectures that Mahan had delivered at the Naval War College. In a letter to Secretary Tracy in May 1890, Mahan wrote that his purpose was to "lay a broad foundation for the study of naval warfare." He acknowledged that several of his colleagues viewed his work "as a mere groping among the dead," but Mahan believed that the understanding of "modern conditions" required the "systematic presentation and analysis of the naval strategy and tactical methods of the past."[30]

In this the first of his seapower books, Mahan laid out the themes that were to dominate naval thought both in the United States and Europe for the next decades. Using the example of the European colonial and maritime wars of the seventeenth and eighteenth centuries, he maintained that British command of the seas was the reason for that nation's predominance. To Mahan, the British experience proved that the main objective of any navy was the destruction, or at least the neutralization, of the opposing fleet. In modern terms and for the United States, he translated this into a requirement for a fleet of armored battleships, the new ships of the line.[31]

Mahan was more important as a propagandist than as a strategic thinker. This was especially evident in his "didactic" first chapter where he called for American expansion in the Caribbean, the rebuilding of the American merchant marine, the eventual building of a canal across the Central American Isthmus, the acquisition of Hawaii, the creation of a battleship fleet, and the establishment of American sea superiority in the waters off both the Atlantic and Pacific coasts. These ideas were not original to Mahan but were ones which many of his naval colleagues commonly held.[32]

Mahan's ideas hit a responsive chord with several of the younger rising Republican political stars such as Theodore Roosevelt and Henry Cabot Lodge. Influenced by European imperialism, the young Republicans were sympathetic to an America "looking outward." They eagerly seized upon the Mahanian concepts of seapower and expansion into the Caribbean and Pacific as the intellectual basis for an American imperialism.[33]

Expansion into the Caribbean had long been an underlying thread of U.S. policy, although immediately after the Civil War, "more like an underground river than a surface stream." By 1890, however, the river had once more risen to the surface. Even traditional policy makers such as Secretary Tracy accepted many of the Mahanian ideas. In fact, since the latter part of 1889, Mahan had served on special assignment in the Bureau of Navigation in Washington. Historians still speculate whether Mahan was the actual author of Tracy's 1889 annual report. In July 1890, Secretary Tracy charged Mahan with the preparation of several contingency plans in the event of war with a European power.[34]

This represented the Navy Department's first formal war-contingency planning. True, in 1885, Commodore Walker's secret orders to Cmdr. Bowman A. McCalla implied some prior thought about plans for an American advanced base off Panama against an unknown enemy. Again the next year when the question of fishing rights and continued resentment against the English by Irish-Americans ruffled Canadian and American relations, Walker asked the Office of Naval Intelligence for information about Canada. He even visited Canada to obtain further intelligence about the country. These were haphazard ventures, at best, and represented no systematic effort to examine the options available to the United States against a European foe.[35]

In mid-1890, Secretary Tracy formed a secret strategy committee consisting of Mahan; Commodore William M. Folger, head of the Bureau of Ordnance; and Prof. James Soley, the assistant secretary of the Navy. Mahan apparently was responsible for developing various contingency plans for the group. In July 1890, he departed Washington for Newport and went from there to New York where he worked on war planning and also continued his historical research. By December 1890, he had completed a plan against England and recommended "taking up next and at once, Germany and Spain" because both of these latter nations were "more nearly equal to ourselves and because with both the ground of meeting would probably be the Gulf and the Caribbean."[36]

Of the contingency plans, only the one involving England still remains extant. Although war with Great Britain in 1890 was most unlikely, the British were in position of all the great powers to do the most damage to the United States. Mahan recognized the great British naval superiority over the United States, and, as a result, his plan reflected an element of desperateness or, as his biographer observed, a certain "Mad Hatter quality."[37]

According to the contingency plan, the U.S. battle fleet would concentrate in New York Harbor. Mahan believed that the British would then attempt to blockade the harbor with their battleships. He assumed American coast defenses and monitors and cruising vessels would be strong enough to fend off British forays against other coastal cities. While the Navy held off the British fleet and gained superiority over the Great Lakes, the U.S. Army would invade central and east-central Canada. The U.S. Navy battle fleet would then somehow slip out of New York, elude the British blockading fleet, and escort transports carrying a landing force of U.S. Army troops and Marines to Nova Scotia and Cape Breton Island. With the American fleet establishing local sea superiority over the defending British squadron, the Marines and Army troops would seize Cape Breton and the port of Halifax in Nova Scotia. Mahan argued that the resulting denial of the coal fields in Nova Scotia and Cape Breton for the use of the British Navy would force the English to lift their blockade of New York for lack of fuel. With Halifax in American hands, the British fleet would have to retire to Bermuda. Although Mahan recognized that the possibility of success was slight, he maintained that the American fleet should undertake the Nova Scotia campaign, even if "there should appear to be one chance in five in our favor." Obviously, Mahan himself had little faith in his plan to overcome the obvious British naval advantages.[38]

Although important as the first systematic contingency planning for war, the Mahan plan had special significance for the Marine Corps. Even with little likelihood of its implementation, the Mahan plan laid out a special role for the Marine Corps: "Allusion has been made to mobilize the Marine Corps in certain contingencies. If this Corps be kept up to the standard of its former efficiency, it will constitute a most important re-enforcement, nay, backbone, to any force landing on the enemy's coast. Measures should be framed by which the whole body could be collected." Mahan was not alone among naval officers in believing that the Marine Corps should be used as a landing force. Capt. Charles H. Davis, who reviewed the plan for the Navy Department, agreed, commenting: "The Marines, as shown by Captain Mahan, could be speedily mobilized to form two battalions of trained regular troops." Even as sharp a critic of the Marine Corps as Lt. William F. Fullam, a former member of the Greer Board, observed in late 1890: "The [Marine] corps would be invaluable as a highly trained, homogeneous, and permanently organized body of infantry, ready at all times to embark and co-operate with the navy in service like that at Panama a few years ago." A Navy staff officer, two decades later, pointed to these discussions in 1890 as the first recognition of the advanced base mission for the Marine Corps to support the new battleship Navy.[39]

Despite this discussion of an expanded role for the Marine Corps, no Marine Corps officers took part in the Navy's war-contingency planning. For the most part, during 1890, the officers turned inward, looking to the succession of the commandancy as Colonel McCawley's tenure in office came to a close. If anything, the Marine officers' proclivity was to hold on to their traditional missions on board ship and at the Navy yards. Having surmounted the challenge of the Greer Board, Colonel McCawley concentrated his efforts on his old concerns of obtaining enough officers and men to carry out these duties.

In March 1890, Colonel McCawley observed to Secretary of the Navy Tracy that the basic requirement for the Marine Corps was "2d lieutenants and privates, and that I have repeatedly so informed the Department for 14 years past." The retirement of several older officers and the resignation or death of others presented unexpected opportunities for the revitalization of the officer corps. By June 1890, the Marine Corps contained 70 officers, 5 below the number authorized by the appropriation act of 1885.[40]

On July 1, 1890, five former naval cadets became Marine second lieutenants. These were John A. Lejeune, ranked sixth in his class; Clarence L. Ingate, ranked fourteenth; Leroy A. Stafford, who stood nineteenth; Eli A. Cole, twentieth; and Theodore P. Kane, twenty-seventh and next-to-last ranking man of his class to be commissioned. All five were Episcopalians and members of families relatively prominent in their region. Ingate, Stafford, and Lejeune were southerners, Stafford and Lejeune from Louisiana, and Ingate from Alabama. Ingate's father was a railroad superintendent in Mobile, Lejeune's father owned a plantation in Pointe Coupee Parish, and Stafford's guardian was a merchant in Alexandria, Louisiana. Cole came from Carmel, New York, where his father was a bank official. Kane, born in Annapolis, was the son of a Navy commander. With the exception of Kane, who had attended only public schools, they had received both public and private schooling. Thus, in most respects, these new officers conformed perfectly to what historian Peter Karsten called the "Naval Aristocracy."[41]

Three of the 5 newly commissioned Marine second lieutenants stood in the lower half of their Academy class, and Ingate ranked fourteenth of 28 class members who received commissions. With the notable exception of the first group of Naval Academy graduates that entered the Marine Corps in 1883, this was the usual pattern. Of the 11 officers commissioned from 1884 through 1890, 8 ranked below most of their Naval Academy classmates who entered the Navy. The Naval Academy Academic Board, which determined service assignments for the new graduates, obviously placed the Marine Corps requirements lower than the Navy on its priority list.[42]

Assigned by the Academic Board as a naval engineer, young Lejeune employed the influence of Louisiana Senator Randell Gibson to reverse the decision. According to Lejeune, he selected the Marine Corps as his first choice only to find himself placed in the Engineer Corps. When he protested, Naval Academy Superintendent William T. Sampson told him that the Academic Board believed that he "stood too high in the class to be assigned to the Marine Corps." Lejeune and Senator Gibson then personally met with Secretary Tracy who agreed that Lejeune should receive his first choice of service.[43]

In his autobiography, Lejeune provided several reasons why he selected the Marine Corps over the Navy. He stated he had no bent for mechanical engineering, which eliminated the Engineering Corps. Having served as a passed midshipman on the *Vandalia* and survived when the vessel sank off Samoa the previous year, he had no great love for the sea. Moreover, according to Lejeune, he believed his best ability lay in handling men and that the Marine Corps offered him the best opportunity to practice this skill. One factor that Lejeune failed to mention in his book but no doubt influenced his decision was that of promotion. In fact the *New York Times* featured an article a few months later, entitled "Shrewd Annapolis Men." The gist of the article was that the Marine Corps offered newly commissioned officers better living conditions and faster advancement. It cited the several recent resignations and approaching retirements in the near future.[44]

The new lieutenants took their initial training at the Brooklyn Navy Yard where they enjoyed rather commodious accommodations. Second Lt. Kane stayed at his father's house in the yard, while the other four shared an apartment with a separate bedroom for each. In addition to the bedrooms, the apartment contained a dining room, a parlor, and a bathroom. The kitchen was in the basement, which also included a servant's quarters and a storeroom. A black woman served as cook for the four young officers while by lot they selected Lieutenant Stafford to be the mess officer.[45]

The officers' training period lasted nearly two months, and Lejeune later remembered that Marine Capt. Richard Wallach "was a very painstaking and conscientious instructor." The training concentrated on drill and the duties of new second lieutenants. Lejeune mentioned to his sister that they had been made officers of the guard "principally for instruction." As an older man, Lejeune told a group of younger officers that when he asked one of his instructors what recent books on military literature he needed to read, the reply was "memorize the drill manual—that's all you'll need to know." Ingate, Stafford, and Cole applied to attend the Army's School of Application for Cavalry and Infantry at Fort Leavenworth, Kansas. Although approved by Maj. Robert W. Huntington, the commander of the Brooklyn Barracks, Marine Corps Headquarters turned down the requests, observing that the officers' services were urgently required elsewhere. At the end of October, the new lieutenants received orders to their new duty stations.[46]

During this period, the Marine Corps continued to emit mixed signals about officer education and professionalization. The previous year, Marine lieutenants Thomas N. Wood and Richard Wallach completed the course of instruction of the Navy Torpedo School. Secretary Tracy offered the commandant of the Marine Corps the choice of permitting the two officers to attend the next session of the Naval War College or to return to duty. Lieutenant Colonel Heywood, who replied for Colonel McCawley, elected to send them to new assignments. Wallach went to the Brooklyn Barracks and

Wood to the USS *Galena*. Yet, in July 1890, three Marine lieutenants served with Col. William B. Remey in the Navy's judge advocate office. One of the officers, 1st Lt. Frank L. Denny, co-authored a legal manual entitled *Naval Summary Courts-Martial*.[47]

Even Marine officers in their late twenties and early thirties found it difficult to decide whether a Marine career held a future for them. Two of the most promising, 1st Lt. William H. Stayton and 1st Lt. Howard K. Gilman, offered their resignations, obviously seeing only limited opportunities. An Academy graduate with an assignment in the Judge Advocate Division, Stayton resigned two weeks after his promotion to first lieutenant. Gilman, the author of two Marine manuals, gave as his reason for resignation, "a very advantageous business offering." Yet, another Marine officer in the Judge Advocate Office, 1st Lt. Charles H. Lauchheimer, withdrew his resignation after receiving his promotion. He half humorously wrote to his Naval Academy classmates, after waiting six years and six months for his advancement, "So you can see promotion is not so rapid but one can become accustomed to the duties of one grade before being promoted to the next higher grade."[48]

This same sense of uncertainty was apparent also in the higher reaches of the Marine Corps. During the year, Colonel McCawley's health continued to deteriorate, and more of the burden of the Corps fell upon Lieutenant Colonel Heywood's shoulders. At the end of May 1890, McCawley wrote to the secretary of the Navy and denied newspaper speculation that he was physically unfit for duty. In July, however, leaving the headquarters under the charge of Lieutenant Colonel Heywood, the commandant took a thirty-day leave because of health problems and then extended it until the end of August. He returned on August 28 but informed the secretary, "Not having derived any benefit from my absence have therefore concluded it was better to . . . resume my duty." Finally on September 4, he told Tracy he could not continue in office because of his deteriorating health. Since he was not eligible to retire until January McCawley asked for a leave of absence until that time. The secretary agreed.[49]

A strange five-month interregnum followed. Instead of leaving Lieutenant Colonel Heywood in command of the headquarters, Secretary Tracy bowed to the tradition of seniority and made Col. Clement D. Hebb acting commandant. Former commander of the barracks in Boston, Hebb was the senior line officer in the Marine Corps and only one year younger than McCawley. According to Hebb, since he was due to retire in 1892, he had mentioned to Lieutenant Colonel Heywood and several other officers that he "would not be a candidate [for the commandancy], as I preferred to remain where I was." Hebb signed the Marine Corps's annual report to the secretary of the Navy in October 1890, using the title "Colonel, Commanding," rather than "Colonel Commandant." In the report, Hebb repeated McCawley's request for more officers and men. Citing as the reason the building of larger ships, he wanted an increase of 300 privates and 8 more second lieutenants.[50]

For the most part, Hebb, as could be expected, identified with the older Marine establishment. According to newspaper accounts, he blocked a petition from several younger Marine officers that would have provided increased standards for officer promotion beyond mere seniority. The reformers wanted a new law requiring Army officers up for promotion to pass both a physical and a mental examination applicable as well to Marine Corps officers.[51]

With the growth of the New Navy, however, reform in the Marine Corps was almost inevitable. Although Colonel Hebb reversed his earlier decision and applied for the commandancy, the press bruited about the names of several officers, including Lieutenant Colonel Heywood, Major Forney, Majors Goodloe and Nicholson of the staff, and even Colonel Remey, the Judge Advocate, as possible successors to Colonel McCawley. Colonel McCawley endorsed Lieutenant Colonel Heywood, writing to the latter: "In severing by reason of my bad health the official relations which have so long and pleasantly existed between you . . . and myself, it gives me much pleasure to testify to your uniform zeal and ability in the discharge of your duty not only in that capacity but in every other in which I have placed you during my long administration of the Office of Colonel Commandant." According to the newspapers, Heywood was the favorite of both officers and men: "They feel that at this time the Corps needs at its head, a strong brilliant man who can sustain its honorable record." According to the *New York Times*, all the New England congressmen and Secretary of State James G. Blaine supported Heywood, who, like Blaine, was from the state of Maine.[52]

While the matter of the succession to McCawley remained open, the subject of the role of Marines on board ship that Marine officers thought had been relegated to the dust bin, had in reality only been swept under the rug. The U.S. Naval Institute accepted for publication an article by Lt. William Fullam of Greer Board fame. In a meeting of the Institute at Annapolis in November 1890, the secretary of the association read Fullam's paper to the assembled officers and caused an immediate furor. The full article with comment and rebuttal was published in the final issue of the 1890 *Proceedings*. In the article, Fullam argued that the presence of Marines on board ship hindered the recruitment of a native-born and better class of seaman for the

Navy. According to Fullam, "The best way to get good men is to raise the standard by establishing the fact that marines are not needed. As long as the Marine remains, the officer will not learn to rely upon the sailor, nor to trust and develop the petty officer." Although referring to the recommendations of the Greer Board and the possible employment of Marines as a ready deployable expeditionary force, the thrust and rhetoric of the article questioned the very existence of the Marine Corps.[53]

Marine officers looked with alarm upon the reaction of the naval officer corps. Of the 18 naval officers whose remarks were printed in the "Discussion," 11 strongly supported Fullam, 3 gave partial support, and only 4 stood opposed. Prominent among the names of the supporters was that of Commodore James A. Greer, who had headed the Board of Organization. Lost in the strident tone of most of the comments were the moderate words of another member of the Greer Board, Cmdr. Harry Glass. Although in general agreement with Fullam, Glass believed that the latter overstated his case. Commander Glass remembered that the Greer Board had recommended the removal of the Marines from the ships mainly "to increase the strength of the corps considerably, with the idea that larger bodies of men being stationed together . . . and [as a result] the Navy Department would have always at hand a compact, thoroughly drilled, and organized force to be used where landing parties were needed." A Navy ensign voiced a more common reaction: "The presence of Marines on shipboard is almost as un-American as would be the control by troops, of citizens."[54]

The argument was not limited to the pages of the *Proceedings*. A series of letters, signed "Fair Play" and possibly authored by Fullam, appeared in the *New York Times*. The letters accused the "conservative" bureaus and officers of "pigeon holing" the Greer Board report and attempting to silence the "intellectual cyclone" caused by the more recent article advocating the withdrawal of the Marines. In a letter to the *Army and Navy Journal*, Fullam stated that his article only reflected the sentiments of many Navy officers and that he was "merely a humble follower of the progressive element."[55]

In a November editorial, the *Journal* praised the Fullam article in the *Proceedings* as "a very hopeful sign of revolt against the hidebound conservatism from which the service has too long suffered." Although claiming that it was not taking sides on the role of Marines, a *Journal* editorial the following month advocated an examination of the issue and said that open discussion "of the best organization for the Navy on ship or ashore will be of ultimate benefit to the Marines as to the Navy proper." To add insult to injury, the *Journal*, normally a warm supporter of the Marine Corps, on January 10, 1891, printed a petition of Navy enlisted men from nine ships of the North

Atlantic Station to the secretary of the Navy requesting "the withdrawal of the marines from service afloat."[56]

This last was too much for Colonel Hebb. In one of his last official acts, he sent a clipping of the petition to Secretary Tracy and formally protested its publication. Although allowing that a right of petition existed, he said- "The method adopted in this instance appears to be not only irregular, but wholly unprecedented, tending to create dissension and discord throughout the enlisted force of the Navy and Marine Corps, and to seriously impair its efficiency and the discipline of the service generally." Hebb stated that he was submitting the material for any action the department "may deem proper." Hebb probably expected no reply and received none from the secretary.[57]

On January 30, 1891, to no one's surprise, Secretary Tracy nominated Lieutenant Colonel Heywood as the official successor to Colonel McCawley as commandant of the Marine Corps. Eleven days later, now Colonel Heywood informed the secretary that he had assumed "command of the Marine Corps." Colonel Hebb returned to the Boston Barracks and awaited retirement. The former commandant, Colonel McCawley, went on the retired list and died the following October. Although McCawley accomplished many minor reforms and provided the setting for a more professional officer corps, he had visualized no new mission or structure for the Marine Corps. Thus, the McCawley commandancy ended as it had begun, with the Marine Corps facing a period of institutional crisis. The threat this time was external to the Marine Corps in the personages of the naval progressives and professionals led by Fullam. Marine Corps officers had yet to establish their area of responsibility within the New Navy.[58]

6. MARINE PROFESSIONALISM, THE NEW NAVY, AND NEW DIRECTIONS, 1891–1893

The first two years of the Heywood commandancy were tumultuous ones. When Colonel Heywood assumed office, the Corps was under attack by the Fullamites and the Navy reformers, but Heywood and his protégé, Capt. Daniel Pratt Mannix, had an agenda of their own. They planned an increased emphasis on professionalization, including advanced officer education and the introduction of officer's examinations for promotions, and they wished to identify more closely the mission of the Marine Corps with that of the New Navy in a period of nascent American expansionism.

In February 1891, at the age of fifty-one, Charles Heywood, the new commandant of the Marine Corps, was hardly the boy colonel any more. Although eleven years younger than Colonel Hebb, Heywood had only two years less service and was less than a year his junior in rank. Over six feet tall and broad shouldered, with a walrus mustache, Heywood towered over most of his contemporaries and conveyed a sense of vigor. Commissioned at nineteen in 1858, Heywood had won early renown as a leader. During the Civil War, he had served with distinction and won two brevet promotions for gallantry in action. He had been the Fleet Marine Officer during the *Virginius* Affair and had commanded the Marine Brigade in Panama. After he took command of the Washington Barracks in 1888, Heywood had become a close adviser to the previous commandant. Long identified with the Marine reform group, Heywood and his cohort, Captain Mannix, had convinced Colonel McCawley to make his ill-fated initiatives to the Greer Board. Although he had been given a more passive role during the Hebb Interregnum, Colonel Heywood now sat in the catbird seat. According to the *Army and Navy Journal*, the selection of Heywood as commandant presaged "the infusion of new life into the Corps."[1]

After the appearance of the Fullam article received a chorus of approval from much of the naval officer corps, the very life of the Marine Corps, let

Col. Charles G. Heywood, ninth commandant of the Marine Corps, succeeded Colonel McCawley in 1891 and inaugurated a series of reform measures. (Marine Corps Historical Center Collection)

alone "new life," was at stake. Following the article's publication, sailors sent a deluge of petitions asking for the removal of Marines from Navy warships. To most Marine officers, the relationship between the petitions and the push by the Fullam faction was obvious. As one service periodical observed, "The fact is that Jack [a popular euphemism of the time for a sailor] will sign anything if properly prepared." On February 15, 1891, Capt. Henry Clay Cochrane wrote to warn Heywood about unnamed persons circulating petitions secretly among the Navy enlisted men on ships in the San Francisco area. According to Cochrane, the enemies of the Corps were "more numerous and active" than he had ever known them to be, and he blamed a certain clique of naval officers working underground like moles to rile up the sailors against the Marines. Cochrane had even heard rumors that Commodore Francis Ramsay, who had relieved Commodore Walker as head of the Bureau of Navigation, favored the movement to put the Marines ashore. The Marine captain then referred to a conversation that he had had with Capt. William T. Sampson, one of the leading naval reformists, who had frankly told Cochrane "that he [Sampson] is in favor of abolishing the Marine Corps."[2]

The internal rancor in the Navy extended beyond the Marine Corps. Navy line officers railed against engineers, and the engineers and other staff corps returned the animosity. A series of disputes erupted in the officer corps, usually centered around questions of perquisites, prestige, authority, and responsibility, and as one naval writer wrote, "Every corps in the Navy was dissatisfied." In 1890, Secretary Tracy reported to the Senate the existence of six unauthorized naval organizations lobbying Congress and representing the interests of almost every corps in the service except the Marine Corps. There was a Line Officers' Association, an Engineer Officers' Organization, and even an ensign organization all trying to obtain legislation that would benefit their particular group.[3]

Like Secretary Tracy, Colonel Heywood decided against a confrontational strategy to meet the challenge presented by the Navy reformers, preferring to act on the priorities that Captain Mannix had outlined two years previously to the Greer Board. He wanted to increase the size of the Corps, build up the morale of the Marine enlisted men, carefully define the mission of the Marines on board ship, further professionalize the officer corps, and establish a School of Application that would serve both as an educational forum and as a ready reserve battalion for any unexpected emergency.[4]

As Heywood clearly realized, he could justify the existence of the Marine Corps and its expansion only in terms of its relationship to the Navy. As the new armored ships authorized by Congress during the previous two administrations came into commission, the commandant wanted a role established for his Marine guards. If the mission of the Marine Corps were closely intertwined with these warships, the pride of the New Navy, he believed the Marine Corps as an institution would be more secure. Seizing upon Colonel McCawley's recommendation to the Greer Board for the Marine guards to man the secondary batteries of the new steel ships, Heywood wanted the secretary of the Navy, and if possible, Naval Regulations to mandate this duty. With more ships, he believed there would be a corresponding need for more Marines.[5]

Before he could persuade the secretary of the Navy and Congress to allocate more Marines, Heywood first needed to convince them that the Marines could do the job, which would be difficult with the enlisted base of the Marine Corps and its desertion rate of over 25 percent. His naval opponents pointedly alluded to the fact that in 1890, the Marine Corps had 948 enlistments, 85 reenlistments, and 520 desertions, with a total enlisted strength of approximately 2,000 men. As Colonel McCawley had written two years previously, many men enlisted "for no other purpose than to secure a home for the winter," and then deserted in the spring. Heywood, like McCawley, however, blamed most of the desertions on the fact that there were not enough men to share the workload.[6]

Despite the slight boost to enlisted morale that certain uniform and equipment modifications may have brought, Heywood's primary goal was a corps of officers and men that could function as ships' artillerymen and man the guns of the secondary batteries. The secondary battery usually consisted of 6-inch rifled guns and smaller caliber rapid-fire cannon and machine guns as opposed to the 13-inch and 8-inch rifled guns of the main turrets on board the new warships. The Marine Corps commandant had already taken some steps to insure that Marine guards that went on board the Navy ships were properly trained and he prevailed upon both Secretary Tracy and Congress to include in the coming year's appropriation $5,000 for the acquisition of both a Gatling and a Hotchkiss machine gun for training purposes at the Washington Marine Barracks. In the interim, Heywood had established an informal training center at the barracks under the new post commander, Captain Mannix and had ordered the new Marine guard for the steamer *Lancaster* to undergo instruction there in both weapons and drill in preparation for their assignment on board ship.[7]

Heywood had even bolder plans for Marine training and education, all centered around the Washington Marine Barracks. Together with Mannix he worked out a scheme for the formal establishment at the barracks of a School of Application. Based on Mannix's original proposal to the Greer

Board, Colonel Heywood, on April 13, 1891, forwarded to Secretary Tracy a detailed course outline for the school so that the Marine Corps would "keep pace with recent progress in the Navy." As an added inducement to the secretary, he asserted that the school would be established without any further appropriation and would offer instruction to officers, noncommissioned officers, and privates. Five days later, Secretary Tracy gave his approval, and on May 1, 1891, Colonel Heywood issued General Order No. 1 which opened with the following statement: "The Colonel Commandant takes pleasure in formally announcing to the Marine Corps the establishment of a School of Application at the headquarters of the Corps."[8]

Heywood's general order named the new school the "School of Application of the United States Marine Corps," and placed it under the "direct care and supervision of the Colonel Commandant." The actual running of the school was the responsibility of the director of instruction, who also functioned as the school commander. He had authority over the post, all instructors, and "such officers and enlisted men as may be assigned to it for duty or instruction." The school itself consisted of two divisions, one for enlisted men and one for officers. The order required all students, both officer and enlisted, to attend all designated classes.[9]

Divided into seven areas of concentration, the curriculum included classes and practical exercises in infantry tactics, gunnery instruction, torpedoes, high explosives, "field service and modern tactics," and field entrenchments, and the medical officer at the barracks offered a mandatory course in medical hygiene. According to Heywood's directive, the noncommissioned officers "and other enlisted men of sufficient intelligence" would receive instruction in "logarithms, solutions of plane triangles, and the practical use in the field of angle-measuring instruments in making military reconnaissances and hasty surveys." The only reference to landing operations was almost an afterthought: "Noncommissioned officers will be instructed also in the duties of guards when embarked, landing and campaigning with the Naval brigade and the best formation for fighting against superior numbers armed with inferior weapons," the traditional naval landing-party mission. The commandant retained authority to require additional officer training.[10]

In the order, Heywood emphasized the personal importance that he placed on the course work, exempting all faculty members, except at the order of the commanding officer of the school, from other duties that "will interfere with . . . performance . . . as instructors and assistant instructors." The instructors were to keep all marks, both class and test scores, and submit them weekly to the director of instruction, who, in turn, would forward them to the commandant. Marks would be based on a standard of three as a perfect score and zero as failure, and the students' grades would be determined in fractions of tenths between those two scores. At the completion of the course work, the commandant would appoint three officers to witness the final examinations. This three-man board would review every aspect of the school and provide the commandant a written report of "its observations and make any recommendations it may deem advisable." The commanding officer of the school was also to submit an annual report to the commandant "of the progress and wants of the school, and he will recommend such alterations in and additions to the programme of instruction and code of regulations as he may from time to time consider necessary or advisable."[11]

Heywood apparently viewed the proposed School of Application as the flagship for a system of satellite schools that would be established at every Marine post. The order called for a modified course based on the curriculum outline "for branch schools." At the moment, however, all the commandant could do was to ask the cooperation of all officers so that the "Marine Corps will be enabled to keep pace with recent progress in the profession of arms." On July 23, 1891, he sent a circular to all Marine commanders with a copy of the general order, exhorting all shore commanders "as far as practicable" to carry out "the 'course of instruction' prescribed therein, for officers and enlisted men at your post."[12]

Even before the actual publication of his general order, Heywood had made arrangements with Commodore William Folger, the chief of the Bureau of Ordnance, who agreed to assist the school as best he could. For the time being, the Marines would use what weapons and equipment were on hand to keep costs down, although additional appropriations could be made in the future for specialized engineering and survey instruments. Heywood had also named Captain Mannix as the director of instruction and commanding officer of the school in addition to his responsibilities as commander of the Marine Barracks.[13]

A graduate of the Army's Artillery School and the Navy's Torpedo School and an instructor for four years at the Chinese naval school, Mannix was better qualified than any other Marine officer. Given his background and his position of trust with both Colonel McCawley and Colonel Heywood, he probably had played more than a passing role in originating the idea of the school and in the actual drafting of the general order. During the summer, he worked on completing the curriculum and preparing for the actual opening of the school. His preparations included visits in August to the Army Artillery School at Fort Monroe, Virginia; the Military Academy at West Point, New York; the Army Engineering School at Willett's Point,

New York; and the Navy Torpedo School and War College at Newport, Rhode Island. According to Mannix's orders, he was to obtain "such information concerning the systems of practical instruction adopted by the schools at those stations as in your judgment may be of use to the School of Application of the U.S. Marine Corps."[14]

Through the early summer, the question of who was to attend the school remained. At one time, the *Army and Navy Journal* reported that a battalion camp would be established at Fort Washington in Maryland near the District of Columbia for the instruction of the new officers entering the Marine Corps from the Naval Academy. In the meantime several junior officers had applied to the commandant for permission to take extra military schooling. In March, 2d Lt. Joseph H. Pendleton had asked for orders to the Army Artillery School at Fort Monroe, but Heywood turned him down, explaining that the limited number of Marine officers made that assignment impractical. In May, two other lieutenants, Theodore P. Kane and John A. Lejeune, wrote to the commandant for orders to the proposed School of Application, but nothing came of their requests, probably for the same reason Pendleton was turned down. Finally, on July 27, 1891, 2d Lt. Clarence L. A. Ingate petitioned Heywood to attend the school. Heywood informed the young lieutenant that the decision had been made to assign the seven most recent graduates of the Naval Academy to the new school.[15]

Given the circumstances, the choice made utmost sense. With several vacancies in the officer corps, most officers could not be spared from their assignments. Some of the older officers had retired, a few of the younger ones had resigned their commissions for better opportunities in civilian life, and one officer had died. The resulting seven openings provided for infusion of new blood, and Heywood could assign the seven new officers to the School of Application without disrupting the rest of the Marine Corps with transfers and reassignments. Moreover, the school could serve as a rite of passage for the new graduates "to supplement the course of the Naval Academy in the administrative and military duties of the Corps." Thus on September 1, 1891, after their graduation and summer leave, 2d Lts. Lewis C. Lucas, Bertram S. Neumann, Charles G. Long, Benjamin H. Fuller, Robert McM. Dutton, Julius Prochazka, and Edward R. Lowndes reported to "Captain D. Pratt Mannix, commanding Marine Barracks for instruction in their duties as officers of the U.S. Marine Corps." Forgoing the enlisted division in its first year, the Marine Corps School of Application was now a reality.[16]

Heywood's enthusiastic support of the establishment of the School of Application and the assignment of the June Naval Academy graduates to its first term was consistent with his overall goal to raise the professional level of

Marine Corps School of Application, class of 1892. From left to right: 1st Lt. Thomas
C. Prince; 2d Lts. Robert McM. Dutton, Lewis C. Lucas, Julius Prochazka, Edward R.
Lowndes, Benjamin H. Fuller, Charles G. Long, Bertram S. Neumann; and Captain D.
Pratt Mannix, the founder of the school. (Marines Corps Historical Center Collection)

the Marine officer corps. Like his predecessor and most of the reform element within the Marine Corps, Heywood placed a high premium on the
professionally educated officers from the Naval Academy. With the seven
second lieutenants who entered the Corps in July 1891, the Marines obtained a few of the more academically able graduates, continuing the precedent of the previous year. Three of the new officers stood in the upper half of
the members of their class who received commissions: Lucas, ranked seventh; Neumann, ranked fourteenth; and Long, ranked fifteenth. The remaining new graduates, except for Fuller who ranked eighteenth, however,
were well at the bottom of the list: Dutton twenty-eighth, Prochazka
twenty-ninth, and Lowndes thirtieth. If the respective class rankings served
as a guide, they showed on the whole, despite some mixing of wheat with
chaff, that the Navy still viewed the Marine Corps as the poor relation.[17]

Outside of their academic records, the seven new lieutenants represented
an interesting social mix. In comparison to the traditional elite as reflected,
for example, in the previous year, this group showed some deviations. Although all of the officers were either Congregationalists, Presbyterians, or
Episcopalians, one of the Episcopalians was Julius Prochazka, hardly a name
indicative of a white, Anglo-Saxon, Protestant background. Prochazka's fa-

ther, Anton, worked as a machinist in Manitowac, Wisconsin, and the young Julius had attended the public schools of the community. Second Lt. Lewis G. Lucas also came from a working-class background; his father was a telegraph operator in Marietta, Ohio. The remaining officers were from the usual upper and upper-middle classes judging by the occupations of their fathers, which included an architect, a judge, a shoe manufacturer, and a fire insurance underwriter.[18]

Heywood's interest in Marine officer professionalism extended beyond the School of Application. Very much aware of the attacks against his Corps, on July 22, 1891, the Marine Corps commandant asked Secretary Tracy for permission to convene a special board "to inquire into and report upon the subject of organization and promotion of officers" together with a broader mandate "to insure a condition of increased efficiency in the Marine Corps." He suggested that the board consist of four officers identified with the reform faction: Maj. Percival C. Pope, in command of the Boston Barracks; Capt. Richard S. Collum, an assistant quartermaster; the ever-present Captain Mannix; and 1st Lt. T. C. Prince, who served under Mannix at the Washington Barracks. The Navy secretary approved the request a week later, and Heywood ordered the board to convene on August 3. Major Pope, as the ranking officer, served as the president of the board and Lieutenant Prince as recorder. Colonel Heywood gave no deadline to the forum except to make its report and recommendations by "an early date."[19]

The press applauded Heywood's initiative. In an editorial, the *Army and Navy Register* suggested that "the Navy at large should appreciate the progressive and energetic policy of the present Colonel Commandant and heartily encourage his recent earnest efforts to increase the efficiency of the corps." The *Register* also offered some advice to the newly appointed board, saying that "a short modest report" was apt to receive more consideration and that "a half loaf is better than none is not a bad principle to follow in such projects."[20]

The Pope Board, however, had a mind of its own and went for the whole loaf. On September 21, it submitted its report to the commandant, who, after some study, on October 17 approved the draft and forwarded it to the secretary of the Navy. The board made its recommendations in the form of a bill which incorporated most of the measures that the Marine reformers had been pushing through the McCawley years. The proposed bill would expand the Marine Corps by 400 men; make the commandant of the Marine Corps a brigadier general; designate the senior Marine officer with a squadron or fleet the fleet Marine officer with a promotion to the next higher rank while serving in that capacity; promote the senior staff officers to lieutenant colonels; limit appointments to the staff to senior line officers; increase the number of officers to 88, including 4 colonels and a like number of lieutenant colonels and majors; reorganize the band; and create 12 post quartermaster sergeants.

The bill, moreover, would permit Marine officers who fought in the Civil War and had thirty years' service to retire at the next highest rank. Marine officers who had twenty years of seniority in one rank would be allowed to take an examination and on passing would be promoted to the next higher grade as long as there was no corresponding increase in the number of officers. The most important feature, however, was the provision that called for the physical, mental, and professional examination of all officers below the rank of major. Congress had passed a similar requirement for Army officers the previous year, and most of the Marine reformers wanted to extend the law to the Marine Corps.[21]

In October, Heywood used the board's study as the basis for his own annual report to the secretary of the Navy. Heywood referred to the officer stagnation in the Corps, especially at the rank of captain, and made reference to the board's recommendations to relieve the situation. He observed that the Marine Corps was the only U.S. service that did not require promotion examinations and stated that he wanted to institute such a program. The commandant then turned to the board's proposal for a 400-man increase in the enlisted force of the Corps. Like his predecessor, Colonel Heywood stressed that the expansion of the Navy caused increased, not fewer, demands on the Marine Corps to provide ships' guards, thus not leaving enough men to carry the burden of protecting the various shore posts.[22]

At this point, Heywood departed from the Pope Board's report—which had touched only superficially upon the Marine mission—to redefine the role of the Marine on board ship. According to the commandant, "It is as artillery men aboard our new floating batteries that their importance must be felt and acknowledged in the future." He declared, "From all the ships of war where the Marines are allowed to man the secondary or main batteries come very gratifying reports as to their accountability for this service." Heywood argued that the provision in the current appropriation that permitted the purchase of the Hotchkiss and Gatling guns was evidence that Congress had "given its stamp of approval to a more extensive field of operation for the Marine Corps." Although as a courtesy many captains already stationed Marines at the secondary battery under their own officers, other commanding officers refused to do so. The commandant asked Secretary

Tracy to formalize the practice of Marines manning the secondary battery with an official Navy Department directive.[23]

Soon after the publication of his report, Heywood mounted a lobbying effort to increase not only the enlisted Marine strength, but to expand and restructure the officer corps. On October 22, 1891, Capt. Henry Clay Cochrane wrote the commandant, thanking him for "moving" in the "deplorable situation" relative to promotions, and assuring him that he would assist in any plausible "scheme" that would further the interests of the Marine Corps. Cochrane exchanged letters with other Marine officers on the east coast and proposed the formation of an organization to further Marine legislation.[24]

In the meantime, on November 18, 1891, Heywood seized upon a request by the commandant of the New York Navy Yard for more Marines to press his demands upon Secretary Tracy. Citing his annual report, he insisted to the secretary that "the number of officers and enlisted men in the Corps is too small." He wanted the secretary to press at the upcoming session of Congress for the increases that he had recommended in his report. Heywood also turned his attention to Congress, convincing Senators Eugene Hale and James McPherson, the leading Republican and Democrat on the Senate Naval Affairs Committee, to introduce bills which incorporated most of the provisions of the Pope Board on Marine Corps reorganization. The commandant sent both of them copies of his annual report, "in which I have presented the wants of the Corps, and which will be so satisfactorily met by the passage of the bill[s] you have introduced." He also wrote the other Senate members of the committee enclosing copies of the Reorganization Board's report. He called their attention to the proposed legislation Senator Hale introduced, suggesting if "it becomes a law [it] will very materially increase the efficiency of the Marine Corps." According to the *Army and Navy Journal*, most Marine officers supported the legislation and suggested that the prospects of its passage looked good, so by the end of the year Heywood had reason to hope that his reforms would take hold.[25]

By this time Secretary Tracy already had enough battles to fight. In April 1891, against the desires of many Republican leaders, he had substituted a merit system for the old political patronage in the selection of foremen in the Navy yards. At the same time, he was attempting to convince Congress to continue the funding of new ships and to win support for a more expansive naval policy in the Caribbean, the Pacific, and South America. With the bipartisan support of congressional leaders like Republican Senator

Eugene Hale and Congressman Hilary Herbert, Congress remained committed to the ship building program, but Tracy met with less success in his endeavor to heed Captain Mahan's call for a "United States Looking Outward."[26]

Secretary Tracy called for the building of a Nicaragua canal and warned
about growing European influence in the Americas. He argued that European commercial supremacy "means the exclusion of American influence"
and that it was "only a step from commercial control to territorial control."
To bolster his designs, Tracy looked for coaling stations in Haiti or San
Domingo, and in the spring of 1891, he tried to influence delicate negotiations with the Haitians by sending Rear Adm. John G. Walker's Squadron
of Evolution to Port-au-Prince as a show of force to join the *Philadelphia*, the
flagship of Rear Adm. Bancroft Gerhardi, already there. This move backfired and resulted in a fiasco with Gerhardi and Walker feuding as to who
should be in command. With the naval demonstration provoking popular
resentment against the Americans, the Haitian leaders broke off negotiations. A similar effort with the Dominican government also ended in stale-
mate.[27]

During this same period, the United States faced a potential crisis with Italy. A New Orleans mob broke into a jail in March 1891 and lynched some
Italian immigrants, supposed members of the Mafia being held on suspicion
of murdering the New Orleans police chief. The Italian government demanded an indemnity and punishment of the mob members. Secretary of
State Blaine expressed his regrets for the incident but refused indemnity on
the basis that the matter was for state officials to deal with, not the federal
government. The Italians recalled their ambassador from Washington, and
newspapers reported talk of armed hostilities between the two nations. For
once, Tracy took a moderate tone within the administration councils, advising President Harrison that the U.S. Navy was unprepared to engage the
stronger Italian fleet. The U.S. eventually agreed to pay a $25,000 indem-
nity. Secretary Tracy used the "war scare" for his own purposes, namely to
campaign for more ships and a buildup of the coast defenses.[28]

The naval secretary played a much more aggressive role, later in the year,
during the crisis with Chile that arose out of the *Baltimore* affair. The *Baltimore*, one of the Navy's newest cruisers, had been in Chilean waters protecting American interests there during a bitter civil war. The rebels, supported
by the Chilean Navy, had succeeded in overthrowing the government. On
October 16, 1891, in Valparaiso, when a barroom brawl broke out between
several members of the *Baltimore* crew and local patrons, a mob killed 2
American sailors and injured 18 others. According to the American ac-

count, police arrived on the scene and arrested 36 sailors, who were later released.[29]

War fever quickly spread through the United States. Since the War of the
Pacific in 1879 when Chile defeated Peru and Bolivia, many American na-
valists had used the specter of Chilean warships bombarding San Francisco
to rouse Americans to build up their own naval defenses. The *Baltimore* incident added fuel to the already unfavorable American image of that South
American nation.[30]

Despite some differences within his administration, President Harrison,
on January 21, 1892, sent an ultimatum to the Chileans. He demanded a re-
traction of their previous statements and an apology for the attack on the
crew of the *Baltimore*, threatening that the United States would break diplomatic relations. Four days later, Harrison sent a virtual war message to Congress.[31]

In the meantime, Secretary Tracy had placed the Navy Department on a
wartime footing. He ordered Captain Mahan to Washington to work with
the Office of Naval Intelligence and Assistant Secretary James R. Soley as an
informal naval strategy group. He also directed work to proceed at the various Navy yards for the fitting out of warships and their supplies and support
ships, including colliers and transports.[32]

On December 31, 1891, Rear Adm. George Brown reported to Secretary
Tracy that the United States could mass a fleet of 12 warships, consisting of
100 guns in the main and 131 in the secondary batteries, and nearly 3,000
crewmen for operations against Chile. This force did not include an additional six ships which could be held in reserve. In the event of war, Brown
recommended that the American fleet blockade Valparaiso, forcing the
Chilean Navy to take refuge under the guns of the various forts there. He
suggested that the Americans use Caldera as a transport rendezvous and
Colquimbo, about 250 miles north of Valparaiso, as a base of operations.[33]

Tracy also had in his possession an unsigned memorandum, presumably
drafted by Captain Mahan and the informal strategy board, comparing the
relative value of Iquique in northern Chile and Lota in the south as operating bases for the U.S. naval forces. Taking a somewhat different tack from
Admiral Brown, the author of the memorandum suggested that the Americans seize Iquique, one of Chile's more important ports and the center of its
nitrate trade, arguing that this action would severely hamper the enemy eco-
nomically and draw the Chilean fleet out of Valparaiso and bring it 1,000
miles closer to the California coast. The memorandum contained the warning, "For effective operations in the north, control of the sea is essential."[34]

Although Captain Mahan had no doubts about the final outcome, he confided to Rear Admiral Luce in early January 1892 that the American forces might "first get some eyeopeners." There were to be no "eyeopeners," because by the end of the month, the Chilean government acquiesced to Harrison's demands and apologized and agreed to pay an indemnity for the incident. One naval officer later exulted to Secretary Tracy that within ten years "you will see us commanding the Pacific and having our will wherever we desire to use it."[35]

At first glance, the *Baltimore* affair would appear to have little involvement with the Marine Corps. Outside of a confidential order forwarded to Colonel Heywood and all the Navy Bureaus on January 26 to see that "the ships . . . fitting out" were fully manned and supplied, the commandant received no specific directives relative to Chile. There appeared no direct mission for the Marines outside of their traditional role as part of the ships' guard.[36]

Beneath the surface, however, the planning for operations against Chile had significant implications for the Marines. Both Admiral Brown's report to Secretary Tracy and the memorandum comparing Iquique and Lota called for the seizure of a port on the Chilean coast as a base of operations for the blockading American fleet. Marine Col. William B. Remey, the Navy judge advocate general who conducted the court of inquiry into the *Baltimore* affair, confided in January to his hometown newspaper in Burlington, Iowa, that the United States action against Chile would be more than a naval demonstration: "An army of occupation would be a necessary adjunct of the naval force. The plan would be undoubtedly to seize upon some Chilean port and make that a base of operations for an invading army." Maj. Gen. John M. Schofield, commanding general of the Army, later recalled that he "was asked to make an estimate of the military force which would be necessary to occupy and hold a vital point in Chilean territory until the demands of the United States were complied with." According to the press, the Army even made some tentative moves to bring its regiments on the West Coast up to a wartime strength of 1,000 men. Still, the most likely force to land first on the Chilean coast would be a Marine battalion or brigade, either formed from Navy Yard Marines from the United States, or more probable, the ships' guards with the fleet. It is even possible that the Navy Department had this consideration in mind when it forwarded to Colonel Heywood the directive that all ships should be at full strength including the Marine guard.[37]

The Navy continued to have an interest in what amounted to amphibious operations. Two officers from the *Baltimore*, Lt. James H. Sears and Ens.

B. W. Wells, submitted to Secretary Tracy a detailed account, later published by the Office of Naval Intelligence, of the Chilean Civil War in which the Chilean Navy had played a large role in the final victory. The authors described at great length a successful unopposed amphibious landing off Quinteros Bay north of Valparaiso in which the rebel troops surprised and outflanked the government defenders. Sears and Wells concluded, "It was necessary that one party . . . should possess itself of place after place along the coast, keep perfect control of the communications in its rear by sea, and gradually to work towards the interior from these ports as bases." Even Lieutenant Fullam, although pushing the theme of taking the Marine guards off the warships, said in a letter to the *New York Times* that he wanted to form the Marine Corps into three permanent well-organized battalions, two on the Atlantic Coast and one on the Pacific, that could be deployed in their own transports and "cooperate with the Navy."[38]

This naval attention to landing operations and the coordination of sea and land operations did not necessarily mean the Marines would receive the responsibility. Although a logical assumption in retrospect, it was not so clear to the men of the time. Naval professional literature was ambivalent on the subject. In the 1891 *Naval Institute Proceedings* prize-winning essay, for example, Ens. A. P. Niblack recommended withdrawing the Marines from warships and having the Navy follow the example of most European nations and "place our sea-coast defenses in the hands of a semi-naval branch of the government." Lt. J. C. Wilson, writing in the June 1891 *United Service*, made the same recommendation. Another naval officer, Lt. Charles C. Rogers, whose article surveyed the European coastal defense systems and in 1891 appeared in an Office of Naval Intelligence publication, added a new wrinkle. He quoted approvingly a British official who suggested that Royal Marines garrison the colonies and would also entrust coast defense and security of "coaling stations abroad to that force which is specially trained to fight both on land and sea."[39]

In the meantime, Colonel Heywood had his own agenda. He and most Marines essentially viewed the naval speculation about coastal defense as another variation of the Fullam theme of getting the Marines off the ships. In January 1892, he found himself attempting to fend off an even more direct assault on the core of his planned rehabilitation of the Marine Corps. Marine 1st Lt. Thomas N. Wood, the Marine officer on board the new cruiser *Newark*, reported that the ship's commander, Capt. Silas Casey, had pulled off the Marine guard from the guns of the secondary battery of the ship. According to Wood, Casey had assigned the Marines under their own officer to the secondary battery at the time the ship went into commission in February 1891 and appeared satisfied with the efficiency of the Marine gun crews. Just after the first of the year, however, Captain Casey received an order from the Bureau of Navigation to take them off, citing 1880 Bureau of Ordnance regulations that Marines should not be responsible for the ships' guns since it interfered with their role as sharpshooters. The Bureau ordered Casey to spread the Marines among the other gun crews of the ship under naval officers, and a Navy ensign replaced Wood in charge of the secondary battery guns.[40]

Before acting, Colonel Heywood first wrote to Captain Casey, asking him for a clarification of the situation and inquiring whether he personally supported the continued assignment of the Marines to the secondary battery. The commandant also discussed the situation with Commodore Folger of the Bureau of Ordnance who saw no reason why Marines could not handle the guns on board ship. After receiving a favorable reply from the *Newark's* captain, Heywood, on January 21, protested directly to Secretary Tracy. According to Heywood, the 1880 regulations cited by the Bureau of Navigation order applied only to the main battery and not to the secondary battery. Arguing that Marines perform better when together than "when mixed with sailors," Colonel Heywood suggested that even if Marines were assigned to the secondary battery, there would be extra men to act as riflemen. He argued that Captain Casey and Commodore Folger upheld his position and that he was "convinced that the majority of the commanding officers of vessels now in commission would express the same opinion." The Marine commandant pointed to the appropriation authorization for the purchase of the Hotchkiss and Gatling guns at the School of Application as an indication of congressional approval and said that the Marines trained with these weapons at shore stations and knew how to use them.[41]

Heywood wanted Secretary Tracy not only to negate the Bureau of Navigation directive, but also to issue a separate order "requiring that the Marines shall man the guns of the Secondary Battery on board ships of the Navy." Wanting harmony with his subordinates and not willing to challenge the Navy line, the secretary of the Navy was not about to override the autocratic Commodore Ramsay, the chief of the Bureau of Navigation, and allowed the new instructions to Captain Casey to remain in effect. The best that Heywood could hope for was that the bureau not issue the same orders to other Navy captains which was unlikely.[42]

During the late winter and the spring of 1892, Heywood lost his earlier high hopes for congressional action leading to an increase in enlisted manpower and a complete restructuring of the officer corps. As the *Army and Navy Journal* observed in April, there was little chance of Congress passing any legislation involving increased costs and numbers. The *Journal* suggested that the Marine Corps would have been better off calling for simpler legislation and concentrating on one or two issues. Taking the *Journal's* advice, Colonel Heywood decided to cut his losses and push for enactment of a single bill that would permit examination of officers before promotion. In May, the House Naval Affairs Committee reported out favorably such a measure, which passed both chambers of Congress in July. Under the new law, every officer below the rank of commandant would take an examination before promotion under the same provisions that applied to officers of the U.S. Army.[43]

Although his Corps still struggled for status and definition of its mission with the New Navy, Colonel Heywood had brought some standardization and professionalism to the officer corps. Winning the fight for officer promotion examinations, Colonel Heywood and Captain Mannix's emphasis on officer education had borne its first fruits. During the School of Application's first year of existence, Captain Mannix had refined the core curriculum as outlined in the original general order and created the following academic departments: the Department of Infantry; the Department of Artillery; the Department of Administration and Sea Service; the Department of Law; the Department of Torpedoes; the Department of Engineering; and the Department of Military Art.[44]

Within each department, Mannix and his one assistant, 1st Lt. Thomas C. Prince, prepared a series of courses that all students took and supposedly mastered. For example, the Department of Infantry consisted of four parts: infantry drill instruction, guard duty, small arms firing regulations, and infantry fire discipline. Included among the subjects were "formation for street riots," duties of the officer of the guard, and "the control and direction of fire." Instruction took the traditional form of "recitations, drills, problems, and field exercises." In the Department of Artillery, Mannix obtained the permission of Commodore Folger and the ordnance officer of the nearby Washington Navy Yard to use the facilities there for the demonstration of the manufacture of ordnance and the rifling and sighting of navy guns. Although he used some standard texts on military subjects, Captain Mannix developed a set of supplementary notes and circulars for the students.[45]

In April 1892, the first class of the School of Application held its graduating exercises under the watchful eyes of a two-man board of review consisting of Colonel Heywood and Maj. H. B. Lowry, the Marine Corps quartermaster. The seven lieutenants demonstrated their newly acquired skills as they put the enlisted men of the Washington Barracks through various infantry and artillery drills, ending with a formal parade. In the classroom, the students passed a 214–question examination covering the complete course of instruction, after which the commandant and Major Lowry assigned each student a question "to answer orally and demonstrate at the blackboard." Although Captain Mannix believed the class had done well under the circumstances, "seven months was too short a period in which to accomplish all that it was desired to teach." Mannix lamented the lack of quarters and additional appropriations as well as the "demand from other stations for the services of officers."[46]

With the continued support of the commandant and the Navy Department, Mannix quickly prepared for the new term of the school. At the urging of Heywood, Commodore Folger of the Bureau of Ordnance acquired for Mannix from the Newport Torpedo School a complete set of spar torpedo boat fittings. The Bureau of Construction and Repair then ordered a steam launch at the Washington Navy Yard to be turned over to the School of Application "for the purpose of instruction in the use of spar torpedoes." From the Bureau of Ordnance, the School of Application received ammunition and a tripod for its new 37-mm Hotchkiss Revolving Cannon and copper for making models of mines and torpedoes. Mannix also received approval from the secretary of the Navy to purchase from the War Department "a set of the Official Records of the War of Rebellion, with accompanying maps." Finally Colonel Heywood assigned two more officers to Mannix's faculty, 1st Lt. Harry K. White, and 2d Lt. Charles G. Long, of the school's first graduating class.[47]

On September 1, 1892, Captain Mannix opened the second term of the School of Application with both enlisted and officer divisions. The enlisted division consisted of fewer than 60 men as opposed to the 150 men that Mannix had originally wanted. Although the course of study for noncommissioned officers in infantry, artillery, torpedoes, and administration followed largely that of the officers, the school placed a larger emphasis in the enlisted division on the field engineering department. In that department, the subjects included military sketching, elementary field fortifications, and a preliminary course in mathematics. A field service course of drills, marches, reconnaissance, outposts, and attack and defense of positions rounded out the enlisted division curriculum. While the school mandated demonstrations and drills for all enlisted students, only the noncommissioned officers had to attend the more theoretical courses. According to Mannix, the "main object" of the enlisted division was to provide a "thorough practical knowledge" of Marine duties.[48]

The officer division in September 1892 was smaller than that of the previous year. Six Naval Academy graduates received Marine Corps commissions on 1 July, one of whom resigned to become an ensign as a result of an unexpected opening in the Navy. The remaining five—2d Lts. Albertus W. Catlin, Lawrence H. Moses, Wendell C. Neville, Cyrus S. Radford, and Thomas C. Treadwell—after their graduation leave, received orders to the School of Application. As opposed to the previous year's class, these new lieutenants all stood in the lower half of their Naval Academy class. Catlin ranked seventeenth while the others placed twenty-second, twenty-third, and twenty-seventh (next to last) among the newly commissioned Marine and Navy officers. Three out of the five were Baptists or Methodists; one, Treadwell, was Episcopalian; and Moses, who described himself as "a follower of Felix Adler," the founder of the American Ethical Society, came from a Jewish background. Catlin, who listed his father's occupation as stonemason, was the only one obviously from a working-class background. While hardly a remarkable group of young officers, Mannix found them ready students.[49]

Mannix saw other advantages to the School of Application besides education. Shortly after the beginning of the course, Mannix lost the bulk of his enlisted student body to quarantine duty at Sandy Hook, Long Island, due to a possible cholera outbreak among newly arrived immigrants. While deploring the lost instruction time, he hailed the establishment of the Marine enlisted battalion at the school. Mannix observed, "It should be remembered that while undergoing training such a battalion would be ready at the hand of the Department for any temporary emergency. That such emergencies arise we know, and we know also that when they do the Marines are always called upon to take a leading part." He wrote in his report to Colonel Heywood, "The corps should be prepared to meet these sudden demands without unduly weakening the force engaged in guarding and protecting the public property at the Navy Yards and stations throughout the country." In his *Annual Report* to the secretary of the Navy, Heywood remarked on the success of the School and his desire "if the corps is increased, to see large classes here in the future, and gradually to have every one in the corps instructed at this school."[50]

By this time, Colonel Heywood had begun to implement the provisions relative to examination for promotion as required in the new legislation. As the *Army and Navy Journal* observed, the turnover in Marine and Navy officer personnel during the period 1891–1892 was "remarkable and has not been exceeded by any similar period since the few years immediately succeeding the Civil War." Overall for both services there were 23 retirements, 5 resignations, and 4 deaths, which for the Marine Corps resulted in 6 vacancies for new second lieutenants and a number of promotions. Even before the enactment of the new law, the commandant refused to recommend one senior captain to the rank of major "in view of his record on file in the Navy Department." In August, the secretary of the Navy appointed the first promotion board to examine the first eligible candidates for higher rank—Capt. Robert L. Meade, 1st Lt. W. F. Spicer, and 2d Lt. Charles G. Long.[51]

On August 23, 1892, on the recommendation of Heywood, the secretary of the Navy issued his guidelines to the president of the Marine board, Lt. Col. McLane Tilton. As president, Tilton was to swear in the board recorder, 1st Lt. Thomas C. Prince, who in turn swore in the four other members of the board, two Marine majors and two Navy surgeons. The doctors first examined each candidate and if they declared the officer unfit for duty, the candidate would not be promoted and possibly forced to retire. If physically fit, the candidate then appeared before the Marine officers who reviewed both his character traits and professional experience. The board could send out "interrogatories" to other officers, but no adverse decision would be made before the candidate "shall have been fully heard in his own behalf." After the interview with the candidate, the board decided on his "fitness for practical service at sea and on shore."[52]

The examining board met with the candidates for three days. On September 1, the medical officers conducted the physical examinations, and the board then adjourned until the next day. On the following morning, Assistant Secretary of the Navy James R. Soley in a message to Lieutenant Colonel Tilton ordered that the professional exam "shall be in the form of written questions and answers and shall form part of the record of the board." These tests lasted the better part of two days, and on September 3, the Tilton board found all three officers "qualified for promotion."[53]

On September 16, 1892, Colonel Heywood forwarded to the secretary of the Navy a proposed order that would "embrace the scope of examination for Marine officers." About a month later, Secretary Tracy issued the directive in the form of a Navy Department general order. It not only confirmed the procedures set out in the letter to Lieutenant Colonel Tilton, but also provided for systematic oral and written tests, which until March 1893, the board would confine to manuals of instruction, Navy regulations, applicable Army regulations, and military law. After March, the board would expand the tests to include most military subjects with increasing complexity for each successive rank. If an officer had successfully completed the School of Application within three years before coming up for promotion, the board automatically assigned credit for proficiency in certain subjects. For promotion to the rank of major, an officer was to write an essay of not fewer than 3,000 words "upon a professional topic, selected by the candidate, and submitted to the Adjutant and Inspector for the approval of the Colonel Commandant of the Marine Corps." But despite these advances in officer education and promotion standards, Marine officers remained insecure within the naval establishment.[54]

During 1892, a series of incidents involving Marine officers caused some embarrassment to the Corps. One was a tragic affair in the spring that involved Col. William B. Remey, the Navy judge advocate general. During the previous year, the colonel had displayed occasional lapses of memory, perhaps caused by a head injury from a runaway horse, but Remey continued to function effectively in his office. In May 1892, however, he walked into a New York hotel lobby, wearing a laurel wreath around his neck, and carrying "an abundance of smilax" in his hat, and bouquets of violets, tuberoses, and yellow rosebuds in his hands. He wore red and white roses in his coat and vest buttonholes. A friend of his came up to him and declared: "You resemble a walking nosegay, Colonel." The judge advocate replied, "Yes I suppose I do; but these are deserved decorations, honors bestowed, yet fully earned, sir." Colonel Remey than began handing flowers to every woman who passed him in the lobby. Placed on the retired list in June, Colonel Remey spent the remainder of his life in an institution for the insane in Massachusetts. The Marine Corps thus lost a prestigious and influential position in the Navy Department because Remey's assistant, a Navy officer, succeeded to the office.[55]

Far more damaging to the prestige of the Marine Corps was an incident in the Venezuelan port city of La Guaira involving Capt. Edwin P. Meeker and the Marine guard of the steel cruiser *Chicago*. In October 1892, a Venezuelan revolutionary Army had defeated the regular forces but had not then entered the city of La Guaira. The regular troops, drunk and out of control, roamed the city, and on October 7, fearing for American lives and property, Rear Adm. John G. Walker, in command of the American naval squadron in port, ordered Captain Meeker and 25 of his Marines ashore to the American consulate. According to Meeker, the consul, Philip C. Hanna had not asked for a guard and told the Marine captain, "I don't need you" but told Meeker to make his men comfortable and stay. The Marine officer did not post any sentries as there was only one way to approach the consulate, and the balcony overlooked this route. Consul Hanna proposed that Meeker accompany him, "dressed in his sword" for a walk around the city so that the populace would know that the Marines were there. Meeker gave orders to his sergeant to look out for the men and went out with Hanna.[56]

Unknown to Meeker, during the thirty to forty-five minutes he was absent, the sergeant of the guard arranged with Hanna's servant to obtain whisky from the liquor store located on the first floor of the building. While the Marine captain and the consul talked, six of the enlisted Marines, including the sergeant, got quietly and then noisily drunk. Aroused by a hullabaloo in the hall caused by the sergeant struggling with the five other troops over a bottle, Meeker broke up the scuffle. Two of the rowdy Marines attempted to escape but were subdued by Meeker and other members of the guard. An American reporter quoted a young Venezuelan clerk working for the consulate: "Last night I no sleep, as I think I was killed by the soldier. Tonight I am more afraid of the Americans than of the Venezuelans. The soldiers inside are more bad than the soldiers outside. If I sleep they rob me."[57]

On the following day, Meeker and the guard returned to the *Chicago*, where the Marine officer reported the events of the preceding day to the ship's captain. When Admiral Walker learned of the incident he was furious. He directed that the *Chicago*'s captain hold a full ship muster and read publicly the following order: "The detachment of Marines sent on shore last evening under command of Captain Meeker of the Marine Corps . . . proving themselves as a body unreliable and worse than worthless . . . and [you] will hereafter never send a detachment of Marines out of the ship on duty without special orders from me." Not satisfied with this public disgrace, he also directed that Meeker stand court-martial. The court at first accepted Meeker's plea that the public reading of Walker's letter was an official reprimand and, therefore, the Marine captain was not subject to further punishment, but Walker refused to accept the judgment of the court arguing that his letter referred to Meeker's command not to Meeker himself. He directed the members to continue with the court-martial, and this time the court found Meeker guilty and ordered him suspended for a year at half pay.[58]

Although both the Navy judge advocate general and Secretary Tracy later reversed the findings of the court-martial and directed Meeker returned to duty, the damage had been done. As Meeker wrote to Colonel Heywood, it was an attack not only on himself but on the entire Marine Corps. There was some justification to Meeker's charge that he was being " 'railroaded' through this business with no opportunity of securing proper counsel, or of properly preparing my case." The *New York World* reporter, W. Nephew King, Jr., and Consul Hanna both testified on behalf of Meeker, but Admiral Walker insisted on prosecuting the Marine captain. Colonel Forney probably represented the views of most Marine officers when he observed in the pages of the *Army and Navy Journal* that the Venezuela incident "has been made a pretence" to get at the Marine Corps.[59]

Even if Walker were sincere in his prosecution of Meeker, the case served as ammunition for those in the Navy who wanted the removal of the Marine guards from ships. The Navy Department continued to give Colonel Heywood mixed signals on the subject. On November 1, 1892, Commodore Ramsay of the Bureau of Navigation asked the Marine Corps to provide guards for seven new ships coming into commission. A few weeks later, the commodore told Heywood that no Marine guard would be required for the *Monterey*, one of the largest of the new vessels. Colonel Heywood protested the decision, declaring that a ship the size of the *Monterey* (4,100 tons) was one "where services of Marines would be so valuable, in manning the guns of either the main or secondary battery." He argued that if berthing space were a problem the Marines could replace an equal number of sailors: "There will be no duty on board this vessel that a Marine cannot perform, and I dare say in a manner as satisfactory, if opportunity is given, as the sailors." Heywood stated that if the Marines were to serve on the *Monterey*, "this will be an opportunity for them to demonstrate their usefulness on a modern fighting ship, which I warrant will be to the satisfaction of all who are in position to observe them." The Department turned down Heywood's appeal, and Assistant Secretary of the Navy James R. Soley in a curt reply wrote: "The berthing capacity of this vessel is so limited as not to permit of the detail of a Marine guard. The directions issued by the Commandant for such a detail will be countermanded."[60]

Together with the Meeker situation, the orders of the Bureau of Navigation removing Marines from the secondary battery, and the recent department failure to assign a Marine guard to the *Monterey*, the Marine officer corps saw itself besieged by enemies on all sides. In late January, Capt. Frank L. Denny, a new assistant quartermaster, with the blessing of Colonel Heywood announced the formation of the " 'Society of Officers of the Marine Corps' for their protective interests." An executive committee in Washington would coordinate society activities with various subcommittees located at major posts. Each member was asked to donate 10 percent of his January salary for dues. At Mare Island, all the officers joined as did one officer assigned to the ship *Alliance*, which was in port.[61]

Although the basic purpose of the organization was to lobby for Marine Corps legislation, some of the officers viewed the society as a means of exchanging opinions and working for reform. Captain Cochrane wrote Marine Captain George Reid that certain things could be done for the Marine Corps without legislation, "particularly in the improvement of quality of men." In response to another officer, "who confirms the growing feeling in Navy adverse to M.C. [Marine Corps]," Cochrane elaborated further about his ideas, stating that he had worked for years "to arouse our people to our steady loss of ground." He credited Commander Fullam for succeeding where he had failed and said the officer society "should not attach too much importance to the Secondary Battery and impossible legislation." Rather, the Marine Corps should place its emphasis on improving the quality of its men: "good men will beget good men and the result will go to windward easily."[62]

As the Harrison administration came to a close in early 1893, the Marine Corps under Heywood remained in a precarious but hopeful situation. While many of the Navy reformers and the press viewed the Marines as "relics of barbarism," the Corps had made some real gains. Colonel Heywood observed in his 1892 annual report that the desertion rate was down by 20 percent, and although this reduction was largely due to the economic downturn and the resulting unemployment in the country, Heywood's improvements in the creature comforts of the enlisted man had contributed to the improvement of morale. The professionalization of the officer corps advanced apace with that of the Navy at large. New officers continued to enter the Marine Corps from the Naval Academy; Marine officers now had to pass both physical and professional examinations for promotion; and the School of Application was about to graduate its second class.[63]

7. THE SOUND AND THE FURY, 1893–1896

The second Grover Cleveland presidency saw for the most part a continuation of the naval policy instituted during the previous Harrison administration. Although less expansionist in foreign policy, the new administration supported the buildup of the battleship Navy. Colonel Heywood, the Marine commandant, sought to assign his men the primary mission of manning the secondary batteries of the new steel ships and also encouraged reforms to raise the professional level of his officer corps. Deep rifts still existed in the Navy Department among both Marine and Navy officers based in part on career anxiety and expectations, but also upon perceived conflicting professional jurisdictions.

In his second administration, Grover Cleveland chose Congressman Hilary A. Herbert, whom the press referred to as the "Congressional secretary of the Navy," to be, in fact, the secretary of the Navy. Although his only military experience was that of a colonel in the Confederate Army, Herbert was well qualified for his new position. In Congress since 1877, he had served three times as chairman of the House Naval Affairs Committee and had been a leading member of the bipartisan coalition in Congress that had funded the new steel Navy. Although not an imperialist, he believed in a close relationship between foreign policy and a strong Navy, and he urged upon President Cleveland the continuing buildup of the battleship Navy, commenting that the "military value of a commerce-destroying fleet is overrated." Impressed by the writings of Mahan, he reversed his initial opposition to the Naval War College and agreed to keep it at Newport as both an education center and a planning staff.[1]

Aware of both the bureaucratic and the political pressures operating within and upon the Navy, Herbert looked with a jaundiced eye on the motivations of both politicians and naval officers alike. He later observed, "Politicians in seeking offices for their friends are necessarily not influenced to any considerable extent by efficiency; they naturally select for appointment, as a rule, such as have the most political influence behind them." He had the same amount of trust for naval officers. Unlike Secretary Tracy, his immediate predecessor, he placed small reliance on naval officer boards: "My opinion always was . . . that what a board of naval officers will decide . . . depends, very largely if not entirely, upon the composition of the board and their prejudices and predilections. . . . it is often difficult for them to keep from being influenced by the natural desire . . . 'Shall I not magnify mine office?' "[2]

Secretary Herbert depended upon a few trusted advisors for most decisions. These included former Rep. William McAdoo of New Jersey, a colleague of his on the Naval Affairs Committee whom he made his assistant secretary, and Rear Adm. Francis M. Ramsay, who continued to head the Bureau of Navigation. McAdoo was responsible for the day-to-day oversight of the Naval War College, the Office of Naval Intelligence, the Marine Corps as well as the Navy Library, and the Bureau of Construction and Repair. Herbert used Ramsay as his chief of staff of the Navy and considered him one of the "most upright and just minded men he had ever known."[3]

Even with a new administration in Washington, the continuing influential position of Rear Admiral Ramsay in the naval establishment promised at best an uncertain future for Colonel Heywood's plans for the Marine Corps. Heywood, nevertheless, persisted in his efforts to expand and define the role of the Marine Corps within the Navy.

In May 1893, the *Army and Navy Journal* editorialized, "The efforts of the Colonel Commandant of the Marine Corps to attain a higher standard of education and professional qualification for his officers are bearing fruit." The new promotion and examination standards had meaning and some bite to them. For example, the previous month, 1st Lt. George T. Bates took his examination for captain. The examining board found Bates "not qualified in professional aspects to perform at next highest grade." Secretary Herbert suspended the Marine lieutenant from promotion for one year, when he again would be permitted to take the exam. Secretary Herbert in his annual report held up the Marine officer examinations as an example for the entire Navy.[4]

Heywood's pride continued to be the Marine Corps School of Application. On April 24, 1893, the school graduated its second class of officers and first class of noncommissioned officers. During their final exercises, the graduates went through their various drills and formations, demonstrated artillery, and concluded with a dress parade. Each graduating officer and non-commissioned officer (NCO) received a certificate of proficiency attesting that he had mastered the "branches of Military Art and Science taught at the School of Application of the United States Marine Corps." A three-man board of visitors, consisting of Lt. Col. Theodore Mosher, the adjutant general of the District of Columbia Militia; Cmdr. Charles M. Thomas of the U.S. Navy; and Capt. Frank L. Denny, assistant quartermaster of the Marine Corps viewed the closing ceremonies and examined the graduates. The board praised the school and its curriculum, observing that the school notes and circulars were "practically a compendium of the military art up to date." In their report, the officers concluded: "The seed thus sown will be sure to bring forth good fruit, and will greatly enhance the usefulness of the school of application and bring to the notice of the Navy at large the excellent work that is now being accomplished."[5]

Less effusive in his appraisal, Capt. Daniel P. Mannix, the director of the school, provided a matter-of-fact description of the school year. He remarked that the course of instruction lasted for seven months, and during the eighth month, the students devoted most of their time to practical exercises including a visit to the naval ordnance proving grounds at Indian Head, Maryland. The curriculum remained much the same as it had the year before with an emphasis on artillery and naval gunnery, infantry tactics, mines and torpedoes, and military engineering. Both the officers and the NCOs were graded and given class standings. The officer grade averages ranged from a high of 94.1 earned by 2d Lt. Albertus Catlin to a low of 83.5 made by 2d Lt. Lawrence H. Moses. The NCO grades varied from a high of 93.7 to a low of 72.1. Mannix believed that both the officers and the NCOs needed more inducements to do well, and recommended that promotions to noncommissioned status be limited to the enlisted graduates of the School of Application. With the close of the term, two of Mannix's instructors, Lts. Thomas Prince and Charles Long, departed for other duties, and Mannix retained 1st Lt. Harry K. White on his staff and selected 2d Lt. Wendell C. Neville, of the present graduating class, as an instructor in the NCO division of the school. By September 1893, 6 new officers and 24 NCOs and privates had reported to Mannix and the school and "are waiting for the wheels to go round."[6]

Like the previous two years, the new officer students came from the graduating class of the Naval Academy. George Richards, one of the new second lieutenants, recalled, "Six of us, with swords in clanking metal scabbards, clothed in sky-blue trousers, and other garments, which felt a little strange to us, came here to Washington, to join the Marine Corps." Richards's prior association with the Marine Corps, like that of most naval cadets, was not of a pleasant nature. An unruly cadet, Richards stood trial for hazing and was only permitted by a presidential pardon to rejoin his classmates. Richards remembered that on two occasions while the rest of his classmates enjoyed their annual leave after their summer cruise, he was a "double dyed" member of two "chain gangs" on board the punishment ship *Santee* docked at the Academy. It was the Marine sentry who "seemed there to hold our 'chain gang' all together, when the rest of you were scattered to the four winds, and having brought us in this way together, he exercised over us all an influence full of restraint." Richards graduated twenty-ninth in his class, next to the last man to receive a commission. The last man, William N. McKelvey, also became a Marine second lieutenant.[7]

None of the other four new Marine officers, 2d Lts. Dion Williams, Rufus H. Lane, Albert S. McLemore, and Elisha Theall, broke any academic records during their tenure at Annapolis. Williams had the best academic record of the new Marines, ranking fifteenth in his class; Lane stood nineteenth; McLemore twenty-first; and Theall, twenty-eighth. Although Lieutenant Williams had a respectable grade average, he had received a waiver after first being denied admittance to the Naval Academy because of defective vision, and McLemore had served a term in solitary confinement while at the Academy for "deliberately disobeying orders." All of the new officers came from a middle- to upper-middle-class background. Their fathers' occupations varied from bookkeeper, railroad agent, schoolteacher, druggist, and merchant, to circuit judge. In effect, the Marine Corps received a rather run-of-the-mill pick of the Naval Academy graduates.[8]

Although hardly receiving the elite of the Naval Academy cadets, neither Colonel Heywood nor Captain Mannix protested the quality of the Marine Corps officers they received from that institution. Because of the 1883 law, there were still fewer openings in the entire naval establishment than there were graduates, and competition for any commission was keen. The young lieutenants for the most part proved to be able and eager students at the School of Application. Captain Mannix observed that the officer students were "aware of the importance of doing well."[9]

At the beginning of its third year of existence, the Marine Corps School of Application had attained somewhat of a minor reputation. In his annual report, Colonel Heywood called attention "to the thoroughness of the instruction in both theory and practice." It had begun to build a professional library, and Lieutenant White earned much praise for his pamphlets "on submarine mines and mining." In December 1893, the school functioned and classes continued uninterrupted when the school's director, Captain

Marine Corps School of Application, class of 1894. From left to right: 2d Lt. Dion Williams, 2d Lt. George Richards, 1st Lt. Wendell C. Neville, 2d Lt. Rufus H. Lane, 1st Lt. Harry K. White, 2d Lt. William N. McKelvy, 2d Lt. Albert S. McLemore, Capt. Paul St. Clair Murphy, and 2d Lt. Elisha Theall. Captain Murphy replaced Captain Mannix as commander of the school in March 1894. (Marine Corps Historical Center Collection)

Mannix, entered the naval hospital in Washington for treatment for what doctors later diagnosed as stomach cancer.[10]

On February 6, 1894, Colonel Heywood announced that Captain Mannix died "at half-past seven o'clock this morning." He described Mannix as "an able zealous and intelligent officer, much interested in his profession and very attentive to his duties. He prepared the course of study at the School of Application . . . and it is to him that much of the credit is due for the successful results attained there."[11]

The Marine commandant was not about to allow the school to lapse with the death of its founder. He appointed Capt. Paul St. Clair Murphy, who had most recently commanded the guard at the Columbian Exposition, to succeed Mannix at the School of Application. Murphy took over on March 8, and on May 3, 1894, the school graduated its third class of officers and its second class of noncommissioned officers with the usual final exercises and

ceremony. According to Heywood, Murphy was "an officer of excellent reputation and tried ability," who would continue to make the school a success.[12]

In the meantime, Colonel Heywood tried to change the composition of his
official staff and generally strove to improve the entire officer corps. Like his
predecessor, Heywood enjoyed mixed results. In 1894, he supported the candidacy of Capt. George C. Reid to replace Maj. Augustus S. Nicholson as
the adjutant and inspector of the Marine Corps. On April 20, 1894, the
Marine commandant observed in a letter to Secretary Herbert that Reid
had thirty years' service and was still a captain although fifty-four years of
age and junior in rank to several officers younger than him. Reid had served
as an aide to General Zeilin during his commandancy and had helped to
found the first Marine officer organization. According to Heywood, Reid
was "an excellent officer . . . a man of most exemplary habits and is well
qualified by age and experience to perform the duties of the position to
which he seeks appointment."[13]

At the close of his letter, Heywood revealed the real reasons for his support of Reid. He noted that according to the 1893 naval regulations that
Reid incidentally had helped to draft, the adjutant and inspector would
function as the commandant of the Marine Corps in the absence of the
commandant. He wrote, "The undersigned is naturally anxious that the
new appointee should be an officer in whom he has confidence and who is
in personal accord with him." Still feeling the loss of Captain Mannix who
had served as an informal adviser, Heywood wanted the new adjutant and
inspector as an ally in his push for reform and had even appointed Captain
Reid as the new commander of the Marine Barracks in place of Mannix.
Secretary Herbert acceded to Heywood's request and made Reid the new adjutant and inspector, which office he assumed on May 2, 1894.[14]

While Heywood made an ally of the adjutant and inspector, his ties with
the other two senior members of the formal staff, the paymaster, Maj. G. C.
Goodloe, and Maj. H. B. Lowry, the quartermaster, soon deteriorated.
Goodloe made no secret of his ambition to be commandant. Prior to Heywood's appointment, the paymaster, the son-in-law of the senior senator
from Kentucky, had made a serious bid for the post, and although correct
and initially respectful toward one another, neither Goodloe nor Heywood
had any great fondness for the other. By November 1892, Heywood reported Goodloe to the secretary of the Navy for willfully disobeying his orders and that of the department and although the department acknowl-

edged that Goodloe's conduct was "reprehensible," it satisfied itself with a letter of reprimand rather than the "more extreme measure" (probably a court-martial) recommended by Heywood.[15]

The commandant's dealings with his quartermaster, Major Lowry, were, if anything, worse. Heywood and Lowry had little difficulty with one another until the commandant discovered that the quartermaster was addressing correspondence directly to the secretary of the Navy. Backed by the department, Colonel Heywood reprimanded Lowry. According to Heywood, the quartermaster stopped "personal intercourse with me and . . . maintained that of only the strictest official character."[16]

Insisting on the betterment of the service rather than the convenience of the individual, Colonel Heywood, like Colonel McCawley before him, attempted to rid the Marine Corps of its more pernicious offenders and raise the professional level of the officer corps. Few officers equaled the notoriety of 1st Lt. T. Glover Fillette, who in January 1893 stood trial by court-martial for indebtedness. The court found Fillette guilty and ordered him to be dismissed from the service. Colonel Heywood approved the sentence, but former Secretary of the Navy Tracy, in one of his last acts of office, overruled both the commandant and the court and returned Fillette to duty, provided the Marine lieutenant paid his creditors $80 per month until he completed payment on all his debts. The *New York Times* commented, "Fillette succeeded in bringing sufficient political influence to his aid to have the sentence mitigated." One Navy wife described the Marine lieutenant as "not the kind of person one would choose for an intimate companion. He may be a gentleman in manners, but his troubles have arisen because he does not pay his debts."[17]

Lieutenant Fillette was soon in trouble again. Colonel Heywood assigned the Marine lieutenant to the Portsmouth, New Hampshire, Navy Yard, but Fillette asked for a delay in his orders because of the illness of his wife. Heywood asked for an investigation since "this officer has not a good reputation for veracity." The commandant wrote to the secretary of the Navy, "Mrs. Fillette and her child were seen yesterday in a street car, apparently in good health, and upon being asked how she and her child were replied that they were 'both well.'" Lieutenant Fillette reported to the Portsmouth Barracks.[18]

In November, Colonel Heywood forwarded two clippings from local Portsmouth newspapers that reflected "very seriously on an officer of the U.S. Marine Corps stationed at the Navy Yard there." Needless to say, the officer was Lieutenant Fillette. Apparently Fillette was carrying on an affair with a local high school girl in the city. The following month, Heywood reported that Fillette's wife "is in such a serious mental condition that she will have to be removed to an asylum for the insane." Undeterred by his wife's health, Fillette in January 1894 wrote a letter to his young high school friend and asked her to elope with him. This last was too much for the Navy commandant of the yard who suspended the Marine lieutenant from duty, "having concluded that this officer was acting in an unbecoming manner in the city of Portsmouth, and had, therefore, lost the respect of his subordinates."[19]

The Navy held a court of inquiry at Portsmouth and directed that Lieutenant Fillette appear before a medical board in Washington "to have his mental condition inquired into." Fillette failed to show up for the examination, and Secretary Herbert ordered Colonel Heywood to arrest the lieutenant and deliver him to the medical director at the naval hospital. Marine 2d Lt. Dion Williams and a Marine sergeant dressed in civilian clothes found Fillette in a Washington theater and escorted him to the Navy hospital where he was placed under guard. Lieutenant Fillette told the examining officers that he did not request a medical board and "had no cognizance of the order convening it until a few hours prior to my arrest." Fillette protested his confinement and claimed "that my mental condition was in good order." The medical board ruled that the Marine lieutenant was "of sound mind" and found no evidence of "abnormal or perverted habits."[20]

Lieutenant Fillette still faced charges, and at the direction of the Navy Department, on May 4, 1894, Colonel Heywood ordered Fillette back to Portsmouth to "report, in arrest to the commandant of the navy yard there." A Navy general court-martial found Fillette guilty of negligence to obedience of orders and "scandalous conduct" and sentenced him to be dismissed from the service. This time both Secretary Herbert and President Cleveland approved the action of the court. On June 29, 1894, Secretary Herbert wrote Fillette that the sentence "takes effect this date, and you accordingly cease to be an officer of the United States Marine Corps." Although Colonel Heywood got rid of one of his bad apples, it took the brazen and flamboyant disregard of both service protocol and the social conventions of the day on the part of Lieutenant Fillette to accomplish this goal. The Marine commandant, nevertheless, was quick to point out that the dismissal of Fillette would permit a certain number of promotions and an additional vacancy in the Marine officer corps.[21]

Promotion opportunities became of increasing concern to Marine officers. In his 1893 annual report, the commandant observed that while retirements and vacancies had led to promotion among lieutenants during the past several years, stagnation continued in the grade of captain. He wanted legislation so that "these old officers, some of whom have served over and many nearly thirty years, may be promoted to field officers while their period of usefulness and activity remains." In thanking Colonel Heywood for his efforts on behalf of the more senior captains, Henry Clay Cochrane remarked that he was now the same age that Heywood was when he made commandant and still faced "nine more years" in the rank of captain. Although Cochrane recommended a more intensified lobbying effort, any prospect for separate legislative action for the Marine Corps appeared dim since the Navy was caught up in an imbroglio over its entire personnel structure, including promotions.[22]

From the very beginning of his taking office, Secretary Herbert had been unhappy with the Navy personnel organization. In December 1892, as one of his last legislative moves as chairman of the House Naval Affairs Committee, Herbert had introduced a concurrent resolution for the House and Senate to form a joint committee to study personnel matters of the Navy, arguing that the existing laws relating to personnel were "inconsistent, unjust, and the result of piecemeal legislation." Although Congress had failed to act at that time, in early 1894, it formed a joint subcommittee from the naval committees of both houses of Congress for that very purpose. On February 2, 1894, the chairman of the joint subcommittee, Senator M. C. Butler, wrote to Secretary Herbert stating that he would "be pleased to receive any suggestions the Department may be inclined to make."[23]

The establishment of the joint committee opened a Pandora's box for almost every special interest group in the naval establishment. Although naval officers complained to the press that Secretary Herbert had placed a "gag rule" on them so that they could not "communicate information on matters connected with the Department except on the express authorization of the Department," this order appeared to be honored more in the breach than in its observance. These anonymous officers charged that the secretary's motives were political in order to secure his own legislative agenda. Each of the various Navy groups, however, had its own agenda as well. There was a lack of unanimity among naval officers and "jealousy and strife between the different corps." Secretary Herbert added fuel to the discord when he resurrected a report made in 1891 by a board headed by Captain Robert L. Phythian to study personnel problems in the Navy and submitted it to the joint subcommittee. The Phythian Report called for the "plucking" or forced retirement of older officers.[24]

Not satisfied with what they considered the halfway measures of the Phythian Report, several Navy line officers lobbied for even more drastic legislation from Congress. On February 5, 1894, Senator Eugene Hale, a member of the congressional joint subcommittee, introduced "by request" a bill in the Senate for the reorganization of the Navy and Marine Corps. Although not identifying the author of the bill, the press speculated that it had official backing, possibly from Commodore Ramsay, the chief of the Bureau of Navigation. This bill not only contained a "plucking" provision, but also called for the eventual abolition of the Marine Corps and the Paymaster Corps and the reduction of the number of engineers and the limitation of their responsibility to ship-construction design.[25]

One anonymous Marine officer replied to the attack on his Corps through the press. He accused the Navy line officers of jealousy and stated that "all the Marines ask is that they be made use of and they will guarantee good service, and that at a great saving to the government." Colonel Heywood decided not to wage his defense of the Corps through the newspapers, but through the joint committee. He forwarded a twenty-one-page report that he wanted Secretary Herbert to consider when the latter presented "the needs of the Naval Service to the Joint Congressional Commission now in session." The descriptive title of the report, "Statements and Arguments Setting Forth the Value and Necessity of a United States Marine Corps to the Navy; Showing that It Will be a Measure of Efficiency, Economy, and Justice to Increase the Corps, Giving It Enough Officers and Men to Efficiently Perform the Duty Expected and Required of It," aptly provides the basic thrust of the document. In a rudimentary form of cost analysis, the Marine commandant enclosed charts that demonstrated that the individual Marine was $1,000 less expensive than the individual sailor. Using past annual reports and studies, Heywood repeated many of his usual refrains: the need for more Marines; the assignment of the Marines under their own officers to the secondary batteries on board ship; the increase in numbers of officers; and the creation of higher ranks for the officer corps, including a brigadier generalship for the commandant.[26]

On March 1, 1894, Secretary of the Navy Herbert forwarded his own recommendations to the joint subcommittee. Like the Hale bill, he called for the forced retirement of a number of senior naval officers but made no reference to the Marine Corps or to any of the Navy staff corps. The subcommittee then began its hearings. On March 24, Rear Adm. John G. Walker, the former chief of the Bureau of Navigation and commander of the Squadron of Evolution, testified on behalf of a bill that he had drafted and which the committee had under consideration. Walker's draft like Herbert's proposal included a "plucking" provision, but also the gradual elimination of the Pay Corps and the Marine Corps. According to Walker, "Marines have been of great service in days gone by—in the days of press gangs and mutinies. . . . their day of usefulness at sea has gone by." Colonel Heywood, making many of the same points that he had made in his formal statement to Secretary Herbert, suggested that the Navy would require fewer sailors if the Marines were employed properly. He argued that with Marines manning the secondary batteries, the Navy would have enough sailors to man the new ships at a saving of over $69,000.[27]

By the end of July, the special joint subcommittee had completed its preliminary deliberations and drafted a tentative personnel bill. Although not formally submitted, subsequent press accounts revealed that the committee rejected all radical proposals to eliminate any of the corps in the naval service and in fact called for an increase in the rank and number of Marine officers. The committee included in its recommendations, however, the "plucking" provision of the Phythian Board and other minor reforms that would raise qualifications for officer promotion throughout the Navy, the establishment of a reserve officer list, and the expansion of opportunities for enlisted men in both the Navy and the Marine Corps. Although supported by the administration, the proposed legislation faced formidable opposition. Each of the conflicting special-interest officer-professional groups within the Navy had its supporters in Congress.[28]

While the joint subcommittee continued to struggle with Navy personnel legislation, the smoldering issue of the role of Marines on board ship lay not far below the surface. In January 1894, Commandant Heywood believed the sentiment among younger naval officers so opposed to the Marine Corps that he undertook a letter-writing campaign to garner the support of more senior officers. In his letter to Commodore Ramsay of the Bureau of Navigation, Heywood suggested that even if the Marines were removed from ships, it would be necessary "to introduce in their places an equal number of men to discharge the duties now performed by them." Given Ramsay's record of general hostility toward the Marines, it is doubtful that he agreed with the commandant's premise. Rear Adm. Stephen Luce, however, reaffirmed his friendship to the Marine Corps and wrote to Heywood, "When a system has worked well for over one hundred years, it seems unwise . . . to change it in the absence of some marked and obvious necessity for improvement." The commandant thanked Luce for his sentiments and declared,"I think they will not abolish or drive us out of ships yet awhile."[29]

In his testimony before the joint subcommittee, Heywood spoke about the reluctance of the Navy, especially of the Bureau of Navigation, to make full use of the Marine complements on board ship. According to Heywood, "As the matter stands now, the Marines are sent on board as sharpshooters, you may say supernumeraries, and they do not render the service which a body of men who are so well organized and drilled could perform." He declared that the captains of the various ships often assigned the Marines to the secondary batteries, but "the guns are taken away from them . . . upon orders from the Bureau of Navigation."[30]

The situation reached a head in the summer of 1894. First Lt. Littleton W. T. Waller, assigned to the Norfolk Navy Yard, obtained copies of a petition being circulated among the crews of several Navy warships at anchor in port. A Navy petty officer told Waller that the purpose of the petition was "to defeat or 'block' the recommendation by the Colonel Commandant for the increase of the Marine Corps." The petition listed the usual grievances against Marines that Commander Fullam had first enunciated in his 1890 *Naval Institute Proceedings* article. Although Waller wrote that he did "not place much credit or belief that an officer received these petitions on any ship," he acknowledged that "rumor has it that the petition is being pushed by a [Navy] officer."[31]

Upon receiving copies of the Navy enlisted petition from Lieutenant Waller, Colonel Heywood protested to Secretary Herbert. He suggested that the petition "savor[s] of conspiracy." Unlike Lieutenant Waller, the commandant had less faith in the innocence of naval officers, and he wondered how the petition could have been placed "on the hatch above the galley on the *Raleigh*, with pen and ink attached ready for the signatures of the crew, without the knowledge of any officer of the ship." Heywood then stated that if officers were involved, "they are engaged in a . . . combination to weaken the lawful authority of their superiors." The commandant also interpreted Navy Regulations as not allowing Navy enlisted men to petition Congress directly without first going through the secretary of the Navy. He then asked Secretary Herbert to form a court of inquiry to investigate the entire matter.[32]

At the end of July, Secretary Herbert issued a circular letter to commanders-in-chief of U.S. naval forces, commandants of Navy yards, and officers commanding vessels in which he largely supported the Marine position. Several years later, he stated that at the time there was a "movement then on foot among certain officers of the line, to induce me to favor the abolition of the Marine Corps." According to Herbert, he credited Major Reid, the Marine adjutant and inspector, for convincing him to retain the Marine Corps intact. In his circular letter, Herbert wrote that the Navy Department "is convinced of the usefulness of that [Marine] corps, both ashore and afloat." In rejecting the enlisted petition, the secretary referred to rumors that Navy officers might have instigated the move, and in a veiled warning,

Herbert stated that the department was "loath, however, to believe that any such officer would lend the influence of his honorable position to the encouragement of dissension between enlisted men of the Navy and the Marine Corps." He referred to such behavior as bordering on the "seditious." Despite his strong words in support of the Marine Corps, Herbert made no mention of Marines manning the secondary batteries on board ship.[33]

In his annual report, Colonel Heywood attempted to renew the issue of the duties of Marines on board ship that had surfaced both in the hearings of the Joint Subcommittee and in the petition movement. His original draft contained a statement requesting once more that Marines man the secondary batteries. He observed that Congress had not authorized any increase in the Navy to man the new ships coming into commission, and he suggested that putting the Marines on the guns would free approximately 1,000 sailors. The commandant argued that Marines "are much cheaper to maintain than sailors [and] that this suggestion is in the direct line of economy."[34]

Fearing more dissension and disruption in the Navy, Secretary Herbert informed Heywood that he thought "it best to revise . . . the portions [of the commandant's report] marked with blue pencil." This portion, of course, was the reference to Marines replacing sailors at the secondary batteries. Taking the not-so-subtle hint, Colonel Heywood deleted the offending phrases but included an appeal for more men to assist in the manning of the new ships now entering into service.[35]

While fending off the Navy's attempts to remove Marines from ships, Heywood suddenly found the Marine Corps the center of another dispute not of its making. This time the instigators were not naval officers, but Army officers. In August 1894, Army artillery reformers, who wished to separate the coast artillery from the field artillery, induced friendly senators to introduce a bill that would form a Marine artillery corps. The bill would combine the coast artillery regiments with the Marine Corps for the purpose of harbor defense. Although the bill called for a brigadier general to command the new Marine artillery organization, Heywood and Marine officers recognized the bill as a direct threat to the Marine Corps. As a Marine board that Heywood formed to study the implications of the proposed legislation related, there was no guarantee that the present commandant of the Marine Corps would be the brigadier general. Heywood understood that junior artillery officers framed the bill for their benefit without consultation of Marine officers or the commandant. The bill allowed for more promotions, but Marine officers would in general rank below their Army artillery counterparts. Heywood recommended to the secretary of the Navy that the latter oppose the bill on the grounds that the Marine Corps "has a distinct sphere of usefulness as a separate military organization which it would be unwise to destroy by any such radical measures as the framers of this bill seek to have adopted." Given the opposition of the commandant, combined with that of the old guard of the Army, the bill had no future. It languished in committee and never appeared on the floor of either house of Congress.[36]

In July 1894, the Marine officer corps received an infusion of graduates from the Naval Academy when 7 new second lieutenants donned their Marine uniforms. Like those of previous years, most of the officers were from the lower half of their class. Only 2d Lt. William C. Dawson, ranked ninth, stood in the top 10. Out of 28 graduates commissioned, the Marines held the seventeenth, nineteenth, twenty-second, twenty-fourth, twenty-sixth, and twenty-eighth positions. In other respects, the Marine lieutenants conformed to the usual Annapolis genteel pattern. All 7 were Protestants, including 5 Episcopalians: Lts. Dawson, Walter Ball, Charles F. Macklin, Theodore H. Low, and John Russell, Jr. Two were sons of military officers: Macklin whose father was in the Army, and Russell whose father was a retired Navy admiral. Second Lt. Austin R. Davis was the son of a Savannah, Georgia, merchant, and Ball's father was a bookkeeper in Washington, D.C. Second Lt. Thomas S. Borden's guardian was Senator A. S. Gibson of Louisiana. Although the sons of widows, Low and Dawson attended public and private schools, indicating that the families had some economic assets at their disposal.[37]

Under the stewardship of Captain Murphy, the Marine School of Application continued to function as the initial entry experience of new Marine lieutenants. Murphy kept much the same curriculum as that developed by Captain Mannix. Like the previous year, the school maintained both an enlisted and an officer division. The enlisted division consisted of 18 men—5 sergeants, 3 corporals, and 10 privates. Second Lt. Rufus T. Lane, who had completed the course of instruction in May, stayed on, relieved Lt. Wendell C. Neville, and headed the enlisted division. In the officer division, 1st Lt. Joseph Pendleton replaced Lt. Harry K. White as the primary instructor. In May 1895, the school once more had its closing exercises. All the officers graduated except for Lieutenant Ball who transferred to the Navy Corps of Engineers. The School's Board of Visitors praised anew the accomplishments of the school in providing "a professional inquiry and study" to supplement the new lieutenants' training at Annapolis. In a defense of the Corps and of the school, the board observed, "The objects sought in the existence of the Marine Corps are peculiar, useful, and important, and seem too often to be misunderstood and unappreciated by those who should be its friends and supporters."[38]

In preparing for the next term, Captain Murphy suddenly faced a paucity of student officers. For the first time in several years, the Marine Corps had only one vacancy, thus permitting only one appointment from the Naval Academy. He was Naval Cadet Louis J. Magill. Magill fit the usual profile of new Marine second lieutenants. He was the son of a Presbyterian Erie, Pennsylvania, dentist and stood eighteenth among 34 commissioned.[39]

Murphy and Colonel Heywood decided to fill out the new class with two more lieutenants—the most junior and senior in their grades. The senior, 1st Lt. Thomas N. Wood, who entered the Marine Corps in 1876, was to be the first student at the School of Application who had not graduated from the Naval Academy. Lieutenant Wood had attended Annapolis, but failed to finish. Heywood selected Wood for the School of Application on the basis of his seniority in grade, however, rather than any tenuous connection to the Naval Academy. Second Lt. John Twiggs Myers, the junior lieutenant, had transferred from the Engineers to the Marine Corps in February 1895.[40]

Myers was a Naval Academy classmate of the lieutenants who had entered the Marine Corps the previous year. Although an Episcopalian, he came from a Jewish background. His father was Abraham C. Myers of South Carolina who had been the quartermaster general of the Confederacy. After the Civil War, the elder Myers spent several years in voluntary exile in Europe before returning to the United States. John Twiggs Myers was born in 1871 in Wiesbaden, Germany. Educated both in Germany and in the United States, the younger Myers entered the Naval Academy in 1887. Although he graduated, he failed to obtain a commission because of his low class standing. Using family influence, Myers became a passed engineer through a special act of Congress, but stating that he did "not know high pressure from low pressure," (except for political pressure), he maneuvered to transfer out of the engineers. He discovered that one of his classmates, Second Lieutenant Ball, was unhappy in the Marine Corps, and convinced Ball to agree to an exchange of service, which was approved by the secretary of the Navy.[41]

In September 1895, the new term of the School of Application opened with its curtailed number of 3 student officers. Perhaps in compensation, the number of enlisted students increased from 18 to 29 privates, 5 corporals, and 7 sergeants. To make up for the lack of actual officers, Captain Murphy used several of the senior sergeants as acting officers in the "practical exercises." In his report to the commandant the following month, Murphy recommended that there should be at least 4 student officers in any class. If there were not enough new second lieutenants from the Naval Academy in any given year, the school superintendent suggested that senior officers make up the difference.[42]

Captain Murphy had more significant recommendations for Marine officer education. He advocated the extension of officer training from eight months to one year. He believed that the Marine lieutenants, once they completed the School of Application in April, should spend one month in studying ordnance at the Washington Navy Yard, and then take the three-month course at the Naval War College in Newport. Murphy noted that both the Army's Infantry and Cavalry School at Fort Leavenworth and the Artillery School at Fort Monroe required two years. Moreover, Murphy argued that the course at the Naval War College "should be availed as early" in an officer's career as possible.[43]

Colonel Heywood agreed with Murphy's proposals about lengthening the school year and mentioned them favorably in his own annual report. In January 1896, the commandant wrote to Secretary Herbert and formally asked that the school term consist of one year to include both the Washington Navy Yard and the Naval War College. The following month, Commodore Ramsay, acting for the secretary, approved the request, and after the School of Application's final exercises in April, all three student officers completed "practical work" at the ordnance shops in the Washington Navy Yard. Only two of the three officers, lieutenants Magill and Myers, went on to the Naval War College which they successfully completed. The third, now Captain Wood, promoted during the school term, received orders for sea duty and was unable to continue.[44]

Officer professionalism in the Marine Corps was still a sometime thing, and personal motives lay behind many actions especially in the commandant's acrimonious relationship with Colonel James Forney, the senior officer in the Marine Corps next to himself. Although Forney had early been aligned with the reform element, his financial management of post funds was often unorthodox and open to question. He also had a reputation for being too fond of his bottle of bourbon or as he called it "Baby John." The fact that Forney's wife had actively campaigned on behalf of her husband for the commandancy in 1891 hardly assuaged the hard feelings between Forney and Heywood.[45]

In April 1895, acting upon reports that the New York Marine Barracks coal accounts were in disorder, the commandant transferred Forney from that large post to the Marine Barracks at Portsmouth, New Hampshire, a much less prestigious command. Referring to his seniority and rank, Forney strongly protested his reassignment stating that he was not "being treated fairly." He admitted, however, that he had received a letter of reprimand from the navy yard commandant, Rear Adm. Bancroft Gherardi, but maintained that he and the admiral had settled their differences. Forney quoted a letter from Gherardi who said that he had "no desire to make a specific report against Colonel Forney."[46]

Colonel Heywood was in no mood to reconsider his decision. He not only refused to return the colonel to New York but launched an investigation into Forney's conduct of his office. In a letter to Secretary Herbert, the Marine commandant observed that Colonel Forney and his officers at the New York Barracks used government coal in their personal quarters, which was against regulations. Colonel Heywood also laid before the secretary conflicting statements between Forney and his officers about the issuance of an order. The commandant believed that the irregularities that had occurred during Forney's tenure at New York required a court of inquiry, and in June, Heywood went even further and recommended a general court-martial.[47]

In Heywood's pursuit of Forney, other officers saw a note of personal animosity. It was no secret that Forney and Heywood had little liking for one another. Rumors abounded that there was also bad blood between the wives of the two men. One wife even suggested that it was Mrs. Forney's "extravagance and love of display" that was responsible for much of Forney's difficulty. Commenting on the forthcoming court-martial, Captain Cochrane wrote to his wife, "Colonel Heywood appears to be after him [Forney], and he may push him to the wall."[48]

In October, the wall came very close. Forney stood trial before a general court-martial, charged on four accounts, from embezzlement, to lying, to using and issuing false papers, and finally to "culpable inefficiency in the performance of duty." Despite Forney's obvious foibles, he still held the sympathy, affection, and even a modicum of respect of many of his contemporaries. During the court-martial, both the present and the preceding adjutant and inspectors, majors George C. Reid and Augustus S. Nicholson, testified to Forney's excellent reputation. As Maj. Robert W. Huntington later remarked about leadership among Marine officers: "Of this quality, Forney has a share, but he is such a fool otherwise."[49]

Apparently the members of the court-martial board held much the same opinion. They acquitted Forney of most of the major charges against him. The major charge of embezzling the coal for his own use had "dwindled down to an instance of omission in the performance of duty." Forney had admitted to using the coal, but claimed precedence, in that former commanding officers had done so for the past thirty years. The court ruled that he was guilty of neglect of duty but directed that his only punishment be a reprimand by the secretary of the Navy, published in General Orders of the Department of the Navy. In the general order, the Navy judge advocate general criticized the court for its conduct of the case and stated that the implication that Colonel Forney had the right to use the coal for his own purpose was untenable. The secretary, however, did not overturn the sentence of the court, and he ordered Colonel Forney released and returned to duty.[50]

The question of Marine Corps promotions surfaced during the trial. As part of the defense, Forney's civilian lawyer, Pennsylvania Congressman Franklin Bartlett, claimed that charges had been brought against his client because of a conspiracy among junior officers at the New York Barracks. The defense argued that the younger officers wanted to get rid of Forney so as to make room for themselves. Perhaps an extreme position, but promotions were not far from the thoughts of officers, or their wives for that matter, junior to Colonel Forney. Captain Cochrane remarked to his wife that "if Colonel Forney comes to grief, I may have to prepare for examination [for promotion] much sooner than expected." His wife, although expressing sympathy, for "poor old Dubbie [Forney]," nevertheless proceeded to express the hope that the court-martial would leave the Marine colonel with a "distaste for active service."[51]

Captain Cochrane, long in the forefront of the Marine reform movement, had also worked hard for the closely related issue of enhanced officer promotions. In October 1894, through official channels, Cochrane addressed a letter directly to Secretary Herbert citing his own case as an example. Cochrane explained that it would be another eight years before he could expect promotion to major. Cochrane stated that he had long refrained from asking for personal relief, but noted, "The years are passing rapidly, my vision is fading, my hair and teeth are going, and it has dawned upon me that I am on the down hill side of life and yet doing practically the same duty that I did more than a quarter of a century ago." He described the unequal distribution of rank, and the resulting "hump," leaving promotion a "lottery." According to Cochrane, the younger officers "have advanced so rapidly as to excite the active envy of their fellow graduates of the Naval Academy," while the older officers remained at the same level. He remarked that because of the vagaries of the "hump," Forney, two months younger than he, was now a colonel while Cochrane was still a captain. He then asked that the secretary support legislation that would permit the promotion of all captains who had forty-one years of service.[52]

Although agreeing in principle with Captain Cochrane, Secretary Her-

A bearded Capt. Henry Clay Cochrane drills a Marine ship guard. Cochrane complained to the secretary of the Navy about the slowness of Marine promotions, stating that he had been performing much the same duty for twenty-five years. (Henry Clay Cochrane Collection, Marine Corps Historical Center)

bert, in effect, rejected the petition. Still in hopes that Congress might pass the omnibus bill recommended by the joint committee of the two naval affairs committees, the secretary did not want any special legislation to jeopardize the whole. He bluntly told Cochrane that he did "not consider this is the proper time to consider this matter."[53]

Despite the denial of the request by Secretary Herbert, Colonel Heywood obviously found some satisfaction in having Captain Cochrane place the matter before the secretary. In November 1895 Heywood rewarded Cochrane with a plum assignment, command of the Newport Marine Barracks at Newport, Rhode Island, and the "position of lecturer at the [Naval] War College." After obtaining a promise from Heywood that if he did not like Newport he would not have to stay there, Cochrane agreed to take the assignment. In such small ways as officer assignments in key billets, the commandant kept the Marine Corps abreast with professional developments in the Navy, even if he was not always able to obtain his legislative objectives or prune out the officers he did not want.[54]

Although somewhat under a cloud during the first years of the Herbert administration, the Naval War College and to a lesser extent the Office of Naval Intelligence remained the intellectual core of the New Navy. Colonel Heywood saw to it that there were Marines assigned to both organizations.

The Marine Corps' relationship with the War College went back almost to the school's beginnings, and several Marine officers had attended the earlier courses. With the formation of the Marine Corps School of Application, however, Marine officer attendance at the Naval War College initially declined. Although unable to send any officers as students in 1894, Colonel Heywood assured Rear Admiral Luce of his keen interest in the War College. At the request of the new president of the college, Commander H. C. Taylor, the Marine commandant sent a Marine captain to assist in the preparations for a summer course at the college and "to fit himself for such lectures as the course demands." Heywood told Taylor, "It has been my endeavor and hope to enlarge the scope of usefulness of the Corps in every possible way, and I am willing and anxious to aid in carrying out any reasonable suggestion towards that end." With the authorization of the Navy Department, Marine Capt. Richard B. Wallach reported to the War College in June 1894.[55]

Commissioned in 1869 and promoted to captain in 1891, Wallach had a penchant for reading military history and gained a small reputation for scholarly attainment. On July 9, 1894, he delivered his first lecture at the War College on the development of infantry tactics. According to a contemporary account, Captain Wallach confined "himself wholly to the cruisers of ancient times." In August, the Marine officer taught a course in combined operations and the following month taught a course in coast defense. Colonel Heywood received excellent reports on Wallach's performance in the classroom and a request from Captain Taylor, the War College's president, to retain the Marine captain for another year on the school's faculty.[56]

Wallach's tenure at the school coincided with the major reforms that

Captain Taylor instituted at the college. In 1894, for the first time, the college had a permanent faculty. Although keeping the lecture format, Taylor divided students into smaller classes, where they studied sections of a larger problem. The course work still required traditional classes in sea power, tactics, signaling, and fleet maneuvers, but also included the study of specific war problems. Retired Navy Lt. William McCarty Little of the faculty staff introduced a naval war game, based in part on the war gaming techniques that the German general staff employed. In an article in the *Naval Institute Proceedings* in 1895, Captain Taylor justified the War College in terms of enabling naval officers to understand their profession and the broader aspects of warfare.[57]

As part of this broader study, the War College looked at both contemporary and past military campaigns. At the outbreak of the Sino-Japanese War in 1894, the Naval War College was engaged in a study of such campaigns. One group of officers actually had played a war game based on a naval conflict between Japan and China with Korea as the area of operations. At the end of the war, Taylor asked Captain Wallach to prepare a series of lectures about Japanese military ground operations to complement the study of fleet operations during the war. Wallach's lectures proved so popular in 1895 that the Naval Institute asked permission to publish them in its *Proceedings*.[58]

In his lectures, Captain Wallach treated events in a straightforward chronological manner and dealt with naval affairs only as they impinged on the three military campaigns in the war—Korea, Port Arthur, and Weihaiwei. He referred, however, as would be expected to Mahan and the importance of command of the sea. In his account, he made several historical analogies and allusions to the Napoleonic campaigns, the Balkan War of 1877, the Prussian-Austrian War, and to a lesser extent to Caesar, the U.S. Civil War, and the Franco-Prussian War. Wallach, nevertheless, used history tentatively and cautioned his readers or listeners: "We must bear in mind that circumstances, which are always different, must decide in each particular case that arises; . . . to make these delicate distinctions and do the right thing at the right time in the right place is a manifestation of a true genius for war."[59]

Although drawing no comparison to the makeup of U.S. forces or U.S. naval strategy, Wallach commented approvingly about the Japanese establishment of bases on the Chinese coast as an adjunct to the fleet and to support ground operations. He also described in great detail the amphibious landing of the Japanese Second Army of nearly 30,000 men near Port Arthur. Over 38 transports accompanied by hundreds of small craft, including 100 steam launches, and protected by 25 warships convoyed the troops from

Hiroshima to the projected landing site, eighty-five miles to the north. The Japanese chose the landing site not because of its accommodation to ships but because it was closer to the Port Arthur road than anywhere else on the Chinese coast. According to Wallach, the water was so shallow that the landing could only be made at high tide. Not only 30,000 troops landed without the loss of a man, the Japanese successfully brought ashore the necessary logistic train including horses, guns, ammunition, wagons, and provisions. Praising the Japanese feat, Wallach stated that such an operation was "recognized as one of the most difficult in war."[60]

In relating the capture of Weihaiwei, Wallach recounted the role played by Japanese "Marines" [in all probability they were Japanese naval infantry]. A force of "Marines" landed in boats from the fleet at Yung Ching on the coast just south of Weihaiwei. The Chinese had covered the landing site with a four-gun battery protected by earthen defensive works, but as the boats approached the shore, their guns dispersed the Chinese defenders and the "Marines advancing in a deep and heavy snow completed the rout." With the beach cleared, the army could then land. A clear theme of Wallach's account was the close connection between the sea and land operations and the "perfection of the combined tactics of the [Japanese] land and sea forces."[61]

Like the War College, the Office of Naval Intelligence also had an interest in the war in the Far East. In July 1895, the office's *Information from Abroad* series featured an article on the "Japan China War." Coincidentally, the co-author of the article was the only Marine assigned to the agency, 1st Lt. Lincoln Karmony. A weapons expert, Karmony had been with the intelligence office since 1892, and the year before had published an article upon "Small Caliber Rifles" used by the navies of the world. In their notes on the Sino-Japanese War, Karmony and his co-author, Navy Lt. H. M. Witzel, confined themselves to a brief narrative of events with little analysis. Like Wallach, they mentioned the many Japanese amphibious operations but again made no comparison to American forces or the mission of U.S. naval forces.[62]

The two studies highlighted the U.S. Navy's interest in the affairs of other nations and developments in modern warfare, both on land and on the sea. In his *Proceedings* article on the War College, Captain Taylor referred to the United States as an expanding power and implied that the nation would play an ever-increasing role among the major powers of the world. Such a role would require larger armed forces, especially a larger Navy. He perceived both the War College and to a lesser extent, the Office of Naval Intelligence, as an embryonic naval general staff to prepare the Navy for its part in the coming modern age. Upon his assumption of the presidency of the War College, Taylor instituted a formal program of war planning to accompany fleet problems and exercises. In 1894 and 1895, the staff based the fleet problems at the War College on the premise of war between England and the United States.[63]

The fleet problem for the summer of 1895 had an unusual degree of reality when Cleveland's secretary of state, Richard Olney, invoked the Monroe Doctrine in a boundary dispute between Great Britain and Venezuela over British Guiana. With the press writing about a ninety-day ultimatum, the North Atlantic Squadron carried out fleet maneuvers based on the problems worked out by the War College. According to the scenario, the American fleet was to concentrate in Nantucket Sound and defend the Atlantic Coast against a British fleet twice its size. The *New York Times* spoke about a "series of naval evolutions and strategic manoeuvres on a larger scale than has ever been attempted before by a United States fleet in time of peace," which included "exercises of landing on a hostile shore in the face of the enemy."[64]

When the British at first refused the American offer of arbitration, a wave of jingoism swept the United States, and Secretary Herbert ordered Captain Taylor to prepare "a scheme of defense in the event of hostilities." According to Taylor, the secretary used the college during the crisis as "a general staff and me as a chief of same with considerable power." The Navy planned on building an improvised fleet on the Great Lakes that would support an Army invasion of Canada. Both the Mahan original plan and the War College problems of 1894 and 1895 suggested that the main American fleet would be concentrated on the East Coast to protect the major population centers there. If an opportunity arose, the American fleet would attack the British base at Halifax and perhaps establish an advance base there. In March 1896, the *New York Times* reported upon a Navy war game in which the U.S. supposedly defeated a much larger fleet which had used Halifax as its main port.[65]

By this time, however, the crisis had passed. Neither the British nor the U.S. military wanted war, and both sides realized that victory would not be an easy matter and could not be assured. The British government cooperated with the boundary commission established by the United States in January 1896 and the following year, through the good offices of the American government, entered into a treaty with Venezuela to arbitrate the dispute.[66]

The Navy Department turned to other matters and problems. Revolution fermented in Cuba. The Naval War College and Office of Naval Intelligence dusted off their old plans for war with Spain. With the growing power of Japan in the Pacific and America's special relationship with Hawaii, the planners also studied possible war with the Japanese. Assistant Secretary of the Navy William McAdoo called for the formation of a permanent board of naval officers to advise the secretary of the Navy on technical and military matters. He also advised more coordination with the Army and the establishment of a joint Army-Navy strategy board. Secretary Herbert in the waning days of the Cleveland administration did appoint a high-level planning board, consisting of the heads of the Bureaus of Navigation and Ordnance, the president of the Naval War College, and the chief of the Office of Naval Intelligence, to review the planning effort for a possible war with Spain over Cuba.[67]

The Naval War College was in the middle of all of this activity. Captain Taylor, the president of the War College, urged upon the department the formation of a general staff on the model of the German Army or the British Admiralty. He found in Washington, however, an overwhelming opposition to the idea. Taylor had hoped that such a staff would come out of the college, "but may to offend nature and have to grow out of a Bureau," specifically the Bureau of Navigation. Although the movement toward a general staff appeared to flounder, the War College took on more and more responsibility in the development of war planning, which normally would be the function of such a staff.[68]

All of the war planning effort at the War College appeared to have little to do with the Marine Corps. Junior Marine officers, after completing the School of Application, took the three-month summer course at the War College, but this again had little relation with the School's planning effort. Captain Cochrane replaced Captain Wallach, who departed Newport in November 1895, but Cochrane had additional duties. He only lectured occasionally at the War College, and usually on the subject of discipline. His main function, in contrast to Wallach, who had no troop responsibility, was the command of the Newport Barracks. During this period, one other Marine officer, 1st Lt. Charles H. Lauchheimer, was a visiting lecturer at the college on "Naval Law and Naval Courts." Lauchheimer generally defined naval law as "synonymous with military law," but said that it had specific connotations that determined the "governing [of] the Navy as a special community."[69]

Although the Marine officers at the War College took little part in the war planning, most of the plans or fleet problems referred to landing operations and to the establishment of a land base to support the fleet. To Navy planners, as Captain Mahan observed in 1890, the Marine Corps would be the "backbone to any force landing on the enemy's coast."[70]

At this point, the Marine Corps' only war planning was limited to its attempts to fend off the assaults of the Navy progressives. On October 24, 1895, Capt. Robley D. Evans, the commander of the new battleship the USS *Indiana*, wrote to Secretary Herbert, "Owing to the extremely limited berthing space in the ship, and the great demand for men in her powder division, I suggest that no Marines be sent to her." Commodore Ramsay, the chief of the Bureau of Navigation, strongly endorsed Evans's recommendation.[71]

Alarmed, Colonel Heywood quickly protested, repeating many of the same arguments that he had used in his testimony before the joint committee the year before. The Marine commandant compared the "modern man of war" to a "floating fort," which "should be manned more by soldiers than sailors, men who are artillerists and accustomed both to the use of great and small arms." As the *Army and Navy Journal* pointed out, Colonel Heywood was well aware, "Should the Department decide to grant Captain Evans' request, it is not probable that Marine Guards will be supplied to any of the other battleships."[72]

As he had the previous year over the seamen's petition, Secretary Herbert came down on the side of the Marine Corps. In his reply to Captain Evans, Herbert wrote that he considered the latter's proposal, but "determined that the 'Indiana' shall be supplied with a Marine guard." The guard was to consist of 60 enlisted men and 2 officers, and the secretary ordered that in addition to their customary duties the Marines were "to be detailed for service at the guns in such manner as the commanding officer may deem expedient." In an obvious rebuke to Evans, Herbert enclosed in his letter a copy of the circular pertaining to Marines that he had issued the previous year.[73]

In his annual report for the year, Secretary Herbert addressed the subject in even stronger terms. He wrote, "There has always been more or less objection on the part of some officers of the Navy to Marines on board ship." The secretary observed, however, that Marines had been part of the naval establishment "both on shore and at sea from its infancy . . . [and] experience has . . . demonstrated the wisdom of maintaining this branch of the service." Herbert referred to the fact that he had recently considered the role of the Marine guards on battleships and then spoke in much the same terms as Heywood. The secretary compared the warship to a "modern fort" and believed that in matters of warfare Marines were as expert as the sailors. He saw no reason why Marine officers could not command gun crews or even gun divisions and believed that the two organizations on board ship "create a healthy competition to excel." He ended with the statement that he had decided to place Marines on the *Indiana* and "will put Marines on the other battleships as they are severally commissioned." In December 1895, Heywood quoted from the report when he recommended that naval regulations be amended to assign Marines to the gun crews under its own officers.[74]

Despite the secretary's remarks in his annual report, the Marine Corps' relationship with naval officers on the role of Marines on board ship remained rocky. Marine Capt. Robert Huntington mentioned "the tyrannical naval superior" as part of the burden of the Marine officer and advised "burning a candle to the devil occasionally" so that "one could be moderately at ease with them." Naval officers, in turn, saw Marines as having undue influence. As one naval officer wrote, "The Col Comdt and his staff pursue a regular campaign of entertainment and they make themselves 'solid' with those who are in power."[75]

Lieutenant Fullam once more led the progressive naval officers' counterattack. Again using the pages of the *Naval Institute Proceedings*, he published an article in the spring 1896 issue on the "Organization of Naval Personnel." In the article, Fullam returned to several of his favorite themes first proposed in the Greer Board in 1889. In true progressive fashion, using terms such as "efficiency" and "objectivity," he argued that the Navy reduce the number of all the various staff officers on board ship and remove altogether the Marines and paymasters. Fullam protested against any assignment of Marines to the secondary batteries and declared that rather than have Marines take over sailors' duties, sailors should assume from the Marines the responsibility for ship discipline. In this article, however, Fullam emphasized the Marine expeditionary role, saying that he would organize the Marine shore establishment into six battalions that the secretary could order concentrated and embarked upon Navy transports for operations on foreign shores.[76]

Colonel Heywood, however, saw the article only as an attack on the Marine Corps. The Naval Institute had sent the commandant, as well as many other officers of the Navy and Marine Corps, a copy of Fullam's article prior to publication for "opinion and criticism." Heywood refused to comment on the draft but asked the secretary of the Navy to suppress it. The commandant observed that Fullam's would-be policies for the Marine Corps directly contradicted those recently enunciated by Secretary Herbert: "I do not attempt to discuss Lieutenant Fullam's article, or to reply to any of his remarks concerning my Corps, but that the Department may be informed as to the persistency with which this officer attacks its policy. . . . I regard it my duty to refer this pamphlet for such action as may be deemed proper." Colonel Heywood also sent a copy of his letter to the secretary to Lieutenant Fullam.[77]

Marines and sailors manning a ship's battery. Navy Lt. William F. Fullam led a movement on the part of Navy officers to have Marines withdrawn from Navy warships. (Henry Clay Cochrane Collection, Marine Corps Historical Center)

Secretary Herbert refused to involve the Navy Department in the imbroglio. He stated that while the department "doubts the advisability of discussions of this character relative to different branches of the naval service, particularly while Congress is in session," it would take no action. The secretary noted that the article was to be published in the *Proceedings* and that he did not want to hinder "full and free discussion in said journal."[78]

The Fullam article did enjoy full and free discussion in the *Proceedings*. More than 30 naval and 2 Marine officers commented on the article. Only 4 of the naval officers took exception to Fullam's views, although, of course both Marines, 1st Lt. Charles Doyen and 1st Lt. Charles Lauchheimer, defended their Corps. They basically argued that Marines and sailors had their specialties and both were necessary on board ship. Doyen rhetorically asked, "Why make a poor Marine out of a good sailor?" Rear Admiral Luce was the strongest defender of the Corps among the naval officers when he stressed that on board ship the Marines "keep alive and foster the military spirit." Most of the other respondents would have done away with the Marine Corps, incorporate them with the Army, or assign them the coast defense mission. One of the more snide comments read that the name Marine "alone has long been a synonym for idleness, worthlessness, and vacuity of intellect."[79]

Only a few officers picked up on Fullam's recommendation to form the Marines into expeditionary battalions. Among these were Richard Wainwright, the head of the Office of Naval Intelligence, and Captain Evans, the commander of the *Indiana*, who wanted to be rid of the Marines on his ship. Calling the Marines the "finest body of soldiers in this country," Evans wanted the Marines formed into an expeditionary brigade of 5,000 men who would continue their present duties of protecting the navy yards, occasionally put down riots, and when necessary "make serious demonstrations on shore." Wainwright would have organized the Marine Corps into a skeleton brigade for expeditionary operations and defense of advanced naval bases. For the moment, however, these suggestions were obscured by the divisiveness over the Marine presence on warships and internecine rivalry among the several officer corps of the Navy.[80]

As before, the internecine warfare among the several groups of the Navy, including Marines, spilled over into the halls of Congress. By the end of 1894, the much-heralded joint committee of Congress had completed its labors and, in January 1895, submitted its final report. Later in the month, the chairman of the joint subcommittee, Representative Adolph Meyer, who was also chairman of the House Naval Affairs Committee, introduced the recommendations of the subcommittee in the form of legislation in the House of Representatives. The ensuing Meyer bill provided for the Marine Corps the rank of brigadier general for its commandant and an additional colonel for the West Coast but called for no change in its organization or size. The bill's most controversial feature was the infamous "plucking" or forced retirement provision. It divided the Navy officer corps into two antagonistic groups, based largely on seniority, each of which formed its own lobbying association for and against the legislation. Marine officers largely supported the bill, but were suspicious of both naval groups.[81]

In the following session of Congress, a plethora of bills appeared favored by one naval officer faction or another. By this time, Secretary Herbert had given up hopes of obtaining the complete revamping of naval officer personnel legislation that he had wanted upon entering office. In December 1895 he switched his support from the Myers bill to a bill introduced by Senator Hale of Maine. Although retaining the "plucking" feature, the Hale bill made several concessions to the naval staff and also would have increased the number of Marine officers and permitted a number of promotions.[82]

Colonel Heywood had his own legislative agenda. Both in his 1895 annual report and in correspondence with the secretary of the Navy, the Marine Corps commandant asked for an expansion of the Corps. In January 1896, he formally requested 500 more enlisted men, reiterating that "the Marine Corps has not been increased to meet the needs of the new Navy." On February 20, 1896, Secretary Herbert forwarded the commandant's letter to Charles A. Boutelle, the chairman of the House Committee on Naval Affairs, and recommended approval "for the reasons therein mentioned."[83]

At the same time, Colonel Heywood informally pushed for more rank for himself and other Marine officers. Both the Hale bill, supported by the administration, and a bill introduced by Senator Chandler, without the notorious plucking provision and supported by the senior naval officers, provided for such an increase. An unofficial Marine lobbying organization backed yet another bill. All of this proposed legislation would have made Heywood a brigadier general and the staff officers lieutenant colonels after thirty years of service.[84]

Although all expanded the officer corps, each bill had different authorizations for the number of officers allowed in each rank. The Hale bill, for example, provided for nine majors, but all of the others, including the one supported by the Marine lobbying association, permitted from a minimum of four to a maximum of six majors. This obviously caused dissension among Marine officers, especially those captains who would be directly affected by the legislation. One Marine captain refused to join the Marine association, calling the legislation it sponsored a "bill to turn the Corps over to the staff." Captain Cochrane, who was in Washington in mid-January, observed to his wife that "they [the Marine association] have a new bill for the reorganization of the Corps in which I am greatly interested and do not like in its present form." Major Huntington, who was more philosophic, recognized that the bill gave the staff "needless advancement, but if a new lease of life can be gained by this I am perfectly willing they should have it." He saw the needs of the Corps in simple terms, an increase in both officers and men and "I think it would be well to take what we can." With the Marine officer corps, like the Navy officer corps, divided against itself, Congress was not about to act. Even the best that the optimistic Huntington believed possible was a favorable report from one of the congressional naval committees, and in fact, all of the officer bills died in committee.[85]

Colonel Heywood's request for additional enlisted men fared much better. On March 24, 1896, the House Naval Affairs Committee reported out the Naval appropriation bill and included a 500-man increase in the enlisted force of the Marine Corps. In explaining the action of the committee to the full House the following day, the chairman, Congressman Boutelle, stated that it was done at the request of both the secretary of the Navy and the commandant of the Marine Corps "in view of the increase of the number of our ships afloat." The House passed the bill and the increase without debate.[86]

The Navy progressives saw the House legislation as another setback in their attempt to remove the Marines from the battleships. They tried to recoup in the Senate where they had some influence with certain members of the Senate Appropriations Committee, including Senator Hale, the Republican chairman of the committee. On April 9, the Senate committee reported the naval appropriation bill without the increase for the Marine Corps. One of Fullam's cohorts gloated that he did not believe the Marines stood a chance to get their 500 men and declared that Marine officers displayed a "lack of wisdom . . . in pushing their claims for additional duties." The Navy officer stated that he "told one of their [Marine] pushers that such action would be sure to do them harm." Richard Wainwright, the chief of the Office of Naval Intelligence, was less sanguine about the Senate committee action: "The Marines are very strong in Washington and we will find it hard work getting rid of them."[87]

Action on the floor of the Senate confirmed Wainwright's fears. On May 2, 1896, the appropriation bill came up for debate. Senator Hale attempted to explain why the committee took out the provision for the 500 additional Marines by saying that the Navy had received 1,000 additional men the previous year, and that they were to receive another additional 1,000 men in the coming fiscal year. Given the additional cost, the committee believed that the Marine request could wait. The Senate rejected the committee's recommendation, and the Marine clause stayed in the bill.[88]

With the final passage of the appropriation bill on June 6, 1896, the Marine Corps had its first significant increase of enlisted personnel since the Civil War. In his annual report, Colonel Heywood observed that he had little difficulty in recruiting the additional men, and by October the Marine Corps was only 90 short of its appropriated enlisted strength. With the increase of the enlisted force, Heywood now argued that there needed to be corresponding growth in the officer corps, and he pointed to the stagnation at the rank of captain and the requirement for new second lieutenants to meet the additional demands for Marines on board ship.[89]

In 1896, as in the previous year, despite Colonel Heywood's request for 3 new second lieutenants to fill vacancies in the officer corps, the Marine Corps received only 1 newly graduated naval cadet from the Naval Academy. For the first time since the passage of the 1882 appropriation bill, there

were more vacancies (45–47), in the entire naval establishment than graduates of the Naval Academy (29). On July 1, 1896, Naval Cadet Melville K.
Shaw received his commission as a second lieutenant of Marines.[90]

Second Lieutenant Shaw matched the prototype of the new Marine officer. He was an Episcopalian and stood in the middle, eighteenth, of his Naval Academy class. His father was George K. Shaw, the editor of the *Minne-
apolis Tribune* and active in Minnesota Republican circles. Thanks to his
father's intervention with then Secretary of the Navy Tracy, the Naval
Academy had granted the younger Shaw a waiver on its physical qualifications after he had failed the entrance eye exam.[91]

Despite the shortage of Marine officers, Colonel Heywood continued the
Marine School of Application and the sending of Marine officers to the War
College. After Lts. Magill and Myers completed the three-month summer
course at the Naval War College, Lieutenant Magill joined the faculty of the
Marine School of Application, replacing Lieutenant Pendleton. Capt. F. H.
Harrington, meanwhile, had relieved Captain Murphy as director of the
school. Like the previous year, Harrington had a full contingent of enlisted
students, but only two officers: Lieutenant Shaw and First Lieutenant Karmony, the latter fresh from his assignment to the Office of Naval Intelligence
and second senior lieutenant in the Corps. Although at least one junior officer officially protested the assignment of officers to the School of Application while others pulled double duty, Colonel Heywood dismissed such
complaints as insubordination. Obviously the commandant considered the
school, with the emphasis in its curriculum on artillery and new technology,
as providing part of the essential education and background for Marine officers serving with the New Navy.[92]

Viewing the Marine Corps role with the New Navy as manning the secondary batteries of the new warships, Colonel Heywood, in the summer of
1896, together with Major Reid, fashioned a plan that he had originally
tried to implement during the Tracy administration. It consisted simply of
organizing and training a Marine guard for several months before assigning
it to a particular ship. On August 21, Major Reid, while acting commandant, apparently without informing the secretary of the Navy, but with the
implicit consent of Heywood, designated 45 men as the guard of the cruiser
Brooklyn, soon to be commissioned. He assigned them to the Newport Barracks to serve under Captain Cochrane together with their officer, 2d Lt.
Thomas S. Borden. As Heywood later explained, Lieutenant Borden who
had never been to sea would benefit from the tutelage of an experienced officer such as Cochrane and would learn to know his men. In the first draft of
his annual report, Colonel Heywood asserted that this new system would

increase the efficiency of the ship guards since it permitted the men to "become accustomed to each other, and there is time to weed out bad elements."[93]

Colonel Heywood suddenly ran into unexpected opposition to his plans. Unaware of the commandant's plans, Secretary Herbert questioned the assignment of both Lieutenant Borden and the enlisted men to Newport. Heywood defended the action, declaring that it was always his "desire to take this action in the cases of all guards intended for ships," but could not due to lack of men. He concluded, "There is nothing exceptional being done, and the only difference between this guard and any other will be that this one will have been instructed as a whole, while the others were not."[94]

The Navy Department, however, accepted no part of the commandant's argument. Although acknowledging that assembling the guard of a ship at one location and drilling them had its advantages, Assistant Secretary McAdoo declared that the commandant and Major Reid had overstepped their authority in moving Marines from one post to another without replacing them. Moreover, according to McAdoo, the Newport station was under the Bureau of Navigation and the department never gave permission for "making it in some sense a school of instruction for the Marine Corps." Although softening the blow somewhat by stating that Heywood did not deliberately violate Navy regulations, the assistant secretary disapproved the commandant's Newport plan, and the Navy Department went so far as to order Heywood to remove any mention of the Newport experiment from his annual report.[95]

Despite the setback to Heywood's training program for the ships' guards, the Marine Corps had fared fairly well under Secretary Herbert's stewardship of the Navy Department. After several years of requesting additional manpower, the Corps received a significant increase in enlisted strength. The fact that the Corps did not receive a corresponding expansion in officers was due to internal divisions among both naval and Marine officers rather than any hostility upon the part of the secretary. Nevertheless, Herbert encouraged Heywood's attempt to further the professionalization of the officer corps through the Marine Corps School of Application and the Naval War College. More important from Heywood's point of view, the secretary not only vetoed every attempt of the Navy progressives to take the Marine guards off the ships, he approved the incorporation into the 1896 Navy Regulations an article that Marines would serve on board ship as a "distinctive" command under their own officers and assigned to certain guns when practicable. Heywood had astutely used the secondary battery mission to link the Marine Corps to the new battleships coming into service.[96]

While some naval progressives worked behind the scenes to remove Marine guard detachments from the new steel Navy, others in the Naval War College explored avenues of naval strategy that would obviously require landing forces, in all probability Marine landing forces. With the mission of the Marines within the new battleship Navy still uncertain, there was no clear jurisdiction for the Marine officer. Thus the Marine and the Navy officer corps, for the most part, were at crosscurrents with one another.

8. POLITICS, PROFESSIONALISM, AND REFORM

Following a policy of "conservative conciliation" in 1897 the newly inaugurated President William McKinley attempted to unite both the nation and the various factions of his own party. Faced with an economic depression, McKinley wanted to concentrate on domestic affairs and make no new bold political departures.[1]

The McKinley administration, therefore, initially foreshadowed little change for the Marine Corps. Given the conservative bent of both the president and his secretary of the Navy, John D. Long of Massachusetts, his Navy Department, like that of his predecessor, would pursue a policy of modest reform intermingled with politics while attempting to balance the conflicting interests within the department. The balancing of these conflicting interests proved no easy task, and outside forces would have an impact both on the Navy and on the Marine Corps.

With much the same political experience, a former congressman and governor of his state, the new secretary was a longtime confidante of the president. Before coming into office, neither McKinley nor Long had supported a large Navy, fearing that it would involve the nation in "foreign complications." Outside of Long's relationship to the president and a reputation as the "scholar in politics"—having translated the *Aeneid* into English—he brought little background or experience to his new position. At the urging of Senator Henry Cabot Lodge of Massachusetts and other eastern Republican leaders of the expansionist wing of the party, the president balanced the selection of Long by the appointment of Theodore Roosevelt as the assistant secretary of the Navy. A naval historian of some note who had lectured at the Naval War College and was active in Republican politics, the young, vigorous Roosevelt was a marked contrast to his chief. As Long himself later observed, Roosevelt's "ardor sometimes went faster than the president or the Department approved."[2]

Despite the conflicting views and personalities of Long and Roosevelt, this "odd couple" partnership in the Navy Department worked together in relative harmony. As one biographer of McKinley wrote, Secretary Long viewed Roosevelt's "push" as a "useful balance to his own cautious habit."[3]

Although on occasion privately censuring a Rooseveltian outburst, Secretary Long relied heavily on his energetic assistant. In effect, Roosevelt, who coordinated the planning activities of the Office of Naval Intelligence and the Naval War College, became the "defacto chief of a naval general staff." Long also assigned to Roosevelt the problem of resolving the Navy personnel knot but still deferred and delegated most of the administrative details to his various bureau chiefs. He made the conservative Capt. Arent S. Crowninshield the head of the key Bureau of Navigation after the more-progressive Capt. Henry C. Taylor turned down the appointment. Thus, in 1897, the Navy Department reflected more the image of the elderly secretary than his younger colleague.[4]

Despite McKinley and Long's caution and personal conservatism, the problems of the world would not go away. The Cuban revolt against the hegemony of Spain in the island confronted the president immediately upon taking office. In a conversation with his predecessor the night before his inauguration, McKinley remarked that he hoped to follow Cleveland's example in avoiding war with Spain. Like Cleveland, the new president in the summer of 1897 called for Spain to end its policy of reconcentration and call a truce with the rebels in Cuba and hinted that the United States might have to act in some manner if the situation did not improve.[5]

In the Pacific another problem confronted the president. On June 16, the McKinley administration negotiated an annexation treaty with the Hawaiian Republic. The Japanese government immediately registered a protest as did Germany, and on June 30, the Navy Department convened a strategy board to consider contingency plans for war against both Spain and Japan.[6]

The crisis with Japan soon diffused itself, and by the end of the year even the tensions with Spain over Cuba appeared to have lessened. Even before the Cuban situation arose, the United States had long standing economic and strategic interests in the Caribbean basin, and an Isthmian canal had been an American objective for several decades. In his message to Congress, President McKinley referred to such a canal as a great highway for American commerce. To protect any projected canal, the United States needed to command the Atlantic approaches, especially the Windward Passage, which Cuba dominated. The apparent disintegration of the once-formidable Spanish empire presented dilemmas for the administration. A weak and vulnerable Cuba was an inviting morsel for the new European imperial powers, especially Germany. Assistant Secretary Roosevelt viewed both Japan and Germany as potential enemies of the United States and wanted to deploy two battleships in the Pacific to protect Hawaii from Japan and four battleships in the Atlantic to uphold the Monroe Doctrine. Although rejected by the administration at the time, a military option to settle the question of Cuba remained open to the United States.[7]

At the start of the McKinley administration, the Marine Corps was hardly involved in such momentous issues as war and peace. Rather the commandant, Colonel Heywood, was engaged in one of his perennial feuds with one of his senior officers or staff. Heywood wanted to retire those officers who, he thought, were unable to function in their respective positions. Two of his prime targets were Maj. H. B. Lowry, the quartermaster, with whom he had a running feud, and the other, Lt. Col. John H. Higbee, now the commander of the New York Marine Barracks. Since his court-martial, Colonel Forney remained in charge of the Portsmouth, New Hampshire, Barracks safely away from both the limelight and the commandant's direct attention.

The same was not true, however, for poor Lieutenant Colonel Higbee. In February 1897, just before the inauguration, Higbee notified Colonel Heywood that because of his rheumatism, he would be unable to command the Marine battalion in the inaugural parade. Heywood wrote to the secretary of the Navy, Herbert, and asked that Higbee appear before a medical board, stating that because of the latter's physical impairment he could not assign him "for active duty in the field or a foreign country." Higbee appeared before the board, but the members ruled that the Marine lieutenant colonel was fit for duty, despite his infirmity.[8]

Two months later, Heywood had another chance at Higbee. The Marines from the New York Barracks were to march in a parade commemorating General Grant's tomb in the city. Higbee had planned to ride a horse at the head of his troops. The marshal of the parade, however, a Navy captain, not sure of his own horsemanship, declined a horse and started out on foot. Colonel Heywood, who was in New York for the occasion, then ordered Higbee to dismount so as not to embarrass his senior. Perhaps with the recent medical survey still fresh in his mind, the Marine lieutenant colonel obeyed, although muttering something beneath his breath about the stupidity of keeping horses and not using them. Higbee kept up the pace for a time, but after climbing a steep hill, he turned over his command to the next senior officer and left the parade. After the incident, Higbee formally protested the order to march on foot to Secretary Long. Answering for the secretary, Assistant Secretary Roosevelt stated that he had referred the matter over to the commandant, who recommended "that your protest be not sustained. The order of the Colonel Commandant will be obeyed."[9]

According to a journalistic account, Colonel Heywood believed "that any officer, to be physically fit for duty, must be able to double several hundred yards and have breath enough left to issue a command." It was obvious that Lieutenant Colonel Higbee did not meet these standards, but for the time being Heywood remained unable to force him to retire. In his defense, Higbee observed that despite suffering from rheumatism he "marched at the head of that battalion for over seven miles, against a cold north wind and in a cloud of dust at the rate of 170 steps per minute which I think was doing pretty well for a man of my build and age."[10]

Colonel Heywood met as much frustration in his dealings with Marine quartermaster Lowry. For several years, the Marine commandant had feuded with his quartermaster over matters ranging from steam heat at the Norfolk Marine Barracks to using "inappropriate language" in official correspondence. In November 1896, Heywood recommended that Lowry be retired for mental and physical deficiencies. At that time, Secretary Herbert declined to move against the quartermaster, but in January 1897, a Navy court of inquiry reprimanded Lowry for permitting a laundry contractor excessive profits in servicing various Marine barracks on the eastern coast. Colonel Heywood renewed his request for a retiring board for the Marine quartermaster, and Secretary Herbert acquiesced.[11]

Once more Heywood was to be disappointed. According to Captain Cochrane who served on the board, the Navy surgeon testified that Lowry suffered from chronic heart disease, but was fit to carry out his duties. At that juncture, the president of the board, Lt. Col. Robert W. Huntington, decided on his own that Lowry should be retained on active duty. A bitter Colonel Heywood remarked in an offhand conversation with Captain Cochrane that Lowry was a "damned little scoundrel."[12]

In June 1897, after all of the furor of the survey board in February, Major Lowry suddenly announced his retirement. This led to a chain reaction. Captain Richard S. Collum, the senior assistant quartermaster, then became quartermaster and then was promoted. Upon his appointment, Collum, in turn, retired. The junior assistant quartermaster, Capt. Frank L. Denny then became the quartermaster, and the department then selected a senior lieutenant, Thomas C. Prince, to fill one of the assistant quartermaster positions. Interestingly, Prince, a native of Canton, Ohio, received his appointment to the Naval Academy in 1878 from then Congressman William McKinley. Even more suspect was the filling of the second vacancy in the quartermaster staff, which went to Charles L. McCawley, the son of the former commandant, a civilian who had for several years been the chief clerk in the commandant's office.[13]

The appointment of McCawley caused disquiet in Congress and in the press as well as resentment in the officer corps. Second Lt. Melville J. Shaw, who would have received a promotion to first lieutenant if an officer had received the position, wrote a protest letter to his senator. The *New York Times* editorialized that staff positions should go to deserving military men rather than to a civilian. The Senate Naval Affairs Committee only approved the appointment by a margin of four votes, and the full Senate delayed its ratification for another week.[14]

Ironically, Roosevelt, the former civil service commissioner and Republican reformer, apparently engineered the entire McCawley affair. In a strange alliance with Richard Olney, the secretary of state in the Cleveland administration, Roosevelt worked behind the scenes. More than a week before the acceptance of Lowry's retirement, he admitted to Olney that he had interceded with the president and believed "I have got young McCawley's matter satisfactorily arranged . . . at any rate, I have done everything that it is in my power to do." The evidence does not indicate that Roosevelt was behind the sudden retirements of Lowry and Collum, but he was certainly aware of the circumstances. According to Captain Cochrane, who quoted another Marine officer, the "Lowry, Collum deal cost $30,000." Whatever the truth about the quartermaster situation, it reflected the close interplay between reform and politics.[15]

Within this setting of political, professional, personal, and bureaucratic juggling, the Marine reform movement continued its uneven progress. New Marine officers still came from the Naval Academy but at a slower pace. In June, the Marine commandant asked that the Marine Corps receive three of the naval cadets from the Naval Academy to fill vacancies in the officer corps, but like the previous year, there were not enough graduating cadets to meet the demands of the respective branches of the Navy. Assistant Secretary Roosevelt denied Heywood's request, agreeing only to give the Marine Corps the two cadets already selected by the Naval Academy Academic Board. There may have been an underlying reason for both the secretary's and the board's decisions. As promotions among the junior Marine officers lagged behind the Navy line and engineers, most naval cadets attempted to avoid the Marine Corps, "which they do not relish."[16]

The 2 new Marine second lieutenants, Newt H. Hall and Philip M. Bannon, fit the general pattern of the new Marine officers. Bannon ranked twelfth and Hall twenty-fifth out of the 25 cadets who received Navy line and Marine commissions in 1897. Hall was an Episcopalian, the son of an attorney from Claiborne, Texas, and had attended private schools before attending the Naval Academy. Bannon deviated somewhat from the norm, being a Roman Catholic and the son of a widow from Jessup, Maryland.[17]

Again because of the low number of new lieutenants and the continuing shortage of Marine officers, Heywood curtailed the size of the officer class of the School of Application. He assigned 1st Lt. Charles A. Doyen, the second senior in his grade, to join the 2 new lieutenants from the Naval Academy. The enlisted division of the school consisted of 43 men: 9 sergeants, 9 corporals, and 25 privates. Captain F. H. Harrington continued on as the commander of the school and director of instruction, and 2d Lt. Magill remained responsible for the enlisted division. The curriculum like that of the previous years emphasized artillery and the new technology.[18]

With the continued stress on technical and artillery skills, Heywood pressed the issue over the assignment of Marines to the secondary batteries of warships. Despite the inclusion of an article in the 1896 Navy Regulations that provided for Marines manning these weapons under their own officers, the Marine commandant found himself fighting a constant battle with naval officers trying to find loopholes. For example, Navy Capt. John J. Read, commanding the *Olympia*, interpreted the regulation to require Marines to man the guns only during instruction. In a long convoluted reply (drafted by Marine Lt. Charles H. Lauchheimer in the Navy judge advocate office), Secretary Long supported the Marine position. Although he recognized that the use of Marines at the guns would vary from ship to ship, Long declared that the intention of the new regulation "is simply to place Marines on a parity with seamen in the matter of assignment to and opportunities for drill and instruction at the guns." Captain Read was "in error in stating that Regulations now in force do not make it imperative upon the commanding officer of a ship to assign Marines as a division or as guns' crews for any other purpose than instruction."[19]

In his annual report for 1897, Colonel Heywood returned to the general subject of the secondary battery mission. He referred to the Navy Regulations of 1896 and then discussed the Newport experiment that he had attempted to implement the year before. The commandant asked Secretary Long to reconsider the department's decision not to permit the training of a ship's guard at the Newport Barracks, because he believed Newport ideal "for the segregation of a detachment of Marines intended for a particular ship."[20]

Although the department did not act upon Heywood's suggestion, Captain Cochrane, commanding the Newport Barracks, had undertaken several innovations in training and providing for the morale and wellbeing of his men. Like former Commandant McCawley, Cochrane identified Marine reform and officer professionalism with the building of the Marine Corps into a military elite. He even went further than Colonel Heywood at first was willing to go. In July 1896, Cochrane had established a post exchange at Newport to replace the old post-trader system. Based on the system recently implemented by the Army, the exchange was a sort of cooperative general store to sell items to the troops not issued by the government for their personal comfort, including beer. Heywood, however, did not support the idea and ordered all Marine post exchanges closed.[21]

Cochrane bided his time and apparently believed with the new administration, he might obtain a different ruling. In June, Assistant Secretary Roosevelt visited the War College and inspected the Marine Newport Barracks. According to Cochrane, Roosevelt complimented the troops "as a fine looking body of men." The Marine captain may also have mentioned the subject of the post exchange to the assistant secretary. At the time, however, Cochrane was most impressed with the reception that Roosevelt received: "Remarkable to see above attention, guns fired and gray bearded officers in epaulets to receive a young man who a month ago was a police commissioner in New York City."[22]

Two months later on August 4, Secretary Long visited the War College, reviewed the troops, and commented favorably on the appearance of the men. Although not clear whether Roosevelt prompted the secretary, Long mentioned to Cochrane that he favored the "Army system . . . and had directed Mr. Roosevelt to look into the matter." Taking up the subject with his usual enthusiasm, the assistant secretary, two days later, wrote Colonel Heywood that the department wanted to compare the "relative merits" of the post exchange as opposed to the post trader. He directed the Marine commandant to use the Newport Barracks under Cochrane as the test case, and although Heywood still had his doubts, Marine Corps headquarters ordered Captain Cochrane to establish an exchange at Newport under the same regulations governing Army post exchanges. On August 18, the Marine post exchange opened with an auspicious beginning, selling eighteen bottles of beer.[23]

Although the original plan was to see how well the exchange worked at Newport, once the assistant secretary took hold of an idea he was not one to let it rest. One week after the opening of the Newport exchange, upon hearing about the death of the post trader at League Island in Philadelphia,

Roosevelt told the Marine commandant to set up an exchange there. A few weeks later in another letter, the assistant secretary declared, "I want to proceed with the substitution of canteens [post exchanges] for post traderships as rapidly as possible." When he believed the commander of the Marine Barracks at Boston, Maj. Robert L. Meade, was dragging his feet, Roosevelt wrote directly to him, stating "there must be no question whatsoever as to the success of the system. . . . It has proved successful elsewhere and it must prove successful at Boston."[24]

Colonel Heywood made no mention of the implementation of the post exchange in his annual report, but Secretary Long spoke of the system in glowing terms. He observed that the department had instituted post exchanges at some of the Marine barracks and intended to open them at all of the posts. According to Long, "Under this plan the profits go to the benefit of the men and not to an outside post trader. . . . They are to be conducted under an officer, and every dollar of profit expended in the improvement of food, the purchase of books . . . the bettering of life in barracks, and the general interest of the Marine service."[25]

Even with the push for reformist measures such as the post exchange to replace the patronage-fed post-trader system, much of the traditional interface between politics and influence continued as before. Secretary Long recorded that a dispute between two members of the Senate over a minor appointment to a low-paying position in the Philadelphia Navy Yard was "like a fight of wolves over a carcass." Assistant Secretary Roosevelt who also knew very well how the system worked wrote a personal note to Colonel Heywood, saying that Senator Hale called on him to intercede in obtaining a discharge for one of his constituents. The assistant secretary asked the Marine commandant to provide a full report on the matter, declaring, "If possible, I am of course anxious to oblige Senator Hale."[26]

The use of such influence among Marine officers was of course more common with their higher social status and often excellent connections to political figures. For example, J. R. Richards, the solicitor general in the McKinley Justice Department, appealed to Roosevelt to assign his brother, 1st Lt. George Richards, to Washington after the latter completed his cruise on the *Lancaster*. Colonel Heywood acceded to the request. At times, however, the Marine commandant stood up to the pressure. He refused a petition by Capt. George Elliott to be placed in command of the Newport Barracks. Senator Thomas Platt of New York had written to Roosevelt on behalf of the Marine captain, but Heywood told the assistant secretary that he intended to keep Captain Cochrane there since he wanted to stay and the naval authorities there were happy with him. The commandant then stated that Captain Elliott was in violation of Navy regulations by writing directly to the Senator, but observed, "I cannot bring this matter officially before the Department as I received the information in a personal letter from you."[27]

The new assistant quartermaster, now Capt. Charles L. McCawley, also knew how to use his political connections. Much to the chagrin of several naval officers, President McKinley selected the younger McCawley to serve as one of his two social aides. According to one of McKinley's biographers, the Marine officer was "an admirable young man, witty, and well bred." It also did him no harm that he belonged to the same tennis club as Assistant Secretary Roosevelt and former Secretary of State Richard Olney. On January 13, 1898, Army Col. Theodore A. Bingham, described as the "major domo" of the McKinley White House, requested the Navy Department to detail Captain McCawley for duty at the Executive Mansion for several days. In his endorsement, Assistant Secretary Roosevelt wrote, "The Colonel Commandant to issue the necessary orders for compliance with this request."[28]

In early 1898 with the retirement or possible retirement of senior Marine officers, other officers began to jockey for favorable assignments. Lt. Col. McLane Tilton had retired the previous year, and Lt. Col. Higbee indicated that he would retire in June. Lieutenant Colonel Huntington filled the vacancy left by Tilton, and Maj. Percival Pope was next in line for promotion awaiting the pending departure of Higbee. Huntington, who did not like New York, wanted to be assigned to Mare Island in California. Colonel Heywood, the past November, had promised Major Pope, who was at Mare Island, to return him to command the Boston Barracks. The unexpected announcement by Higbee that he was retiring caught Colonel Heywood off guard, and he then changed his plans and decided to send Pope to New York. Pope protested, and on February 16, Heywood received a note from Roosevelt stating that Secretary Long particularly wanted Pope assigned to Boston. Given no choice, Heywood revoked the orders and sent Huntington to New York in Pope's stead. As one Marine officer observed, "It was Pope's friends who got him to Boston. The Comd't couldn't stand the pressure. As New York is the apple of his [Heywood's] eye, the other lt. col. has to go there."[29]

Although political pressure played a role in officer assignment, Colonel Heywood with the full support of the department and the Marine officer reformers attempted further to adjust the promotion system to reflect merit as well as seniority. In September 1897, the Department published a new general order pertaining to officer promotion. As before, the order was applicable to all line officers and assistant quartermasters below the rank of major.

It contained several recommendations made by an officer board the previous year to streamline the examination process. More detailed than previous directives, the order called for more standardization with the commandant providing the examining board with a list of specified questions and attached values. The examiners, however, would not be limited by the list and could ask any question from any of the publications recommended for study. The order cautioned examining boards that they should keep in mind "that the object of examinations is to determine the actual professional fitness of officers for promotion. Boards should so conduct examinations that the qualifications for promotion will be developed by the officer's ability to make practical application of all he has learned, rather than the committal to memory of equations and data, which, he would, under ordinary conditions, obtain from books of reference." The board would make its judgment on the qualification of the officer for the next rank based upon a combination of the officer's record, physical and mental fitness, and professional efficiency.[30]

In February 1898, Capt. Henry Clay Cochrane was one of the first officers to come up for promotion under the new order. Cochrane arrived in Washington on February 7 to appear before the board, which consisted of Lieutenant Colonel Huntington, the president; Major Denny, the quartermaster; Major Reid, the adjutant and inspector; and two surgeons. First Lieutenant Doyen served as the recorder. On the first day, the two doctors examined Cochran and declared him fit. The board then reviewed Cochrane's record. From February 8 through February 11, he took a battery of tests ranging from infantry and artillery drill regulations, to military law, to minor tactics. Part of the test involved the physical drilling of two companies on the Marine parade ground. He was then given a military map problem that he was to take back to his hotel and provide a solution to the next day. After completing this task, Cochran was informed by the board that he had passed. From Cochrane's activities during this period and the late hours he spent studying the various references, he obviously took the exam very seriously.[31]

The emphasis on officer examination was only one aspect of a much larger effort on the part of the Navy Department to rationalize the officer structure of both the Marine Corps and the Navy. Like Secretary Herbert before him, Secretary Long was unhappy about officer promotion stagnation and the constant feuding within the department among the various officer factions and branches. As he stated in his report in 1897, "some better adjustment of the different elements of the Naval Corps can be had whereby present frictions can be diminished and the whole service strengthened and

stimulated in all its parts." He assigned the finding of the solution to his in-
defatigable assistant, Theodore Roosevelt.[32]

According to Secretary Long, he had pondered the problem of Navy officer
personnel for some time and had discussed the situation with Congressman
Francis H. Wilson, who had championed the engineers. In the meantime,
Assistant Secretary Roosevelt visited with various officers from every corps
to obtain differing points of view and see if there was any common ground.
On November 4, 1897, Long appointed Roosevelt as president of a special
board "to consider the reorganization of the personnel of the Navy." In his
instructions, Long charged the board to make a report of its findings and to
prepare a draft of a "bill which it will submit for the further consideration of
the Department." The composition of the board consisted of six voting line
officers and four engineer officers, including Chief Engineer George W.
Melville and Capt. Arent S. Crowninshield, the chief of the Bureau of Navigation. Each member, with the exception of the recorder, who was a line officer, was to have one vote.[33]

Apparently much of the spade work for the committee had been completed. Secretary Long later wrote that he had limited the representation on
the board to engineers and line officers "because the main question was between the line and engineer corps." According to the *Army and Navy Register*, the board was to study a plan drawn up by a Harvard professor, I. N.
Hollis, a former naval engineer, and amended by Lt. Cmdr. Richard
Wainwright, a line officer and member of the board. In any event, at one of
the first meetings of the Roosevelt Board, Captain Evans proposed the amalgamation of the line and engineer officer corps, but Secretary Long observed that the "plan all along had been in the mind of the Department and
of the Board." Although the board on November 8 practically agreed to the amalgamation proposition,
referring it to a subcommittee to work out
the details, most engineers were still wary and unhappy that they were in
the minority on the board. Chief Engineer Melville remembered that when
Evans recommended the amalgamation proposal, "engineers, mindful of his
record, wondered if it could have been made in good faith, and there were a
great many who believed and stated that the ostensible scheme was only a
cover for getting rid of the separate engineer corps."[34]

Other naval officer corps and especially that of the Marine Corps soon became uneasy when they learned about the activities of the personnel board.
The same day that it considered the amalgamation of the line and engineers,
two additional propositions surfaced. These related to the integration of the of-

ficers of the Paymaster Corps and Marine Corps with the line. On November 9, Assistant Secretary Roosevelt wrote to Colonel Heywood inviting the Marine commandant to appear before the board about the possible "transfer of the officers and men of the Marine Corps to the Line."[35]

On November 11, Heywood came before the board and learned that Navy Capt. A. H. McCormick, one of the line members, had suggested that the Marines, in effect, be dissolved. Heywood received two proposals that he should take back and canvas his officers for their opinion on and then return on November 22 and testify before the board. In a round robin letter, Heywood conducted an informal survey of the Marine officer corps on the two questions, the first being, "That the officers and men of the Marine Corps be transferred to the line of the Navy." The second provided two alternatives: "That it is desirable that marines be not embarked as a part of the complement of seagoing ships; and if so embarked, that the officers should perform duty both as watch and division officers, as is now done by line officers of the Navy."[36]

The response of the Marine officers was what would be expected. Most had little objection to the second part of the second proposition. They all opposed the first proposal and few showed any willingness to accept doing away with the Marine guards on board ship. The angry reply of Captain Cochrane was typical. He sarcastically began his letter saying that Marine officers and enlisted men by integrating with the Navy line "would benefit immediately by having their pay in most cases doubled, their rations improved, their enlistments shortened, their duties lightened and their opportunities multiplied by ten if not twenty." As the Marine officer observed, the "chief value of the Marine to the Navy is due to the differences of thought, habit, training, action, and purpose which characterize him, and which have caused him to survive the fads of centuries." Deprived of his distinctive character, declared Cochrane, the Marine "would promptly become a blue-jacket in a button-up coat, who could no more be expected to represent authority and enforce law and order than the average of his new comrades."[37]

At this point, Cochrane stated that he would personally prefer the Marines being absorbed by the Army. He believed the Marine Corps could answer the Army's requirements for additional artillery regiments to man the coastal defenses. Continuing in a more sardonic vein, the Marine officer wrote that the trend of the Navy in the last twenty years was "away from the reefing jacket and in a military direction, [and] that it may prove, when all is revealed and properly stated, that it virtually wants to transfer to us and organize sea battalions." Cochrane placed his hopes on Roosevelt, saying that he understood that "the President of the Board before which you are to appear seeks the truth and likes candor. Being a civilian, he may well be presumed to be without those service prejudices which become imperceptibly a part of ourselves."[38]

In the other letters that the commandant received in response to his original inquiry, only 1st Lt. George Barnett, Capt. H. K. White, and possibly Capt. Paul St. Clair Murphy, the former commander of the Marine School of Application, picked up on the theme of "sea battalions" that Cochrane had obliquely mentioned. Almost all of the other Marine officers, if they spoke of Marine mission at all, confined themselves to the defense of the Marine guards or the possible transfer to the Army as coast artillery. In his remarks, Captain Murphy emphasized that the Marine Corps was a "fundamental part of the Navy" and that it had "proved itself equal to every emergency, a well drilled, disciplined, and equipped body of soldiers, ready at a moment's notice to go, if need be, to the ends of the earth." Captain White compared the Marine Corps to mounted cavalry or torpedo boats, declaring only "a very mobile body like this [the Marine Corps] accustomed to the sea . . . can be readily transported by sea (and even sustain itself there if necessary)."[39]

Lieutenant Barnett was the most direct about the possibility of transforming the Marine Corps into an expeditionary force. In very much of a minority opinion, he was not especially opposed to removing Marine guards from small ships. He stated, however, that Marines on board ship served a useful purpose in that they assisted in both the general work and handling the guns and provided a trained force for landing parties. Barnett believed the chief role of the Marines both "on shore and at sea must be considered as an expeditionary force for use in any part of the world and not merely as a collection of watchmen."[40]

On November 22, 1897, fortified by the support of his officers, Colonel Heywood returned to the Roosevelt Board to defend his Corps against its detractors. In a long passionate appeal, he traced the history of the Corps from the days of the Revolution to the present and mentioned in passing various landings by the Marines, their role in the 1877 labor strike, and the rapid mobilization of the Corps for the Panama intervention in 1885. The commandant observed that the Marines were specialists and that it would be necessary for some other organization to take their place without the advantage of Marine pride and esprit de corps. Heywood then spoke about his own service and dedication of forty years to the Corps. He used the example of the British Royal Marines to justify the existence of the American Corps. Despite the sentiments of White, Murphy, and Barnett, Heywood defined the main mission of the Marine Corps in the traditional role of ships guards with the added duty of manning the secondary batteries. He concluded his presentation with the suggestion that Marine officers should be represented on the board if it was going to recommend modifications to the organization and duties of the Corps.[41]

By this time, the board had decided on its own to confine its work to the integration of engineer officers with the line and the forced retirement ("plucking") of senior officers. The press quoted one of the members, Capt. William T. Sampson, as stating that the board was "undertaking a little at a time." On December 4, the *Army and Navy Register* carried a story that Secretary Long did not intend to have the agreement on engineers and the line "jeopardized by loading it down with provisions for other branches of the Navy." Five days later, Assistant Secretary Roosevelt transmitted the board's final report to the secretary of the Navy. As expected, the board recommended the integration of the line officers and the engineers and a modification to the Navy seniority system to allow for the forced retirement of senior officers. There was no mention of Marines or any other officer corps of the Navy.[42]

The completion of the report hardly insured action by Congress. As the *New York Times* editorialized, the writing of the report would be only the "beginning of the real battle." Senator Hale, the floor manager of the Roosevelt bill, agreed. He stated that the bill would be the most "vexatious" and "most fought over question" and probably would result in no action. In March 1898, Roosevelt appeared before the House Naval Affairs Committee and asked that the personnel bill be included in the appropriation bill. The committee informed Roosevelt that it could not conform to his wishes. At that point, the assistant secretary requested that the appropriation bill not contain any personnel provisions as it would dilute his bill. With Congress caught up in the war fever over the sinking of the battleship *Maine*, there would be no personnel bill in 1898, and the Marine Corps had escaped once more the knives of its enemies.[43]

For the Marine Corps during the first years of the McKinley administration, the forces of reform intermeshed with officer professionalism and institutional and individual self-interest. Influenced by political and foreign-policy considerations as well, this strange amalgam dominated relations between the Navy and the Marine Corps. Despite internal disputes and the attacks of the naval reformers, Heywood still attempted to identify the Marine Corps with the new battleship Navy, and thus his determined push for the secondary battery mission. But events outside of the Marine Corps and its commandant—war and its aftermath—would settle the questions of organization and mission, and in a sense Marine officer professionalism.

9. THE SPANISH-AMERICAN WAR AND AFTERMATH

The McKinley administration wanted to avoid war with Spain over Cuba, but not at any price. Circumstances over which the United States had little control persuaded the president that he had little choice but to force Spain to grant the Cubans their independence. For the Marine Corps and its officers, still uncertain about their role in the naval establishment, the resultant war and its aftermath served to delineate a mission for their Corps and themselves with the New Navy in the defense of America's new colonial possessions.

The publication of the Spanish Minister Depuy de Lome's letter critical of the American president in the *New York Journal* and the sinking of the U.S. battleship *Maine* in Havana Harbor in February 1898 galvanized American popular opinion against the Spanish. President McKinley attempted to defuse the situation by appointing a board of naval experts to determine the cause of the explosion on the American warship. Headed by Capt. William T. Sampson, the Navy court of inquiry reported on March 21, 1898, that a submarine mine, exterior to the hull, set off the forward magazines of the *Maine*. A Spanish investigating team, on the other hand, blamed an internal explosion in the forward magazines for the disaster. McKinley forwarded the Sampson Board's findings to Congress without comment. Even as moderate a figure as Secretary Long, however, later observed that the sinking of the *Maine* "would inevitably lead to war, even if it were shown that Spain was innocent of her destruction."[1]

While the war fever spread through the country, the Navy Department reexamined its strategy in the event of a conflict with Spain. In March 1898, Secretary Long appointed an advisory war board consisting of Assistant Secretary Roosevelt as chairman and three naval officers, including the heads of the Bureau of Navigation and the Office of Naval Intelligence. By the time of its establishment, the board had the benefit of the extensive ad hoc planning effort that had continued through both the Cleveland and McKinley administrations. Since 1895, the Office of Naval Intelligence, the War College, and the temporary strategy boards had developed several contingency plans for war with Spain. Through the contradictions and different formulations of the various American planning documents, certain features appeared and reappeared: a blockade of Puerto Rico and Cuba, a possible land campaign against Havana, a blockade or assault against Manila in the Philippines, and a possible naval attack in Spanish home waters. Indeed, on February 25, 1898, even before the formation of the war board, Theodore Roosevelt on a quiet Sunday afternoon cabled Commodore George Dewey, the commander of the Asiatic Squadron, at Hong Kong "to keep full of coal." He ordered Dewey "in the event of declaration of war with Spain" to undertake "offensive operations in the Philippine Islands" after first insuring that the Spanish naval squadron "does not leave Asiatic coast."[2]

The war board recommended to the secretary that the Navy take the offensive and not be relegated to a passive coast-defense role. Based on the consensus of the earlier war-planning effort, the board suggested the close blockade of Cuba and its extension to Puerto Rico. The Navy was to concentrate as well on the poorly defended outposts of Spain's insular empire, including the Philippines. As Secretary Long later explained, Spain's "undoing lay in her possessions in the East and West Indies." There Spain was the most vulnerable and would be forced to send both scarce men and ships to shore up her defenses. The board rejected any immediate operations aimed at the Spanish homeland in favor of a strategy of American sea dominance in the Caribbean and Pacific.[3]

As the naval plans became more serious, the military prepared for what appeared inevitable. Congress passed on March 9, 1898, a $50-million emergency appropriation to be shared between the War Department and the Navy Department. The Army received $20 million, which mostly went into the coast fortification program. War Department planners visualized only a limited mobilization. They expected the National Guard to man the coast defenses while the Regular Army expanded from its 28,000-man peacetime strength to form an expeditionary corps of 75,000–100,000 men. This corps would land in Cuba only after the Navy established its mastery over the Spanish fleet. War Department officials failed to stock supplies for a large army because they simply "did not expect to raise one" in a war against Spain.[4]

The Navy, on the other hand, used a good portion of its approximately $30 million of the emergency appropriation to augment the fleet. At Hampton Roads, the Navy maintained what it called the "Flying Squadron," consisting of two battleships, the *Texas* and *Massachusetts*, and four supporting vessels. The department concentrated the preponderance of its warships in the North Atlantic Squadron at Key West, Florida.[5]

This naval buildup also applied to the Marine Corps. On March 10, 1898, Secretary of the Navy Long provided Colonel Heywood, the Marine commandant, with guidelines on the use of the Navy's share of the emergency appropriation. The commandant was to incur expenses under the appropriation only after making an estimate of expenses and receiving the approval of Secretary Long and the president, "all in writing." All told, the Marine Corps would eventually receive $106,529.64 under the emergency appropriation. The expenditures included the purchase of 1 million rounds of ammunition for the newly issued Lee rifles.[6]

Although both Secretary Long and Marine Commandant Heywood wanted to expand the Marine Corps to meet anticipated demands, the role of the Corps in any pending conflict was still vague. In a March communication to the chairman of the House Committee on Naval Affairs, Secretary Long explained the need for more Marines in terms of their traditional missions. The usually authoritative *Army and Navy Journal*, nevertheless, carried a story on March 12, 1898, saying that the Navy secretary had ordered Colonel Heywood to form two battalions ready to deploy at short notice. According to the account, "Two battalions have been made up on paper, and all the available officers of the Corps assigned to places in different companies." About the same time, the *Naval Institute Proceedings* published as one of its prize articles a piece by Lt. Cmdr. Richard Wainwright. While not specifically mentioning Marines, Wainwright referred to advanced bases as the first line of defense in conjunction with the fleet. He advocated that such bases "should require such protection as is necessary to render the base safe against cruiser raids, or such light attacks as might be attempted during the temporary absence of the guarding fleet." The only obvious readily available source to establish and provide such protection for an advanced base would be the Marine Corps.[7]

The correspondence of Lt. Col. Robert Huntington, commander of the New York Barracks and the most likely commanding officer of any Marine expeditionary force, reflected the uncertainties of the Marine role and the questionable readiness of its aging officer corps. Coincidentally, on the same day as the sinking of the *Maine*, Huntington wrote to Colonel Heywood expressing his concerns about the officer corps, especially in the field-grade ranks and among the senior captains. Most had entered the Marine Corps during the Civil War or shortly afterward and had over thirty years of service. Huntington observed that they were "fit for service in barracks, but

age has decreased . . . the power of resisting the hardship and exposure incident to service in the field." He remarked that "under favorable circumstances as to weather I presume we should be effective. In cold or wet
weather I incline to think we should give out. Still we should accept the service without hesitation in the hope that our age and other infirmities might
not unfit us, but that we should be able to render effective service."[8]

On March 30, 1898, with the possibility of war much closer, Huntington
speculated in a letter to his son about the mission of the Marines. He
thought that Heywood planned to send him "to Key West to guard a coal
pile. This prospect of glory fills me with lively anticipation of plenty of trouble on pay days." Huntington did say, however, "There is of course a possibility that we might go to Cuba. I cannot say I enjoy the prospect very
much, but as my view of the war is, that it is one of humanity, I am willing
to take the personal risk." Huntington proved right on both counts; he and
his Marines later went both to Key West and to Cuba.[9]

Although President McKinley still desired peace and may have hoped for
some miracle on the diplomatic front, he at the same time hardened the
American stance on the Cuban question. At the end of March, under increasing pressure for action from both public opinion and Congress, McKinley insisted on Cuban independence. On April 11, 1898, he sent a message
to Congress asking for the authority to use "the military and naval forces of
the United States as may be necessary."[10]

By early April, the Navy had completed its initial preparations for operations against the Spanish. At Key West, the North Atlantic Squadron, under the command of Captain Sampson consisted of three armored battleships, several cruisers and torpedo boats, and support vessels. Backed by
many captains of his fleet, Sampson proposed a direct naval attack against
Havana immediately upon the declaration of war. Secretary Long on the advice of his strategy board vetoed the idea, because the department did not
wish to risk armored ships against shore batteries, and, furthermore, the
Army had no forces "to hold strongholds." Instead, on April 6, 1898, Secretary Long ordered Sampson on the outbreak of hostilities to capture all
Spanish warships in the West Indies and to establish a blockade of Cuba.
Although still insisting that he could attack Havana successfully, Sampson
admitted "the force of . . . [Long's] reasoning that we would have no troops
to occupy the city if it did surrender." He, nevertheless, remonstrated, "yet,
Mr. Secretary, it will be very unfortunate, besides a great loss of time, if we
must delay until the rainy season is over." Sampson asked Long to recon-

sider the decision, predicting that it would take until October for the blockade to have any effect.[11]

Whether influenced by the lack of readiness on the part of the Army or as part of the general mobilization, Captain Sampson asked Secretary Long for the deployment of two battalions of Marines to serve with the fleet at Key West. On April 16, Colonel Heywood received verbal orders to make the necessary arrangements, and the following day, a Sunday, he met with the headquarters staff and sent out telegrams to Marine commanding officers at the various East Coast navy yards. Planning to mount the first battalion out of New York within the week, the commandant, on April 18, departed Washington to supervise personally the preparations. Back at Marine headquarters, Maj. George C. Reid, the adjutant and inspector and acting commandant, asked for and received $20,000 out of the emergency appropriation to transport and equip the expedition. By Wednesday, April 20, the Marines had assembled 450 men from various East Coast navy yards at the New York Barracks. At that point the Department decided against the formation of a second battalion but increased the one battalion by another 200 men. At the time of its embarkation, two days later, the 1st Battalion of Marines, under the command of Lieutenant Colonel Huntington, consisted of 631 enlisted men, 21 officers, and 1 surgeon organized into 6 companies, 5 infantry and 1 artillery.[12]

On Friday, April 22, 1898, the newly purchased Navy transport *Panther*, formerly the *Venezuela*, docked at the Brooklyn Navy Yard. At the battalion's morning formation, Lieutenant Colonel Huntington told the men that they would embark that night for Hampton Roads, Virginia. The troops greeted the news with loud cheers and song and then formed working parties to assist sailors in loading the ship. About 5:00 P.M., "The 'assembly' was sounded and the battalion formed in line in heavy marching order, headed by the Navy Yard band." An hour later, the Marines marched out of the entrance of the navy yard, down Flushing Avenue, and then wheeled into the yard through the east gate. By eight o'clock that night, to the refrain of the "Girl I Left behind Me," the *Panther* set sail to join the fleet.[13]

On board the *Panther*, conditions were crowded and uncomfortable. The Navy had purchased the ship to carry a battalion of about 400 men, not 600 plus. Furthermore, the troops carried on board the equipment and supplies, which included mosquito netting, woolen and linen clothing, heavy and lightweight underwear, provisions for three months, wheelbarrows, push carts, pick axes, shovels, barbed wire cutters, tents, and medical supplies. In addition, the artillery company took four 3-inch rapid-fire guns. Colonel

Heywood observed that the hatches for loading freight and two small venti-
lators in the aft section provided the only ventilation for the ship. Still, morale among the men and officers was high. Major Henry Clay Cochrane,
second in command to Huntington, remarked on the quality of officers:
"We have a very nice set aboard and are starting out well."[14]

The specific mission of the Marine battalion still remained unclear. At
the time of the formation of the unit, Major Reid wrote that the Marines
"are to have no connection whatever with the army, and are to report, and
be at the disposal of the Commander-in-Chief of the North Atlantic Fleet."
More than that, Reid stated that he did "not feel at liberty to speak at
present." In a message to Captain Sampson on April 21, Secretary Long referred to the Navy Department studying the possibility of "occupying the
[northern Cuban] port of Matanzas by a military force large enough to hold
it." He later declared that the Marine "battalion was organized especially for
service in Cuba." Among the officers and men of the battalion, however,
speculation abounded as to their final destination. According to Major
Cochrane, "Porto Rico is rumored," but he believed that "some port near
Havana is more likely."[15]

By the time the battalion departed New York, the uncertainties and confusion of the general U.S. mobilization forced both the Army and Navy to
reconsider many of their initial assumptions. Acting upon the president's
message of April 11, Congress on April 19 passed a joint resolution that recognized the independence of Cuba, demanded the withdrawal of the Spanish military forces, disclaimed any intention of the United States to an-
nex the island, and authorized the president to use the armed forces of
the United States to carry out the policy. McKinley signed the resolution
the following day and sent an ultimatum to the Spanish government. In the
meantime, after Congress rejected a War Department measure that would
have increased only the Regular Army, the administration agreed with congressional leaders to support the establishment of a volunteer Army as well
as expanding the regular forces. As war approached, however, the Army unlike the Navy, was not yet ready.[16]

On April 20, President McKinley held his first council of war with his
principle military advisers as well as the secretaries of the Army and the
Navy. At the meeting, Maj. Gen. Nelson A. Miles, the commanding general
of the Army, reported that the Army would not be ready for any large expeditionary campaign for at least two months. Like many other veterans of the
Civil War, General Miles opposed frontal assaults against well-entrenched
positions. He advocated blockade by the Navy, small raids by the Army
along the Cuban coast in support of the Cuban rebels, and the seizure of

Puerto Rico. The Army's position surprised Secretary Long and the other naval officers. While rejecting Sampson's initial assault plans against Havana, Secretary Long and his Navy planners had expected the Army in conjunction with the Navy to prepare for an offensive against the Cuban capital before the rainy season began. In fact, a joint Army-Navy board had earlier in the month proposed the landing of a small Army force at Mariel, a port town about twenty-five miles west of Havana, to establish a base of operations against the larger city. President McKinley, who had served in the Civil War as a major, overruled Long and the Navy and supported General Miles's position.[17]

The conference enunciated a rather cautious military strategy in the Caribbean. McKinley approved the imposition of a blockade of Cuba, the resupply and other logistic support of Cuban insurgents, and limited U.S. land operations in Cuba, and the Navy was to assume the main burden of the war. On April 21, 1898, Secretary Long promoted Captain Sampson to rear admiral and ordered him to "blockade coast of Cuba immediately from Cardenas to Bahia Honda" in the north and possibly the southern city of Cienfuegos, "if it is considered advisable." The following day, the North Atlantic Squadron under Rear Admiral Sampson set out for the Cuban coast to initiate its new orders. In the meantime, most of the Army regular infantry regiments remained in encampments at Tampa, Mobile, and New Orleans.[18]

On the evening of the day Sampson's squadron left Key West for Cuban waters, April 22, the Navy transport *Panther*, with the 1st Marine Battalion embarked, pulled out of New York Harbor for Hampton Roads and Fortress Monroe. Arriving there the following evening, Lieutenant Colonel Huntington reported to Capt. Winfred S. Schley, the commander of the Navy's Flying Squadron. Huntington received orders that the battalion would stay on board the *Panther* and await a warship that would escort the transport to Key West. Two more Marine officers, Maj. Percival C. Pope and 1st Lt. James E. Mahoney, joined the battalion at Fortress Monroe, bringing the number of officers to their full complement of 23. Pope, because of his seniority, became second in command, while Major Cochrane remained on the battalion staff. Cochrane, in somewhat of a huff, wrote in his diary that he and Pope were unsure of their positions in the battalion and Huntington had not asked for a "conference, suggestion, or assistance."[19]

Huntington took advantage of the short interlude at Fortress Monroe to drill the troops and hold firing exercises. On the afternoons of April 24 and 25 the infantry companies practiced "volley and mass firing," while all four guns of the artillery company fired at least one round. The new Lee rifles, after earlier modifications, appeared reliable, although Major Cochrane reported that two of the muzzles expanded after firing. Morale remained high, although two of the enlisted men came down with high fevers that developed into pneumonia and another man fell off a rope ladder and was evacuated to the Army hospital ashore with a fractured limb.[20]

The men remained in good spirits when the cruiser *Montgomery* arrived to accompany the *Panther* to Key West. At 8:05 on Tuesday, April 26, the transport steamed out of port and passed the battleships *Texas* and *Massachusetts* and the cruiser *Brooklyn* of the Flying Squadron still at anchor. As the *Panther* went by the other ships, the crews crowded the decks and "sent up cheer after cheer," and the Marines returned the cheers, although several of the older officers had their reservations. Major Cochrane observed, "Some of us felt anything but jolly at leaving behind the beauties of spring to be replaced by the perils of the sea and the hardships of war." On April 29 after a three-day voyage, including a somewhat stormy passage around Cape Hatteras, the two ships arrived at Key West.[21]

By then the country was officially at war. On April 24, Spain had declared war on the United States, and the following day Congress formally declared war against Spain retroactive to the April 21. Five days after the American declaration, on April 29, a Spanish squadron of seven ships, consisting of three cruisers, one battleship, and three destroyers, under Admiral Pascual Cervera, departed the Portuguese Verde Islands and headed west. This departure of the Spanish fleet caused the Army to postpone indefinitely a planned 6,000-man "reconnaissance in force" on the southern coast of Cuba. The Navy simply did not have enough ships to escort the Army transports and still watch for the Spanish squadron which could appear at any time. Apparently the departure of the Spanish squadron may also have caused the postponement of a Marine landing in Cuba. In letters to his sons and wife, Major Cochrane observed that the Marines had expected to "land in Cuba last Saturday [April 30], but now we must lie here [at Key West] for a week." On April 30, Lieutenant Colonel Huntington, on board the *Panther* and sick with the grippe, wrote to his son, "This ought to be my chance, but I think I am all of ten years too old for this business."[22]

While the U.S. fleet in the Caribbean waited for the Spanish squadron under Cervera to make its appearance, the Asiatic Squadron under Commodore George Dewey had already taken the offensive. Having forewarned Dewey in late February to attack the Spanish in the Philippines in the event of hostilities, the Navy Department, on April 24, 1898, informed the commodore that war had begun and that he "was to proceed . . . to the Philippines" and to "commence operations at once." Acting upon these orders, Dewey and his squadron shortly after midnight on Sunday, May 1, 1898, slipped into Manila Bay under the cover of darkness. Although challenged by a few rounds from Spanish shore batteries on El Fraile Island near the entrance of the bay, the American naval squadron successfully eluded the Spanish defenses. Lying at anchor outside the protection of the land batteries at Manila, the older Spanish vessels were no match for Dewey's relatively modern cruisers. In the ensuing uneven battle which lasted a little more than seven hours, the American squadron sank or left as burning hulks all the enemy warships. At a cost of nine crewmen slightly wounded, the Americans had inflicted more than 370 casualties on the Spaniards, including 161 killed.[23]

Despite his overwhelming victory in the Philippines, Dewey's options to exploit his success were limited. As he informed Washington, "I can take city [Manila] at any time, but not sufficient men to hold." He estimated, "To retain possession and thus control Philippine Islands would require . . . [a] well-equipped force of 5,000 men." In the meantime, Marine 1st Lt. Dion Williams and a detachment of Marines from the cruiser *Baltimore* occupied the Spanish naval station at Cavite, which served as a base of operations for the fleet until reinforcements from the United States could arrive.[24]

The news of Dewey's victory electrified American public opinion and reinforced the demand for a similar initiative in the Caribbean. Even before he officially heard the news from Manila, President McKinley had reversed his earlier decision to refrain from a major land campaign against Havana, and in a conference on May 2, the president approved an expedition against Mariel that he had rejected at the earlier April meeting. The vanguard of these forces were to be the troops encamped at Tampa under Gen. William Shafter, idle since the canceled "reconnaissance in force" mission. The plans for this operation went through several reiterations as there were major differences of opinion among many of the principals, including Secretary of War Russel A. Alger and General Miles, as well as between the Army and Navy. Although overruled by the president, General Miles still opposed any major land campaign until after the rainy season. Admiral Cervera's squadron also remained a wild card. As Secretary Long informed Admiral Sampson on May 3, "No large army movement can take place for a fortnight and no small one will until after we know the whereabouts of the Spanish armored cruisers and destroyers."[25]

While the Army and Navy planners examined the feasibility of a Cuban campaign, the Marine battalion remained on board ship at Key West. On

The Marine battalion drilling at Key West, Florida. One officer described the battalion parade as "a little Army, little Navy, and some Marine Corps." (Robert Huntington Collection, Marine Corps Historical Center)

April 30, Lieutenant Colonel Huntington reported to Admiral Sampson on board the latter's flagship, although the Navy commander at that time had no orders for the Marine commander "as the plan of campaign had not yet been completed." Huntington's adjutant, 1st Lt. Herbert L. Draper, told Major Cochrane that Sampson stated "he did not want the Marines to go away to the Army. [He] had use for them." On May 3, Sampson departed Key West with a small task force in the hopes of intercepting Cervera's squadron off Puerto Rico, leaving the Marine battalion to fend for itself.[26]

At Key West, the Marine battalion settled into a routine of morning drills, almost daily disputes with the Navy commander of the *Panther*, and rumormongering. Every morning the Marine battalion went ashore for drills. Although most of the officers had several years of service, the enlisted men of the battalion were largely raw recruits and required both discipline and training. Major Cochrane overheard another Marine officer describe a battalion parade as "a little Army, little Navy, and some Marine Corps."

Even Huntington mentioned to his son that the men "have little idea of obeying orders" and that some were prone "to steal."[27]

On May 23, the *Panther* received orders to tow the monitor *Amphitrite*, which had been in Key West for repair, back out to the American blockading fleet. Forced to disembark in the early hours the following morning, the Marine battalion established a camp site on the beach, in effect, marooned at Key West without its transport.[28]

While Huntington futilely protested his forced "grounding," his subordinate officers speculated about their mission and, indeed, about their futures and the future of the Marine Corps. In typical fashion, the ubiquitous Major Cochrane reflected much of this sentiment. Writing to his wife in early May, Cochrane observed that the Marines "are not hurrying very much to get to Cuba—unless we can have the prestige of being first. Every forward plan is suspended until the Spanish fleet is encountered." Most of his correspondence with his wife represented the Marines' hopes for new legislation that would increase the Corps and permit promotions for the officers. Cochrane's wife, Betsy, noted that the war "should be an immense advantage to the Marine Corps." By late May and early June, however, Major Cochrane's optimism for favorable legislation had diminished: "When I think that war was declared on the 25th of April . . . , and that we embarked on the 22d, organized, equipped, and ready for duty, it annoys me that so little benefit comes from it."[29]

As Huntington and his officers vented their frustrations against the Navy and against their forced inactivity on the white sandy beaches of Key West, Colonel Heywood and his staff in Washington busied themselves in placing the Marine Corps on a wartime footing and lobbied for permanent legislation to benefit the Marine Corps. The Marines were more successful in the former activity than the latter.

At the beginning of the crisis, Heywood hoped to obtain from Congress a significant increase in manpower and a restructuring of the officer corps, but as events turned out the commandant settled for much less. This was due, in part, to the legislative strategy of the McKinley administration, which opposed any dilution of the reforms proposed by the Roosevelt Board and did not want half measures attached to the appropriation bill.[30]

On March 28, 1898, Colonel Heywood submitted to Secretary Long a formal request for proposed legislation for the restructuring of the Marine officer corps. The recommended bill contained many of the same provisions that the Corps had pushed through the years: the rank of brigadier general for the commandant, promotion for most other senior officers, an increase in the total number of officers, the temporary increase of rank for the fleet Marine officer, and the requirement that the president appoint all new staff officers in accordance with seniority in the staff and then from the list of senior Marine captains of the line. This bill contained one new wrinkle, however, in that it provided for the appointment of one-quarter of the new second lieutenants from the ranks of meritorious noncommissioned officers who passed the required examinations. Secretary Long forwarded the bill to the House Naval Affairs Committee, and in its report, the committee incorporated Heywood's bill with the reform measures suggested by the Roosevelt personnel board.[31]

The incorporation of the Marine bill with the broader Navy personnel legislation, however, had its disadvantages. Because of the administration's admonition to the House Naval Affairs Committee, Congress would not consider the restructuring of the officer corps in the Naval appropriation bill. But in the appropriation legislation, because of the war, the Marine Corps realized some expansion in its enlisted ranks and in the number of temporary officers. Congress authorized the inclusion of 473 enlistments already tentatively approved into the permanent organization and permitted the Corps to recruit another 1,640 men for the emergency. The final appropriation measure signed on May 4, 1898, contained a stipulation that allowed the president to appoint "if an exigency may exist" such officers to the Marine Corps as may be necessary from civilian life or from the ranks of meritorious noncommissioned officers of the Marine Corps. These officers could serve only through the emergency and could not be appointed above the rank of captain.[32]

If Major Cochrane's reaction was typical, Marine officers with the Marine battalion considered the measure to be grossly inadequate. He wrote to his wife in disgust that "the bill has caused great indignation among the lieutenants in our party," who probably had expected to be promoted to captain. He observed that the new second lieutenants from civilian life would all probably be the "sons of post traders." Cochrane also disapproved the making of officers of noncommissioned officers, writing that their temporary appointments would make them "unfit for their duties after the war." He reserved his greatest criticism, however, for what was not in the legislation. He believed that in the same situation, the "Army would have gotten three colonels and so on with them, and thirty-six captains." All the Marines received, according to Cochrane, were some additional men and "acting second lieutenants to officer them." In agreement with her husband, Cochrane's wife replied, "I cannot see that the condition of the officers in the

Corps has been improved one bit and it was such a chance to have gotten a really good organization."[33]

Colonel Heywood miscalculated in his legislative stratagem. He went along with the Navy Department policy to divorce the wartime mobilization from the permanent reform of the Navy and Marine officer corps, apparently believing that Congress would pass the Navy Department sponsored personnel bill which would amalgamate the line and engineers. This bill now included the changes that Heywood had forwarded relating to the Marine Corps officers. Despite assurances from Heywood that the legislation was "sure to go through," many Marine officers, including Major Cochrane, remained skeptical. The skeptics proved correct. Congress was not about to touch the controversial amalgamation and "plucking" issues in the midst of the war when there were more pressing matters. Despite last-minute efforts on the part of Heywood and his staff to separate the Marine legislation from the overall naval personnel bill, the attempt failed, and there was no major wartime reformation of the Marine officer corps.[34]

With the temporary officer appointments permitted by the appropriation act, however, the Marine officer corps at least gained a wartime infusion of new blood. A jaundiced Major Cochrane provided his wife with advice for a young relative who wanted to obtain one of the new Marine commissions from civilian life. According to Cochrane, "the usual plan should be pursued," meaning the candidate should first "make written application supported by testimonials . . . from well known men as to his character, ability, and general meritoriousness, and then to follow that up with any political, naval or social influence that he or his father or friends may have." Observing that Secretary of the Navy Long was from Boston, Cochrane suggested that the young man should try to find someone from Massachusetts who could "in political parlance 'reach' him [the secretary]." If the candidate could not obtain someone who knew Long, "perhaps he can 'reach' Senator Lodge, Senator Hoar, or a Boston M.C. [member of Congress]." Cochrane concluded rather sardonically, "Permission to be examined once secured and the rest is easy."[35]

The system was not quite as cut and dried as Cochrane described it. Although influence certainly helped in obtaining a commission, it was not enough to ensure one. As far as being from Massachusetts and knowing Secretary Long, this more often worked against an aspirant than for him. After recommending two young men from Massachusetts for commissions, Secretary Long directed that no further appointments be made from that state. Even after receiving an endorsement of both the secretary of the Navy and the commandant of the Marine Corps, the candidates had to appear before an examining board. The Navy Department and Marine Corps were inundated with young and some not-so-young applicants who wanted to go to war as Marine second lieutenants. To weed out the unfit, the board tested the applicants for physical, mental, moral, and military attributes and ranked each candidate by merit. By May 21, Colonel Heywood wrote Secretary Long "that the number of candidates already authorized to appear before the board for examination is more than sufficient to fill all the places created by the Act of May 4, 1898."[36]

By early June, the examining boards had selected 24 men from civilian life to serve as Marine second lieutenants. Of this number, 1 was the son of a member of Congress, 1 the nephew of a member of Congress, at least 7 were the sons or close relatives of military officers, and most of the others had some military education or experience. Although the law actually left the number of temporary commissions open ended, Secretary Long and Colonel Heywood had decided upon 28 new officers for the time being. With the completion of the selection of the officers from civilian life, the remaining 4 officers were to come from the ranks of meritorious noncommissioned officers. Eventually the Navy Department raised the quotas so that 43 officers served as temporary Marine second lieutenants through the end of the war. Of this total, 40 were from civilian life and 3 were former noncommissioned officers.[37]

The selection of the new lieutenants from the enlisted ranks was somewhat different from that of the officers from civilian life. A noncommissioned officer who wanted an appointment had to have the strong endorsement of his commanding officer. He submitted his application through official channels to the commandant who would recommend whether the man would be permitted to take the officer examination.[38]

Even here, however, political influence played its role. Sgt. Frank A. Kinne, hardly representative of the Marine enlisted ranks, was one of the selectees. He came from a comfortable middle-class family. His father, C. Mason Kinne, was the assistant secretary of the Pacific Coast division of a prominent international insurance company. The elder Kinne had enlisted in the Volunteers during the Civil War and rose to the rank of colonel. He was a past master of the Grand Army of the Republic and knew Secretary of War Alger. The father imposed on Alger to recommend his son for one of the second lieutenant openings. Frank Kinne was a high school graduate and had received an appointment to the U.S. Military Academy at West Point but had been unable to attend because of illness. He had then joined the Marine Corps and had had five years of service; at the time of his application, he was an acting lieutenant on board the cruiser *New York*. Secretary Alger penned a short note to Secretary Long, describing the elder Kinne as "an old personal friend and his statements are entitled to every consideration." Sergeant Kinne received a commission.[39]

The remaining two noncommissioned officers, Sgt. Robert E. Devlin and Sgt. Charles G. Andresen, were both with the deployed 1st Battalion before receiving their commissions. In his letter of recommendation in which he stated that he knew each "to be a worthy and capable noncommissioned officer," Colonel Heywood asked that both men be examined at the 1st Battalion headquarters rather than called back to Washington. Andresen came from a much more typical enlisted background than Sergeant Kinne. Born in Norway, Andresen had immigrated to the United States as a young man and enlisted in the Marine Corps. Showing an aptitude as a soldier, he had risen quickly through the ranks. At Fisher's Island in Long Island Sound, apparently during a fleet landing exercise, he had served as first sergeant to Capt. Littleton W. T. Waller. He so impressed the latter that Waller highly recommended Andresen for a commission when the opportunity presented itself. Thanking Waller for his efforts, Andresen wrote: "Through your kindness and good will, I am allowed to address you as a brother officer. . . . Without your kindly assistance and advice it would have been impossible for me to have reached the place, where I now find myself."[40]

Although the selection process of the new officers was subject to the vagaries of political influence, it still provided an objective criteria to determine qualifications. The system rejected more than one candidate with impeccable social and personal background because of physical or mental failings. With the possible exception of the noncommissioned officers, however, most of the candidates came from middle-class or upper-middle-class families, and almost all had completed high school. Given the large number of candidates seeking commissions, the examining boards had the luxury to select only those who showed the most promise for a military career.

The training of the new officers was quick and pragmatic. After the outbreak of the war, the Marine Corps School of Application graduated its class in April 1898 at the Washington Barracks and temporarily suspended operations. The Corps then used the barracks and school's facilities to indoctrinate the new officers. As Colonel Heywood observed, "The newly appointed officers were hurriedly drilled and otherwise prepared for duty as rapidly as possible, and distributed among the auxiliary cruisers, the various posts, and the First Marine Battalion."[41]

By June 1898, the days of the Marine battalion at Key West were numbered. On May 18, 1898, having eluded both Sampson's North Atlantic Squadron and Commodore William S. Schley's Flying Squadron, Admiral Cervera and his small fleet entered the harbor of Santiago de Cuba on the southern coast of Cuba. For several days, the whereabouts of the Spanish fleet remained unknown to the Americans, and on May 27, Commodore Schley, whose ships had just missed sighting the Spanish flotilla earlier, asked permission to abandon the quest for Cervera temporarily and return to Key West for recoaling. Following the advice of his Navy War Board, Secretary Long denied the request, suggesting that Schley use the Guantanamo Bay area, about forty miles to the east of Santiago, for a coaling station. On May 29, Schley, off Santiago, reported the "enemy in port."[42]

At the same time that he had cabled Schley, apparently concerned that the latter would not be able to stay off Santiago, Secretary Long also sent a message to Admiral Sampson at Key West asking him if he could blockade Santiago and also seize Guantanamo and "occupy as a coaling station." Responding affirmatively, Sampson declared that he could "blockade indefinitely; think that I can occupy Guantanamo." Commodore Schley reported that he would remain off Santiago, and Admiral Sampson ordered him to maintain the blockade at all costs.[43]

On May 31, Capt. Charles D. Sigsbee, the captain of the cruiser St. Paul, who was departing Santiago with dispatches from Schley, recommended to Secretary Long that Guantanamo "should be seized, and the shores garrisoned by United States troops." He believed it "a fine base for operating against Santiago." The occupation of Guantanamo also would prevent the Spanish from placing "plunging fire" on ships attempting to use the bay for recoaling. Sigsbee reported that Admiral Sampson agreed with his appraisal. According to Sampson, after "the establishment of the blockade [of Santiago], my first thought was to find a harbor which could serve as a coaling station and as a base for the operations of the fleet pending a decisive action." In any event, whether at the urging of the Department or on his own initiative, the admiral ordered the reembarkation of the Marine battalion still at Key West. He also directed the cruiser Marblehead under the command of Cmdr. Bowman H. McCalla to reconnoiter Guantanamo.[44]

The Marines were more than ready to depart. The forced inactivity was causing some discord among the officers and some bad press. On June 2, 1898, Major Cochrane stated at the officers' mess that Marine Capt. George Elliott "was so loud in his clamor for war as to be disquieting." Lieutenant Colonel Huntington retorted that the New York Herald contained a statement that "Marines would rather eat than fight." Two days later a telegram ordering the battalion to prepare for reembarkation broke the tedium of the camp routine, and by June 6, the battalion was back on board the Panther, except for a small guard detachment left behind and Major Pope, who was ill. The *Panther* sailed to join the fleet off Santiago the following day to "great cheering" from the crews of the ships still in port."[45]

With their spirits revived, the Marines still had no idea of their mission. Major Cochrane speculated that they were to reinforce Army transports in an attack on Santiago. On the morning of June 10 when the *Panther* joined the fleet off Santiago, Admiral Sampson informed Huntington that the Marine battalion was to land at Guantanamo and seize a base for the fleet, and Commander McCalla, the commander of the *Marblehead*, would serve as the overall commander of the expedition. Earlier, the *Marblehead* had bombarded Spanish positions and landed a small reconnaissance detachment under the command of Capt. M. C. Goodrell, the fleet Marine officer. Goodrell selected a camp site for the Marine battalion on a hill near an abandoned Spanish blockhouse and then returned to the ship. The *Panther* rendezvoused with the *Marblehead* on the afternoon of June 10, and McCalla sent Goodrell on board the *Panther* to brief Huntington on the situation ashore. As the Marine battalion landed, the first company formed a skirmish line and ascended the hill. According to Huntington, "We went ashore like innocents and made a peaceful camp and slept well on the tenth."[46]

Although Marine pickets heard strange noises and saw some lights during the night, there was no sign of the Spanish except for abandoned equipment, some personal belongings, and two old muzzle-loading field artillery pieces. The next morning, the Marines destroyed most of this material and the blockhouse fearing the spread of disease. They also continued unloading their heavy equipment and moved it to their campsite. Huntington and his officers were not too happy with the selection of their base camp. They were in a clearing on top of a hill, surrounded by thickets and dense underbrush, but overlooking the water. Captain McCawley, the battalion quartermaster, called the site a "faulty one" from a "military point of view." About 1,100 yards to the front was a larger ridgeline which dominated the Marine-held hill. According to McCawley, "had the enemy been at all energetic or possessed of an ordinary amount of military knowledge they could have, in occupying this hill with sharpshooters, rendered our positions untenable."[47]

On June 11, although not occupying the hill, Spanish troops made their presence known in the evening. About 5:00 P.M., Spanish snipers killed two Marines on an outpost. Huntington sent out a patrol, but it failed to locate the Spanish. The Marine commander, however, still felt secure. As he later wrote his son, "I do not know why I did not expect a night attack for we had a flurry in the P.M., but I did not." The enemy, however, returned on five occasions during the night. Major Cochrane, who had been directing the movement of supplies across the beach, came up to the Marine camp, now called Camp McCalla in honor of the Navy commander, with reinforcements from the working parties during one of the lulls. First limiting themselves to minor probes, the Spaniards attacked in force after midnight. Cochrane called it "The beginning of 100 hours of fighting."[48]

Despite the heavy intensity of firing in the darkness, Marine casualties were relatively low, although the Navy surgeon with the battalion received a mortal wound in the first major attack. About daybreak, the enemy struck in force again and killed a Marine sergeant and wounded three other men. The fighting continued sporadically during April 12, but the Marines took no further casualties during the day. Cochrane wrote his wife: "We have been having no end of racket and excitement. . . . We are all worn out with the tension of fighting the scoundrels all night and all day and have another night coming on. Bullets went over my head and cannonading and fusilading all around but never close enough to hurt."[49]

With the continuing attacks on the afternoon of April 12, several of the Marine officers thought that the Spanish would overrun their camp if they remained. The Marines entrenched the top of the hill and moved their base camp to a lower site. Believing the enemy was bringing up more reinforcements, some of the company commanders even proposed that the battalion reembark on board the *Panther*. Major Cochrane argued forcibly against any such move, but Lieutenant Colonel Huntington remained noncommittal. Huntington reported back to Commander McCalla and referred to the possible evacuation of the battalion. Reputedly, the commander replied, "You were put there to hold that hill and you'll stay there. If you're killed I'll come and get your dead body." The matter of withdrawal soon became moot as about 60 Cuban insurrectionists, familiar with the terrain and area, reinforced the Marines.[50]

The Spaniards continued to harass the American outposts and lines through the night and the next day. According to the battalion's journal, "During the night many persistent and trifling attacks were made on the camp in reply to which we used a good deal of ammunition." Major Cochrane was more direct, stating there "was a vast deal of panicky, uncontrolled, and unnecessary fire." Again casualties were low, but the Marines lost their sergeant major, Henry Good, a victim of a sniper's bullet.[51]

At this point, Lieutenant Colonel Huntington was ready to take the offensive. The Cubans informed him that the enemy numbered some 400 to 500 troops and made their headquarters six miles to the south in the village of Cuzco, whose well contained the only source of water for the Spaniards. On April 14, Huntington sent two companies under the command of Captain Elliott to destroy the well. Moving through dense underbrush and rugged terrain and encountering stiff opposition along the way, the Marines accomplished their mission, although 3 were wounded and heat prostration felled several men. Their Cuban allies lost 1 man and suffered several wounded. Supported by ships' batteries from below, the Marines took a heavy toll of the enemy, capturing 1 lieutenant and 17 enlisted men. According to the prisoners, the Spaniards had sustained heavy casualties and morale was low. A few days later, Huntington sent out a 50-man patrol to recover some of the enemy bodies. He noted: "The expedition found many dead but the intolerable stench from the dead made it impossible to continue search. Also the formation of the ground prevented any disposition of the bodies."[52]

The destruction of their water supply drove the Spanish troops from the immediate environs of the Marine camp. The nearest enemy was the Spanish garrison at the city of Guantanamo twelve miles to the north, which the Marines estimated ranged from 3,000 to 7,000 men. With Cuban insurrectionists in control of the countryside, the Americans had little to fear from the garrison. Commander McCalla received reports that large numbers of Spanish troops would surrender "were they not prevented by their officers." On June 22, Rear Admiral Sampson wrote Secretary Long that the "Spanish forces in the vicinity of Guantanamo are in great straits for food." The Marines made an unspoken modus vivendi with the garrison. As Lieutenant Colonel Huntington observed to his son, "The Spaniards do not trouble us and [we] only talk of troubling them."[53]

Following the action of June 14, the Marine battalion spent the rest of its time at Guantanamo improving their fortifications and camp. They also began to bask in the first publicity of their exploits. On the second day, several news correspondents arrived at Guantanamo, including Stephen Crane, the novelist, and immediately began to file their dispatches. A few articles were critical. For example, the reporter for the *New York Times* observed "that given a free rein with repeating rifles, 500 nervous troops can waste 10,000 rounds of ammunition, killing shadows, in a single night, and not think even then that they have done much shooting."[54]

The *Times* article was very much the exception rather than the rule. More often the headlines spoke of "First in the Fight" and "The Gallant Marines." Crane, who represented the *New York World*, was particularly friendly to the men of the 1st Battalion. In an article entitled "The Red Badge of Courage was His Wig Wag Flag," Crane stated that Captain Elliott's attack on the Cuzco well "was the first serious engagement of our troops on Cuban soil." The novelist told about the heroics of Sgt. John

In an obviously staged photograph, Marines of Huntington's battalion pose for the camera at their camp near Guantanamo. They are armed with the new Lee "straight-pull" 6-mm., 5-shot, magazine-fed rifle. (Defense Department [Marine Corps] photo #514982, Marine Corps Historical Center Collection)

Quick who exposed himself to enemy fire in order to signal an American ship to cease a bombardment that threatened the Marine advance. Crane also had high praise for Lieutenant Colonel Huntington, referring to him as the "grey old veteran . . . and the fine old colonel" who provided a brave example to his men. The Marines returned the affection. Captain Elliott in his report declared that Crane accompanied him on the expedition to Cuzco and "was of material aid during the action, carrying messages to fire volleys, etc., to the different company commanders." An enlisted Marine several decades later remembered meeting Stephen Crane and rolling "a smoke with him." Not lost on the public was the fact that the Marines had landed and fought the Spanish while the Army under General Shafter still remained at Tampa.[55]

The question about the launching of the Army expedition against Cuba had preoccupied the military commanders and government policy makers since President McKinley, on May 2, had approved the proposed assault against Mariel. With the arrival of Cervera's fleet in the Caribbean, American planners abandoned plans for a direct attack against Havana. Instead, at a meeting at the White House on May 26 with the Naval War Board, the secretaries of War and the Navy, and Maj. Gen. Nelson Miles, the president agreed to an Army campaign against Santiago based on the assumption that Cervera's fleet had taken refuge there.[56]

Reflecting this decision, Secretary Long the next day cabled Commodore Schley off Santiago Bay—who at the time still had not determined the exact location of Cervera's ships—that the Army was prepared to send 10,000 troops, "which are ready to embark," to assist the Navy in the capture of the city and harbor of Santiago. On May 31, after Schley had confirmed the presence of Cervera at Santiago, Secretary Long repeated the information about the proposed Army expedition to Admiral Sampson. He stated that the Army's V Corps at Tampa, under Brig. Gen. William Shafter, stood ready to send nearly 25,000 men to Santiago as soon as the Navy determined that, indeed, Cervera's entire fleet was in port.[57]

On May 31, the War Department delineated Shafter's mission. As soon as possible, the corps commander was to embark his troops on Army transports which, accompanied by Navy escort vessels, would steam to a position off Santiago. The corps would then land either east or west of the city. Shafter was to move on Santiago, capture the Spanish garrison, and assist the Navy in the reduction of Cervera's squadron.[58]

The War Department badly underestimated the difficulties of organizing an amphibious operation from Tampa. Even General Shafter, on the scene, believed that he would be able to embark his force and sail for Cuba within three days. With no roads and only a single railroad track between the city and the wharfs at the port, the embarkation would have been daunting under the best of circumstances. As it was, the scene at Tampa bordered on the chaotic: the commander lacked experience, the supplies piled up, and the continual arrival of new troops compounded the situation. By June 4, the scheduled day of departure, the corps commander admitted that he required a few more days. An unfounded rumor about sightings of unidentified Spanish ships in Caribbean waters delayed the departure of the Army transports even further. On June 6, off Santiago, an exasperated Admiral Sampson cabled Secretary Long: "If 10,000 men were here city and fleet would be ours within forty-eight hours. . . . Every consideration demands Army movement." Finally, on June 14, the Army convoy set sail from Tampa for Cuba.[59]

The delays in the departure of the Army ships from Florida hardly made for harmony in the relations between the Army and Navy off Cuba. Although the first meeting between General Shafter and Admiral Sampson went relatively smoothly, it resulted in a misunderstanding. On June 20, the two met with the senior Cuban commanders at Aserradero, eighteen miles west of Santiago and under the control of the insurgents. One of the Cuban commanders, General Calixto Garcia, proposed that the Army expedition land at Guantanamo, but both Sampson and Shafter rejected Guantanamo because of the poor roads between there and Santiago and, instead, favored Daiquiri, only eighteen miles southeast of Santiago. Sampson later wrote that he "was pleased that my ideas in this matter so nearly accorded with those of the general." According to the admiral, Shafter "declared it to be his intention to attack the shore batteries [protecting the entrance to Santiago Bay] in the rear, and make it possible for the navy to clear the channel and get inside the harbor, it being his main object to assist the navy in destroying the Spanish fleet." Shafter, on the other hand, remembered the meeting differently. He believed the only feasible strategy was to take the city of Santiago at the top of the bay rather than assault the fortified heights at the lower end of the bay: "It would have been the height of folly and endangered the safety of the army to have attempted to carry out the plan desired by the Navy and it never for one minute met with my approval."[60]

The issue in dispute between the two commanders revolved around the Spanish fortifications near the entrance of Santiago Bay. At the entrance, high cliffs dominated a narrow, winding channel. A Spanish minefield, restricting the water entryway, and gun batteries positioned on the eastern and western banks, known as the Morro and Socapa Heights, respectively, supplemented the natural defenses already afforded the Spanish. Unwilling to expose his armored ships to either the mines or the artillery, Admiral Sampson wanted the Army to attack the Morro Heights while he used the Marine battalion, reinforced by Marines from the fleet, to take the western, or Socapa, heights. Such an attempt would have required close Army-Navy planning; it was not forthcoming.[61]

In the meantime, on June 22, as agreed, Shafter's force came ashore at Daiquiri. Opting for a decisive land battle, Shafter advanced upon the city of Santiago. On July 1, despite a tenuous line of communications to the sea resulting in haphazard resupply, the American Army expeditionary corps defeated the Spanish in two hard-fought battles: San Juan Hill and El Caney. Shafter's victorious troops soon held the strategic high ground overlooking Santiago while the Spanish defending garrison retreated into the city. Although holding the upper hand, Shafter had his doubts whether he could continue the attack on Santiago and seriously considered falling back to positions closer to his supply base at Siboney on the coast.[62]

Admiral Sampson and General Shafter were each concerned about the dangers to their respective forces, and they still remained far apart on objectives and strategy. Sampson's main purpose was the destruction of Cervera's fleet, and Shafter's was the surrender of the city of Santiago and its defending garrison. In an exchange of messages on July 1 and 2, General Shafter asked Admiral Sampson to force the entrance into Santiago Bay and take the city under fire, but Admiral Sampson insisted that he could not force the entrance until someone cleared the channel of mines. Shafter tartly replied that he was "at a loss to see why the Navy can not work under a destructive fire as well as the Army."[63]

In order to obtain a meeting of the minds, Admiral Sampson asked General Shafter to confer with him, and on July 3, Sampson on board his flagship, the cruiser *New York*, steamed to meet with Shafter at the latter's headquarters. According to Capt. French E. Chadwick, Sampson's chief of staff, the admiral was going to "explain the situation and lay our plans . . . , which were to countermine the harbor, going in at the same time and also trying . . . to carry the Morro by assault with a thousand Marines. . . . The Army is ignorant to an inconceivable degree of what you may call the military conditions."[64]

The meeting with Shafter did not take place that day. About half an hour after setting out, Admiral Sampson on the quarterdeck of the *New York* spotted smoke near the entrance of Santiago de Cuba harbor. Admiral Cervera had decided to leave and encountered the American blockading ships. Ironically, by the time Sampson reached the fleet, the battle raged. In the four-hour engagement, the Spanish lost all their ships and sustained casualties of 474 killed and wounded, and Admiral Cervera and 1,750 of his men were taken prisoner. The cost to the American fleet was relatively low, 1 sailor dead and 1 wounded.[65]

Despite the result of the lop-sided sea battle, the dispute between Shafter and Sampson remained unresolved. Although Cervera's fleet was no longer a factor, the Army had not yet taken the city of Santiago. On both political and military grounds, the Washington authorities insisted that the Army continue the campaign against the city, and President McKinley directed that Shafter and Sampson meet and determine how they would cooperate to force the surrender of Santiago. Sampson agreed to meet Shafter at Siboney, but fell ill and sent Chadwick to represent him.[66]

At the conference with General Shafter on July 6, Captain Chadwick again presented Sampson's proposal that the Marines and Army capture the Socapa and Morro Heights to permit the Navy to clear the mines. Eventually the two reached an agreement of sorts. The Navy would first shell the city of Santiago at long range with its great guns. If at the end of the bombardment, the Spanish had not surrendered, Marines from the fleet with the assistance of Cuban troops would attack the Socapa Heights. At the same time, Sampson would attempt to force the entrance with some of his smaller ships. It was unclear whether Shafter would provide troops to assist in the taking of the Morro.[67]

The commanders implemented only part of the agreement. Although on July 10 and 11, Sampson's ships fired upon the city from outside the harbor entrance, the admiral and Shafter soon reverted to their original positions. Shafter continued to want Sampson to force the entrance of the harbor, and Sampson refused to do so until the ground troops had reduced the artillery batteries. The arguments even reached the White House. On July 13, Secretary Long cabled Sampson, "The Commanding General of the Army urges, and Secretary of War urgently requests that Navy force harbor." Long directed the admiral to consult with the Army commander and do "all that is reasonably possible to insure the surrender of the enemy." Still, Long left to Sampson's discretion how to accomplish this and, furthermore, warned "that the United States armored vessels must not be risked."[68]

The subject of the capture of the artillery batteries remained a divisive issue and one of mutual recriminations between senior Army and Navy commanders. At the heart of the question was the feasibility of an assault on the Morro: the Army said it was not, and the Navy said it was. For his part, Marine Maj. Robert L. Meade who would have commanded the Marine assault force on the Morro, agreed with Admiral Sampson, with some qualifications. After examining the terrain following the surrender of Santiago, he wrote: "The most difficult part . . . would be in reaching the crest from the beach through almost impassable maniqua plants." According to Meade, "Nothing but a narrow trail reached the crest. . . . Under such circumstances an inferior force could conduct a defense with success if properly handled." He concluded, nevertheless, that "the army in the near vicinity had successfully assaulted positions similarly defended [and] I was certain that my assault would have been successful also, if undertaken."[69]

Events, however, overtook the dispute. With continuing Army reinforcements from the United States, including 1,500 troops under General Miles, Shafter squeezed the vise around the city. Finally on July 15, after extended negotiations and in the face of overwhelming odds, the Spanish commander of the Santiago garrison agreed to surrender. The formal ceremony took place the following day.

With the aborting of the campaign against the heights, the 1st Marine Battalion, even after the destruction of Cervera's fleet and the surrender of the city of Santiago, remained at Guantanamo Bay until the beginning of August. There had been some discussion about the Marine battalion joining General Miles and his planned expedition against Puerto Rico. The War Department, however, vetoed the Marine participation.[70]

At Guantanamo, the Marines established a garrison routine. Three of the temporary lieutenants joined the battalion together with enlisted replacements. The Marines maintained their vigil and manned their outposts, but at the same time entered into a more relaxed regimen. They, nevertheless, held to a high standard of health discipline, using only distilled water from the ships, burning their garbage, and changing their clothes whenever they could. One of the Marine battalion's first orders related to basic toilet habits: "Men are forbidden to ease themselves except at the latrine, and will not urinate inside the Fort or near the ramparts." On July 23, Major Cochrane observed that "our camp continues healthy, and we are trying to keep it so." In contrast to the Army, the Marines did not suffer one case of yellow fever and sustained only a 2 percent sickness rate.[71]

By the end of July, the Marine battalion was prepared to depart Guantanamo. In order to place further pressure on the Spanish in Cuba, the Naval War Board wanted to extend the naval blockade to western Cuba where the Spanish still used ports on the southern coast that were connected by rail to Havana. The board directed that the Marine battalion seize the Isle of Pines off the southwestern coast as a "secure base for coal and against hurricanes, for the small vessels which alone could operate in the surrounding shoal water." Lieutenant Colonel Huntington at this point had some private doubts about the capability of the older officers to continue. He believed that another campaign "would clear Huntington, Harrington, Elliott, and Spicer off the rolls of this battalion." Huntington stated, however, that "Cochrane . . . takes such selfish care of himself that he might last, unless somebody killed him."[72]

Fortunately for Huntington and his officers and men, they did not have to endure the hardships of further strenuous ground combat in a tropical climate. On August 9, escorted by the cruiser *Newark*, the battalion departed Guantanamo on board the Navy transport *Resolute* for the Isle of Pines. Joined the following day by another two ships off Cape Cruz, Cmdr. Casper

F. Goodrich, the captain of the *Newark* and task force commander, decided upon a small digression. Acting upon a suggestion of one of his ship captains, he ordered, en route to the Isle of Pines, the capture of the city of Manzanillo, west of Santiago. Although the Navy ships bombarded the city on August 12, the news of the signing of the peace protocol calling for an armistice halted the proposed landing of the Marine battalion.[73]

Although Commander Goodrich and Lieutenant Colonel Huntington expressed disappointment about not attaining additional glory for American arms, other Marine officers were much less enthusiastic. Captain McCawley, the battalion quartermaster, later observed that the Americans badly underestimated the size of the Spanish garrison. According to McCawley, the Spanish troops numbered nearly 4,500, not the 800 that Goodrich and his commanders thought to be the case. Although reinforced by Cuban forces to the north of the city and by naval gunfire, the Marine battalion might have faced an almost impossible task. As McCawley later wrote tongue in cheek, "One Marine could dispose of two or three Spaniards, but it is questionable whether he could accomplish the defeat of ten." Aptly and succinctly, Marine Maj. Henry Clay Cochrane concluded: "The whole affair [at Manzanillo] was unnecessary and unwise." The Marine battalion stopped briefly at Guantanamo and then returned to the United States.[74]

For the Marine Corps and the nation at large the war was over. The protocol of August 12 between the two countries ended hostilities and called for a peace treaty to be negotiated at Paris. Spain agreed to relinquish Cuba, give Puerto Rico to the United States, and permit the United States to occupy Manila until the conclusion of the formal treaty determined the fate of the Philippines. Ironically, on August 13, the day after the protocol was signed, American forces captured Manila after token resistance by Spanish defenders. In the final Treaty of Paris, signed on December 10, 1898, and ratified in February 1899, the Spanish ceded the Philippines to the United States. Almost completely unnoticed during the war, the United States had also formally annexed the Hawaiian Islands. Thus, the immediate result of the Spanish-American War was to make the United States an imperial power in both the Caribbean and the Pacific.

The Spanish-American War also had a lasting result on the Marine Corps. Although nearly 75 percent of Marine strength was on board ship, it was Huntington's battalion that caught the public eye and also signaled portents for the future. As Colonel Heywood quickly remarked, the Marine battalion with the fleet "showed how important and useful it is to have a body of troops which can be quickly mobilized and sent on board transports, fully equipped for service ashore and afloat, to be used at the discre-

The Marines of the 1st Battalion at their camp at Portsmouth, New Hampshire, after their return from Cuba. Colonel Heywood used the battalion to herald the success of the Marine Corps in the Spanish-American War. (Marine Corps photo #312851, Marine Corps Historical Center Collection)

tion of the commanding admiral." Heywood also pointedly observed that the Marine force stood "always under the direction of the senior naval officer," and thus posed no "conflict of authority" inherent in Army-Navy relations.[75]

Upon the return of the Marine battalion from Cuba, Colonel Heywood exploited the Marine record in the war to enhance the Corps' status within the naval and military establishment. Rather than immediately dissolving the 1st Battalion, he kept the unit together at Portsmouth, New Hampshire, for over three weeks. Ostensibly, the reason was to permit the men "to rest and get the malaria" out of their system. On September 10, Colonel Heywood visited the Marine encampment and reported to Secretary of the Navy Long that "the men are looking very well, none of them being sick, and there has not been a death by disease since the battalion left for Cuba." The Navy Department and the press were not slow to compare the 2 percent sickness rate of the Marine battalion with the ravages that malaria and yellow fever caused among Shafter's troops at Santiago.[76]

Finally, before disbanding in mid-September, the 1st Battalion paraded before the president and other dignitaries in Washington. In a heavy rain, but before a large cheering crowd, the Marines dressed in their campaign uniforms passed in review to the strains of a "Hot Time in the Old Town Tonight" played by the Marine Corps Band. President McKinley complimented the men on their appearance and declared, "They have performed magnificent duty and to you, Colonel Heywood, I wish to personally extend my congratulations for the fine condition your men are in."[77]

Although the Marine leadership accepted with great satisfaction the public acclaim received by the Marine battalion, it still perceived the secondary battery mission a primary one for Marines with the fleet. Even before the end of the war, on August 9, 1898, Colonel Heywood had sent out letters to selected ship commanders and to ship detachment Marine officers to determine the effectiveness of Marine gunnery in the sea battles of Santiago and Manila Bay. In his annual report, the commandant claimed that the secondary batteries caused the greatest damage to the Spanish ships at Santiago and that their raking fire forced the enemy to abandon their guns. He also observed that a large percentage of the guns were manned by Marines.[78]

The accounts by both Marines and naval officers were less conclusive than Heywood professed for them. On the *Indiana*, for example, Marine Captain Waller reported that only about a third of the Marine detachment actually manned the guns. As Capt. A. C. Taylor, the ship commander, pointed out, the Marines on the secondary battery fired about half the number as the seamen because the Marines manned the "port battery of 6-pounders, while the starboard battery was the one engaged." Taylor then wrote to the secretary of the Navy, "While valuing very highly the services of the Marine guard I respectfully state that I look upon their services and their conduct in battle as being of equal merit with the other divisions of the ship, all of these divisions distinguishing themselves alike by bravery and skill." Another ship's commander, Captain Evans of the *Iowa*, seconded Captain Taylor's sentiments: "I do not think it desirable to single out an individual division of this ship's company for special report. All the ship's company, of which the Marine Guard forms a division, have done their work in a manner creditable to themselves and their ship." Even more to the point, however, was the fact that naval gunnery during both the battles of Santiago and Manila Bay was notoriously poor. American naval guns of all calibers averaged between 1 and 5 percent hits for ammunition expended. As one naval study concluded, "War ships of the present day will generally be placed hors de combat by conflagration and the destruction of their personnel before they are sunk by gun fire."[79]

Still, neither the public nor Congress was overly concerned with the technicalities of naval gunfire. In fact, the inadequacies of the aimed firing during the two sea battles did not come out until several months later, and then appeared only in professional journals and published official reports. Heywood's report containing lists of Marines breveted for gallantry in action and accounts of Marines in battle both on land and sea served to satiate the nation's appetite for heroes. As the *New York Times* shrewdly noted, "This is the sort of stuff that members of Congress will read when they receive the request of [the] Colonel Commandant . . . to have an increased allowance of men and money to the Marine Corps in the next naval appropriation bill."[80]

The acquisition of the new possessions in the Pacific was to have more bearing on the post Spanish-American War Marine Corps than all the public relations blandishments of Colonel Heywood. As the United States soon discovered, it was to be much easier to take the Philippines from the Spanish than to decide what to do with them. President McKinley remarked, "It is not a question of keeping the islands of the east, but of leaving them." In the end, McKinley decided to retain the Philippines as the result of various diverse pressures placed upon him, not the least of which were America's own expansionist impulse and a possible scramble for the Philippines among the European powers and Japan if the United States did not take them. By the end of 1898, the United States Army in the Philippines was engaged in a full-fledged military campaign to suppress the Filipino insurrectionists.[81]

Marine and naval officers were quite aware of the implications of colonial possessions for their services. As early as June 1898, Major Cochrane wrote, "The apparent intention of establishing a colonial empire suggests foreign duty for all grades of the Marine Corps." In December 1898, Colonel Heywood elaborated on this theme in a letter to the secretary of the Navy. He observed that several "prominent naval officers" believed "there should be a force of 20,000 well drilled and equipped Marines, who could be placed on board naval transports, at very short notice, and sent to any of the many possessions recently captured by the Navy without the necessity for calling on the Army." On March 9, 1899, Admiral Dewey requested "a battalion of Marines to garrison the Naval Station at Cavite [in the Philippines] as soon as possible." A few days later, the *New York Times* carried a report that the Navy Department planned to send eventually 1,000 Marines to Cavite in order "to take care of the Navy's interests there."[82]

This new colonial mission placed demands on the limited manpower resources of the Marine Corps that Colonel Heywood had already anticipated. On November 9, 1898, Heywood sent a lengthy memorandum to Secretary Long asking for an extensive increase in both the enlisted and officer strength of the Marine Corps. He stressed that the "new territories" required an adequate size force and argued that a Marine Corps of 6,000, an increase of 1,268 over its wartime force, "would give the Navy a well organized and well drilled body of men, who would be always available for any duty, to act in conjunction with the Navy, in any service they may be called upon to perform." Colonel Heywood also insisted that the Marine officer corps needed to be restructured and expanded. He referred to the bill for the reorganization of the Marine Corps that he had submitted the previous spring. Although the bill was still on the House calendar for action, the commandant stated that its provisions were no longer valid as they were "based on the requirements of the Navy before any large increase was contemplated." He asked permission to submit a new bill that would include his present recommendations to Congress. In his annual report published shortly afterward, Secretary Long pointed to the "general efficiency" of the Marine Corps and supported its increase "to at least 5,000 men and necessary officers."[83]

The following month, on December 12, Colonel Heywood followed up on his previous memorandum. At some length, the commandant reiterated much of the same rationale, and although acknowledging the secretary's request for a 5,000-man Marine Corps, he insisted that the altered circumstances because of the war and its outcome required "at least 6,000 men at the present time." Heywood warned, however, that this number would only be adequate for five years and that the expansion of the fleet would then necessitate 10,000 and possibly even 20,000 Marines. The commandant then enclosed a copy of his proposed bill that would provide for a 6,000-man Marine Corps and a doubling of its officer corps. The officer corps would include 60 second lieutenants who would come from the Naval Academy, the temporary lieutenants appointed during the war, meritorious noncommissioned officers, and civilian life. Heywood gave preference to the Naval Academy graduates and the wartime temporary officers.[84]

Secretary Long approved Colonel Heywood's recommended legislation and forwarded it to the House Naval Affairs Committee for its consideration. On January 5, 1899, Major Cochrane visited Marine Corps Headquarters and observed that the Marine Corps commandant was "jubilant over" the prospects of congressional action. On January 17, 1899, Representative Adolph Meyers from Louisiana, the leading Democrat on the House Naval Affairs Committee, with the unanimous support of the full committee, offered an amendment to the naval personnel bill, which incorporated the changes wanted by Heywood. The full House agreed to the amendment with little debate by a vote of eighty-eight to fifty-five, but took out the provision which would have made the commandant a major general. It would, however, promote Heywood to the rank of brigadier general. The House then passed the entire naval personnel bill, which included the amalgamation of the Navy line with the Navy engineer corps as well as the expansion of the Marine Corps, and sent it to the Senate.[85]

The Senate acted without delay. Making only a few changes in the overall bill, the senior body passed the legislation a month later. On March 1, a House-Senate conference committee worked out the differences between the two versions. The House agreed to the revised bill on the same day, and on the following day the Senate voted to enact the measure. On March 3, 1899, President McKinley signed the bill into law. The new law provided the Marine Corps not only with the 6,000 enlisted Marines but with an authorized officer corps of 201 line officers, including the new rank of brigadier general commandant. In addition, it permitted the Marine Corps 5 new staff officers and promoted the paymaster, adjutant and inspector, and the quartermaster to the rank of colonel. As a result of the legislation, the authorized number of Marine line officers consisted of 1 brigadier general, 5 colonels, 5 lieutenant colonels, 10 majors, 60 captains, 60 first lieutenants, and 60 second lieutenants.[86]

As would be expected, the Marine officers were exultant over their success. Many, such as Major Cochrane; Maj. George Reid, the adjutant and inspector; Maj. Frank C. Denny, the Marine Corps quartermaster; and Capt. Charles McCawley, the assistant quartermaster, had openly lobbied for the bill. Several of the junior officers had also used whatever influence they had. First Lt. John A. Lejeune asked his sister to thank a friend "for his very successful effort in behalf of our bill." As Lejeune confided, "Everybody worked hard for it, and no opposition to the Marine Corps developed in the Senate." Major Cochrane openly stated his own self-interest in the legislation, noting in his diary on February 17: "Naval Personnel bill passed the Senate. Marine Corps all right. Will promote me to Lt. Col."[87]

The new law completely transformed the Marine officer corps and resulted in wholesale promotions. Heywood, of course, became a brigadier general. Two officers received promotions from lieutenant colonel to colonel and 1 a promotion of two ranks, from major to colonel. Another 3 officers went from major to lieutenant colonel and 2 from captain to lieutenant colonel. The same explosive pattern of promotions followed in the lower officer ranks: 10 captains became majors, and all the lieutenants, both first and second, became captains. Of the 43 temporary officers who had served during the Spanish-American War, 35 took the qualifying examination and 30 received commissions as Marine first lieutenants, bypassing the rank of second lieutenant. Out of the 3 noncommissioned officers who took advantage of the law to apply for a commission, only 1, Sgt. Thomas F. Lyon, passed the qualifying examination. Because of the promotion fluidity, he also became a first lieutenant. Except for General Heywood, all of the newly promoted officers passed a written and physical examination. Secretary of the Navy Long ruled that the newly reappointed former temporary officers, however, did not have to take an additional examination for their appointments as first lieutenants but would be commissioned, "in the order of merit" that they passed the entrance examinations.[88]

With the new law permitting the appointment of 45 new second lieutenants in 1899 and 15 more after the new year, General Heywood immediately proposed guidelines in accordance with the legislation for the appointment of the new officers. Immediately after the enactment of the personnel bill, the Marine Corps commandant proposed to Secretary Long selection procedures and a uniform examination for all officer aspirants. Applicants for a Marine commission were to first obtain from the commandant permission to take the officer examination. He would include in his application certificates of previous military training, a diploma from an educational institution, or a recommendation from its faculty. If granted permission by the commandant, the candidate would then appear before a military board, much the same procedure followed during the Spanish-American War. He would have to pass a physical examination, the same as required for the troops. The board would report on the individual's moral character and "if addicted to use of intoxicating liquors." After he cleared those hurdles, the candidate then would face a barrage of written tests in English, geography, history, constitutional law, surveying, and math to include plane trigonometry and logarithms. Each of these tests would be weighted and then graded on a scale of 100. Each candidate would have to score at least 65 percent on each test and a minimum average of 70 percent overall. Secretary Long approved these recommendations and issued a Navy circular which incorporated them.[89]

Although the procedures provided a rational basis for officer selection, political influence still played a role, but not always a dominant one. For example, former Assistant Secretary Roosevelt recommended a former lieutenant in his Rough Riders for a Marine commission. According to Roosevelt, the man had been "wounded by my side twice on San Juan Hill and . . . was promoted twice for good conduct and for gallantry." For whatever reason, Roosevelt's nominee did not become a Marine officer. On the other hand, Hilary A. Herbert, Jr., the son of the former congressman and secretary of the Navy, later received an appointment as a Marine second lieutenant. The elder Herbert described his son as not developing "rapidly, either mentally or physically." Although a Democrat, Herbert still obtained from President McKinley, a former colleague on the House Ways and Means Committee, a Marine Corps commission for his son.[90]

With the Marine Corps expansion, professionalism was still in the eye of the beholder. Although General Heywood wanted to reopen the School of Application to train his new officers, the continued drain on his manpower resources prevented him from doing so. At the request of the president of the Naval War College, however, the Marine commandant detailed six Marine officers in June 1900 to Newport. In November of that year, the Marine Corps reopened its School of Application at the Marine Corps Barracks in Washington.[91]

During this time, the Marine presence in the Pacific continued to grow. By November 1899, in the Philippines alone the Marines had three battalions stationed at Cavite, consisting of 43 officers and 976 enlisted men. Although these units only played a marginal role in the pacification of the Philippines, they were the first sent into China during the Boxer emergency in the spring and summer of 1900. By September of that year, nearly 2,000 Marines were in the Far East, about one-third of total Marine Corps strength.[92]

Although General Heywood continued to stress the role of Marines as gunners on board Navy warships, the Navy's newly formed General Board under the leadership of Admiral Dewey looked to a new mission for the Corps. At its first meeting in April 1900, the board assigned its Marine member, Col. George Reid, the adjutant and inspector, to come up with the "number and organization of a force of Marines sufficient" to defend several proposed bases in the Caribbean. Owing to the volatility of the situation in China, the General Board also studied attaining and defending an advanced base off the Chinese mainland. On October 6, 1900, Admiral Dewey signed a memorandum from the General Board to the secretary of the Navy advocating the immediate formation of a 400-man Marine battalion that could serve as the nucleus for a 1,000-man Marine force, in the event of a war, to defend an advanced base in support of a naval campaign in Asiatic waters. The board suggested that "the Marines would be best adapted and most available for immediate and sudden call" for the establishment of such a base and the throwing up of hasty defenses and gun positions and the laying of mines to channelize the approaches. If more permanent defenses were then decided upon, Army units could be sent to relieve the Marines who then would be available "for other duty." The following month, General Heywood agreed to the proposal, but warned that the preparations would "necessitate very careful consideration, and considerable time will be necessary for accomplishing it."[93]

Marine relations with the Navy had come full circle. As General Heywood testified before Congress that year, "Naval officers are almost a unit as to the necessity for a larger number of Marines to act in cooperation with the Navy, especially now, since our outlying possessions will in all [make] such cooperation necessary." He observed that "many of the naval officers who . . . were opposed to the . . . Marine Corps are now firmly convinced of the necessity for a large corps." In essence, the naval establishment recognized the Marine Corps as an essential part of the Navy and provided the Marine officer his professional jurisdiction.[94]

10. CONCLUSION

During the last two decades of the nineteenth century, the Marine officer corps demonstrated the interdependence between the professionalization of the Marine officer and his "jurisdictional links" to both his organization and to the profession of military officer. For the Marine officer, these jurisdictional links revolved around mission and the interrelationship between the Marine Corps and the Navy, and in the broadest connotation, the larger society. In essence, these links determined what the Marine officer did and what he claimed as his area of expertise. The irony was that Marine officer professionalism developed during a period of transition when the Marine officer's jurisdictional areas were in flux. Jurisdictional links also brought up questions about the Marine role within the Navy and, in a sense, of the Marine officer's identity of himself and of his organization.[1]

Throughout this period, Marine officer professionalism and the Marine reform movement complemented one another. Such fledgling steps as Captain Forney's trip to Europe and the formation of the secret Marine officer associations in the 1870s intermingled both individual and organizational aspirations. Even granting that these reform and professional impulses were based in part on individual and institutional self-aggrandizement, there still lay behind them a genuine desire to improve the caliber of the individual Marine officer and the Corps as a whole. Colonel McCawley's initial efforts to rid the Marine Corps of its unsuitable officers and to raise the level of the enlisted Marines were indicative of such interest.

The greatest impediment to this initial Marine reform movement was its lack of a coherent unifying theme or strategy. For many Marine officers, perhaps even the majority, their devotion to reform and change had a direct correlation to what advantages it brought, mostly in the form of promotions, to themselves. Although Colonel McCawley allied with the reformers in an attempt to push a legislative agenda through Congress, this proved a dismal failure. On one hand, McCawley wanted to take officer selection and promotion out of the political patronage system, but, on the other, he wanted to use the political system to enhance the Corps, which proved an impossible task. There was little agreement among the Marine officers themselves and no common broad vision for their service.

Thus, for the most part, Marine professionalism during the late 1870s and much of the decade of the 1880s was individualistic and iconoclastic. Despite the apparent disparity and lack of cohesiveness, there was a constant thread in this nascent professionalism. It centered around small unit tactics, discipline, technical training in ordnance and gunnery, and even military law. Marine officers attended both the Army Artillery School and the Navy Torpedo School; Marine Capt. William Remey became the judge advocate general of the Navy, in effect the Navy's chief lawyer and judge; and 1st Lt. Daniel Pratt Mannix, a graduate of both the Artillery School and the Torpedo School, established a naval artillery school for the Chinese Navy. The Marine Corps nexus with the Navy, however, made for the uniqueness of the Marine officer.

It is the exploration and redefinition of this relationship of the Marine Corps within the Navy during the latter decades of the nineteenth century that made for the jurisdictional link of the Marine officer within his profession. Navy officers, however, for the most part, were responsible for this redefinition and development of the Marine jurisdictional links.

Throughout this same period, the Navy officer corps was in intellectual ferment. Technology had transformed the nature of naval warfare. Steel and armor-plated oceangoing vessels began replacing the wooden steamers of the immediate post–Civil War Navy. In the 1880s, such reformist secretaries of the Navy as William Hunt, William Chandler, and William Whitney supported by a bipartisan coalition in Congress provided the initial funding for the new ships. The pages of the *Proceedings of the Naval Institute* served as the unofficial forum of naval thought. At the same time, such naval reformers as Rear Adm. Stephen Luce and Capt. John J. Walker, the head of the Bureau of Navigation, established the Naval War College and the Office of Naval Intelligence, two institutions that became the intellectual nucleus of the New Navy.

The beginnings of the New Navy also coincided with a more outward looking American foreign policy. The same technology that made for new ships and new armaments also made the oceans highways rather than barriers. It also meant the possibility of European fleets in American waters. At the same time, American naval officers recognized the strategic importance of an Isthmanian canal across Central America and viewed with suspicion the French activity in Panama. The American intervention in Panama in 1885 was a result in part of the recognition of American strategic and economic interests in the region. In fact, leading naval officers used the crisis in an aborted attempt to establish a possible permanent presence on the Isthmus.

The American military worried about its ability to defend the extensive, vulnerable U.S. coastline, let alone to protect the nation's economic and strategic interests abroad. During the first Cleveland administration, the president created a joint Army-Navy Board to refurbish American coastal defenses. The Army had the more passive role, the manning of the forts to repulse a hostile fleet, and the Navy was to take the offensive against any potential foe. For U.S. naval leaders this necessitated a reshaping of American naval strategy.

In the Naval War College, in the publications of the Office of Naval Intelligence, and in articles appearing in the *Naval Institute Proceedings*, intellectuals developed a consensus about the employment of naval force. The writings and lectures of Alfred Thayer Mahan at the Naval War College provided the synthesis of this consensus. As opposed to the American traditional concepts of coastal defense and cruiser raiding, American naval strategists advocated a more forward policy based upon a battleship fleet large enough to defeat a potential enemy fleet on the high seas and possibly even to carry the fight to the enemy's home waters. Such a strategy required not only more ships but a large train and advanced support bases. Although not fully developing their ideas, American naval officers included in their writings on the new concepts the projection of force ashore. Indeed, Cmdr. Bowman McCalla's recommendation after the Panama intervention to form the Marine Corps shore establishment into part of a permanent naval expeditionary brigade equipped with its own transports reflected in part this concern.

The paradox was that leading Marine professionals took little part in this discussion about landing operations. Colonel McCawley opposed any suggestion of restructuring the Corps, and even such members of the reform element as Forney, Mannix, and Cochrane contributed little to the debate. Although supporting a more structured permanent organization, their interests continued to revolve around issues of training, recruiting, discipline, and expanding the Marine officer and enlisted base. With no clear jurisdictional link to the New Navy, Marine professionals struck out in several different directions.

Indeed, the most significant change in the commissioning of new Marine officers came from the naval establishment and Congress rather than from the efforts of the Marine professionals. This was of course the passage of the 1882 appropriation bill which provided for the selection of graduates of the Naval Academy into the Marine officer ranks. To McCawley's credit, he quickly acted upon this measure to ensure that the Marine Corps received its share of graduates.

From 1883 through 1897, 52 Annapolis graduates became Marine officers. Although their appointments to the Naval Academy usually depended on some form of political patronage, they still had to meet relatively stringent physical and mental requirements. Furthermore, their four years at the academy as well as their two years as passed midshipmen provided another test of their military aptitude. While for the most part not the top members of their classes, the new Marine second lieutenants had attained a relatively high class standing because the provisions of the 1882 law restricted commissions to actual vacancies in the Navy. It was not unusual during these years for less than 50 percent of any Naval Academy class to receive any kind of commission. Thus, the new Naval Academy graduates brought to the Marine officer corps a certain elan and more positive self-image. They also provided a constant factor which differentiated the Marine officer corps both from the stagnation of the 1870s and the expanding Marine Corps after the Spanish-American War.

Corresponding with the raised officer entrance requirements, the last years of the McCawley administration and the first years of Colonel Heywood's commandancy witnessed several new initiatives to raise the professional proficiency of the Marine officer corps. These included the establishment of the School of Application and vigorous promotion examinations, the providing of both students and faculty for the Naval War College, coastal defense training, and the attempt to identify the Marine Corps with the New Navy by assigning the Marines the responsibility to man the secondary batteries on the new ships.

At the same time, however, when the Marine officer showed increasing professional proficiency, his Corps came under unexpected attack by the young Navy reformers. Beginning with the Greer Board in 1889 and led by such officers as Lt. William Fullam, the Navy progressives demanded the removal of Marines from the new steel ships so as to attract a better quality Navy recruit and to improve morale among the Navy seamen. With the support of either a sympathetic secretary of the Navy or key congressmen, the Marine Corps successively resisted the onslaught of the naval progressives. The differences among the various officer corps within the Navy forestalled any legislation to rationalize Navy and Marine Corps officer restructuring. During the 1890s, the Navy consisted of a cacophony of conflicting jurisdictions: Navy line officers versus the various staff corps; younger line officers versus more senior ones; line officers versus engineers; and most naval officers versus Marines. Although the engineers and the line officers compromised their differences in 1897, the Marine officers reached no such accommodation.

All of this left the Marine officer betwixt and between. On one hand, he was the poor relation of the Navy, and on the other, he had attained all the outward appurtenances of the modern professional: he was preselected; he received a formal education in his profession; he received special advanced training; he lived according to a strict code of conduct and concept of honor; and he advanced in rank by meeting specific professional requirements. Still, his professional status depended upon the relationship of his Corps to the Navy. It was becoming abundantly clear that Navy officers were willing to give only limited authority to the Marine officer on board the modern steel ships. Some of the Marine reform element, such as Captain Cochrane, even suggested that the Marine officer not force the secondary battery mission but instead concentrate on improving the quality of their enlisted force in the simple belief that "good men will beget good men" and the Marine Corps could only benefit from the result.

The criticism of the naval progressives, however, had little to do with the quality of the Marine officer or enlisted men but rather with the relevance of the Marine Corps to the Navy. Most of the younger line officers were in agreement with Fullam's analysis. They simply did not want Marines on board Navy warships. By 1897, when the Navy Personnel Board examined the amalgamation of the Marine officer corps with the Navy, these doubts shook the Marine officer corps. Many Marine officers, such as Captain Cochrane, wondered aloud whether they had any role with the Navy and even suggested half seriously the incorporation of the Marine Corps into the coast artillery regiments of the Army.

Such considerations were not entirely unthinkable given the dissident lobbying activity in 1894 by Army artillery reformists to separate coast defense from the field artillery. Even Marine reformists at one time or another proposed such a role for the Marine Corps. In fact, much of the curriculum of the Marine Corps School of Application supported a coastal defense role for the Marine Corps.

Paradoxically, although one set of Navy line officers wanted to do away with the Marine Corps and Marine officers themselves had doubts about their future, many of the planners at the Naval War College and in the Office of Naval Intelligence saw the Marine Corps in another light. In his initial war plan against England, Capt. Alfred Thayer Mahan wanted to use the Marine Corps to project power from the sea onto an enemy's shore for the seizure of a base of operations for the fleet. Later war plans required some sort of advanced base although the Marine Corps was not specifically mentioned. Naval writers also made references to the requirements for landing forces with the fleet, and even Lieutenant Fullam called for Marine battalions to be embarked on board Navy transports. By the time of the Spanish-American War, naval strategists had determined that Marine ground forces might prove useful in a naval war but had articulated no specific mission or doctrine.

The Spanish-American War proved to be a defining period for the Marine Corps. Although not fully knowing how they would use it, naval authorities immediately ordered the establishment of a Marine battalion with its own transport. Numbering less than a quarter of the active Marine Corps, this battalion's activities not only received public approbation but also had implications for the future relationship of the Marine Corps with the Navy. Despite a somewhat rocky start, the Marine 1st Battalion proved itself in combat by seizing the heights on Guantanamo and providing a safe anchorage for Navy ships. In effect, the Marines seized and protected an advance base for the fleet blockading Santiago.

Navy strategists and planners also learned another lesson from the war. They quickly realized that Army and the Navy officers may have very different and even possibly conflicting goals in a military campaign. The dispute between the Army and the Navy at Santiago reflected the separate approaches of professional Army and Navy officers. For General Shafter and his staff, the vital objective was the capture of the Spanish garrison and the city of Santiago. But Admiral Sampson and the Navy's aim was the destruction of Cervera's fleet. For his part, General Shafter designed an overland campaign to capture the city and was unwilling to sacrifice men to take the Morro and Socapa Heights overlooking the narrow channel into Santiago Bay. At the same time, Admiral Sampson refused to chance the loss of any of his ships by running the channel. Although both commanders attained their desired ends, their basic conflict remained unresolved. The Navy felt that it could not depend upon the Army to secure land-based sites for naval purposes. The Navy required its own land force, which it had in the Marine Corps.

The attainment of an American insular empire in the Caribbean and the Pacific also affected Navy requirements and dependence on the Marine Corps. Like naval bases and stations in the United States, the Navy required a Marine security force for its newly acquired bases in the Philippines. Most important, however, the newly created Navy General Board in

1900 formally assigned to the Marine Corps the advance base mission. In essence, the Navy provided the Marine Corps with a clear area of jurisdiction.

As important, however, as all of this may have been to Marine professionalism, the basic factor that stands out was the inherent insecurity of the Marine officer. Throughout this entire period, it appeared no matter how much the Marine officer tried to improve himself, he was rebuffed by his naval colleagues. Although a small minority of naval officers may have looked to the Marine Corps as a possible landing force for the Navy, most looked upon it as largely a relic of the age of sail. The circumstances of the Spanish-American War and its consequences, however, forced the Navy progressives to reexamine their views about the Marine Corps. This still left the Marine officer in an innocuous position and resulted in a certain amount of institutional and professional schizophrenia and paranoia. For example, although Colonel Heywood and other Marine officers accepted the new advanced base mission in 1900, they continued to resist any attempt to abandon any of their traditional relationships with the Navy. Heywood and his successors continued to argue the viability of the assignment of Marines on board Navy warships. Indeed, the largest crisis over the ship's guard issue occurred in 1908 when certain Navy officers convinced President Theodore Roosevelt to issue an executive order taking the Marines off Navy warships. Behind the scenes, Army general Leonard Wood wanted Roosevelt to incorporate the Marine Corps into the Army as a sort of colonial infantry. Although Congress reversed the presidential dictum, Marine officers continued to fear for the existence of their Corps. They constantly defined, redefined, and justified their roles and missions to both themselves and to everyone else.[2]

Grudgingly, however, the Navy officer eventually accepted the Marine officer as a military professional, albeit in his lights an inferior one. Over time, Navy strategists came to the realization that they needed a Marine Corps not only to hold advance bases but to project naval power ashore. After the Spanish-American War, while the rhetoric of the secondary battery and Marine guards on board Navy warships occasionally ruffled the Marine and Navy connection, there developed during the next decades a "continuity and consensus" about the Marine mission with the Navy. The consensus centered around the advance base and expeditionary roles of the Marine Corps.[3]

What then can be concluded about Marine officer professionalism? From one aspect, it was self-directed and simulated the same features as that of any professional military officer. In a very real way, the Marine officers' concerns with military discipline, tactics, and questions of enlisted morale and desertion rates were very similar to those of Army officers. These resulted in a certain elitism and esprit de corps. They had almost nothing, however, to do with mission or with the establishment of an area of professional jurisdiction. If the Marine officer had had to depend only on these acquired professional traits, he and his Corps would have disappeared entirely or been absorbed completely by the Army. The intersection of the jurisdiction and responsibilities of the Marine officer with that of his naval counterpart, therefore, provides the best approach for the analysis of Marine officer professionalism. That professionalism consisted of two separate but related strains. In the first instance, it consisted of the outward traits that characterized most professionals. The second strain related to the professional jurisdiction that the Marine officer had to carve out for himself within the Navy.

The question then became, How did the Marine fit into the naval service? In a sense, during the period under consideration, 1880–1898, some Marine officers and Navy officers searched to find and define this role. Mostly, those years were a time of missed connections. Although both realized that this function would have to fit into the new naval technology, the Marine reformers viewed the secondary battery mission on board the new armored warships and some aspect of coast defense as the special domain of the Marine. Naval strategists, on their part, were looking for some means to project force ashore as well as to protect the vulnerable advance bases of the fleet. After the Spanish-American War, Marine guards would continue to serve on board naval vessels, but it would be the expeditionary and advance base missions that would provide the professional jurisdiction for the Marine officer and ensure both his professional and institutional survival.

In the broadest sense, then, all professionalism, not only Marine officer professionalism, consists of relationships that are constantly changing. These relationships do not exist in an abstract vacuum, but rather in what has been defined as interlocking jurisdictional links. These links connect the individual professional to his profession, to his organization if the profession exists in an organization, and to the larger society. Time and events alter and occasionally break these links so that they have to be constantly reforged.

The Marine officer participated in, affected, and was affected by the society and forces around him. He was a part of the basic search for structure that characterized much of American life during the last decades of the nineteenth century. As seen, this search for structure took place in a confused arena where the old forms continued to have full play and competed with the new. The new professionalism coexisted with partisan politics, competing interest groups, personal and institutional self-interest, advancing technology, and an America beginning to look outward.

NOTES

CHAPTER 1. INTRODUCTION: PROFESSIONALISM AND REFORM

1. Henry Clay Cochrane Diary, General Entry, 1880, Henry Clay Cochrane Papers, PCS 1, Marine Corps Historical Center (MCHC); Commandant of the Marine Corps, *Annual Report, 1880*, 529; Capt. Woodhull S. Schenck to SecNav, March 10, 1880, Letters Received, 1880, RG 80, General Records of the Department of the Navy, National Archives and Records Agency (NARA); *New York Times*, February 12, 1880, 5; *Army and Navy Journal*, July 3, 1880, 978.

2. Maj. James Forney, "The Marines," *United Service* (Apr. 1889): 89 and 94-95.

3. "Authorized Strength of United States Marine Corps, 1798-1916," May 13, 1916, File 6758, RG 80, NARA; Henry Clay Cochrane, *A Resuscitation or a Funeral*, October 1, 1875, Cochrane Papers, MCHC; *New York Times*, December 29, 1875, 5; Forney, "The Marines," 89 and 94-95.

4. Daniel Beaver, "The American Military and the 'New' Institutional History" (Paper delivered at the annual meeting of the Organization of American Historians, May 1985), 2-4; James L. Abrahamson, *America Arms for a New Century: The Making of a Great Military Power* (New York, 1981), xii; Kenneth E. Boulding, *The Organizational Revolution: A Study in the Ethics of Economic Organization* (Chicago, 1968), 49, 202; Robert H. Wiebe, *The Search for Order* (New York, 1967), vii-ix, xiii-xiv, 11-43; Alfred D. Chandler, Jr., *The Visible Hand: The Managerial Revolution in American Business* (Cambridge, MA, 1977), 1-14; Thomas Haskell, *The Emergence of Professional Social Science: The American Social Science Association and the Nineteenth Century Crisis of Authority* (Urbana, IL, 1977), 3-4, 234; the quote is from pp. 3-4.

5. The general sources for this and the following paragraph are Boulding, *The Organizational Revolution*, xvi, xxvii-xxviii; Chandler, *The Visible Hand*, 1-14, 130-33, 143; William E. Nelson, *The Roots of American Bureaucracy, 1830-1900* (Cambridge, MA, 1982), 103; Richard H. Hall, "Introduction," in Richard H. Hall, ed., *The Formal Organization* (New York, 1972), 3.

6. Additional sources for this paragraph are Burton Bledstein, *The Culture of Professionalism: The Middle Class and the Development of Higher Education in America* (New York, 1976), 80; Ralph S. Bates, *Scientific Societies in the United States* (Cambridge, MA, 1965), 85, 105, 121.

7. Magali Sarfatti Larsen, *The Rise of Professionalism: A Sociological Analysis* (Berkeley, CA, 1977), 17, 193-94; Gerald L. Geison, "Introduction," in Gerald L. Geison, ed., *Professions and the French State* (Philadelphia, 1985), 1-12; Allan Millett, *Military Professionalism and Officership in America* (Columbus, OH, 1977), 5-6; Andrew Abbott, "Perspec-

tives on Professionalization" (Paper delivered at annual meeting of the Organization of American Historians, May 1985), 6–8, 12–15; Haskell, *The Emergence of Professional Social Science*, vi–vii, 65–66.

8. A. P. Carr-Saunders and P. A. Wilson, *The Professions* (Oxford, 1933), 3; Harold L. Wilensky, "The Professionalization of Everyone?" *American Journal of Sociology* (Sep. 1964): 137–58; Terence J. Johnson, *Professions and Power* (London, 1972), 23; Eliot Freidson, *Professional Powers* (Chicago, 1986) 30–32; Geoffrey Millerson, *The Qualifying Associations: A Study in Professionalization* (London, 1964), 4–5; Geoffrey Millerson, "Dilemmas of Professionalism," *New Society* (June 1964): 15–16; W. J. Goode, "The Theoretical Limits of Professionalization," in A. Etzioni, *The Semi-professions and Their Organization* (New York, 1969), 266–313. The quotation is from Johnson, *Professions and Power*, 22.

9. Among sociologists who have written most extensively on the subject, there are at least three identifiable schools on the subject of professionalism. For convenience, they can be designated the functionalists, the structuralists or "traitists," and the "monopolists" or power theorists. The functionalists, largely associated with Talcott Parsons, submit that the professions provide the vital functions of society. With an emphasis on "cognitive rationality" and the social responsibility of the professions, Parsons and his adherents focus largely on the expert-client relationship. For discussion of the functionalist perspective in the literature, see Talcott Parsons, "Professions," *International Encyclopedia of the Social Sciences*, ed. David L. Sills, vol. 12 (New York, 1968), 536–47; Johnson, *Professions and Power*, 23, 32–37; Bernard Barber, "Some Problems in the Sociology of the Professions," *Daedalus* (Fall 1963): 669–88; Michael F. Winter, *The Culture and Control of Expertise* (New York, 1988), 42–44; Andrew Abbott, *The System of Professions: An Essay on the Division of Expert Labor* (Chicago, 1988), 15; and Abbott, "Perspectives on Professionalism," 2–3.

In contrast to the functionalists, the structuralists concentrate on the structure or attributes of the professions and attempt to identify the defining characteristics of any given profession. The difficulty, however, is that there are probably more differences among the structuralists than between the structuralists and the functionalists. For discussion on the literature of the structuralists, see Abbott, *The System of Professions*, 15; Abbott, "Perspectives on Professionalism," 2–3; Johnson, *Professions and Power*, 23–30; Winter, *The Culture and Control of Expertise*, 21–3, 26–27, 37, and 119; Millerson, "Dilemmas of Professionalism," 15; Bengt Abrahamsson, *Military Professionalism and Political Power* (Beverly Hills, CA, 1972), 14–15; and Wilensky, "The Professionalization of Everyone?" 137–58.

Beginning in the 1960s, writers began questioning the validity of both the structuralist and the functionalist position. Such scholars as Eliot Freidson, Magali S. Larson, and Terence Johnson contended that both schools emphasize the positive while ignoring the negative aspects of professionalism. Criticizing the older scholarship for too much concern with form and structure, Freidson, Johnson, and Larson argued that the new scholarship should concentrate upon the concept of professions as ideologies to control the work place. Rather than accepting the older view of collegiality and mutual trust as the trademark of professional life, they insisted that "dominance and autonomy" are its chief characteristics. For extended discussion of the power theorists, see Eliot Freidson, "Professions and the Occupational Principle," in Freidson, ed., *The Professions and their Prospects* (Beverly Hills, CA, 1973), 19–38; Freidson, *Professional Powers*, 28–29, 211; Abbott, *The System of Professions*, 5; Johnson, *Professions and Power*, 32, 37–39; Larson, *The Rise of Professionalism*, xvi–xviii; and Winter, *Culture and Control*, 44–45, 50.

10. Abbott, "Perspectives on Professionalism," 10; Abbott, *The System of Professions*, 8–9, 18–20, 86–91, 318, 320–21.

11. Abbott, "Perspectives on Professionalism," 13–15; Abbott, *The System of Professions*, 2–3, 33, 35, 59, 69; 86–91, 111–12.

12. Much of the examination of military professionalization has ignored the question of professional military jurisdictions, except for the differences between line and staff officers in the Army and line and engineers in the Navy. Historian Peter Karsten perhaps skirts the fringes of professional jurisdictions when he argues that it was "career anxiety" that accounted for the professionalization of the so-called naval aristocracy. Carol Ann Reardon touches upon a jurisdictional dispute, not between rival groups of military officers, but between professional historians and Army officers in the use and understanding of military history. For the most part, however, most writers on military professionalization have largely ignored the jurisdictional areas that both differentiate and link together the various military professionals. See Peter Karsten, *The Naval Aristocracy: The Golden Age of Annapolis and the Emergence of Modern American Navalism* (New York, 1972), 292–93, and Carol Ann Reardon, "The Study of Military History and the Growth of Professionalism in the U.S. Army before World War I" (Ph.D. dissertation, University of Kentucky, 1987), 8, 34–36, 38. It is interesting to compare the confrontation between Army officers and historians in contrast to the accommodation reached by naval officers and the profession of history. Rear Adm. Alfred Thayer Mahan, the proponent of history and seapower, served a term as president of the American Historical Association, and Rear Adm. French E. Chadwick, the chronicler of the Spanish-American War, was also a respected member of the historical community.

13. Although there has been some question among scholars whether military officership is a profession, as Allan Millett suggests, the viewpoint depends somewhat upon one's concept about the morality of war and the need of society for military force. In the early 1930s, British sociologists A. M. Carr-Saunders and P. A. Wilson dismissed discussion of the military officer "because the service which soldiers are trained to render is one which it is hoped they will never be called upon to perform." Thirty years later, American sociologist Magali S. Larson denied military officers professional status because they did "not transact their services on the market." See Allan Millett, *Military Professionalism and Officership in America* (Columbus, OH, May, 1977), 12–13; Carr-Saunders and Wilson, *The Professions*, 3; and Larson, *The Rise of Professionalism*, xvi–xvii.

The literature on military professionalism has largely concentrated on such attributes as education, inculcation of military ethics, and socialization of the officer corps. Much of the discussion has dealt with the professionalization of both the individual officer and of the officer corps in general. A large concern is the correlation of the professionalization of the military officer corps to its relationship, both political and professional, to the civilian community. Most writers accept political scientist Samuel B. Huntington's definition of military professionalism: "expertise [in the management of violence], responsibility, and corporateness." On the other hand, most recent military historians disagree with Huntington's contention that this professionalism occurred in isolation from the rest of the American community. American military officers were not separated from the general trends of society but interacted with them and the rest of the American community. See William B. Skelton, "Professionalization in the U.S. Army Officer Corps during the Age of Jackson," *Armed Forces and Society* (August 1975): 443–71; Timothy K. Nenninger, "The Fort Leavenworth Schools; Post Graduate Military Education and Professionalization in the U.S. Army, 1880–1920," (Ph.D. dissertation, University of Wisconsin, Madison, 1974), 2–3; Timothy K. Nenninger, *The Leavenworth Schools and the Old Army: Education, Professionalism, and the Officer Corps of the United States Army, 1881–1918* (Westport, CT, 1978), 3–20; Samuel B. Huntington, *The Soldier and the State: The Theory and Politics of Civil Military Relations* (Cambridge, MA, 1957), 7–10, 19–54; Abrahamsson, *Military Professionalism*, 12–13, 15–17, 19, 36, 59–60, 69; Millett, *Military*

Professionalism, 2, 4–5, 12–13, 18–22; Allan R. Millett, "Professional Military Education and Marine Officers," *Marine Corps Gazette* (November 1989): 46–56; Morris Janowitz and Roger W. Little, *Sociology and the Military Establishment*, 3d ed. (Beverly Hills, CA, 1974), 123–24, 127, 142; Abrahamson, *America Arms for a New Century*, xiii–xv, 33–36, 40, 48, 147–48, 150; John Gates, "The Alleged Isolation of U.S. Army Officers in the late 19th Century," *Parameters, Journal of the U.S. Army War College* (September 1980): 32–45; John Gates, "The 'New' Military Professionalism," *Armed Forces and Society* (Spring 1985): 427–36; Edward M. Coffman, *The Old Army: A Portrait of the American Army in Peacetime, 1784–1898*, (New York, 1986), 96, 270; Sam C. Sarkesian "Moral and Ethical Foundations of Military Professionalism," in James Brown and Michael J. Collins, eds. *Military Ethics and Professionalism: A Collection of Essays* (Washington, D.C., 1981), 1–22; Sam C. Sarkesian, *Beyond the Battlefield: The New Military Professionalism*, (New York, 1981), ix–xi, 7, 9–13, 42, 254; Ronald Spector, *The Naval War College and the Development of the Naval Profession*, (Newport, RI, 1977) 1–26; and Reardon, "The Study of Military History," 1–5, 11, 15, 40.

Perhaps voicing a somewhat dissident opinion, Russell Weigley in his most recent work suggests that military forces are in large measure autonomous from the rest of society. See Weigley, *The Age of Battles: The Quest for Decisive Warfare from Breitenfeld to Waterloo*, (Bloomington and Indianapolis, 1991) xvi.

This may be the case of the European armies of the seventeenth through the early nineteenth centuries, but I would hold not true of the American military of the late nineteenth century.

14. Allan Millett and Peter Maslowski, *For the Common Defense: A Military History of the United States of America* (New York, 1984), 126–30; Russell F. Weigley, *The American Way of War: A History of United States Military Strategy and Policy* (New York, 1973), 80–81; William H. McNeill, *The Pursuit of Power, Technology, Armed Force, and Society since A.D. 1000* (Chicago, 1982), 216–18; Theodore Ropp, *War in the Modern World*, revised ed. (New York, 1962), 160; Millett, *Military Professionalism*, 15; Correlli Barnett, "The Education of Military Elites," in Walter Laqueur and George L. Mosse, eds., *Education and Social Structure in the Twentieth Century* (New York, 1967), 15–35; Morris Janowitz and Roger W. Little, *Sociology and the Military Establishment*, 3d ed. (Beverly Hills, CA, 1974), 44–47, 59–62. Weigley argues quite convincingly that modern European military officer professionalism saw its origins in the early seventeenth century. See Weigley, *The Age of Battles*, xiii, 5, 540–1.

15. Barnett, "The Education of Military Elites," 16–21; McNeill, *Pursuit of Power*; Ropp, *War in the Modern World*, 155–57; Weigley, *The Age of Battles*, 459–61; Walter Millis, *Arms and Men* (New York, 1958), 137–38. See also Martin Van Crevold, *The Training of Officers, From Military Professionalism to Irrelevance* (New York, 1990), 19–28.

16. Millis, *Arms and Men*, 136–37; Janowitz and Little, *Sociology and the Military*, 59–62; Morris Janowitz, "Appendix, Sociological Notes on the Analysis of Military Elites," in *The Military in the Political Development of New Nations: An Essay in Comparative Analysis* (Chicago, 1964), 107–25; Millett, *Military Professionalism*, 15.

17. Millett and Maslowski, *For the Common Defense*, 126–30; Weigley, *American Way of War*, 80–81; Skelton, "Professionalization in the U.S. Army Officer," 443–71; Huntington, *The Soldier and the State*, 193–221; Coffman, *The Old Army*, 96–102; Upton quote is from Stephen E. Ambrose, *Upton and the Army* (Baton Rouge, LA, 1964), 12.

18. Theodore Ropp, "Rise of American Miliary Forces," in Stephen E. Ambrose, ed., *Institutions in Modern America: Innovation and Structure in Modern America* (Baltimore, MD, 1967), 105; Millett and Maslowski, *For the Common Defense*, 227, 229.

19. Millett and Maslowski, *For the Common Defense*, 249–55; Russell F. Weigley, *History of the U.S. Army* (New York, 1967), 278; Abrahamson, *America Arms for a New Cen-*

tury, 19–20; Peter Karsten, ed., *Soldiers and Society: The Effects of Military Service and War on Americans* (Westport, CT, 1978), 11.

20. Timothy K. Nenninger, *The Leavenworth Schools and the Old Army* (Westport, CT, 1978), passim; Abrahamson, *America Arms for a New Century*, 19–20; Millis, *Arms and Men*, 138–41; Weigley, *American Way of War*, 171; Reardon, "The Study of Military History," 1–5; Stephen E. Ambrose, *Duty, Honor, Country: A History of West Point* (Baltimore, MD, 1966), 209–10.

21. Millett and Maslowski, *For the Common Defense*, 255–56; Adm. D. D. Porter, "Naval Education and Organization," *The United Service* (July 1879): 470–86, 473; Walter R. Herrick, *The American Naval Revolution* (Baton Rouge, LA, 1966), 30–31; Abrahamson, *America Arms for a New Century*, 48.

22. Abrahamson, *America Arms for a New Century*, 33–34; Millis, *Arms and Men*, 138–41; Ambrose, *Upton*, 139; Nenninger, *Fort Leavenworth Schools*, 16–31; Reardon, "The Study of Military History," 10; Millett and Maslowski, *For the Common Defense*, 255–56; Weigley, *History of U.S. Army*, 273–74; Emory Upton to Col. Henry A. Dupont, April 1, 1877, in Peter S. Michie, *The Life and Letters of Emory Upton, Colonel of the Fourth Regiment and Brevet Major General, U.S. Army* (New York, 1885), 418.

23. Lawrence C. Allin, "The United States Naval Institute: Intellectual Forum of the New Navy," (Ph.D. dissertation, University of Maine, 1976), 24, 35–36, and 73; Theodorus B. M. Mason, "The United States Naval Institute," *The United Service* (April 1879): 290–96; Jeffrey Dorwart, *The Office of Naval Intelligence: The Birth of America's First Intelligence Agency* (Annapolis, MD, 1979), 8–9; *Proceedings of the United States Naval Institute* 1 (1874), 1–14.

24. John M. Gates, "The 'New' Military Professionalism," *Armed Forces and Society* (Spring 1985), 427–36, 428–29; Abrahamson, *America Arms for a New Century*, 34–36. The quote is from Weigley, *The American Way of War*, 171.

25. Gates, "The New Military Professionalism," 427–36; Gates, "The Alleged Isolation of U.S. Army Officers," 32–45; Abrahamson, *America Arms for a New Century*, 34–36, 40; Peter Karsten, "Armed Progressives: The Military Reorganized for the American Century," in Jerry Israel, ed., *Building the Organizational Society* (New York, 1962), 197–232; Millett and Maslowski, *For the Common Defense*, 249–55; Millett, *Military Professionalism*, 18–22. The quote is from p. 21.

26. Daniel Beaver, "The American Military and the 'New' Institutional History," 12–14.

27. Huntington, *Soldier and the State*, 163–92; Gates, "New Military Professionalism," 432–33; Leonard D. White, *The Republican Era: A Study in Administrative History 1861–1901* (New York, 1958), 26–27; Ambrose, *Upton*, 135; Millett and Maslowski, *For the Common Defense*, 256–58; Abrahamson, *America Arms for a New Century*, 150. The first quote is from White, and the second is from Abrahamson.

28. Peter Karsten, *The Naval Aristocracy*, 277, 292–93; Beaver, "The American Military," 7. The first quotation is from Karsten while the second is from Beaver; Karsten quotes Elting E. Morison about the Navy being "the paradise . . . for society's response to change."

CHAPTER 2. THE OLD CORPS: A FEW TENTATIVE STEPS, 1865–1880

1. Allan R. Millett, *Semper Fidelis: The History of the U.S. Marine Corps* (New York, 1980), 92; "Register of Officers, U.S. Marine Corps, 1798–1903," in Richard S. Collum, *History of the United States Marine Corps* (New York, 1903), 430–49; Lt. Robert W. Huntington, letter to father, March 20, 1864, Huntington Papers, MCHC; Henry Clay

Cochrane, "A Scrap of Marine Corps History," Folder 101, and Henry Clay Cochrane Journal, 1869–, vol. 55, Cochrane Papers, MCHC.

2. "Examining Board of the Marine Corps," n.p., n.d. (circa 1866), Clipping File, Cochrane Papers, MCHC; CMC letter to Charles G. Petit, February 25, 1874, Letter Book 20, Letters Sent, 506, RG 127, Records of the U.S. Marine Corps, NARA; D. D. Porter letter to Rep. B. F. Butler, February 9, 1870, Box 18, D. D. Porter Papers, Manuscript Division, Library of Congress (LC).

3. Robert T. Huntington, letter to his father, June 22, 1871, Huntington Papers, MCHC.

4. Undated clipping, John W. Forney Papers, LC; SecNav letter to Bvt. Lt. Col. James Forney, July 10, 1872 (copy), attached to Capt. James Forney, letter to SecNav, July 20, 1876, Letters Received Marines, July-December 1876, RG 80, NARA; Forney, "The Marines," 394; Lewis R. Hamersly, *The Records of Living Officers of the U.S. Navy and Marine Corps*, 4th ed. (Philadelphia, 1890), 376; Forney letters to SecNav, June 3, 1873, and September 24, 1873, Marine Corps Letters, 1873, RG 80.

5. Capt. James Forney, USMC, Report on the Marine Corps of Other Nation's Marine Corps, Report and Synopsis, September 15, 1873, Subject File VR, RG 45, Naval Records Collection of the Office of Naval Records and Library, NARA.

Although the report is dated September 15, 1873, correspondence between Forney and the Secretary of the Navy indicates that Forney was still working on the report in late September and early October 1873. See Forney letter to SecNav, September 24, 1873, Marine Corps Letters, 1873, RG 80, and SecNav letter to Capt. James Forney, October 11, 1873, "N," Letters Received, RG 127, NARA.

6. Forney Report, September 1873, RG 45, NARA.

7. Ibid.

8. Ibid.; *Army and Navy Journal*, October 18, 1873, 150, 152–53; Secretary of the Navy, *Annual Report, 1873*.

9. *Army and Navy Journal*, November 28, 1874, 247, and December 12, 1874, 281; Record of Minutes and Resolutions of Marine Officer Meeting, December 4, 1874, Unorganized Collection, Field/McCawley Papers, MCHC.

10. Marine Officer Meeting, December 4, 1874, Field/McCawley Collection, MCHC; *Information in Regard to the United States Marine Corps* (Washington, 1875), 30–31, and passim.

Although the pamphlet lists no group or individual responsible for its publication, it can be assumed that the Marine officer association had some involvement with its reissuance because it was one of the recommendations made at the association's December meeting.

11. Capt. Richard S. Collum Notebook, January 6, 1873, in Notebook Folder, Wood Family Papers, LC; Collum letter to Cochrane, February 25, 1875, and October 14, 1877, Folders 19 and 22, Cochrane Papers, MCHC; M. Almy Aldrich, *History of the United States Marine Corps* (Boston, MA, 1875), passim; Collum, *History of the U.S. Marine Corps*, 5.

12. Aldrich, *History of USMC*, passim; Collum, *History of the U.S. Marine Corps*, 5.

13. Aldrich, *History of USMC*, 15–18, 21–30; *Army and Navy Journal* March 6, 1875, 472–73.

14. Henry Clay Cochrane, *A Resuscitation or a Funeral*, October 1, 1875, Cochrane Papers, MCHC.

15. Ibid.

16. *Army and Navy Journal*, September 4, 1875, 55, and September 11, 1875, 73; clipping from *Washington Chronicle*, November 9, 1875, Scrapbook, 71, Cochrane Papers, MCHC.

17. Cochrane Diary, entry for August 25, 1876, Cochrane Papers, MCHC; CMC, *Annual Report, 1876,* October 25, 1876, in SecNav, *Annual Report, 1876,* 283–84.

18. Robert Huntington letter to father, October 21, 1870, and February 25, 1877, Huntington Papers, MCHC; William H. Russell, "The Genesis of Fleet Marine Force Doctrine: 1879–1899," pt. 1, *Marine Corps Gazette,* April 1951, 52–59; Millett, *Semper Fidelis,* 108–9; "Changes in the Marine Corps, which suggested themselves to father before he became Col. Comd't," presented to HQMC, Oct. 17, 1921 (Charles L. McCawley Papers, Personal Papers Collection, MCHC).

The original list is not extant. On the copy, Maj. Gen. Charles L. McCawley, USMC, the son of the commandant, wrote: "The above memorandum in his own hand writing, was written by my father the late Col. Comd't. C. G. McCawley before his appointment as comd't, probably in 1875 or 1876."

19. CMC letters to SecNav, March 28 and April 30, 1877, Letters Sent, vol. 23, 392–93, 443, RG 127; SecNav letter to 2d Lt. J. C. Shailer, Letters Sent, Marine, vol. 9, RG 80; CMC letters to SecNav, May 8 and 12, 1877, Letters Sent, vol. 23, 459, RG 127; CMC letter to SecNav, May 4 and 12, 1877, and 1st Lt. E. T. Bradford letter to SecNav, 15 May 1877, Letters Received, Marine, 1876–77 Supplement, RG 80; Capt. James Forney letter to CMC, June 25, 1877, Letters Received, Historical Branch, RG 127; 2d Lt. Andrew Stevenson letter to SecNav, August 20, 1877, Letters Received, Marine, 1876–77 Supplement, RG 80; 1st Lt. R. S. Collum letter to 1st Lt. H. C. Cochrane, August 14, 1877, Folder 22, Cochrane Papers, MCHC; *Army and Navy Journal,* November 24, 1877, 247.

20. Senator McPherson letter to SecNav Thompson, April 17, 1877, PC 50, Folder 7, Broome Papers, MCHC, and Col. M. R. Kintzing letter to SecNav, April 20, 1877, with endorsement by Navy Department, Letters Received, Marine, 1876–77 Supplement, RG 80, NARA.

21. Allan R. Millett, *The American Political System and Civilian Control of the Military: A Historical Perspective* (Columbus, OH, 1979), 14–15; George C. Remey letter to wife, March 11, 1877, in "Life and Times of George C. Remey," MS, vol. 4, pt. 1, 286, Remey Family Papers, LC; D. D. Porter letter to President, March 9, 1877, Letter Book 1869–84, 647–49, D. D. Porter Papers, LC; *Army and Navy Journal,* March 24, 1877, 526; Maj. Green Clay Goodloe letter to SecNav Thompson, March 22, 1877, Letters Received, Marines, 1876–77 Supplement, RG 80, NARA; Maj. Green Clay Goodloe letter to Lewis Hamersly, n.d., L. R. Hamersly Letters, Officers, U.S. Navy Volume, Hamersly Collection, New York Historical Society.

22. Jerry M. Cooper, *The Army and Civil Disorder: Federal Military Intervention in Labor Disputes, 1877–1900* (Westport, CT, 1980), 43–83.

23. Ibid., 237–60; Abrahamson, *America Arms for a New Century,* 30–31; Capt. Richard S. Collum, letter to H. C. Cochrane, October 14, 1877, Folder 22, Cochrane Papers, MCHC; Karsten, *The Naval Aristocracy,* 10–11; Stephen E. Ambrose, "The Armed Forces and Civil Disorder," in Stephen E. Ambrose and James A. Barber, eds., *The Military and American Society, Essays and Readings* (New York, 1972), 241–48.

Allan Millett points out the difference between the rhetoric and the actual use of the military in labor disputes. From 1877 until 1903 there were about 50,000 strikes in the United States, and the Regular Army was only used in three of them. See Millett, *Civilian Control of the Military,* 18.

24. SecNav letter to CMC, August 17, 1877, Letters Received, "N," RG 127, NARA; USMC General Order No. 1, August 21, 1877, in Navy and Marine Corps Orders, 1877–1903, Library, MCHC; CMC, "Annual Report," November 16, 1877, in SecNav, *Annual Report, 1877.*

25. H. C. Cochrane, "The Naval Brigade and the Marine Battalions in the Labor Strikes of 1877," *The United Service,* pt. 1, (Jan. 1879), 115–29, pt. 2, (October 1879),

617–23; Maj. James Forney, "The Marines," *The United Service* (April 1889): 393–401; Richard S. Collum, *The History of the U.S. Marine Corps*, revised ed. (New York, 1903), 216–32; Capt. James Forney Report to CMC, September 1, 1877 (copy), encl. to Forney letter to SecNav, September 6, 1877, Letters Received, 1877, Marines, RG 80.

26. Richard S. Collum letter to H. C. Cochrane, October 14, 1877, Folder 22, Cochrane Papers, MCHC; 2d Lt. Frank Scott letter to SecNav, April 10, 1876, Letters Received, Marines, January-June 1876, RG 80.

27. CMC letter to 2d Lt. J. C. Shailer, April 9, 1875, Letters Sent, Letter Book 21, and HQ Arty School Special Order No. 54, May 1, 1876, Letters Received, "H," 1876, RG 127, NARA; Maj. A. S. Nicholson letter to 1st Lt. D. P. Mannix, May 2, 1876, Mannix Scrapbook, MCHC; Military Record of Daniel Pratt Mannix and unsigned letter January 9, 1965, giving genealogy of Mannix family, Mannix Papers, MCHC; D. Pratt Mannix letter to Louis R. Hamersly, February 24, 1878, Hamersly Collection, New York Historical Society; Clipping, "Commencement at Artillery School," *Army and Navy Journal*, April 27, 1878, Mannix Scrapbook, MCHC; SecNav letter to CMC, March 23, 1878, Letters Sent, Marines, vol. 10, p. 99, and 1st Lt. W. S. Muse letter to SecNav, February 24, 1880, Letters Received, Marine, RG 80, NARA. Quote is from *Army and Navy Journal* clipping.

28. Maj. Aug S. Nicholson letters to Mannix, May 7, and October 3, 1878, Mannix Scrapbook, MCHC; Forney letter to CMC, April 19, 1879, Letters Received, Marines, RG 80, and SecNav letter to CMC, April 26, 1879, Letters Received, "N," 1879, RG 127, NARA; George Remey, letter to Wife, June 16, 1878, in "Life and Letters of George Remey," vol. 4, pt. 2, 450, LC. Quote is from Remey letter to his wife.

29. CMC, *Annual Reports*, 1876–1880; CMC letter to 1st Lt. F. H. Harrington, October 16, 1879, Letters Sent, Letter Book 25, 232, RG 127, and CMC endorsement, May 8, 1880, on 1st Lt. F. H. Harrington letter to SecNav, March 7, 1880, Letters Received, Marines, RG 80, NARA.

30. Capt. Homer A. Walkup, JAGC, USN, "A Summary History of the Office of the Judge Advocate General of the Navy," Judge Advocate General Anniversary Ball Souvenir Program (1980), 8–9, Remey Biographical File, MCHC; Charles Mason Remey, "The Remey Family of the United States of America, 1654–1957," typescript, 1957 (copy in Library of Congress), 55–79; Clippings, n.p., n.d., in C. M. Remey, "Life and Letters of Adm. George C. Remey," vol. 8; D. D. Porter draft of letter to P. Whyte, February 5, 1880, D. D. Porter Papers, Box 19, LC.

31. Capt. C. D. Hebb letter to SecNav and SecNav endorsement, September 13, 1873, and SecNav letter to Remey, November 28, 1873, Marine Officer Letter Supplement, 1870–75, RG 80, NARA; George C. Remey letters to wife, May 1874 and October 4, 1875, copies in "Life and Letters of Rear Adm. George C. Remey," vol. 3, pts. 1 and 2, Remey Family Papers, LC; Walkup, "Summary History of . . . Judge Advocate General," 8–9.

32. Walkup, "Summary History" pp. 6–9; SecNav letter to Capt. William B. Remey, February 12, 1879, Letters Received, "N," RG 127, NARA; 46th Congress, 2d Session, *Congressional Record*, House and Senate, January, February, June, 1880, 338, 962, 4102, 4133–34; Porter letter to Whyte, February 5, 1880, Porter Papers; SecNav letter to Col. William B. Remey, June 12, 1880, Letters Sent, Marine, vol. 10, RG 80, NARA.

33. Charles Mason Remey, "Reminiscence of Colonel William Butler Remey United States Marine Corps and Lieutenant Commander Edward Wallace Remey, United States Navy," typescript, 1955 (copy in Library of Congress), 14–15, 19–24; Clippings, n.p., n.d., in C. M. Remey, ed., "Life and Letters of RAdm. George C. Remey," vol. 8, Remey Family Papers, LC.

34. H. C. Cochrane entry for March 9, 1878, Cochrane Diary, 1878, Cochrane Pa-

pers, MCHC. The diaries for 1878–1879 provide an excellent record of the daily routine of a Marine officer during this period.

35. Louis E. Fagan letter to Cochrane, September 11, 1877, Cochrane Papers, MCHC; Capt. Henry J. Bishop letter to SecNav, January 21, 1878, and Capt. P. C. Pope letter to Rear Adm. G. H. Scott, Letters Received, 1878, Marine, RG 80, NARA.

36. Karsten, *Naval Aristocracy*, 106–7; Capt. McLane Tilton letter to Nannie, November 30, 1877, Folder 4, Tilton Papers, PC 122, McLane Tilton Papers, MCHC.

37. Tilton letter to Nannie, November 29, 1877, Tilton Papers.

38. Entry for April 17, 1879, Cochrane Diary, 1879; Cochrane letter to sister, April 19, 1879, Folder No. 24; Lt. William Zeilin letter to Cochrane, October 3, 1877, and A. W. Owen letter to Cochrane, October 29, 1877, Folder 22, Cochrane Papers, MCHC; H. Wayne Morgan, *William McKinley and His America* (Syracuse, NY, 1963), 81–82.

39. CMC letter to SecNav, September 6, 1879, Letters Sent, Letter Book 25, p. 197, RG 127; CMC letter to SecNav, June 26, 1878, Letters Received, Marine 1878, RG 80, NARA. For examples of letters showing attempts to circumvent assignments, see Charles Foster letter to SecNav, October 25, 1878, Letters Received, Marine, 1878, RG 80; CMC letter to SecNav, November 1, 1878, Letters Sent, Letter Book 24, p. 469, RG 127; CMC letter to SecNav, December 12, 1877, Letters Received, Marine, 1876–77 Supplement, RG 80, NARA.

40. CMC letter to Maj. J. S. Broome, March 21, 1878, Letters Sent, Letter Book 24, p. 269, RG 127. For examples of letters relating to retirements, court-martials, and resignations, see CMC letter to SecNav, November 19, 1877, Letters Received, Marines, 1876–77 Supplement, RG 80; CMC letter to SecNav, February 11, 1878, Letters Sent, Letter Book 24, RG 127, p. 232; 1st Lt. James Breese, letter to CMC, August 16, 1879, Letters Received, Marines 1879, RG 80; and SecNav letter to Mr. Andrews, April 25, 1879, Letters Sent, vol. 10, Marines, RG 80.

41. SecNav letter to new second lieutenants, June 16, 1880, Letters Sent, Marine, vol. 10, RG 80, NARA; *Navy and Marine Corps Register, 1880*; *Military Academy Register, 1876*; George Denny Scrapbook (Rare Book Collection, Marine Corps Library, MCHC); Clipping, "Career of Maj Waller," n.p., n.d., Entry 46, Clipping Book 2, RG 127, NARA.

42. Entry December 31, 1880, Cochrane Diary, Cochrane Papers, MCHC; CMC letter to Capt. W. A. T. Maddox, January 3, 1880, Letters Received, Marine, RG 80, NARA; Capt. Woodhull S. Schenck letter to SecNav, March 10, 1880, Letters Received, Marine, RG 80, NARA; *New York Times*, March 3, 1880, 1; *Army and Navy Journal*, March 13, 1880, 646–47; Commandant of the Marine Corps, *Annual Report, 1880*, 529.

CHAPTER 3. NEW DIRECTIONS AND OLD BATTLES, 1880–1885

1. Robert L. Meade, ZB File, Operational Archives Branch, Naval Historical Division; C. M. Remey, ed., "Life and Letters of RAdm George C. Remey," ch. 5, p. 111, Remey Family Papers, LC; E. Digby Baltzell, *Philadelphia Gentlemen: The Making of a National Upper Class* (Glencoe, IL, 1958), 145; SecNav letter to CMC, October 29, 1879, Letters Sent, Marine, vol. 10, p. 346, RG 80, NARA; CMC letter to SecNav, November 6, 1879, Letter Book, Letters Sent, vol. 25, RG 127, NARA.

2. Lt. Col. J. L. Broome letter to Cmdre. John H. Upshur, April 17, 1882, Letters Received, Historical Division, January-June 1882, RG 127; JAG letters to CMC, July 26, 1882, Letters Received "N," RG 127; SecNav letter to Capt. R. L. Meade, April 18, 1884, Letters Received "N," RG 127, NARA.

3. "Our Social Marines," clipping from the *Philadelphia Times*, January 7, 1882, Ma-

rine Corps Scrapbook, 1880–1898, RG 127, NARA. See also "Our Social Marines," clipping from the *Washington Republican*, January 9, 1882, Thomas N. Wood Papers, LC.

4. Benjamin F. Cooling, *Benjamin Franklin Tracy: Father of the Modern American Navy* (Hamden, CT, 1973), 60–61; Daniel H. Wicks, "New Navy and New Empire: The Life and Times of John Grimes Walker" (Ph.D. dissertation, University of California, Berkeley, 1979) 1, 111–12; James L. Abrahamson, *America Arms for a New Century: The Making of a Great Military Power* (New York, 1981), 61–62; Peter Karsten, "Armed Progressives: The Military Reorganized for the American Century," in Jerry Israel, ed., *Building the Organizational Society* (New York, 1972) 197–232, 207–9; Robert Seager II, "Ten Years before Mahan: The Unofficial Case for the New Navy, 1880–90," *The Mississippi Valley Historical Review* (June 1953): 491–512, 503–5; Thomas H. Coode, "Southern Congressmen and the American Naval Revolution, 1880–98," *Alabama Historical Quarterly* (Fall and Winter 1968): 89–110; Milton Plesur, *America's Outward Thrust: Approaches to Foreign Affairs, 1865–1890* (DeKalb, IL, 1971), 89; Peter Karsten, *The Naval Aristocracy: The Golden Age of Annapolis and the Emergence of Modern American Navalism* (New York, 1972), 354; Harold and Margaret Sprout, *The Rise of American Naval Power, 1776–1918* (Princeton, NJ, 1946), 183–84.

5. Charles O. Paullin, *Paullin's History of Naval Administration, 1775–1911*, (Annapolis, 1968), 390–91; Wicks, "New Navy," 9; Sprout and Sprout, *The Rise of American Naval Power*, 183–84.

6. Secretary of the Navy, *Annual Report, 1883*, 8–9.

7. A&I to 1st Lt. D. P. Mannix, October 17, 1878, Mannix Scrapbook, MCHC; *Army and Navy Journal*, October 12, 1878, p. 150, and December 14, 1878, p. 306; Journal, *Ticonderoga*, World Cruise, vol. 3, Shufeldt Papers, LC; Shufeldt letter to "Moll," January 9, 1880, General Correspondence, Shufeldt Papers; Mannix memo to Shufeldt, July 29, 1880, Korea Correspondence, 1880–81, Subject Files, Shufeldt letter to Moll, September 9, 1880, General Correspondence, Shufeldt letter to James B. Angell, August 30, 1880, Letter Press Book 2, pp. 214–16; Shufeldt letter to SecNav, August 30, 1880, Korea Correspondence, all in Shufeldt Papers. See also Shufeldt letter to Li Hung-chang, September 2, 1880 (copy), Mannix Scrapbook, MCHC. See also Frederick C. Drake, *The Empire of the Seas: A Biography of Rear Admiral Robert Wilson Shufeldt, USN* (Honolulu, HI, 1984), chs. 10 and 11, and pp. 238–45.

8. Li Hung-chang letter to Shufeldt, September 21, 1880, Shufeldt Papers and Li Hung-chang letter to Mannix, September 21, 1880, Mannix Scrapbook, MCHC.

9. Yung Wing, Chinese Legation letter to Secretary of State, February 23, 1881 (copy), and CMC endorsement, March 2, 1881 (copy), both in Mannix Scrapbook; SecNav letter to Lt. D. Pratt Mannix, March 2, 1881, (copy), encl., SecNav letter to CMC, March 2, 1881, Letters Received, "N," RG 127.

10. Charles L. Fisher letter to Shufeldt, March 3, 1881, Korea Correspondence, Shufeldt papers.

11. St. Louis and San Francisco newspaper clippings, n.d., (ca. Mar.-Apr. 1881), Mannix Scrapbook.

12. Secretary of State James Blaine letter to Cmdre. Robert W. Shufeldt, May 9, 1881, China Correspondence, Shufeldt Papers; Drake, *The Empire of the Seas*, 260–61, 355–62.

13. *The North China Herald and Supreme Court and Consular Gazette*, May 20, 1881, p. 473; Rear Adm. Daniel Pratt Mannix, Jr., "Hewers of Wood," MS, n.d., ch. 1, p. 10, Mannix Papers, MCHC; D. Pratt Mannix letter to SecNav William H. Hunt, November 15, 1881, Letters Received, Marine, 1881, RG 80, NARA; Translation of Agreement between Lin Taotsi and D. P. Mannix, June 28, 1880, Mannix Scrapbook.

14. Mannix letter to Hunt, November 15, 1881; *North China Herald and Supreme Court and Consular Gazette*, August 26, 1881, p. 215; Clipping from *Shanghai Daily News*, n.d., Mannix Scrapbook. From 1872 to 1875, Chinese students were sent to the United

States to be educated in American schools. In 1881, fearing that these students would be corrupted by Western values, the Chinese government brought them back early. See Cyrus H. Peake, *Nationalism and Education in Modern China* (New York, 1932), 9.

It was from this group that Mannix made his selection for his advanced group. Although not entirely confirmed by the evidence, Mannix apparently conducted classes both at the School of Application at Taku and the Naval School at the Tientsin Arsenal.

15. Mannix letter to Hunt, November 15, 1881, with endorsements by CMC and SecNav, January 17, 1882, Letters Received, Marines, 1881, RG 80.

16. Table Showing the Course of Instruction for Students in Torpedoes and Coast Defense, n.d., encl. to 1st Lt. D. Pratt Mannix letter to CMC, November 15, 1882, Letters Received "M," RG 127, NARA.

17. *The North China Herald and Supreme Court and Consular Gazette*, November 29, 1882, 590.

18. First Lt. D. Pratt Mannix letter to SecNav, November 15, 1882, encl. to Mannix letter to CMC, November 15, 1882, Letters Received, "M," RG 127, NARA; Extract of report of Capt. R. M. Lang to Li Hung-chang, n.d., [Nov. 1882], Mannix Scrapbook.

19. First Lt. D. Pratt Mannix letter to SecNav, November 15, 1882, with endorsement, CMC letter to SecNav, January 15, 1883, and SecNav letter to CMC, January 21, 1883, encl. to 1st Lt. Mannix letter to CMC, November 15, 1882, Letters Received "M," RG 127.

20. Rear Adm. Daniel Pratt Mannix, Jr., "Hewers of Wood," MS, n.d., ch. 1, pp. 1, 10-11, Daniel Pratt Mannix Papers, MCHC.

21. First Lt. D. Pratt Mannix letter to SecNav, November 15, 1883, with CMC endorsement, January 9, 1884, and SecNav endorsement, January 10, 1884, Letters Received, Marine, 1883, RG 80, NARA; Lo, Superintendent of Taku Forts letter to D. P. Mannix, April 15, 1884, Mannix Scrapbook; Mannix letter to CMC, May 20, 1884, Letters Received, "M," RG 127, and Mannix letter to SecNav, May 20, 1884, Letters Received, Marine, RG 80, NARA.

22. Agreement between Gen. Lo, Superintendent of Taku Forts, and D. Pratt Mannix, May 26, 1884, Mannix Scrapbook.

23. Mannix, "Hewers of Wood," ch. 1, p. 16; CMC letter to SecNav, August 24, 1884, Letters Sent to the Secretary of the Navy, RG 127, NARA (hereafter referred to as LSSN), vol. 1, p. 67.

24. J. Russell Young letter to Lt. Mannix, November 11, 1884, Mannix Scrapbook; 1st Lt. D. Pratt Mannix letter to John Russell Young, November 17, 1884, Letters from Presidential and Executive Officers, NARA microfilm, M-517, Roll 49; Cyrus H. Peake, *Nationalism and Education in Modern China* (New York, 1932), 10.

25. Young letter to Mannix, November 11, 1884; SecNav letter to 1st Lt. D. Pratt Mannix, January 2, 1885, Letters Sent, Marine, vol. 11, p. 327, RG 80, NARA; Li Hung-chang letter to Mannix, April 22, 1885, and clipping from *Congressional Record*, June 9, 1886, Mannix Scrapbook.

26. Cmdre. Robert W. Shufeldt, "The Chinese Navy," Proposition submitted by request to H. E. the Viceroy, n.d., Korean Treaty Folders, 1881-1882, Shufeldt Papers.

27. Karsten, *Naval Aristocracy*, 277-317; Abrahamson, *America Arms for a New Century*, 22, 48-54, 61-62; John A. S. Grenville and George B. Young, *Politics, Strategy, and American Diplomacy: Studies in American Foreign Policy* (New Haven, CT, 1966), 5-6, 37-38; Wicks, "New Navy," 10-12, 162-68, 190-91, 206; Charles S. Campbell, *The Transformation of American Foreign Relations, 1865-1900* (New York, 1977), 72-73, 76-82, 86-87, 158-59; Kenneth J. Hagan, *American Gunboat Diplomacy* (Westport, CT, 1973), 7-10; Sprout and Sprout, *The Rise of American Naval Power, 1776-1918*, 184-85; Seager II, "Ten Years before Mahan," 491-512; Plesur, *America's Outward Thrust*, 198-236; SecNav, *Annual Report, 1883*, 8-9.

28. William H. Russell, "Genesis of FMFPac Doctrine," pt. 1, *Marine Corps Gazette*, April 1951, p. 56; CMC letters to Col. J. H. Jones, May 31, 1879, and June 12, 1879, Letters Sent, vol. 25, pp. 101 and 113–14, RG 127; Navy Department, General Order 273, August 23, 1881, Navy Department General Orders, 1863–87, p. 200, RG 80, NARA.

29. C. D. Hebb letter to CMC and CMC letter to Hebb, August 9, 1882, Letters Received, "H," RG 127; CMC letters to SecNav and to C. D. Hebb, December 5, 1882, Letters Sent, vol. 27, pp. 296–97, RG 127, NARA.

30. Brig. Gen. Jacob Zeilin letter to SecNav, October 28, 1873, Letters Received, Marines, RG 80, and C. G. McCawley letter to Naval Solicitor, John A. Bolles, August 2, 1877, Letters Received, Historical Division, RG 127, NARA.

31. Marine Corps Circular Order, August 4, 1877, and Marine Corps General Order, December 29, 1877, *Navy and Marine Corps General Orders, 1877–1903*, Rare Book Collection, MCHC; Navy Department General Order 237, March 12, 1878, Navy Department General Orders, 1863–1887, RG 80, NARA; Marine Corps Order, December 10, 1878, Letters Received Historical Division, 1878, RG 127; CMC letter to Commanding Officers, June 22, 1880, Letters Sent, vol. 25, p. 536, RG 127. For Marine Corps desertion figures, see Maj. George P. Houston letter to CMC, May 30, 1882, Letters Received "H," 1882, RG 127 and Memo, n.d., copies of Letters Now on File recommending sale of Malt Liquors, Letters Received Historical Division, 1878, RG 127.

32. Maj. Nicholson letter to CMC, February 7, 1882, Lt. Col. C. D. Hebb letter to CMC, April 18, 1881, and Lt. Col. J. L. Broome letter to CMC, October 8, 1881, Letters Received, Historical Division, 1881–July 1882, RG 127, NARA.

33. CMC letter to SecNav, February 15, 1882, Letters Sent, vol. 27, p. 16, RG 127, and SecNav letter to CMC, February 15, 1882, Letters Received, "N," 1882, RG 127, NARA.

34. Lt. Col. C. D. Hebb letter to Cmdre. O. C. Badger, November 20, 1882, Letters Received, Historical Division, July-December 1882; CMC letter to SecNav, November 27, 1882, Letters Sent, vol. 27, pp. 288–89; and SecNav letter to CMC, March 16, 1883, Letters Received, "N," 1883, RG 127, NARA.

35. Jack D. Foner, *The United States Soldier between Two Wars, 1865–1898* (New York, 1970), 223; Peter Karsten, *Soldiers and Society: The Effects of Military Service and War on Americans* (Westport, CT, 1978), 29; Capt. James Forney letter to CMC, November 29, 1880, Letters Received "F," RG 127, NARA.

36. CMC letter to Maj. J. S. Broome, December 23, 1878, Letters Sent, vol. 24, p. 526, RG 127; CMC letter to SecNav, September 6, 1879, Letters Received, Marine, 1879, RG 80; Forney letter, November 29, 1880; Capt. James Forney letter to CMC, October 7, 1881, Letters Received "F," RG 127; Millett, *Semper Fidelis*, 103.

37. CMC letter to Maj. George Butler, September 14, 1881, Letters Received, Historical Division, July-December 1881, RG 127, NARA.

38. CMC, "Annual Report," October 1878 in SecNav, *Annual Report, 1878*, 283; *Army and Navy Journal*, April 30, June 11, and June 18, 1881, pp. 817, 938, and 968; Col. William B. Remey letter to SecNav, March 6, 1882, and Capt. James Forney letter to Senator J. D. Cameron, July 2, 1882, Letters Received, Historical Division, RG 127, NARA.

39. Henry Clay Cochrane, draft of letter to Col. Comdt. Heywood, December 30, 1893, Folder 41, Cochrane Papers, MCHC; 46th Congress, 3d Session, *Congressional Record*, House and Senate, December 1880–February 1881, pp. 11, 16, 257, 710, 904; *Army and Navy Journal*, op. cit.; Senate, Naval Affairs Committee, *Appointments and Promotions in the Marine Corps*, 46th Congress, 3d Session, Senate Report 762, January 1881.

40. Entry for January 14, 1881, Cochrane Diary, Cochrane Papers, MCHC; U.S. Congress, Senate, Naval Affairs Committee, *Appointments and Promotions*; U.S. Congress, House, Committee on Naval Affairs, *Appointments and Promotions in the Marine Corps*, 46th Congress, 3d Session, House Report 314, February, 1881.

41. 47th Congress, 1st Session, *Congressional Record*, House and Senate, December 1881–January 1882, pp. 3, 166, and 398; U.S. Congress, Senate, Naval Affairs Committee, *Appointments and Promotions in the Marine Corps*, 47th Congress, 1st Session, Senate Report 15, December 1881; *Army and Navy Journal*, December 24, 1881, 450; CMC letter to SecNav, May 9, 1882, Letters Sent, vol. 27, pp. 104–5, RG 127, NARA; *Army and Navy Journal*, May 20, 1882, 966; Capt. H. C. Cochrane letter to CMC, August 16, 1882, Letters Received, Historical Section, RG 127, NARA.

42. *Congressional Record*, House, 47th Congress, 1st Session, March 13, 1882, p. 1838, and Senate, July 26, 1882, p. 6501.

43. Paullin, *Naval Administration*, 336–77, 387; Robert G. Albion, *Makers of Naval Policy, 1798–1947*, Rowena Reed, ed. (Annapolis, 1980), 113; Sprout and Sprout, *The Rise of American Naval Power*, 378–79; Robert Seager II, "Ten Years Before Mahan," 491–92; Thomas H. Coode, "Southern Congressmen and the American Naval Revolution, 1880–98," 89–110; Karsten, *Naval Aristocracy*, 380.

44. Wicks, "New Navy and New Empire," 3–5, 22–25, 41–45, 66–78, 479–80; Albion, *Makers of Naval Policy*, 72; Jeffrey Dorwart, *The Office of Naval Intelligence: The Birth of America's First Intelligence Agency* (Annapolis, MD, 1979), 12.

45. Wicks, "New Navy," 36–37; Walter Millis, *Arms and Men* (New York, 1958), 145–46; Walter R. Herrick, *The American Naval Revolution* (Baton Rouge, LA, 1966), 20–23; Karsten, *Naval Aristocracy*, 279.

46. Secretary of the Navy, *Annual Report, 1881*, 3–6; Report of the Advisory Board, November 7, 1881, in Secretary of the Navy, *Annual Report, 1881*; Cooling, *Tracy*, 53–54; Walter R. Herrick, *The American Naval Revolution* (Baton Rouge, LA, 1966), 25–28; Paullin, *Naval Administration*, 390–99; Albion, *Makers of Naval Policy*, 74–77, 206; Hagan, *Gunboat Diplomacy*, 39–41.

47. Paullin, *Naval Administration*, 418–19, Karsten, *Naval Aristocracy*, 285–86, 289; *Congressional Record*, Senate, 47th Congress, 1st Session, July 26, 1882, p. 6501; *U.S. Statutes at Large*, 47th Congress, 1881–1883, vol. 22, ch. 391; Karsten, "The Armed Progressives," 199–201.

48. Karsten, "Armed Progressives," 199–201; Lt. Cmdr. Allan D. Brown, "Naval Education," *U.S. Naval Institute Proceedings*, 1879, pp. 305–21; Lt. Cdr. C. F. Goodrich, "Naval Education," *U.S. Naval Institute Proceedings*, 1879, pp. 323–44; Capt. W. T. Truxton, "Reform in the Navy," *United Service* (July 1879): pp. 378–82; Bowman H. McCalla, "Memoirs of a Naval Career," MS, Navy Library, Naval Historical Center, ch. 12, pp. 15–16; *U.S. Statutes at Large*, 47th Congress, 1881–1883, vol. 22, ch. 391.

49. James Forney, "The Marines," *United Service*, April 1889, pp. 393–401; "Editorial Notes," *United Service*, August 1882, p. 225; Mdmn. John Hood letter to CMC, September 29, 1881, Letters Received, "H," Cadet Engr. Jno. L. Worthington letter to CMC, May 1, 1881, Letters Received, Historical Section, CMC letter to Cadet Mdmn. Henry W. Finley, November 15, 1880, Letters Sent, vol. 26, pp. 104–5, and Cadet Mdmn. Francis R. Wall letter to CMC, October 11, 1882, Letters Received, Historical Section, RG 127, NARA; *Navy and Marine Registers*, 1883–1898.

50. CMC letter to SecNav, September 1, 1882, Letters Sent, vol. 27, pp. 206–7, RG 127, NARA; SecNav, *Annual Report, 1882*, 24–25; CMC letter to SecNav, February 3, 1883, Letters Received, Marines, 1881, letter misfiled, RG 80, NARA; Exchange of letters between Senator Eugene Hale and SecNav, February 12, 1883 (copies), provided to CMC for his information, Letters Received "N," RG 127, NARA.

51. *Congressional Record*, Senate, 47th Congress, 2d Session, February 23, 1883, pp. 3153–54; SecNav, *Annual Report, 1883*, p. 29.

52. F. M. Ramsay letters to Chandler, October 19, 1882, January 31, 1883, and February 2, 1883, vol. 59, William E. Chandler Papers, LC; Peter Karsten, *The Naval Aristocracy, The Golden Age of Annapolis and the Emergence of Modern American Navalism* (New

York, 1972), 5-6; Merrill Bartlett, "Cadet Midshipman Barnett," MS, 13 and 20; Jack Sweetman, *The U.S. Naval Academy: An Illustrated History* (Annapolis, MD, 1979), 117; SecNav, *Annual Report, 1883*, p. 29.

53. J. G. Walker, Ch BuNav letters to CMC, July 2, 1883, and October 15, 1883, Letters Received, "N," RG 127, NARA; *Navy and Marine Registers, 1883-84*; F. M. Ramsay letter to Chandler, July 2, 1883, vol. 62, Chandler Papers, LC.

54. CMC letter to 2d Lt. F. J. Moses, July 6, 1883 (identical letters to other members of the class), Letters Received, Marine, 1883, RG 80, NARA; George Barnett, "Soldier and Sailor Too," MS, ch. 5., pp. 7-8, Barnett Papers, MCHC; Heywood letter to CMC, October 12, 1883, Letters Received, "H," RG 127, NARA; CMC, "Annual Report," in SecNav *Annual Report, 1883*, 366.

55. CMC letter to SecNav, May 22, 1884, LSSN, vol. 1, p. 36, RG 127, NARA; SecNav, *Annual Report, 1884*, 37; and *Navy and Marine Register, 1884.*

56. U.S. Congress, House, 47th Cong., 1st Sess., June 29, 1882, *Congressional Record*, 5522-26; *Army and Navy Journal*, April 14, 1883, p. 841; United States Naval Academy, Candidates for Admission, 1876-84, RG 405, Records of the U.S. Naval Academy, NARA; "Obituary, Francis Eskridge Sutton," in USNA, Class of 1881, *Report of 1891* (copy in U.S. Naval Academy Library); F. B. Simkins, "Moses, Franklin J.," *Dictionary of American Biography*, ed. Dumas Malone, vol. 7 (New York, 1934), 275-76.

57. *Navy and Marine Registers*, 1883-1884; United States Naval Academy, Candidates for Admission, 1876-84, RG 405, Records of the U.S. Naval Academy, NARA.

58. In Karsten's sample of 1,560 Naval Academy candidates between 1847 and 1900, the largest percentage of appointments (18 percent) came from the sons of merchants, followed by sons of attorneys and judges (12 percent) and then by sons of officers and farmers (10.3 and 10.0, respectively). The representation from the other occupational categories were as follows: sons of doctors, druggists, and engineers, 9.6 percent; sons of government officials, 7.9 percent; sons of manufacturers, 7.3 percent; sons of shopkeepers, agents, and hotel keepers, 7.1 percent; sons of artisans and clerks, 6.5 percent; sons of bankers, 5.5 percent; and sons of clergymen, educators, and artists, 5.1 percent. Karsten, *Naval Aristocracy*, 9; quotation from *Army and Navy Journal*, April 14, 1883, p. 841.

Interestingly enough, Edward M. Coffman in a similar study of the Military Academy found less than 31 percent of the West Point cadets to come from the highest strata of society as compared to more than half for the Naval Academy. Although admitting that all such analyses are at best tentative, Coffman convincingly makes the point that the American Army officer corps was more representative of American society than Karsten's sample of Naval Academy candidates. Edward M. Coffman, *The Old Army: A Portrait of the American Army in Peacetime, 1784-1898*, (New York, 1986), p. 222.

59. James G. Courts, Clerk, Committee of Appropriations letter to SecNav, January 15, 1884 (copy), encl. to SecNav letter to CMC, January 16, 1884, Letters Received "N," RG 127; CMC letters to SecNav, January 17, 1884, and February 11, 1884, Letters Sent, vol. 28, pp. 44-45, and p. 71, RG 127, NARA; *Congressional Record*, 48th Congress, 1st Session, House, February 12, 1884, and March 6, 1884, pp. 1072 and 1666.

60. CMC letter to SecNav, March 11, 1884, with inclusive memoranda, Letters Received, Marine, 1884, RG 80; *Congressional Record*, 48th Congress, 1st Session, Senate, April 14, 1884, p. 2924.

61. SecNav letter to Senator Eugene Hale, January 12, 1885 (copy), Letters Received, "N," RG 127, NARA; *Congressional Record*, 48th Congress, 2d Session, Senate, January 14, 1885, p. 686, Senate, January 27, 1885, p. 1019, and House, January 28, 1885, p. 1041; *Army and Navy Journal*, January 31, 1885, p. 523.

62. Ronald H. Spector, "Professors of War: The American Naval War College and the Modern American Navy" (Ph.D. dissertation, Yale University, 1969), 43-44, 52; Ronald

H. Spector, *Professors of War: The Naval War College and the Development of the Naval Profession* (Newport, RI, 1977), 11–26; Russell F. Weigley, *The American Way of War: A History of United States Military Strategy and Policy* (Bloomington, IN, 1973, 1977), 172; Stephen B. Luce letter to William C. Church, November 2, 1882, in W. C. Church Papers, LC; Donald J. Sexton, "Forging the Sword: Congress and the American Naval Renaissance, 1880–1890" (Ph.D. dissertation, University of Tennessee, 1976), 200–216.

63. Spector, "Professors . . . American Navy," 27–35; Spector, *Professors . . . Naval Profession*, 27–29; Weigley, *American Way of War*, 172; Robert Seager II, *Alfred Thayer Mahan* (Annapolis, MD, 1977), 164–65; S. B. Luce letter to W. C. Church, December 23, 1884, W. C. Church Papers, LC; SecNav, *Annual Report, 1885*, p. xi; S. B. Luce letter to Porter, December 21, 1885, David D. Porter Papers, LC.

64. Cmdr. William Bainbridge-Hoff, *Examples, Conclusions, and Maxims of Modern Naval Tactics*, Office of Naval Intelligence, *Information from Abroad, General Information Series* 3 (Washington, 1884), 19–21, 89, 146–47.

65. Lt. T. B. M. Mason, "On the Employment of Boat Guns as Light Artillery for Landing Parties," *United States Naval Institute Proceedings*, 1879, pp. 207–23; Lt. John C. Soley, "The Naval Brigade," *USNIP*, May 1880, pp. 271–90; Lt. Carlos G. Calkins, "How May the Sphere of Usefulness Be Extended in Time of Peace with Advantages to the Country and the Naval Service," *USNIP*, 1883, pp. 155–94. See also William H. Russell, "The Genesis of Fleet Marine Force Doctrine: 1879–1899," *Marine Corps Gazette*, April-July 1951, pp. 49–50, 53.

66. Lt. Cmdr. Casper F. Goodrich, *British Operations in Egypt, Office of Naval Intelligence, Information from Abroad, General Information Series* (Washington, 1883), 339–40.

67. Bainbridge-Hoff, *Modern Naval Tactics*; Mason, "Landing Parties"; Calkins, "How May the Sphere"; Soley, "The Naval Brigade"; Goodrich, *British Operations in Egypt*, 204–8.

68. Albert Gleaves, *The Life and Letters of Rear Adm. Stephen B. Luce* (New York, 1925), 197–99; "The Landing of the Naval Brigade on Gardiner's Island," in ONI, *Papers on Naval Operations during the Year Ending July 1885, Information from Abroad, General Information Series* 4 (Washington, D.C., 1885), 101–10.

CHAPTER 4. THE TRANSITIONAL YEARS, 1885–1889

1. Jack Shulimson, "U.S. Marines in Panama, 1885," in Lt. Col. Merrill L. Bartlett, USMC (Ret.), ed., *Assault from the Sea: Essays on the History of Amphibious Warfare* (Annapolis, MD, 1983), 107–20. For general accounts of the revolution in Panama, see E. Taylor Parks, *Colombia and the United States, 1765–1934* (Durham, NC, 1935), 202–28; Kenneth Hagan, *American Gunboat Diplomacy and the Old Navy* (Westport, CT, 1973), 158–87; Gerstle Mack, *The Land Divided: A History of the Panama Canal and Other Isthmian Canal Projects* (New York, 1944), 350–54; Richard S. Collum, *History of the United States Marine Corps*, rev. ed. (New York, 1903), 234–53; Clyde Metcalf, "The Naval Expedition to the Isthmus of Panama," MS, Geographic Files, Reference Section, MCHC; Daniel H. Wicks, "Dress Rehearsal: United States Intervention on the Isthmus of Panama, 1885," MS; Bowman H. McCalla, "The U.S. Naval Brigade on the Isthmus of Panama," in ONI, *Papers on Naval Operations during the Year Ending July 1885, Information from Abroad, General Information Series*, 4 (Washington, D.C., 1885), 41–100 (hereafter, McCalla, "The U.S. Naval Brigade"); Milton Plesur, *America's Outward Thrust: Approaches to Foreign Affairs, 1865–90* (DeKalb, IL, 1971), 176–78; David M. Pletcher, *The Awkward Years: American Foreign Relations under Garfield and Arthur* (Columbia, MO, 1962), 232–33 and 347.

2. Mark D. Hirsch, *William C. Whitney, Modern Warwick* (New York, 1948), 270;

Wicks, "Dress Rehearsal," 9; SecNav letter to Jouett, April 1, 1885, Letters to Officers, vol. 8, pp. 510–11, Entry 16, RG 45, NARA; SecNav letter to J. B. Houston, April 1, 1885, Letters from Officers Commanding Expeditions, Naval Expedition to the Isthmus of Panama, McCalla, Feb.-May 1885, Entry 25, Subseries 13, RG 45, NARA (hereafter cited as Expedition to Panama, Entry 25, Subseries 13, RG 45).

3. Wicks, "Dress Rehearsal," 10; Bowman H. McCalla, "Memoirs of a Naval Career," MS, Navy Library, Navy Historical Center, Ch. 14, p. 2. See also SecNav letter to Chandler, April 2, 1885, Expedition to Panama, Entry 25, Subseries 13, RG 45.

4. SecNav letter to Jouett, April 3, 1885, Letters to Officers, vol. 8, pp. 513–14, Entry 16, RG 45, NARA. See also exchange of telegrams between Whitney and Houston, April 5, 1885, Expedition to Panama, Entry 25, Subseries 13, RG 45; SecNav letter to CMC, April 5, 1885, Letters to Officers, vol. 1, p. 468–69, Entry 18, RG 45, NARA.

5. J. G. Walker letter to B. H. McCalla, April 6, 1885, General Letterbook, 1885–89, John G. Walker Papers, LC.

6. See Hagan, *Gunboat Diplomacy*, 148–89, and Wicks, "Dress Rehearsal," 15. For suspicion of French interests see Ens. W. I. Chambers letter to Chandler, January 9, 1885, vol. 72, pp. 3080–88, William E. Chandler Papers, LC, and Wicks, "Dress Rehearsal," 15-6. For Jouett's repudiation of his interview see his letter to SecNav, May 1, 1885, Squadron Letters, M-89, Roll 296, RG 45, NARA.

7. Jouett letters to SecNav, April 29 and 30, 1885, Squadron Letters, M-89, Roll 296, RG 45; Collum, *History of the United States Marine Corps*, 250, 252–53; David G. McCullough, *The Path between the Seas: The Creation of the Panama Canal, 1870-1914* (New York, 1977), 178–79.

8. Jouett letter to SecNav, May 7, 1885, Squadron Letters, M-89, Roll 296, RG 45, NARA; Henry Clay Cochrane Diary, Entries for April 16, 1885, and for May 5, 1885, Cochrane Papers, MCHC; McCalla, "Memoirs," 9–10.

9. CMC letter to SecNav, April 8, 1885, LSSN, vol. 1, pp. 155–58, RG 127, NARA.

10. Ibid. Frank E. Sutton letter to Naval Academy classmates, November 2, 1885, printed in *Second Annual Report of the Class of 81, U.S. Naval Academy* (Butler, PA, 1886), 38.

11. McCalla, "The U.S. Naval Brigade," 61.

12. CMC letter to SecNav, July 13, 1885, LSSN, vol. 1, pp. 193–204, RG 127, NARA.

13. SecNav letter to CMC, July 27, 1885, Letters Received, "N," RG 127, NARA.

14. The general sources for this and the following paragraph are Hirsch, *Whitney*, 255–336; Charles O. Paullin, *Paullin's History of Naval Administration, 1775-1911* (Annapolis, MD, 1968), 378–79; Ronald Spector, *Professors of War: The Naval War College and the Development of the Naval Profession* (Newport, RI, 1977), 50–51; Leonard D. White, *The Republican Era: A Study in Administrative History, 1869-1901* (New York, 1958), 162–69. The quote in the paragraph is from Hirsch, *Whitney*, 263.

15. Additional sources for this paragraph are SecNav, *Annual Report, 1887*, iii-v, and *Annual Report, 1888*, iii-iv; Paullin, *Naval Administration*, 398–99; Harold and Margaret Sprout, *The Rise of American Naval Power, 1776-1918* (Princeton, NJ, 1946), 189–90; James L. Abrahamson, *America Arms for a New Century: The Making of a Great Military Power* (New York, 1981), 37–40; B. Franklin Cooling, *Benjamin Franklin Tracy: Father of the Modern American Navy* (Hamden, CT, 1973), 56–57; John D. Alden, *The American Steel Navy* (Annapolis, MD, 1972), 31–32; John D. Long, 2 vols., *The New American Navy* (New York, 1903) 1: 40.

16. Robert G. Albion, *Makers of Naval Policy, 1798-1947*, ed., Rowena Reed (Annapolis, MD, 1980), 155–56; Hilary A. Herbert, "Grandfather's Talks about His Life under Two Flags," MS, p. 14, in Hilary A. Herbert Papers, Southern Historical Collection, University of North Carolina Library, Chapel Hill, NC.

17. Herbert, "Grandfather Talks," 5-6; Hugh B. Hammett, *Hilary Abner Herbert: A Southerner Returns to the Union* (Philadelphia, 1976), 111; Rear Adm. Stephen B. Luce, "Naval Administration," *United States Naval Institute Proceedings* (June 1888), 561-88.

18. Hirsch, *Whitney*, 337-41; Hammett, *Herbert*, 138-39; Cooling, *Tracy*, 57-58; Donald J. Sexton, "Forging the Sword: Congress and the American Naval Renaissance, 1880-1890," (Ph.D. dissertation, University of Tennessee, 1976), 193-94; Abrahamson, *America Arms for a New Century*, 187; Daniel H. Wicks, "New Navy and New Empire: The Life and Times of John Grimes Walker," (Ph.D. dissertation, University of California, Berkeley, 1979), 174-75, 180-82; Robert Seager II, *Alfred Thayer Mahan* (Annapolis, MD, 1977), 145-46; Peter Karsten, "Armed Progressives: The Military Reorganized for the American Century," in Jerry Israel, ed., *Building the Organizational Society* (New York, 1972), 197-232, 204-5; Hagan, *Gunboat Diplomacy*, 34-35.

19. Allan R. Millett and Peter Maslowski, *For the Common Defense, A Military History of the United States of America* (New York, 1984), 253-54; Russell F. Weigley, *History of the U.S. Army* (New York, 1967), 284; Abrahamson, *America Arms*, 37-39.

20. Millett and Maslowski, *For the Common Defense*, 253; Walter R. Herrick, Jr., *The Naval Revolution* (Baton Rouge, LA, 1966), 35; *Congressional Record*, 50th Congress, 1st Session, House, August 22, 1888, p. 7848.

21. Hammett, *Herbert*, 141-43; Wicks, "New Navy," 96-97, 103-10, 153; Cooling, *Tracy*, 57-58; Abrahamson, *America Rearms*, 22, 187; Hagan, *Gunboat Diplomacy*, 7-10; Robert Seager II, "Ten Years before Mahan: The Unofficial Case for the New Navy, 1880-1890," *Mississippi Valley Historical Review* (June 1953): 491-512; Lt. Carlos G. Calkins, "What Changes in Organization and Drill Are Necessary to Sail and Fight Effectively Our War Ships of Latest Type," *United States Naval Institute Proceedings* 12 (1886), 269-316; Bradley A. Fiske, *From Midshipman to Rear-Admiral* (New York, 1919), 88.

22. Calkins, "What Changes," 277.

23. "Discussion of Prize Essay for 1886," *United States Naval Institute Proceedings* 12 (1886), 317-60.

24. Lt. C. T. Hutchins, "The Naval Brigade: Its Organization, Equipment, and Tactics," *United States Naval Institute Proceedings* 13 (1887), 303-40.

25. Ens. William L. Rogers, "Notes on the Naval Brigade," *United States Naval Institute Proceedings* 14 (1888), 57-96; William H. Russell, "The Genesis of Fleet Marine Force Doctrine: 1879-1899," *Marine Corps Gazette*, pt. 2, May 1951, 53.

26. CMC, *Annual Reports*, 1885-1888; CMC letter to SecNav, December 1, 1887, LSSN, vol. 1, pp. 492-93, and CMC letter to SecNav, May 21, 1888, LSSN, vol. 2, pp. 37-38, RG 127, NARA.

27. *Army and Navy Journal* August 20, 1887, 67.

28. Ibid., August 27, 1887, 80.

29. Ibid., September 3, 1887, pp. 106-7. Cochrane notes in his diary on August 28, 1887, that he wrote the editor of the *Army and Navy Journal* "a reply to Col. Commandant's McC's letter 'On Reckless Recruiting.'" See entry, August 28, 1887, Cochrane Diary, Cochrane Papers, MCHC; CMC, "Annual Report," October 1, 1888, in SecNav, *Annual Report, 1888*, 525.

30. SecNav letter to 2d Lt. T. G. Fillette, October 10, 1885, Letters to Marines, vol. 11, p. 388, RG 80; Maj. George W. Collier letter to CMC, November 1, 1885, "C," Letters Received, RG 127; CMC letter to SecNav, December 3, 1885, LSSN, vol. 1, p. 257, RG 127; Acting SecNav letter to 1st Lt. W. P. Biddle, December 5, 1885, Letters to Marines, vol. 11, p. 403, RG 80, NARA.

31. First Lt. Robert G. Benson letter to SecNav, October 9, 1886 (copy), attached to JAG letter to CMC, October 23, 1886, and JAG letter to SecNav, February 14, 1887, Letters Received, "N," RG 127, NARA.

32. CMC letter to SecNav, February 21, 1887, LSSN, vol. 1, p. 318, Acting SecNav letter to CMC, May 25, 1887, Letters Received, "N"; CMC letter to SecNav, June 6, 1887, LSSN, vol. 1, pp. 419-20, RG 127, NARA.

33. CMC letter to SecNav, December 13, 1886, Letters from Marines, RG 80; CMC letters to SecNav, December 13, 1886, and February 18, 1887, LSSN, vol. 1, pp. 351 and 386, RG 127, NARA.

34. SecNav letter to CMC, December 9, 1887; J. G. Walker letter to 1st Lt. O. C. Berryman, October 10, 1887; Department of Navy, General Court-Martial Order No. 61, November 14, 1888, attached to JAG letter to CMC, December 12, 1888, all in Letters Received, "N," RG 127.

35. U.S. Congress, Senate, Committee on Naval Affairs, *To Equalize the Grades of Officers of the Marine Corps, Report 931 to Accompany Bill S. 2049*, 50th Cong., 1st session, 1888, passim.

36. Entries, February 22, 1888, April 21, 1888, and May 31, 1888, Cochrane Diary; Cochrane letter to Capt. Louis E. Fagan, May 15, 1888; Cochrane draft of letter to Lieutenant Lauchheimer, May 31, 1888, Folder 33 (Cochrane Papers, MCHC).

37. Cochrane letter to Fagan, May 15, 1888; and Committee on Naval Affairs, *To Equalize the Grades of Officers of the Marine Corps*, 1888.

38. Cochrane letter to Fagan, May 15, 1888.

39. *Congressional Record*, 50th Congress, 1st Session, Senate, May 17, 1888, 4313.

40. Cochrane letter to Fagan, May 15, 1888.

41. McCalla, "The U.S. Naval Brigade," 61; *Army and Navy Journal*, July 18, 1885, 1037.

42. Lt. H. K. White letter to CMC, January 17, 1885, Letters Received, Historical Section, 1817-1915, RG 127; SecNav letter to CMC, May 26, 1885, Letters Received, "N," RG 127; CMC letters to 2d Lt. F. E. Sutton, August 17, 1885, and Capt. George F. Elliott, 1886, LSSN, vol. 1, p. 293, RG 127.

43. CMC letters to Commanding Officers of Marine Posts, September 5, 1885, Letters Sent, Letter Book 31, p. 148; J. G. Walker, Acting Secretary, letter to CMC, August 20, 1886, Letters Received, "N," RG 127; J. G. Walker, Acting Secretary, letter to CMC, Letters Received, "N," August 20, 1886, RG 127; CMC letter to SecNav, August 21, 1886, LSSN, vol. 1, p. 316, RG 127; Acting SecNav letter to CMC, August 23, 1886, Letters to Marines, vol. 11, p. 468, RG 80, NARA.

44. D. B. Harmony, Acting SecNav, letter to CMC, August 29, 1887, and SecNav letter to CMC, October 31, 1887, Letters Received, "N," RG 127, NARA; C. H. Lauchheimer to Naval Academy classmates, November 7, 1887, printed in *Fourth Annual Report of the Class of 81, U.S. Naval Academy* (Washington, D.C. 1888), 38-39.

45. SecNav letter to CMC, April 10, 1888, Letters Received "N," RG 127, NARA; George Barnett letter to Naval Academy classmates, January 5, 1889, printed in "Fifth Annual Report of the Class of 81, 1889" in U.S. Naval Academy, *Report of Class of 81*, 2d-6th ed. (Annapolis, 1886-1890), 1-2.

46. Howard K. Gilman, *Marines' Manual* (Washington, 1885) passim. See also CMC letter to SecNav, August 22, 1885, LSSN, vol. 1, p. 227, RG 127, NARA; HQMC, General Order No. 7, September 15, 1885, in *Navy and Marine Corps Orders, 1877-1903*, Library Rare Book Collection, MCHC; Joe A. Simon, "The Life and Career of General John Archer Lejeune" (MA thesis, Louisiana State University, 1967), 76.

47. Howard K. Gilman, *The Naval Brigade and Operations Ashore* (Washington, 1886), passim.

48. Second Lt. H. K. White letter to SecNav, June 29, 1885, and CMC endorsement, July 1, 1889, Letters Received, Marine, 1885, RG 80; CMC letter to SecNav, July 9, 1885, LSSN, vol. 1, p. 188, and SecNav letter to CMC, November 13, 1888, RG 127, NARA.

49. Maj. Gen. George Barnett, "Soldier and Sailor, Too" MS, ch. 6, pp. 1-6, and ch. 8, pp. 3-4, George Barnett Papers, MCHC.

50. George Barnett letter to Naval Academy classmates, October 15, 1885, printed in *Second Annual Report of the Class of 81, U.S. Naval Academy* (Butler, PA, 1886), 4-5; Barnett, "Soldier and Sailor," ch. 8, pp. 3-4; George Barnett, Sitka Letter Book, 1884-86, Barnett Papers, MCHC; George Barnett letter to Naval Academy classmates, January 15, 1888, printed in "Fourth Annual Report of the Class of 81, 1888" in U.S. Naval Academy, *Report of Class of 81*, 4-6.

51. CMC letter to SecNav, January 28, 1885, LSSN, vol. 1, p. 128, RG 127, NARA.

52. Charles A. Doyen letter to classmates, October 25, 1886, Francis E. Sutton letter to Classmates, n.d., [1886?], C. Marrast Perkins, October 1, 1886, printed in "Third Annual Report of the Class of 1881, 1887" in U.S. Naval Academy, *Report of Class of 81*, 17, 45, 48; J. E. Mahoney letter to classmates, November 14, 1887, printed in "Fourth Annual Report of the Class of 81, 1888," in U.S. Naval Academy, *Report of the Class of 81*, 42.

53. H. C. Haines letter to classmates, October 6, 1886, and C. L. Lauchheimer letter to classmates, October 27, 1886, printed in "Third Annual Report of the Class of 1881, 1887" in U.S. Naval Academy, *Report of Class of 81*, 23-24, 29; J. E. Mahoney letter to classmates, December 6, 1885, printed in *Second Annual Report of the Class of 81, U.S. Naval Academy*, 27-28.

54. Clipping from *Army and Navy Journal*, n.d., [1888], HQMC Clipping Book, RG 127, NARA; SecNav, *Annual Report, 1889*, vol. 2, 824; "Obituary: Francis Eskridge Sutton," *Report of Class of 1881*, 7th ed. (Annapolis, 1891), n.p.

55. Hirsch, *Whitney*, 345-47; Charles S. Campbell, *The Transformation of American Foreign Relations, 1865-1900* (New York, 1977), 76-82; Milton Plesur, *America's Outward Thrust: Approaches to Foreign Affairs, 1865-1890*, paperback ed. (DeKalb, IL, 1971), 202.

56. Ibid. See also Wicks, "New Navy," 176-79, 189-90.

57. Hagan, *Gunboat Diplomacy*, 7-10; John A. S. Grenville and George Berkeley Young, *Politics, Strategy, and American Diplomacy: Studies in Foreign Policy, 1873-1917* (New Haven, CT, 1966), 39-40; Seager, "Ten Years before Mahan," 509, 511; Wicks, "New Navy," 180-82.

CHAPTER 5. MARINE PROFESSIONALISM AND THE NEW NAVY, 1889-1891

1. Milton Plesur, *America's Outward Thrust: Approaches to Foreign Affairs 1865-1890* (DeKalb, IL, 1971), 234-35; H. Wayne Morgan, *From Hayes to McKinley: National Party Politics, 1877-1896* (Syracuse, NY, 1969), 287, 289-90; John A. S. Grenville and George Berkeley Young, *Politics, Strategy, and American Diplomacy: Studies in Foreign Policy, 1873-1917* (New Haven, CT, 1966), 90; B. Franklin Cooling, *Benjamin Franklin Tracy: Father of the Modern American Navy* (Hamden, CT, 1973), 64-65; Charles O. Paullin, *Paullin's History of Naval Administration, 1775-1911* (Annapolis, MD, 1968), 367-68; Walter R. Herrick, Jr., *The Naval Revolution* (Baton Rouge, LA, 1966), 41-43.

2. Quoted in Cooling, *Tracy*, 62. See also *Paullin's History of Naval Administration*, 367-68; Herrick, *The Naval Revolution*, 41-43; and Morgan, *From Hayes to McKinley*, 324.

3. Cooling, *Tracy*, 69-70; Herrick, *The Naval Revolution*, 44-49; Daniel H. Wicks, "New Navy and New Empire: The Life and Times of John Grimes Walker" (Ph.D. Dissertation, University of California, Berkeley, 1979), 194-96.

4. Wicks, "New Navy," 208-9, 214-19, 247; Daniel H. Wicks, "The First Cruise of the Squadron of Evolution," *Military Affairs* (April 1980), 64; Harold and Margaret Sprout, *The Rise of American Naval Power, 1776-1918* (Princeton, NJ, 1946), 217.

5. Stephen B. Luce, "Our Future Navy" and "Discussion," *United States Naval Institute Proceedings* 15 (1889), 541–59.

6. SecNav, *Annual Report, 1889*, passim.

7. Ibid. See also Sprout and Sprout, *The Rise of American Naval Power*, 207–8; Herrick, *The Naval Revolution*, 56; and Cooling, *Tracy*, 79–87.

8. Sprout and Sprout, *The Rise of American Naval Power*, 209–10; Cooling, *Tracy*, 72; Alan R. Millett, *Semper Fidelis: The History of the United States Marine Corps* (New York, 1980), 122.

9. H. K. White letter to Naval Academy classmates, December 20, 1889, in "Sixth Annual Report of the Class of 81, 1890," in U.S. Naval Academy, *Report of Class of 81* 2d-6th ed. (Annapolis, 1886–1890), 110; Wicks, "New Navy," 196–200; James L. Abrahamson, *America Arms for a New Century: The Making of a Great Military Power* (New York, 1981), 26.

10. SecNav, *Annual Report, 1887*, xii–xiii, Appendix 6, 72–73; SecNav, *Annual Report, 1888*, Appendix 3, 21; U.S. Congress, Senate, Naval Affairs Committee, *Appropriations for the Naval Service*, Senate Report 2430, 50th Cong., 2d Sess., 1889; *Congressional Record*, House, 50th Congress, 2d Session, March 2, 1889, pp. 2279–80; *U.S. Statutes at Large*, vol. 23, "Naval Appropriation Act," March 2, 1889, 50th Congress, 2d Session, ch. 396, pp. 878–79; Superintendent of the Naval Academy, "Annual Report," in SecNav, *Annual Report, 1889*, 427; *Naval Register, 1889*; SecNav letter to CMC, July 16, 1889, Letters Received, "N," RG 127, NARA.

11. SecNav letter to Lt. Col. John L. Broome, March 8, 1888, Letters Received "N," 1888; CMC letter to SecNav, July 1888, LSSN, vol. 2, p. 51; Mannix letters to CMC, February 13, 1889, and April 19, 1889, Letters Received "M," 1889; J. G. Walker letter to SecNav, August 18, 1889, Letters Received "N," 1889, RG 127, NARA; *Army and Navy Journal*, Mar. 3, 1888, 632, and Mar. 17, 1888, 677; Millett, *Semper Fidelis*, 117.

12. Mannix letter to H. C. Cochrane, September 14, 1889, Folder 35, Henry Clay Cochrane Papers, MCHC.

13. CMC letter to SecNav, October 1, 1889, LSSN, vol. 2, pp. 188–89, RG 127.

14. Cmdre. James A. Greer letter to SecNav, October 12, 1889, Subject File, NF, 1889, RG 45.

15. CMC letter to Commodore James A. Greer, October 18, 1889, and attached memoranda, Subject File, NF, 1889, RG 45.

16. Cdr. Henry Glass, memorandum, August 31, 1889, File 4715, General Correspondence Files, RG 80, NA; entry, May 13, 1892, Cochrane Diary, Henry Clay Cochrane Papers, MCHC; Col. C. G. McCawley letter to S. B. Luce, December 18, 1889, Stephen B. Luce Papers, LC; Millett, *Semper Fidelis*, 122. Glass may have moved, as Cochrane claims, that the Board recommend the removal of Marines from Navy warships, but William F. Fullam was certainly the point man on the issue.

17. "The Marine Corps," *New York Times*, Nov. 13, 1889, 5; *Army and Navy Journal*, Dec. 7, 1889, 296–97.

18. McCawley letter to Luce, December 18, 1889. The Greer Board did not make an overall report but a series of recommendations varying from signaling lanterns to employment of artillery. E.g. President of the Board letters to SecNav, November 5, 1889, File 5229; November 9, 1889, File 5261; December 10, 1889, File 5779, RG 80, NA. The only formal reference to the recommendation about Marines is an entry that shows the Navy Department received a letter from the Board of Organization on November 19, 1889, relative to the duties of Marines. A note states that the letter went to the chief clerk. (Briefing Book, 1889, Entry 5412, RG 80, NA.) A search of pertinent records and finding aids failed to locate the actual recommendation or the secretary's action. In all probability, the letter was destroyed.

19. Peter Karsten, *The Naval Aristocracy: The Golden Age of Annapolis and the Emer-*

gence of Modern American Navalism (New York, 1972), 299; Wicks, "New Navy," 66, 68, 70–72, 75–78.

In 1890, the average age of a Navy ensign was thirty-two, for the next rank of lieutenant junior grade, it was thirty-four, and for lieutenant, forty-four. Secretary Tracy predicted that at the then existing rate of promotion, the Navy would be populated by lieutenants (the Navy equivalent of the Marine and Army rank of captain) ranging in age from thirty-seven to fifty-four. SecNav, *Annual Report, 1890,* 27–29.

20. Karsten, *The Naval Aristocracy,* 206; Lieutenant Richard Wainwright, "Modern Naval Education," *The United Service* (January 1890): 11–21.

21. Karsten, *The Naval Aristocracy,* 214, 228, 398; Peter Karsten, "Armed Progressives: The Military Reorganized for the American Century," in Jerry Israel, ed., *Building the Organizational Society* (New York, 1972), 197–232, 197; Wicks, "New Navy," 7–8, 96–97; Charles S. Campbell, *The Transformation of American Foreign Relations, 1865–1900* (New York, 1977), 159–60; Abrahamson, *America Arms for a New Century,* 48–54, 61–62, 187.

Karsten emphasizes the institutional and career anxiety of naval officers; Wicks downplays the actual dangers facing the U.S., emphasizing the large role that the naval bureaucracy and officer class played in foreign policy; while Campbell cites Richard Hofstadter's concept of a "psychic crisis" in American society at large in the 1890s as lying behind the U.S. naval buildup in that period. While acknowledging the validity of much of the above, Abrahamson, nevertheless, stresses that European imperialism and rivalry as well as the advances in military technology made war a realistic possibility. He also observes that even if the European powers were not an actual threat, the American military perceived them as such.

22. Sprout and Sprout, *The Rise of American Naval Power,* 209–11; Herrick, *The Naval Revolution,* 62–63; Cooling, *Tracy,* 79–87; Walter Millis, *Arms and Men* (New York, 1958), 157–58; Paullin, *Naval Administration,* 404–5; Wicks, "The First Cruise," 65; Capt. C. M. Chester letter to S. B. Luce, February 18, 1890, Luce Papers, LC.

23. Wicks, "New Navy," 233–34; Wicks, "The First Cruise," 66, 68.

24. John G. Walker letter to Tracy, April 27, 1890, General Correspondence, Tracy Papers, LC.

25. Wicks, "New Navy," 247; Wicks, "The First Cruise," 64.

26. W. E. Chandler letter to W. C. Church, February 19, 1890, Church Papers, LC; Herrick, *The Naval Revolution,* 67–68, 71–74; Cooling, *Tracy,* 79–87; Robert G. Albion, *Makers of Naval Policy, 1798–1947,* Rowena Reed, ed. (Annapolis, MD, 1980), 143, 145–46, 151–52.

27. Herrick, *The Naval Revolution,* 73–74; Sprout and Sprout, *The Rise of American Naval Power,* 213.

28. Walter Millis, *Arms and Men,* 158–59; Herrick, *The Naval Revolution,* 73–74.

29. Capt. W. T. Sampson, "Outline of a Scheme for the Naval Defense of the Coast," *United States Naval Institute Proceedings* 15 (1889), 170–232. By 1890, Army engineers, as recommended by the Endicott Report, had started upon the rebuilding of American harbor defenses. Although many areas of overlapping jurisdiction existed, both services agreed that the main responsibility lay with the Army. Jamie W. Moore, "National Security in the American Army's Definition of Mission, 1865–1914," MS, September 1981 (paper read at 1982 meeting of the American Military Institute); Abrahamson, *America Arms for a New Century,* 37–39.

30. A. T. Mahan letter to Tracy, May 30, 1890, General Correspondence, Tracy Papers, LC; Philip A. Crowl, "Alfred Thayer Mahan: The Naval Historian," in Peter Paret, ed., *Makers of Modern Strategy: From Machiavelli to the Nuclear Age* (Princeton, NJ, 1986), 444–77.

31. Capt. A. T. Mahan, *The Influence of Sea Power upon History, 1660-1783* (Boston, 1890), passim.

32. Ibid., 25-89; Crowl, "Mahan," 462-64; Robert Seager II, "Ten Years before Mahan: The Unofficial Case for the New Navy, 1880-1890," *Mississippi Valley Historical Review* (June 1953): 491-512; Walter Millis, *Arms and Men*, 161-63.

33. Richard Hofstadter, "Manifest Destiny and the Philippines," in Daniel Aaron, ed., *America in Crisis* (New York, 1952), 173-200.

34. Richard W. Van Alstyne, *The Rising American Empire* (New York, 1966), 161-66; Campbell, *Transformation of American Foreign Policy*, 66; Seager, "Ten Years Before," 512; Russell F. Weigley, *The American Way of War: A History of United States Military Strategy and Policy*, paperback ed. (Bloomington, IN, 1977), 181-83; Herrick, *Naval Revolution*, 41-43; Cooling, *Tracy*, 52, 92; Crowl, "Mahan," 470-71; Robert Seager, *Alfred Thayer Mahan* (Annapolis, MD, 1977), 219. The quote is from Van Alstyne, *The Rising American Empire*.

35. Jeffrey M. Dorwart, *The Office of Naval Intelligence: The Birth of America's First Intelligence Agency* (Annapolis, MD, 1979), 28-29.

36. Herrick, *Naval Revolution*, 78; Cooling, *Tracy*, 99; Seager, *Mahan*, 219, 223, 226-27; Mahan letter to Charles H. Davis, December 23, 1890, in Robert Seager II, and Doris D. Maguire, eds., *Letters and Papers of Alfred Thayer Mahan*, vol. 2 of 3 vols, 1890-1901, (Annapolis, MD, 1975), 35-37.

37. Seager, *Mahan*, 227-31. See also Richard A. Preston, *The Defence of the Undefended Border: Planning for War in North America, 1867-1939* (Montreal, Canada, 1977), 97. Preston observes that in this period both the British and the U.S. authorities considered war unlikely, but "it was considered wise to plan against the possibility of an Anglo-American war."

38. "Contingency Plan of Operations in Case of War with Great Britain," New York, December, 1890, reprinted in Seager and Maguire, *Letters and Papers of Alfred Thayer Mahan*, vol. 3, pp. 559-82 (copy of the plan exists in the OAB, NHD). See also Seager, *Mahan*, 227-31.

39. "Contingency Plan," Seager and Maguire, *Letters and Papers of Alfred Thayer Mahan*, vol. 3, p. 573; Capt. C. H. Davis, comments on Captain Mahan's plan, December 13, 1890 (true copy) OAB, NHD; Lt. William F. Fullam, "The Systems of Naval Training and Discipline Required to Promote Efficiency and Attract Americans," *United States Naval Institute Proceedings* 16 (1890), 473-95; Cmdr. R. H. Jackson, "History of Advanced Base," May 15, 1913, Navy General Board Records, File 408, OAB, NHC.

40. CMC letters to SecNav, March 28, 1890, and June 26, 1890, vol. 2., pp. 235-37 and 268, LSSN, RG 127, NARA.

41. Record of Eli K. Cole, Record of Clarence L. A. Ingate, Record of Theodore P. Kane, Record of John Archer Lejeune, and Record of Leroy A. Stafford, Reel 23, M. 991, Naval Academy Academic and Conduct Records, Records of the U.S. Naval Academy, RG 405, NARA; *Naval Register, 1890*; Karsten, *The Naval Aristocracy*, 7-19.

42. *Naval Registers, 1884-90*.

43. The source for this paragraph and the following is Maj. Gen. John A. Lejeune, *The Reminiscences of a Marine* (Philadelphia, 1930), 90-96. See also Lt. Col. Merrill A. Bartlett, "The Road to the Commandancy, 1890-1920," MS, p. 3, and Bartlett, "Naval Cadet Lejeune," MS, p. 11.

44. Additional source for this paragraph is *New York Times*, September 8, 1890, 8.

45. Lejeune letter to sister, September 3, 1890, Box 16, Lejeune Papers, LC.

46. Lejeune, *Reminiscences*, 99; Lejeune letter to sister, October 6, 1890, Box 16, Lejeune Papers. Remark about the drill manual quoted in Joe A. Simon, "The Life and Career of General John Archer Lejeune" (MA thesis, Louisiana State University, 1967), pp. 73-74; HQMC Endorsement No. 388, September 20, 1890, Endorsement Book 6, RG 127, NARA; HQMC order to Lejeune, October 28, 1890, Box 3, Lejeune Papers, LC.

47. SecNav letter to CMC, July 25, 1889, "N," Letters Received, and Lt. Col. Heywood letter to SecNav, July 27, 1889, vol. 2, p. 127, LSSN, RG 127; Col. William Remey telegram to Lt. F. L. Denny, July 30, 1890, and Clipping "New Publications," n.d., Denny Scrapbook, Library Rare Book Collection, MCHC.

48. First Lt. W. K. Gilman letter to CMC, January 7, 1890, and SecNav letter to CMC, April 19, 1890, "N," Letters Received, RG 127; CMC letter to 1st Lt. H. K. Gilman, June 10, 1890, Letter Book 36, p. 191, Letters Sent, RG 127; *Army and Navy Journal*, September 6, 1890, 23; C. H. Lauchheimer letter to classmates, January 15, 1890, in "Sixth Annual Report of the Class of 81, 1890," in U.S. Naval Academy, *Report of Class of 81* 2d-6th ed. (Annapolis, 1886-1890), 64-65.

49. CMC letters to SecNav, May 27, July 7, August 28, and September 4, 1890, and Lt. Col. Heywood letter to SecNav, August 6, 1890, vol. 2, pp. 256-57, 270-71, 282, 284, and 289-90, LSSN, RG 127, NARA.

50. Hebb letter to SecNav, November 22, 1890, vol. 2, pp. 315-16, LSSN, RG 127, NARA; CMC, *Annual Report, 1890*, 607. See also "A Brief of the Facts Pertaining to the Detail of C. N. Hebb as Acting Commandant of the Marine Corps," n.d., Richard A. Long Files, MCHC.

51. *Army and Navy Journal*, September 6, 1890, 1, September 20, 1890, 23 and 58, and January 31, 1891, 390; "Promotion of Merit," *New York Times*, January 31, 1891, 3.

52. Hebb letter to SecNav, November 22, 1890, LSSN, vol. 2, RG 127; Col. C. G. McCawley letter to Lt. Col. Charles Heywood, September 5, 1890, Maj. Gen. Charles Heywood Record Book, RG 127; entry for October 20, 1890, Cochrane Diary, Henry Clay Cochrane Papers, MCHC; "History of a Soldier," n.p., n.d., [1890?], HQMC Scrapbook, vol. 1, 1890-98, RG 127; "Commander of the Marines," clipping from *Baltimore Sun*, October 8, 1890, Denny Scrapbook; *Army and Navy Journal*, November 8, 1890, 173; "To Command the Marines," *New York Times*, October 9, 1890, 5; "Col. Heywood Promoted," *New York Times*, January 31, 1891, 8, "Service Salad," *United Service* (Feb. 1891): 211-12; Charles Mason Remey, *Reminiscent of Colonel William Butler Remey, United States Marine Corps 1842-1894 and Lieutenant Edward Wallace Remey, United States Navy* (n.p., 1955) (copy in Library of Congress), 19-20.

53. John B. Briggs, USNI, letter to William F. Fullam, October 31, 1890, William F. Fullam Papers, LC; "Lt. Fullam's Paper Creates a Decided Sensation," *New York Times*, November 22, 1890, 2; Fullam, "The Systems of Naval Training and Discipline Required," 473-95.

54. "Discussion" of "The Systems of Naval Training and Discipline Required," *United States Naval Institute Proceedings* 16 (1890), 495-536.

55. *New York Times*, December 7, 1890, 10, December 14, 1890, 2, December 21, 1890, 9, and December 28, 1890, 3; *Army and Navy Journal*, December 6, 1890, 247.

56. *Army and Navy Journal*, November 29, 1890, 228-29, December 6, 1890, 247, and January 10, 1891, 327.

57. Hebb letter to SecNav, January 15, 1891, vol. 2, pp. 342-43, LSSN, RG 127, NARA.

58. Heywood letter to SecNav, February 10, 1891, vol. 2, p. 351, LSSN, RG 127, NARA.

CHAPTER 6. MARINE PROFESSIONALISM, THE NEW NAVY, AND NEW DIRECTIONS, 1891-1893

1. Brig. Gen. Charles Heywood Biographical File, Reference Section, MCHC; "Colonel Charles Heywood," *United Service* (April 1890): 455-56; *Army and Navy Journal*, January 31, 1890, 390.

2. "Service Salad," *United Service* (May 1891): 538–39; Capt. H. C. Cochrane letter to Heywood, February 15, 1891, Folder 37, Cochrane Papers, MCHC.

3. Charles O. Paullin, *Paullin's History of Naval Administration, 1775–1911* (Annapolis, MD, 1968), 416–17; U.S. Congress, Senate, *Organizations among Naval Officers*, S. Ex. Doc. 86, 51st Cong., 1st sess., March 15, 1890; Peter Karsten, *The Naval Aristocracy: The Golden Age of Annapolis and the Emergence of Modern American Navalism* (New York, 1972), 355.

4. CMC letter to Cmdre. James A. Greer, October 18, 1889, and attached memoranda, Subject File, NF, 1889, RG 45, NARA; CMC, *Annual Report, 1891*, 3–5; CMC letter to Col. James Forney, March 23, 1891, Letters Sent, LB 37, p. 171, RG 127, NARA.

5. CMC letter to SecNav, October 1, 1889, LSSN, vol. 2, pp. 188–89, RG 127, NARA; CMC, *Annual Report, 1891*, 4–5.

6. CMC, *Annual Report*, in SecNav *Annual Report, 1890*, 607; Ensign A. P. Niblack, "The Enlistment, Training, and Organization of Crews for Our New Ships," *USNIP* 17, no. 1, 3–49; CMC, *Annual Report*, in SecNav *Annual Report, 1889*, 825.

7. U.S. Congress, Senate and House, *Congressional Record*, 51st Cong., 1st sess., February 11 and February 24, 1891, vol. 22, pp. 2495 and 3228; *Army and Navy Journal*, April 4, 1891, 547.

8. CMC letter to SecNav, April 13, 1891, LSSN, vol. 2, p. 336, RG 127; Headquarters, Marine Corps, General Order No. 1, May 1, 1891, in Marine Corps General and Special Orders, Rare Book Collection, MCHC.

9. Marine Corps General Order No. 1.

10. Ibid.

11. Ibid.

12. Ibid.; Marine Corps Circular to all Shore Commanders, July 23, 1891, Order Book 19, p. 394, RG 127, NARA.

13. Report of Capt. D. P. Mannix, Commanding School of Application, October 1, 1892, as reprinted in Richard S. Collum, *History of the United States Marine Corps* (New York, 1903), 288–98; *Army and Navy Journal*, April 4, 1891, 547, and April 25, 1891, 602.

14. Adjutant and Inspector (A&I) letter to Capt. D. P. Mannix, August 4, 1891, Order Book 19, p. 455, RG 127, NARA.

15. *Army and Navy Journal*, June 27, 1891, 753; CMC letter to 2d Lt. Joseph H. Pendleton, March 23, 1891, LB 37, p. 172, RG 127; 2d Lt. T. P. Kane letter to CMC, May 16, 1891, Letters Received, "K," RG 127; 2d Lt. John A. Lejeune letter to CMC, May 10, 1891, Letters Received, "L," RG 127; 2d Lt. C. L. A. Ingate letter to CMC, July 27, 1891, Letters Received, "I," RG 127; CMC letter to Ingate, July 28, 1891, LB 39, p. 646, RG 127, NARA.

16. CMC, *Annual Report, 1891*, 8; Mannix Report, p. 289; *Army and Navy Journal*, September 5, 1891, 27.

17. Record of Robert McM. Dutton, Record of Ben H. Fuller, Record of Charles G. Long, Record of Edward R. Lowndes, Record of Lewis G. Lucas, Record of B. S. Newmann, Record of Julius Prochazka, Reel 24, M. 991, Naval Academy Academic and Conduct Records, Records of the U.S. Naval Academy, RG 405, NARA; *Naval Register, 1891*.

18. See note 17.

19. CMC letter to SecNav, July 22, 1891, LSSN, vol. 2, p. 402; SecNav letter to CMC, July 29, 1891, Letters Received, "N"; CMC letter to Maj. P. C. Pope, July 31, 1891, Order Book 19, p. 437, RG 127.

20. *Army and Navy Register*, August 8, 1891.

21. CMC letter to SecNav, October 17, 1891, LSSN, vol. 2, pp. 442–43, RG 127,

NARA; Board of Reorganization letter to CMC, September 21, 1891, reprinted in *Army and Navy Register*, October 24, 1891, 681–82.

22. CMC, *Annual Report, 1891*, 3–4.

23. Ibid., 4–5.

24. Cochrane letter to Heywood, October 22, 1891, Folder 37, and entries for November 26, and December 6, 12, 15–16, 1891, Cochrane Diary, Cochrane Papers, MCHC.

25. CMC letter to SecNav, November 18, 1891, LSSN, vol. 2, pp. 471–74, RG 127; CMC letters to senators Eugene Hale and J. R. McPherson, December 17, 1891, and CMC letters to members of the Senate Naval Affairs, December 18, 1891, LB 38, pp. 368–69, 372, RG 127, NARA; *Army and Navy Journal*, December 26, 1891, 311.

26. Paullin, *Naval Administration*, 408; R. Franklin Cooling, *Benjamin Franklin Tracy: Father of the Modern American Navy* (Handen, CT, 1973), 103; A. T. Mahan, "The United States Looking Outward," *Atlantic Monthly*, December 1890.

27. SecNav, *Annual Report, 1891*, pp. 31–38; Cooling, *Tracy*, 110–15; Walter R. Herrick, Jr., *The American Naval Revolution* (Baton Rouge, LA, 1966), 99–102.

28. Richard B. Morris, *Encyclopedia of American History* (New York, 1953), 284; Cooling, *Tracy*, 119–20.

29. SecNav, *Annual Report, 1891*, 21–30; Herrick, *The American Naval Revolution*, 109–19; Cooling, *Tracy*, 118; Winfield S. Schley, *Forty-Five Years under the Flag* (New York, 1904), 203–34; Robley D. Evans, *A Sailor's Log: Recollections of Forty Years of Naval Life* (New York, 1901), 259.

30. Thomas H. Coode, "Southern Congressman and the American Naval Revolution, 1880–1898," *Alabama Historical Quarterly* (Fall and Winter 1968): 89–110; Cooling, *Tracy*, 165.

31. Herrick, *American Naval Revolution*, 119–29.

32. *Army and Navy Journal*, January 2, 1892, 326; Paullin, *Naval Administration*, 420; SecNav, *Annual Report, 1892*, 38.

33. List of Vessels of U.S. Navy ready in view of possible service against Chili [sic], attached to Rear Adm. George Brown report to SecNav, December 31, 1891, Box 31, B. F. Tracy Papers, LC.

34. Unsigned Memorandum, Comparison of Iquique and Lota, n.d., Box 31, Tracy Papers; Evans, *Sailor's Log*, 294–95. Robert Seager argues in his biography of Mahan that the latter was generally shunted aside in the Navy Department and prepared no war plan. Apparently Seager did not come across the above memorandum in the Tracy Papers which appears to be consistent with Mahan's concept of the decisive naval battle. Joyce S. Goldberg, who also credits Mahan as author of the memo, drew my attention to both the Brown and Mahan memos in the Tracy Papers. See Robert Seager II, *Alfred Thayer Mahan* (Annapolis, MD, 1970), 235–38, and Goldberg, *The Baltimore Affair* (Lincoln, NE, 1986), 119, 178.

35. Mahan letter to Luce, January 10, 1892, in Robert Seager II and Doris D. Maguire, eds., *Letters and Papers of Alfred Thayer Mahan*, vol. 2 of 3 vols., 1890–1901, (Annapolis, MD, 1975), p. 63; Chadwick letter to Tracy, May 21, 1892, in Doris D. Maguire, *French Ensor Chadwick: Selected Letters and Papers* (Washington, DC, 1981), 172–75.

36. James R. Soley letter to CMC, January 26, 1892, Letters Received, "N," RG 127; A search of Marine Corps correspondence from the secretary of the Navy in RG 127 failed to show any significant reference to the Chilean affair except that noted above.

37. Brown report to SecNav, December 31, 1891, Tracy Papers; Unsigned Memorandum, n.d., Tracy Papers; Clipping from Burlington, Iowa newspaper, n.d., [January 1892], in "Life and Letters of George Remey," vol. 7, Remey, Family Collection, LC; Lt. Gen. John M. Schofield, *Forty-Six Years in the Army* (New York, 1897), 489–90; "The Navy in Excitement," *New York Times*, January 15, 1892, 1.

38. Lt. James N. Sears and Ens. B. W. Wells, Jr., *The Chilean Revolution of 1891*, ONI, *War Series No. IV, Information from Abroad* (1893), 8; "Americanizing the Navy," *New York Times*, May 2, 1892, 10.

39. Ensign A. P. Niblack, "The Enlistment, Training, and Organization of Crew for Our New Ships," *Proceedings of the United States Naval Institute* 17 (1891), 3–49; Lt. J. C. Wilson, "Suggestions on the Reorganization of the Personnel of the Navy, pt. II," *United Service* (July 1891): 28–40; Lt. Charles C. Rogers, "The Coast Defense Systems of Europe," ONI, *General Information Series No. I, Information from Abroad* (July 1891), 318–383.

40. CMC endorsement No. 13, January 9, 1892, Endorsement Book 17 and CMC letter to SecNav, January 21, 1892, LSSN, vol. 2, pp. 489–91, RG 127, NARA.

41. CMC endorsement No. 13, January 9, 1892, Endorsement Book 17 and CMC letter SecNav, January 21, 1892, LSSN, vol 2, pp. 489–91, RG 127, NARA.

42. CMC endorsement No. 13, January 9, 1892, Endorsement Book 17; CMC letter to SecNav, January 21, 1892, LSSN, vol. 2, pp. 489–91, RG 127, NARA; Paullin, *Naval Administration*, 375; CMC, *Annual Report, 1892*, 5.

43. *Army and Navy Journal*, April 9, 1892, 575; U.S. Congress, House, *Promotions in the Marine Corps*, H. Report 1502, 52d Cong., 2d Sess., May 27, 1892; U.S. Congress, House and Senate, *Congressional Record*, 52d Cong., 1st Sess., July 21 and 26, 1892, vol. 23, pp. 6539 and 6743; CMC, *Annual Report, 1892*, 4.

44. Mannix Report, 288–94.

45. Ibid., 288–96.

46. Ibid., 296–97.

47. Ibid., 297–98; William B. Folger, Chief, Bureau of Ordnance, letter to CMC, March 7, 1892, Letters Received, "N," RG 127; CMC letter to Folger, May 7, 1892, Letters Sent, Letter Book 39, p. 95, RG 127; CMC letters to SecNav, May 6, June 23, and June 30, 1892, LSSN, vol. 2, pp. 537, 573, and 578, RG 127; Capt. Mannix letters to CMC, May 3 and 6, 1892, Letters Received, "W," RG 127; Darius A. Greer, Acting Chief of Bureau of Construction and Repair, letter to CMC, June 29, 1892, and William B. Folger letter to CMC, September 1, 1892, Letters Received, "N," RG 127; A&I letter to SecNav, April 27, 1897, LSSN, vol. 6, pp. 564–65, RG 127, NARA.

48. Mannix Report, 294–95 and 297–98; CMC letter to SecNav, June 30, 1893, LSSN, vol. 3, p. 105.

49. Record of Albertus C. Catlin, Record of Lawrence N. Moses, Record of Wendell C. Neville, Record of Cyrus S. Radford, Record of Thomas C. Treadwell, Reel 25, M. 991, Naval Academy Academic and Conduct Records, Records of the U.S. Naval Academy, RG 405, NARA; *Naval Register, 1892*.

50. Mannix Report, 297–98; CMC *Annual Report, 1892*, 6.

51. *Army and Navy Journal*, August 20, 1892, 901, and September 3, 1892, 93; CMC letter to SecNav, July 11, 1892, LSSN, vol. 2, p. 585, and Copy of SecNav Order to Lt. Col. McLane Tilton, August 23, 1892, Letters Received, "N," RG 127, NARA.

52. Sources for this and the following paragraph are SecNav Order to Tilton, August 23, 1892, and JAG letter to CMC, September 6, 1892, Letters Received, "N," RG 127, NARA.

53. Additional sources for this paragraph are Records of Proceedings of Marine Examining Board, Cases of 1st Lt. William F. Spicer and 2d Lt. Charles G. Long, September 1892, in Proceedings of Naval and Marine Examining Boards, 1890–1941, Entry 62, RG 125, Records of the Navy Judge Advocate General, NARA. The proceedings of the examining board relative to Captain Meade were not found. The actual questions and answers of the examination were not contained in either of the Spicer or the Long case files.

54. CMC letter to SecNav, September 16, 1892, LSSN, vol. 2, p. 626; Navy Depart-

ment General Order 403, October 14, 1892, Entry 45, Scrapbook of Navy Department Issuances, 1885–1900, RG 127.

55. *Army and Navy Journal*, January 26, 1895, 359; Entry for January 10, 1892, Cochrane Diary, Cochrane Papers, MCHC; Charles Mason Remey, *Reminiscent of Colonel William Butler Remey United States Marine Corps, 1842–1894 and Lieutenant Commander Edward Wallace Remey, United States Navy* (n.p., 1955) (copy in Library of Congress), 17, 24–25.

56. Sources for this and the following paragraph are Navy Department, General Court Martial Order No. 9, January 31, 1893, William F. Fullam Papers, LC; Capt. E. P. Meeker letter to CMC, October 28, 1892, encl. to SecNav letter to CMC, January 31, 1893, Letters Received, "N," 1893, RG 127, NARA. Quotes are from Meeker letter to CMC.

57. Additional source for this paragraph is W. Nephew King, "Men from the Chicago Go Looting," clipping from *New York World* (Oct. 17, 1892) in HQMC Scrapbook, vol. 1, RG 127, NARA.

58. Navy Department General Court-Martial Order No. 9; North Atlantic station, U.S. Flagship *Chicago*, General Court-Martial Order No. 1, October 27, 1892, encl. to SecNav letter, January 31, 1893; Rear Adm. J. G. Walker letter to Capt. John F. McGlensey, October 8, 1892, encl. to SecNav letter, January 31, 1893.

59. Navy Department, General Court-Martial Order No. 9; SecNav letter to CMC, January 31, 1893; Philip C. Hanna letter to Capt. E. P. Meeker, October 16, 1892, W. Nephew King, Jr., letter to Meeker, October 16, 1892, and Meeker letter to CMC, October 28, 1892, enclosures to SecNav letter, January 31, 1893; *Army and Navy Journal*, November 5, 1892, 173.

60. F. M. Ramsay letter to SecNav, November 1, 1892, Letters Received "N"; CMC letter to Asst. SecNav, November 30, 1892 and Asst. SecNav endorsement, December 14, 1892, Letters Received "N," RG 127.

61. Cochrane letter to Capt. F. L. Denny, February 3, 1893, Folder 41, Cochrane Papers, MCHC. See also entries for January 30, February 2–3, 5–6, 1893, Cochrane Papers, MCHC.

62. Entries February 11, 19, and 26, 1893, Cochrane Diary; Cochrane to Maj. P. C. Pope, March 3, 1893, Folder 41, Cochrane Papers, MCHC.

63. "Abolish the Marines," Clipping from *New York Herald*, March 17, 1893, in HQMC Scrapbook, vol. I, RG 127, NARA; CMC, *Annual Report, 1892*, 5.

CHAPTER 7. THE SOUND AND THE FURY, 1893–1896

1. Hugh B. Hammett, *Hilary Abner Herbert: A Southerner Returns to the Union* (Philadelphia, 1976), 141–43, 158–60; Charles O. Paullin, *Paullin's History of Naval Administration, 1775–1911* (Annapolis, MD, 1968), 367–68. For Mahan's influence on Herbert, see French E. Chadwick letter to Mahan, August 10, 1893, in Doris D. Maguire, *French Ensor Chadwick: Selected Letters and Papers* (Washington, DC, 1981), 179–80; and SecNav, *Annual Report, 1893*, 36–37.

2. Hilary A. Herbert, "Grandfather Talks," MS, 318, 323, Hilary A. Herbert Papers, Southern Historical Collection, University of North Carolina Library, Chapel Hill, North Carolina, Microfilm, Reel 1.

3. Ibid., 321; Hammett, *Herbert*, 151–53; Paullin, *Naval Administration*, 370.

4. *Army and Navy Journal*, May 13, 1893, 631; copy of SecNav letter to 1st Lt. George T. Bates, May 23, 1893, Letters Received, "N," RG 127, NARA; Proceedings of Examining Board, Mar.-Apr. 1893, case of 1st Lt. George T. Bates in Proceedings of Naval and Marine Examining Boards, 1890–1941, Entry 62, RG 125, Records of the Navy Judge

Advocate General, NARA; SecNav, *Annual Report, 1893*, 53. Unfortunately for Lieutenant Bates, the following year, when he came up again for promotion, he failed the physical examination because of a heart condition he had developed in the intervening period. He was forced to retire as a first lieutenant. See Proceedings of Examining Board, April 1894, Case of 1st Lt. George T. Bates in Proceedings of Naval and Marine Examining Boards, 1890–1941.

5. *Army and Navy Journal*, April 29, 1893, 597; Headquarters, School of Application, USMC, May 1, 1893, letter to 2d Lt. Thomas C. Treadwell, Letters Received, Historical Section, 1893, RG 127, NARA; "Report of Board of Visitors of School of Application," April 26, 1893, in CMC, *Annual Report, 1893*, 9.

6. "Report of Commander of School of Application," September 15, 1893, in CMC, *Annual Report, 1893*, 9–10; Mannix letter to H. C. Cochrane, September 10, 1893, Folder 41, H. C. Cochrane Papers, MCHC.

7. Record of George Richards, Reel 26, M. 991, Naval Academy Academic and Conduct Records, Records of the U.S. Naval Academy, RG 405, NARA; Col. George Richards, "The Marine Corps," June 1911, speech to Naval Academy Class of 1891, in RG 127, NARA; *Naval Register, 1893*.

8. Records of Dion Williams, Rufus H. Lane, Albert S. McLemore, Elisha Theall, and George Richards, Reel 26, M. 991, Naval Academy Academic and Conduct Records, RG 405, NARA; *Naval Register, 1893*.

9. "Report of Commander of School of Application," September 15, 1893, in CMC, *Annual Report, 1893*, 9.

10. CMC, *Annual Report, 1893*, 5–6; "Report of Commander of School of Application," October 1, 1894, in CMC, *Annual Report*, 7; Entry December 17, 1893, Cochrane Diary, H. C. Cochrane Papers, MCHC; "The Obituary Record," *New York Times*, February 7, 1894, 4.

11. CMC letter to SecNav, February 6, 1894, LSSN, vol. 3, p. 295, RG 127, NARA.

12. CMC, *Annual Report, 1894*, and "Report of Commanding Officer of School of Application," October 1, 1894, in CMC, *Annual Report, 1894*, 7.

13. CMC letter to SecNav, April 20, 1894, LSSN, vol. 3, p. 386, RG 127, NARA.

14. Ibid. See also clipping from *Washington Evening Star*, May 4, 1894, HQMC Scrapbook, vol. 1, RG 127, NARA; and see the *Army and Navy Journal*, February 25, 1893, 447, for the revision of naval regulations and Capt. Reid's appointment to the Board.

15. For Goodloe's ambitions for the commandancy, see Entries, January 10, 13, and 18, 1891, Cochrane Diary, Cochrane Papers, MCHC; and SecNav letter to CMC, November 15, 1892, enclosing letter of reprimand to Maj. G. C. Goodloe, Letters Received, "N," 1892, RG 127, NARA.

16. F. M. Ramsay letter to CMC, October 20, 1892, Letters Received, "N," 1892, and CMC letter to SecNav, February 2, 1897, LSSN, vol. 6, pp. 398–406, RG 127, NARA.

17. SecNav letter to CMC, January 9, 1893, and SecNav letter to 1st Lt. Fillette, March 2, 1893, Letters Received, "N," RG 127, NARA; "Naval Sentences Mitigated," *New York Times*, March 7, 1893, 4; Mary Remey letter to Charles Remey, March 9, 1893, in "Life and Letters of Mary J. M. Remey," typescript, vol. 4, Remey Family Papers, LC.

18. CMC letter to SecNav, March 10, 1893, LSSN, vol. 3, p. 23, RG 127, NARA.

19. CMC letters to SecNav, November 4 and December 21, 1893, LSSN, vol. 3, pp. 214 and 246, RG 127; M. Sicard letter to SecNav, February 5, 1894, Letters Received, "N," RG 127; clipping from *Washington Post*, July 20, 1894, in HQMC Scrapbook, vol. 1, RG 127, NARA.

20. C. H. Lauchheimer (for JAG) letter to CMC, February 23, 1894, SecNav letter to CMC, March 1, 1894, and Proceeding of Naval Medical Board, encl. to JAG note to CMC, Letters Received, "N," RG 127; CMC letter to SecNav, March 2, 1894, LSSN, vol. 3, p. 332, RG 127, NARA.

21. CMC letter to Fillette, June 4, 1894, encl. to SecNav letter to Fillette, June 4, 1894, and SecNav letter to Fillette, June 29, 1894, Letters Received, "N," RG 127; CMC letter to SecNav, LSSN, vol. 3, p. 488, RG 127; clipping from *Washington Post*, July 20, 1894, in HQMC, Scrapbook, vol. 1, RG 127, NARA.

22. CMC, *Annual Report, 1893*, 4; H. C. Cochrane draft of letter to CMC, December 30, 1893, Folder 41, H. C. Cochrane Papers, MCHC; "Small Chance for Promotion," *New York Times*, January 4, 1894, 10.

23. U.S. Congress, House, *Personnel of the Navy*, H. R. Misc. Doc. 38, 52d Cong., 2d Sess., 1892; "The Personnel of the Navy," *New York Times*, December 28, 1893; Senator M. C. Butler letter to SecNav, February 2, 1894, File 655/1894, RG 80, NARA.

24. Clipping from *Boston Daily Advertiser*, January 16, 1894, in Clipping Book, vol. 9, Hilary A. Herbert Papers, Southern Historical Collection, University of North Carolina Library, Chapel Hill, North Carolina, Microfilm, Reel 2; Paullin, *Naval Administration*, 420; U.S. Congress, Senate, *Report of a Board . . . to Report upon Stagnation, September, 1891*, S. Misc. Doc. 98, 53d Congress, 2d session, 1894.

25. U.S. Congress, Senate, *Statement to Accompany Bill to Reorganize and Increase the Efficiency of the Personnel of the Navy, February 7, 1894*, S. Misc. Doc. 76, 53d Congress, 2d session, 1894; *New York Times*, February 6, 1894, 6, and February 19, 1894, 4; clipping, "Shaking up the Navy," n.d., n.p., HQMC Scrapbook, vol. 1, RG 127, NARA.

26. Unidentified clipping, n.d., n.p., HQMC Scrapbook, vol. 1, RG 127, NARA; CMC letter to SecNav, February 16, 1894, File 2205/1894, RG 80, NARA.

27. SecNav letter to Joint Committee, March 1, 1894, File 1210/94, RG 80, NARA; U.S. Congress, House Naval Affairs Committee, *Personnel of the Navy*, January 12, 1895, House Report 1573, 53d Congress, 3d Session, 1895, pp. 116–17 and 256. Although Colonel Heywood's testimony is not reprinted in the report, it is quoted in the following sources: Maj. H. B. Lowry, "The United States Marine Corps Considered as a Distinct Military Organization," *Journal of the Military Service Institution* (May 1895): 523–29, and clipping from "Marines at Guns," *Washington Star*, October 12, 1894, HQMC Scrapbook, vol. 1, RG 127, NARA.

28. *Army and Navy Journal*, July 14 and 28, 1895, 810–11, 847–48; William McAdoo, "Reorganization of the Personnel of the Navy," *The North American Review* (October 1894), 457–66.

29. CMC letter to Cmdre. F. M. Ramsay, January 22, 1894, Subject File VR, RG 45, NARA. There is no record of Ramsay's reply to Heywood. See also, Heywood letter to Luce, January 22, 1894, Luce draft to Heywood, February 15, 1894, and Heywood letter to Luce, June 8, 1894, Box 10, Luce Papers, LC.

30. Heywood's testimony before the committee is quoted in U.S. Congress, House, *Congressional Record*, 53d Cong., 3d sess., February 20, 1895, 27, p. 2459.

31. First Lt. Littleton W. T. Waller letter to CMC, with encl., July 17, 1894, Letters Received "W," RG 127, NARA.

32. CMC letter to SecNav, July 20, 1894, LSSN, vol. 4, pp. 13–15, RG 127, NARA.

33. For reprints of the secretary's circular letter of July 31, 1894, see *Army and Navy Journal*, August 4, 1894, 863, and various clippings in HQMC Scrapbook, vol. 1, RG 127, NARA. For references to Herbert's evaluation of the Marine Corps, see SecNav, *Annual Report, 1895*, xxxvii–xxxviii, and *Annual Report, 1896*, 34–35. For Major Reid's influence, see Herbert letter to President, June 2, 1903, vol. 7, p. 1202, William N. Moody Papers, LC.

34. CMC letter to SecNav, October 1, 1894, LSSN, vol. 4, pp. 96–97, RG 127, NARA.

35. Ibid.; SecNav letter to CMC, October 26, 1894, Letters Received, "N," RG 127, NARA; CMC, *Annual Report*, 3.

36. U.S. Congress, Senate, *Congressional Record*, 53d Cong., 2d Sess., August 24,

1894, 26, p. 8648; "A Marine Artillery Corps," *New York Times*, August 26, 1894, 1; CMC letter to SecNav, December 20, 1894, LSSN, vol. 4, pp. 226–28, RG 127, NARA; *Army and Navy Journal*, December 22, 1894, 274.

37. Records of Walter Ball, Austin R. Davis, Thomas S. Borden, T. H. Low, William C. Dawson, John H. Russell, Jr., and Charles F. Macklin, Reel 27, M. 991, Naval Academy Academic and Conduct Records, RG 405, NARA; *Naval Register, 1894*.

38. "Report of Commander of School of Application," October 1, 1894, in CMC, *Annual Report, 1894*, 7; "Report of Commander of School of Application," October 1, 1895, in CMC, *Annual Report, 1895*, 14–15; "Report of Board of Visitors to School of Application," September 1, 1895, in CMC, *Annual Report, 1895*, 17–18.

39. CMC, *Annual Report, 1895*, 6; Record of Louis J. Magill, Reel 28, M. 991, Naval Academy Academic and Conduct Records, RG 405, NARA; *Naval Register, 1895*.

40. CMC, *Annual Report, 1895*, 6; *Naval Registers, 1894–95*. See also Wood Family Papers, LC.

41. Record of John Twiggs Myers, Reel 27, M. 991, Naval Academy Academic and Conduct Records, RG 405, NARA; *Army and Navy Journal*, July 21, 1900, 1106, and September 1, 1900, 17; BuNav letter to 2d Lt. Walter Ball (copy), February 7, 1895, Letters Received "N," RG 127, NARA.

42. "Report of Commander of School of Application," October 1, 1895, in CMC, *Annual Report, 1895*, 14–15, and "Report of Commander of School of Application," August 25, 1896, in CMC, *Annual Report, 1896*, 9.

43. "Report of Commander of School of Application," October 1, 1895, in CMC, *Annual Report, 1895*, 14–15. See also CMC letter to SecNav, January 24, 1896, LSSN, vol. 5, pp. 295–97, RG 127, NARA. Murphy's sentiments about when an officer should attend the War College were quite in contrast with those of the college's founders, Luce and Mahan, who emphasized the postgraduate aspect, but in line with Secretary Herbert's and Commodore Ramsay's views. See Hammett, *Herbert*, 138–39 and 158–60.

44. CMC, *Annual Report, 1895*, 6; CMC letter to SecNav, January 24, 1896, and Ramsay letter to CMC, February 15, 1896 (insert), LSSN, vol. 5, pp. 295–97, RG 127, NARA; "Report of Commander of School of Application," August 25, 1896, in CMC, *Annual Report, 1896*, 9.

45. For some of Forney's idiosyncrasies, see Forney letter to CMC, March 16, 1890, Letters Received, "M," and CMC letters to Forney, March 24 and 26, 1890, Letters Sent, LB 36, pp. 82 and 86, RG 127, NARA. See also entries for September 2 and 3, 1890, in Cochrane Diary, Cochrane Papers, MCHC. For Forney's campaign for the commandancy see J. W. Wanamaker, Postmaster General, letters to Secretary Tracy, January 22 and 27, 1891, Benjamin F. Tracy Papers, LC.

46. Col. James Forney letter to CMC, April 21, 1895, Letters Received, Historical Division, RG 127, NARA.

47. CMC letter to SecNav, May 10 and June 17, 1895, LSSN, vol. 4, pp. 402, 407–9, 453–59, RG 127, NARA.

48. Capt. H. C. Cochrane to Betsy, August 17, 1895, Folder 46, and Betsy letter to Cochrane, November 7, 1895, Folder 48, H. C. Cochrane Papers, MCHC.

49. Sources for this paragraph and the following are Navy Department, General Court-Martial Order No. 88, October 21, 1895, in James Forney Record Book, RG 127, St. Louis Records Center; *Army and Navy Journal*, October 5, 1895, 66; Huntington letter to Cochrane, February 16, 1896, Folder 49, Cochrane Papers, MCHC. The quotation is from Huntington letter to Cochrane.

50. Additional sources for this paragraph are Record of Service in Forney Record Book; *Army and Navy Journal*, November 23, 1895, 203; *New York Times*, November 20, 1895, 9.

51. *Army and Navy Journal*, October 5, 1895, 66; Cochrane letter to Betsy, September

11, 1895, and Betsy to Cochrane, September 16, 1895, Folder 47, Cochrane Papers, MCHC.

52. H. C. Cochrane letter to SecNav, October 22, 1894, File 7294, RG 80, NARA.

53. SecNav to Capt. H. C. Cochrane (copy), December 29, 1894, Letters Received, "N," RG 127, NARA.

54. Cochrane letters to Betsy, November 30 and December 25, 1895, and January 20, 1896; Betsy letter to Cochrane, December 5, 1895, Folders 48–49; and entries, November 25 and 30, 1895, and February 10–11, 1896, Cochrane Diary, Cochrane Papers, MCHC.

55. Heywood letter to Luce, June 8, 1894, Box 10, Luce Papers, LC; Heywood letter to Cmdr. H. C. Taylor, December 29, 1893, U.S. Naval War College Naval Historical Foundation Collection, Miscellaneous, LC; Taylor letter to SecNav, April 25, 1894, Letters Received "N," RG 127, NARA; CMC, *Annual Report, 1894*, 4–5.

56. *Navy Register, 1894*; "The Torpedo in Warfare," *New York Times*, July 10, 1894, 9; "Report of the President of the War College and Torpedo School," September 24, 1894, encl. to SecNav, *Annual Report, 1894*, 208–12; CMC, *Annual Report, 1894*, 4–5.

57. Ronald H. Spector, "Professors of War: The American Naval War College and the Modern American Navy,"(Ph.D. dissertation, Yale University, 1967), 114–62; Ronald H. Spector, *Professors of War: The Naval War College and the Development of the Naval Profession* (Newport, RI, 1977), 64–82; Paullin, *Naval Administration*, 414–16; Capt. H. C. Taylor, "Naval War College," *U.S. Naval Institute* (1895), 199–208.

58. Capt. H. C. Taylor, "Introduction," to Capt. Richard Wallach, "The War in the East," *U.S. Naval Institute Proceedings* (1895): 691, and "Report of President of Naval War College," October 5, 1895, encl. to SecNav, *Annual Report, 1895*.

59. Wallach, "War in the East," 691–745, passim, and 701.

60. Ibid., 708 and 730–31.

61. Ibid., 718 and 721–22.

62. Lt. Lincoln Karmony, "Notes on Small Arms," *Information from Abroad*, ONI, *General Information Series*, July 1894 (Washington, 1894), 155–74; Lt. H. M. Witzel, USN, and Lt. L. Karmony, "Preliminary Notes on the Japan China War," *Information from Abroad*, ONI, *General Information Series*, July 1895 (Washington, 1895), 215–34.

63. Taylor, "Naval War College," 199; "Statement of Rear Adm. H. C. Taylor," in 58th Congress, 2d session, House Committee on Naval Affairs, *General Board Hearings*, April 1904 (Washington, 1904), 950–51; H. C. Taylor, "The Fleet," *U.S. Naval Institute Proceedings* (1903): 797–807; Spector, *Professors of War*, 71–73. See also Henry Taylor letters to Stephen B. Luce, January 13 and 22, 1896, Luce Papers.

64. Spector, *Professors of War*, 85; Robert Seager, *Alfred Thayer Mahan*, 331, 333, 646–47; Mahan letter to H. C. Taylor, July 19, 1895, in Robert Seager and Doris D. Maguire, *Letters and Papers of Alfred Thayer Mahan*, vol. 2, (Annapolis, MD., 1975), 425–28; "Will Be a Mighty Fleet," *New York Times*, July 30, 1895, 1; "Fleet Off for Newport," *New York Times*, August 9, 1895, 9.

65. C. G. Goodrich letter to Asst. SecNav, n.d., reprinted in *Army and Navy Register*, November 20, 1897, 333; H. C. Taylor letter to S. B. Luce, January 22, 1896, Luce Papers, LC; H. C. Taylor, "The Fleet"; "Contingency Plan of Operations in Case of War with Great Britain," December 1890, in Seager and Maguire, *Letters and Papers of Alfred Thayer Mahan*, vol. 3, 559–76; Jeffrey Dorwart, *The Office of Naval Intelligence: The Birth of America's First Intelligence Agency* (Annapolis, MD, 1979), 53; Hammett, *Herbert*, 203; Richard A. Preston, *The Defence of the Undefended Border: Planning for War in North America, 1867–1939* (Montreal, 1977), 131–35; Spector, *Professors of War*, 88–89; "A Naval Fight on Paper," *New York Times*, March 6, 1896, 16. As Spector observes, little documentation exists about Taylor's actual planning efforts in January 1896. One must depend on secondary sources, memories of some of the participants, and on the basis of previous plans and problems involving Great Britain.

66. Preston, *Defence of the Undefended Border*, 7, 104, 126, 128, 130, 135.

67. Spector, "Professors of War," 185–247; Spector, *Professors of War*, 88–94; Hammett, *Herbert*, 203; William McAdoo, "Naval War College," *U.S. Naval Institute Proceedings* (1895), 429–45.

68. Taylor letters to Luce, January 13 and 22, 1896, Luce Papers, LC; and Spector, *Professors of War*, 88–94; Taylor in *General Board Hearings* (1904), 950–51.

69. "Report of President of the Naval War College," October 10, 1896, in SecNav, *Annual Report, 1896*, 147–48, 151; entries, January-July 1896, Cochrane Diary, Cochrane Papers, MCHC; Charles H. Lauchheimer, "Naval Law and Naval Courts," *U.S. Naval Institute Proceedings* (1897): 85–125.

70. "Contingency Plan of Operations in Case of War with Great Britain," December 1890, in Seager and Maguire, *Letters and Papers of Alfred Thayer Mahan*, vol. III, 573.

71. SecNav letter (copy) to Capt. Robley D. Evans, November 1, 1895, Letters Received, Historical Section, 1895, RG 127, NARA; *Army and Navy Journal*, November 2, 1895, 135.

72. CMC letter to SecNav, October 31, 1895, LSSN, vol. 5, pp. 170–75, RG 127, NARA; *Army and Navy Journal*, November 2, 1895, 135.

73. SecNav letter (copy) to Capt. Robley D. Evans, November 1, 1895.

74. SecNav, *Annual Report, 1895*, xxxvii–viii; CMC letter to SecNav, December 18, 1895, LSSN, vol. 5, p. 235, RG 127, NARA.

75. CMC letter to SecNav, February 29, 1896, LSSN, vol. 5, pp. 328–34, RG 127, NARA; Huntington letter to Cochrane, February 16, 1896, Folder 49, H. C. Cochrane Papers, MCHC; P. F. Harrington letter to William F. Fullam, May 5, 1896, William F. Fullam Papers, LC.

76. Lt. William F. Fullam, "The Organization, Training, and Discipline of the Navy Personnel as Viewed from the Ship," *U.S. Naval Institute Proceedings* (1896): 83–116.

77. CMC letter to SecNav, April 14, 1896, LSSN, vol. 5, pp. 375–76, RG 127, NARA. See also copy of letter in Fullam Papers, LC. On his copy of the letter, Fullam wrote, "This must not be published; but it is perfectly proper to give publication to the fact that such a report was made against me by the Col. Comdt. in an attempt to stop discussion."

78. SecNav letter to CMC, April 20, 1896, Letters Received, Historical Section, 1896, RG 127, NARA.

79. "Discussion" of "The Organization . . . Navy Personnel," *U.S. Naval Institute Proceedings* (1896): 116–97.

80. Ibid., 118 and 157.

81. U.S. Congress, House Naval Affairs Committee, *Personnel of the Navy*, January 12, 1895, House Report 1573, 53d Congress, 3d Session, 1895; U.S. Congress, House, *Congressional Record*, 53d Cong., 3d sess., January 12, 1895, 27, p. 910; Peter Karsten, "Armed Progressives: The Military Reorganized for the American Century," in Jerry Israel, ed., *Building the Organizational Society* (New York, 1972), 197–232, 211–14.

82. *Army and Navy Journal*, December 14, 1895, 251 and 261; U.S. Congress, Senate, *Congressional Record*, 54th Cong., 1st Sess., December 4, 1895, 28, p. 34; *New York Times*, December 10, 1895, 9.

83. CMC, *Annual Report, 1895*, 4–5; CMC letter to SecNav, January 14, 1896, and SecNav letter to C. A. Boutelle, February 20, 1896 (copy), LSSN, vol. 5, p. 271, RG 127, NARA.

84. *Army and Navy Journal*, December 14, 1895, 251, January 25, 1896, 369, and February 15, 1896, 423 and 431; U.S. Congress, Senate, *Congressional Record*, 54th Cong., 1st Sess., December 4, 1895, 28, p. 34; U.S. Congress, House, *Congressional Record*, 54th Cong., 1st Sess., January 31, 1896, 28, p. 1197; U.S. Congress, Senate, *Congressional Record*, 54th Cong., 1st Sess., January 29, 1896, 28, p. 1069.

85. Ibid.; Capt. Muse letter to Cochrane, February 7, 1896; Cochrane letter to Betsy, January 20, 1896; and Huntington letter to Cochrane, February 16, 1896, all in Folder 49, Cochrane Papers, MCHC. See also entries for January 20–22, 1896, in Cochrane Diary, Cochrane Papers, MCHC.

86. U.S. Congress, House Committee on Naval Affairs, *Appropriations for the Naval Service*, H.R. Report No. 904, 54th Cong., 1st Sess., March 24, 1896; U.S. Congress, House, *Congressional Record*, 54th Cong., 1st Sess., March 25, 1896, 28, p. 3194.

87. U.S. Congress, Senate, Committee on Appropriations, *Appropriation Report*, Senate Report 652, 54th Cong., 1st Sess., April 9, 1896; Buss Buckingham letter to Fullam, April 20, 1896, and Richard Wainwright letter to Fullam, April 11, 1896, William F. Fullam Papers, LC.

88. U.S. Congress, Senate, *Congressional Record*, 54th Cong., 1st sess., May 2, 1896, 28, pp. 4728–29.

89. CMC, *Annual Report, 1896*, 3, 5–6.

90. CMC letter to SecNav, June 19, 1896, LSSN, vol. 5, pp. 478–79, RG 127, NARA; *Naval Register, 1896*; *New York Times*, April 8, 1896, 1.

91. Record of Melville J. Shaw, Reel 29, M. 991, Naval Academy Academic and Conduct Records, RG 405, NARA; *Naval Register, 1896*; George K. Shaw letter to Tracy, October 8, 1890, Benjamin F. Tracy Papers, LC.

92. "Report of School of Application," July 8, 1897, in CMC, *Annual Report, 1897*, 7; CMC, *Annual Report, 1896*, 6; CMC letter to SecNav, September 26, 1896, LSSN, vol. 6, pp. 148–49, RG 127, NARA.

93. Maj. Reid, Acting CMC letter to SecNav, August 21, 1896; CMC letters to SecNav, October 9 and 12, 1896, LSSN, vol. 6, pp. 86–87, 184–88, and 194–95. On the copy of Major Reid's letter, the clerk wrote: "Letter canceled: Personally attended to by Major Reid."

94. SecNav letter to CMC, October 10, 1896, Letters Received, "N"; CMC letter to SecNav, October 12, 1896, LSSN, vol. 6, pp. 184–88, RG 127, NARA.

95. Acting SecNav McAdoo letter to CMC, December 4, 1896, Letters Received, "N," and CMC letter to SecNav, typescript of annual report, October 9, 1896, LSSN, vol. 6, pp. 194–95, RG 127, NARA.

The annual report typescript contains the following statement: "The following paragraphs have been omitted by secretary's directions." Although there is no documentary evidence, it is not too farfetched to believe that Commodore Ramsay of the Bureau of Navigation may have been behind the Department's decision to veto the experiment with the Marine guard at Newport. The fact that the Newport facility came under his jurisdiction gives some credibility to this supposition, as does the fact that he had tried to deny the assignment of Marines to the secondary battery. The guard of the *Brooklyn* actually trained at Newport, not departing until November 30, 1896. See Cochrane letter to CMC, December 1, 1896, Letters Received, "N," RG 127, NARA.

96. For the 1896 revision of Navy Regulations, see "Changes in Naval Rules," *New York Times*, July 9, 1896, 11; Acting SecNav (McAdoo) letter to Capt. James H. Sands, February 4, 1897, Letters Received, "N," RG 127, NARA; CMC, *Annual Report, 1897*, 8.

CHAPTER 8. POLITICS, PROFESSIONALISM, AND REFORM

1. H. Wayne Morgan, *William McKinley and His America* (Syracuse, NY, 1963), 261, 276, and 527. See also Margaret Leech, *In the Days of McKinley* (New York, 1959), 531–52, and Walter LaFeber, *The New Empire: An Interpretation of American Expansion, 1860–1898* (Ithaca, NY, 1963), 327–33. From a revisionist point of view, LaFeber argues

rather unconvincingly that McKinley looked "to crown his presidency with American control of the markets of the world."

2. Morgan, *McKinley and His America*, 261; Leech, *In the Days of McKinley*, 137; Walter R. Herrick, Jr., *The American Naval Revolution* (Baton Rouge, LA, 1966), 196; Leonard D. White, *The Republican Era: A Study in Administrative History, 1869-1901* (New York, 1958), 157; John D. Long, *The New American Navy*, 2 vols. (New York, 1903), 2: 174-75.

3. Long quoted in Leech, *In the Days of McKinley*, 156.

4. William R. Braisted, *The U.S. Navy in the Pacific 1897-1909*, (Austin, TX, 1958), 10-11; Leech, *In the Days of McKinley*, 156; Long, *The New American Navy*, 2: 174-75. For Taylor's declining of the Bureau of Navigation post, see H. C. Lodge letter to Luce, April 7, 1897, Stephen B. Luce Papers, LC.

5. David F. Trask, *The War with Spain in 1898*, The MacMillan Wars of the United States (New York, 1981), 13-18; David F. Healy, *The United States in Cuba, 1888-1902—Generals, Politicians, and the Search for Policy* (Madison, WI, 1963), 12-13.

6. Herrick, *American Naval Revolution*, 199-201; Braisted, *U.S. Navy in the Pacific*, 11-15; Charles S. Campbell, *The Transformation of American Foreign Relations, 1865-1900*, The New American Nation Series (New York, 1977), 231-32; Outten J. Clinard, *Japan's Influence on American Naval Power, 1897-1917* (Berkeley and Los Angeles, 1947), 8-16; ONI, Plans of Campaign Against Spain and Japan, June 30, 1897, War Portfolio 11, Operational Archives Branch, Naval Historical Division.

7. Campbell, *Transformation of American Foreign Policy*, 66; Sprout and Sprout, *Rise of American Naval Power*, 241; Clinard, *Japan's Influence on American Naval Power*, 31-32; Braisted, *U.S. Navy in the Pacific*, 11-15.

8. CMC letter to SecNav, February 19, 1897, LSSN, vol. 6, pp. 430-32, and Acting SecNav McAdoo letter to CMC, February 20, 1897, Letters Received "N," RG 127, NARA; Entry for March 3, 1897, Cochrane Diary, Henry Clay Cochrane Papers, MCHC; clipping "Col. Higbee Had to March," May 1, 1897, n.p., HQMC Clipping Book, vol. 2, RG 127, NARA.

9. CMC letter to SecNav, April 9, 1897, and Acting CMC letter to SecNav, April 26, 1897, LSSN, vol. 6, pp. 521 and 555; Acting SecNav letter to Lt. Col. J. H. Higbee, April 26, 1897, Letters Received, "N"; "Col. Higbee Had to March," HQMC Clipping Book, vol. 2, RG 127, NARA.

10. "Col Higbee Had to March," HQMC Clipping Book, vol. 2, RG 127, NARA; Lt. Col. John Higbee letter to Navy Capt. W. Sigbee, Commandant of the New York Navy Yard, May 14, 1897, in response to evaluation report by Sigbee, May 13, 1897, various fitness reports and correspondence, 1894-97, Case of Lt. Col. John Higbee, Proceedings of Naval and Marine Examining Boards, 1890-1941, Entry 62, RG 125, Records of the Navy Judge Advocate General, NARA. Higbee's case file does not contain any of the proceedings of any of the examining boards. In Sigbee's evaluation of May 13 on Higbee, the Navy captain wrote that he did not believe the Marine officer's "health sufficiently robust for the discharge of such duties."

11. JAG letter to CMC, October 17, 1895, and SecNav letter to Lowry (copy), Letters Received, "N"; CMC letter to SecNav, November 14, 1896, CMC letter to SecNav, January 30, 1897, and CMC letter to SecNav, February 2, 1897, LSSN, vol. 6, pp. 254, 338-39, and 398-406; Acting SecNav letter to CMC, February 17, 1897, Letters Received, "N," RG 127, NARA; *Army and Navy Journal*, January 23, 1897, 371.

12. Entry for March 3, 1897, Cochrane Diary, Henry Clay Cochrane Papers, MCHC.

13. CMC, *Annual Report, 1897*, 9; Acting SecNav letters to Maj. Horatio B. Lowry, June 18, 1897, and to Maj. Richard S. Collum, June 26, 1897, Letters Received, "N"; JAG letters to CMC, June 21, June 30, and July 23, 1897, Letters Received, "N," RG 127,

NARA; Entry for Thomas C. Prince, Candidates for Admission, 1876–84, Records of the U.S. Naval Academy, RG 405, NARA.

14. Entry for July 10, 1897, Cochrane Diary, Cochrane Papers, MCHC; "At the National Capital," *New York Times*, July 11, 1897, 4; *Army and Navy Register*, July 10, 1897, 18, July 17, 1897, 34, and July 24, 1897, 54.

15. Roosevelt letter to Richard Olney, June 9, 1897 in Elting E. Morison, ed., *The Letters of Theodore Roosevelt*, 18 vols., (Cambridge, MA, 1951–54), 1: 623; Entry for August 21, 1897, Cochrane Diary, Cochrane Papers, MCHC.

16. CMC letter to SecNav, June 12, 1897, LSSN, vol. 6, pp. 670–71; Asst. SecNav letter to CMC, June 15, 1897, Letters Received, "N," RG 127, NARA; "Favor the Engineer Corps," *New York Times*, February 1, 1897, 7.

17. *Naval Register, 1897*; Records of Philip M. Bannon and Newt N. Hall, Reel 30, M. 991, Naval Academy Academic and Conduct Records, RG 405, NARA.

18. CMC, *Annual Report, 1897*, 8–9; Capt. F. H. Harrington, Director of Instruction letter to CMC, April 18, 1898, Letters Received, History Section, RG 127, NARA.

19. Copy of SecNav (CHL) letter to Capt. John R. Read, May 24, 1897, Letters Received, History Section, RG 127, NARA. See also *Army and Navy Register*, June 12, 1897, 384–85.

20. CMC, *Annual Report, 1897*, 7–8.

21. Capt. H. C. Cochrane letter to CMC, July 16, 1896, Letters Received, "N," RG 127, NARA. The Army established its post-exchange system in 1895. See Russell F. Weigley, *History of the U.S. Army* (New York, 1967), 270.

22. Entry for June 1, 1897, Cochrane Diary, Cochrane Papers, MCHC.

23. Entries for August 4, 7, and 18, 1897, Cochrane Diary, Cochrane Papers, MCHC; Acting SecNav letter to CMC, August 6, 1897, and SecNav letter to CMC, October 17, 1901, Decision in Regard to Status of the Post Exchange in the Marine Corps, with attachments, Letters Received, "N," RG 127, NARA. See also *New York Times*, August 18, 1897, 3.

24. Acting SecNav letters to CMC, August 25 and September 6, 1897, and to Maj. Robert L. Meade, October 27, 1897, Letters Received, "N," RG 127, NARA.

25. SecNav, *Annual Report, 1897*, 29–30.

26. Long is quoted in Robert G. Albion, *Makers of Naval Policy, 1798–1947*, Rowena Reed, ed. (Annapolis, MD, 1980), 142; Roosevelt letter to CMC, December 29, 1897, Letter Book, December 1897–April 8, 1898, Series 2, Reel 315, p. 9, Theodore Roosevelt Papers, LC.

27. J. R. Richards letter to Asst. SecNav, December 1, 1897, Letters Received, History Section; CMC letter to Mr. Roosevelt, December 16, 1897, LSSN, vol. 7, pp. 51–52, RG 127, NARA. It is interesting to speculate whether Heywood knew that Platt had tried to block Roosevelt's appointment to the Navy Department. If he did, he may have felt secure in denying Elliott's request, figuring there was no apparent love lost between Roosevelt and Platt.

28. Leech, *In the Days of McKinley*, 468; clipping from the *North American Press*, January 6, 1902, Charles L. McCawley Personal Papers, MCHC; Col. Theo A. Bingham, USA, letter to SecNav, January 13, 1898, Letters Received, History Section, RG 127, NARA.

29. CMC letter to SecNav, January 13, 1897, LSSN, vol. 6, p. 354; Asst. SecNav letter to CMC, February 16, 1898, Letters Received, "N"; CMC letter to SecNav, February 18 and March 15, 1898, LSSN, vol. 7, pp. 153–54 and p. 191, RG 127, NARA; Entries for February 2, 9, 12, 1898, Cochrane Diary, and Capt. W. S. Muse letter to Cochrane, March 13, 1898, H. C. Cochrane Papers, MCHC.

30. CMC letter to SecNav, May 29, 1896, LSSN, vol. 5, pp. 451–52; SecNav letter to CMC, with enclosures, June 15, 1896, Letters Received, "N"; Navy Department General

Order No. 478, September 4, 1897, Entry 45, Scrapbook of Navy Department Issuances, 1885–1900, RG 127, NARA.

31. Proceedings of Examining Board, February 1898 case of Capt. Henry C. Cochrane in Proceedings of Naval and Marine Examining Boards, 1890–1941, Entry 62, RG 125, Records of the Navy Judge Advocate General, NARA; Entries for February 7–11, 1898, Cochrane Diary, H. C. Cochrane Papers, MCHC.

32. Long, *The New American Navy*, 1: 82–83 and SecNav, *Annual Report, 1897*, 36.

33. Long, *The New American Navy*, 1: 82–83; SecNav Long letter to Asst. SecNav Roosevelt, November 4, 1897, attached to copy of letter from SecNav to Charles A. Boutelle, chairman, Committee on Naval Affairs, HR, January 12, 1898, Case File 5288/6, RG 80, General Records of the Department of the Navy, NARA.

34. Long, *The New American Navy*, 1: 82–84; *Army and Navy Register*, November 6 and 13, 1897, 302 and 318; Robley D. Evans, *A Sailor's Log: Recollections of Forty Years of Naval Life* (New York, 1901), 403; Rear Adm. George W. Melville, "Engineering in the United States Navy," n.d., (Mar. 1909?), George W. Melville Papers, LC.

35. *Army and Navy Register*, November 13, 1897, 318; Asst. SecNav letter to Erwin Stewart, Paymaster General, November 9, 1897, File 5288/3, RG 80; Asst. SecNav letter to CMC, November 9, 1897, File 5288/4, RG 80, NARA.

36. Heywood letter to Lt. Col. J. H. Higbee, November 10, 1897, attached to Higbee letter to Stephen B. Luce, November 13, 1897, Luce Papers, LC; CMC letter to President of the Board of Reorganization of Naval Personnel, November 22, 1897, LSSN, vol. 7, pp. 1–14, RG 127, NARA; *Army and Navy Register*, November 20, 1897, 334.

37. Capt. H. C. Cochrane letter to CMC, November 19, 1897, Letters Received, History Section, RG 127, NARA.

38. Ibid.

39. Capt. Paul St. Clair Murphy letter to CMC, November 16, 1897, and Capt. H. K. White letter to CMC, December 12, 1897, Letters Received, History Section, RG 127, NARA.

40. First Lt. George Barnett letter to CMC, November 16, 1897, Letters Received, History Section, RG 127, NARA. For other samples of Marine officers' replies, see 1st Lt. Dion Williams letter to CMC, November 27, 1897; 1st Lt. Charles L. Lauchheimer letter to CMC, November 19, 1897; 1st Lt. B. S. Neumann, letter to CMC, November 13, 1897; Maj. Robert L. Meade letter to CMC, November 13, 1897; Capt. Charles L. McCawley letter to CMC, November 16, 1897; Capt. W. S. Muse letter to CMC, November 15, 1897; Capt. F. H. Harrington letter to CMC, November 13, 1897; Capt. William F. Spicer letter to CMC, November 13, 1897; Capt. O. C. Berryman letter to CMC, November 26, 1897; Capt. J. M. T. Young letter to CMC, December 18, 1897; and Lt. Col. Robert W. Huntington letter to CMC, November 15, 1897. All in Letters Received, History Section, RG 127, NARA.

41. CMC letter to President of the Board of Reorganization of Naval Personnel, November 22, 1897, LSSN, vol. 7, pp. 1–14, RG 127, NARA.

42. *New York Times*, November 28, 1897, 24; *Army and Navy Register*, 366; U.S. Congress, House, *Reorganization of Naval Personnel, HR 10403, with Accompanying Report*, HR 1375, 55th Cong., 2d Sess, 1898.

43. *New York Times*, November 9, 1897, 6; *Army and Navy Journal*, December 11, 1897, 267; *New York Times*, March 25, 1898, 3.

CHAPTER 9. THE SPANISH-AMERICAN WAR AND AFTERMATH

1. David F. Trask, *The War with Spain in 1898*, The MacMillan Wars of the United States (New York, 1981), xii–xiv, 35; John D. Long, *The New American Navy*, 2 vols.

(New York, 1903), 1: 141. In a seminal essay, historian Richard Hofstadter stated that the Spanish-American War resulted from what he called the "psychic crisis of the 1890s." He suggested that economic depression, perceived social and political convulsions, and the "maturation and bureaucratization of American business" combined to create almost a schizoid America. He believed the Spanish-American War "served as an outlet for aggressive impulses while presenting itself, quite truthfully as an idealistic and humanitarian crusade." Hofstadter, like Trask, played down the role of the press, observing that it "must operate roughly within the framework of public predispositions." Richard Hofstadter, "Manifest Destiny and the Philippines," in Daniel Aaron, ed., *America in Crisis* (New York, 1952), 173-200.

2. Trask, *The War with Spain*, 72-78, 88-90; *Appendix to the Report of the Chief of the Bureau of Navigation*, SecNav, *Annual Report, 1898*, vol. 2, p. 23. See also William R. Braisted, *The U.S. Navy in the Pacific, 1897-1909*, (Austin, TX, 1958), 21-22, 25; Margaret Leech, *In the Days of McKinley* (New York, 1959), 195-96; Long, *The New American Navy*, 1: 162-63; Ronald Spector, *Admiral of the New Empire: The Life and Career of George Dewey* (Baton Rouge, LA, 1974), 32-35, 43; J. A. S. Grenville, "American Naval Preparations for War with Spain, 1896-98," *Journal of American Studies* (April 1968), 33-47.

For copies of some of the original plans, see Lt. William Kimball, "War with Spain," June 1, 1896; Plan of Operations Against Spain, December 17, 1896; and Plans of Campaign against Spain and Japan, June 30, 1897, all in War Planning Portfolio 11, OAB, Naval Historical Division.

Theodore Roosevelt's instructions to Cmdre. George Dewey to undertake offensive operations in the Philippine Islands in the event of war were not as remarkable as historians once thought. Almost all of the past contingency plans took into consideration naval operations against the islands.

3. Trask, *The War with Spain*, 83-90; Long, *The New American Navy*, 1: 165-66.

4. Graham A. Cosmas, *An Army for Empire: The United States Army in the Spanish-American War* (Columbia, MO, 1971), 87-89. See also Trask, *The War with Spain*, 145-49, and Russell F. Weigley, *History of the U.S. Army* (New York, 1967), 299.

5. Trask, *The War with Spain*, 82-88; Leech, *In the Days of McKinley*, 195-96; Walter Millis, *Arms and Men* (New York, 1958), 170-71.

6. SecNav letters to CMC, March 10, April 6, and April 11, 1898, Letters Received, "N," RG 127; CMC letters to SecNav, March 13 and 15, and April 6 and 9, 1898, LSSN, vol. 7, pp. 187, 194-95, 245-46, 252, RG 127, NARA; CMC, *Annual Report, 1898*, 6. In 1892, the Army adopted for the infantry and cavalry the .30-caliber 5-shot, magazine-fed, Krag-Jorgenson rifle to replace the .45-caliber, single-shot, breech-loading Springfield rifle, model 1873. The Navy Department, which had also used the Springfield as its standard rifle, refused to go along with the selection of the "Krag," choosing instead the Lee "Straight-pull" 6-mm, 5-shot, magazine-fed rifle for the Marine Corps and Navy. Navy small arms experts argued that the smaller-caliber, lighter Lee because of its faster muzzle velocity could cause as much if not more damage than the heavier, larger-caliber Krag. The Marine Corps began partial distribution of the new Lee rifles in 1897. Russell F. Weigley, *History of the U.S. Army* (New York, 1967), 268-69; Cosmas, *An Army for Empire*, 8; SecNav, *Annual Report, 1895*, xiv-v; CMC, *Annual Report, 1897*, 4-5.

7. SecNav letter to CMC and copy of letter to C. A. Boutelle, March 10, 1898, Letters Received, "N," RG 127; *Army and Navy Journal*, March 12, 1898, 515; Lt. Cmdr. Richard Wainwright, "Our Naval Power," *United States Naval Institute Proceedings* (March 1898), 39-87.

8. Lt. Col. R. W. Huntington letter to CMC, February 15, 1898, Letters Received, "N," RG 127, NARA.

9. Huntington letter to Bobby, March 30, 1898, Col. R. W. Huntington Papers, MCHC.

10. McKinley quoted in Trask, *The War with Spain*, 53. See also Charles S. Campbell, *The Transformation of American Foreign Relations, 1865-1900*, The New American Nation Series (New York, 1977), 273 and 278.

11. Long letter to CinC, U.S. Naval Force, NA, April 6, 1898, and Sampson letter to SecNav, April 9, 1898, reprinted in *Appendix to the Report*, 171-73; Trask, *The War with Spain*, 90-91; Long, *The New American Navy*, 1: 243; Chief, Bureau of Navigation letter to CMC, March 25, 1898, Letters Received, "N," RG 127, NARA.

Captain Robely D. Evans, one of Sampson's officers, later wrote that he believed the fleet could have captured Havana two days after the declaration of war if Sampson's original plan had been followed. Rear Adm. A. T. Mahan, who joined the Navy's Strategy Board after Assistant Secretary Roosevelt resigned to form a volunteer regiment, defended the decision to implement the blockade: "Its importance lay in its two-fold tendency to exhaust the enemy's army in Cuba, and to force his navy to come to the relief. No effect more decisive than these two could be produced by us before the coming of the hostile navy, or the readiness of our own army to take the field." Robley D. Evans, *A Sailor's Log, Recollections of Forty Years of Naval Life* (New York, 1901), 407, and A. T. Mahan, "The War on the Sea and its Lessons," *McClures* 3 (December 1898?): 353-62, in Printed Material Folder, H. C. Taylor Papers, LC.

12. CMC letters to SecNav, April 18 and 23, 1898, LSSN, vol. 7, pp. 250-52, and 266, RG 127; Acting CMC letter to SecNav, April 19, 1898, Letters Received, "N," RG 127; Entries for April 17-22, 1898, and Battalion Orders 1-3, April 19-20, 1898, in Journal of the Marine Battalion under Lt. Col. Robert W. Huntington, Apr.-Sep. 1898, RG 127, NARA; CMC, *Annual Report, 1898*, 7 and 10; "Report of the Adjutant and Inspector of the USMC," September 20, 1898, in CMC, *Annual Report, 1898*, 50 and 56; Charles L. McCawley, "The Marines at Guantanamo," n.d., MS, 2-4, Maj. Gen. Charles L. McCawley Papers, MCHC; "Marine Battalion at Guantanamo," reprinted in *Appendix to the Report*, 440-41. Graham A. Cosmas observed that the "Marine mobilization coincides in time with the order for concentration of most of the Regular Army at Chickamauga Park, New Orleans, Mobile, and Tampa, which went out on 15 April [1898]." Graham A. Cosmas, comments on author's draft chapter, March 1990.

13. "Marines to Start Tonight," clipping from *Brooklyn Eagle* (Apr. 22, 1898), General Clipping File, Cochrane Papers, MCHC; *New York Times*, April 23, 1898, 4; Charles L. McCawley, "The Marines at Guantanamo," n.d., MS, 2-4, Maj. Gen. Charles L. McCawley Papers, MCHC; "Marine Battalion at Guantanamo," 440-41; CMC, *Annual Report, 1898*, 6.

14. "Marine Battalion at Guantanamo," reprinted in *Appendix to the Report of the Chief of the Bureau of Navigation*, 440-41; CMC letter to SecNav, April 23, 1898, LSSN, vol. 7, pp. 250-52, RG 127, NARA; Cochrane letter to Betsy, April 22, 1898, H. C. Cochrane Papers, MCHC.

15. Maj. George C. Reid letter to Pendleton, April 19, 1898, in Maj. Gen Joseph H. Pendleton Papers, MCHC; Long message to Sampson, April 21, 1898, reprinted in *Appendix to the Report*, 174-75; Cochrane letter to Betsy, April 23, 1898, H. C. Cochrane Papers, MCHC; Long, *The New American Navy*, 2: 5.

16. Trask, *The War with Spain*, 56, 150-52; Cosmas, *An Army for Empire*, 93-102.

17. Leech, *In the Days of McKinley*, 198-99; Trask, *The War with Spain*, 153-54; Cosmas, *An Army for Empire*, 102-7; Long, *The New American Navy*, 2: 9.

18. Trask, *The War with Spain*, 108, 153-54; Cosmas, *An Army for Empire*, 107; Long letter to Sampson, April 21, 1898, reprinted in *Appendix to the Report*, 174.

19. Entries for April 23-26, 1898, in Journal of the Marine Battalion, Apr.-Sep. 1898, RG 127 NARA; entries for April 23-28, 1898, Cochrane Diary, H. S. Cochrane Papers,

MCHC; Lt. Col. R. W. Huntington report to CMC, April 30, 1898, Letters Received, History Section, RG 127, NARA; McCawley, "The Marines at Guantanamo," 8–10; CMC, *Annual Report, 1898,* 6.

20. Entries for April 23–26, 1898, in Journal of the Marine Battalion, Apr.-Sep. 1898, RG 127; entries for April 23–28, 1898, Cochrane Diary, H. S. Cochrane Papers, MCHC; Lt. Col. R. W. Huntington report to CMC, April 30, 1898. Modifications continued to be made on the Lee rifles. See Chief, Bureau of Ordnance letter to CMC, July 22, 1898, Letters Received, "N," RG 127, NARA.

21. Entries for April 26–29, 1898, in Journal of the Marine Battalion, Apr.-Sep. 1898, RG 127; Henry Clay Cochrane letter to Betsy, April 26, 1898, Folder 51, H. C. Cochrane Papers, MCHC; McCawley, "The Marines at Guantanamo," 8.

22. Trask, *The War with Spain,* 162–63; Cosmas, *An Army for Empire,* 111–12; Leech, *In the Days of McKinley,* 198–99; Cochrane letter to Betsy and boys, May 4, 1898, Cochrane Papers, MCHC; Huntington letter to Bobby, April 30, 1898, R. W. Huntington Papers, MCHC.

23. Long letter to Dewey, April 24, 1898, and Dewey report to SecNav, May 4, 1898, reprinted in *Appendix to the Report,* 67 and 69–72; Trask, *The War with Spain,* 95–107.

24. Dewey to Long, May 4 and 13, 1898 reprinted in *Appendix to the Report,* 68 and 97–98; Trask, *The War with Spain,* 105; Bernard C. Nalty, *The United States Marines in the War with Spain,* rev. ed. (Washington, 1967), 6.

25. Cosmas, *An Army for Empire,* 121–30; Leech, *In the Days of McKinley,* 214–16; Trask, *The War with Spain,* 163–67; Long letter to Sampson, May 3, 1898, reprinted in *Appendix to the Report,* 366. Graham A. Cosmas observed it was his understanding that "McKinley had unofficial reports of Dewey's victory at the time he began to revise strategy on 2 May." Cosmas comments to author, March 1990.

26. Entry for April 30, 1898, in Journal of the Marine Battalion, Apr.-Sep. 1898, RG 127; McCawley, "The Marines at Guantanamo," 10; Entry for May 3, 1898, Cochrane Diary, H. S. Cochrane Papers, MCHC; Trask, *The War with Spain,* 114.

27. Entries for May 1–24, 1898, in Journal of the Marine Battalion, Apr.-Sep. 1898, RG 127; entry for May 31, 1898, Cochrane Diary, H. S. Cochrane Papers, MCHC; Huntington letter to Bobby, May 27, 1898, R. W. Huntington Papers, MCHC.

28. Huntington letters to CMC, May 25 and November 3, 1899, Maj. Charles L. McCawley letter to CMC, January 8, 1900, and Cmdre. George C. Remey endorsement to CMC, May 25, 1898, Letters Received, Historical, RG 127, NARA; Huntington letter to Bobby, May 27, 1898, R. W. Huntington Papers, MCHC.

29. For examples of this correspondence, see Cochrane letters to Betsy, May 6, 9, 12, 28, and June 1, 1898, and Betsy letters to Cochrane, April 24 and 25, 1898, Folder 51, Cochrane Papers, MCHC.

30. *New York Times,* March 25, 1898, 3.

31. CMC letter to SecNav, March 28, 1898, with enclosures, LSSN, vol. 7, pp. 210–27, RG 127, NARA; U.S. Congress, House, *Reorganization of Naval Personnel, HR 10403, with Accompanying Report,* HR 1375, 55th Cong., 2d sess., 1898, pp. 12–13.

32. U.S. Congress, Senate, *Congressional Record,* 55th Cong., 2d sess., April 29, 1898, 31, 4422; CMC, *Annual Report, 1898,* 11.

33. For the Cochrane correspondence, see Henry letters to Betsy, May 6, 9, 12–13, 1898, and Betsy letter to Henry, May 12, 1898, Folder 51, Cochrane Papers, MCHC.

34. U.S. Congress, House, *Congressional Record,* 55th Cong., 2d sess., May 19, 1898, 31, 5058–59; CMC, *Annual Report, 1898,* 16–17; SecNav, *Annual Report, 1898,* 54–57; Cochrane letters to wife, May 12 and 28, 1898, Folder 51 and entry, Cochrane Diary, June 4, 1898, Cochrane Papers, MCHC.

35. Cochrane letter to wife, June 1, 1898, Folder 51, Cochrane Papers, MCHC.

36. Sources for this and the following paragraph are CMC letter to SecNav, May 5, 9,

13-16, 17, 18, 20, 21, 25, and June 6, 1898, LSSN, vol. 7, pp. 305, 308-14, 329-45, 353, 370-74; Asst. SecNav letter to CMC, May 3-4, 1898, Letters Received, "N," RG 127, NARA.

37. Additional sources for this paragraph are CMC, *Annual Report, 1898*, 11. The records do not indicate why a fourth NCO was not commissioned, although Sergeant Henry Good, the sergeant major of the Marine battalion under Huntington was nominated. One can surmise that his untimely death at Guantanamo prevented his appointment and that the war ended before another choice could be made.

38. CMC letter to SecNav, June 18, 1898, LSSN, vol. 7, p. 415, RG 127, NARA.

39. C. Mason Kinne letter to SecWar, Gen R. A. Alger and attached letters and endorsements, June 24, 1898, Letters Received, Historical Section, RG 127, NARA.

40. CMC letter to SecNav, June 6, 1898, LSSN, vol. 7, pp. 372-74, RG 127, NARA; Lt. Charles G. Andresen letter to Waller, May 5, 1899, LWT Waller Papers, 1896-1902, MCHC.

41. Capt. F. H. Harrington, School of Application letter to CMC, April 18, 1898, Letters Received, Historical Section, RG 127, NARA; CMC, *Annual Report, 1898*, 11 and 15. See also Hans Schmidt, *Maverick Marine, General Smedley D. Butler and the Contradictions of American Military History* (Lexington, Kentucky, 1987), 7.

42. Exchange of messages between Long and Schley, May 27-29, 1898, reprinted in *Appendix to the Report*, 397-400.

43. Exchange of messages, May 28-30, 1898, reprinted in ibid., 398-400.

44. Sigsbee letter to SecNav, May 31, 1898, reprinted in ibid., 412-14; Rear Adm. William T. Sampson, "The Atlantic Fleet in the Spanish War," *Century Magazine*, n.d., 886-913, 903, in Printed Material Folder, H. C. Taylor Papers, LC.

45. Entries for June 1-7, 1898, in Journal of the Marine Battalion, Apr.-Sep. 1898, RG 127; Entries for June 1-7, 1898, Cochrane Diary, H. C. Cochrane Papers, MCHC.

46. Entry for June 4, 1898, Cochrane Diary, H. C. Cochrane Papers, MCHC; McCalla letter to Sampson, July 19, 1898, reprinted in Maj. Richard S. Collum, *History of the United States Marine Corps* (New York, 1903), 348-49; McCawley, "The Marines at Guantanamo," 9; Nalty, *The United States Marines in the War with Spain*, 9; Huntington letter to Bobby, June 19, 1898, R. W. Huntington Papers, MCHC.

47. McCawley, "The Marines at Guantanamo," 15-17.

48. Sources for this paragraph and the following are ibid.; Entries for June 11-12, 1898, in Journal of the Marine Battalion, Apr.-Sep. 1898, RG 127; Huntington letter to Bobby, June 19, 1898, R. W. Huntington Papers, MCHC; Entries for June 11-12, 1898, Cochrane Diary, H. C. Cochrane Papers, MCHC.

49. Additional source for this paragraph is Cochrane letter to wife, June 12, 1898, Folder 51, H. C. Cochrane Papers, MCHC.

50. Entries for June 11-12, 1898, in Journal of the Marine Battalion, Apr.-Sep. 1898, RG 127. The discussion about the proposed evacuation is contained in Cochrane's diary (entries for 11-12 June and August 25, 1898, and in the flysheet in the back of the diary for 1898, H. C. Cochrane Papers, MCHC) referring to interviews with several other witnesses. He also mentions the incident in a letter to his wife (Cochrane letter to wife, June 14, 1898, Folder 51, Cochrane Papers). Cochrane was not a witness to McCalla's refusal and gives conflicting accounts. In a separate report, Commander McCalla only stated: "The mistake of locating the camp between the main position and the outpost was corrected . . . at my suggestion." McCalla letter to Sampson, July 19, 1898, reprinted in Collum, *History of the United States Marine Corps*, 348-49.

51. Entries for June 12-13, 1898, in Journal of the Marine Battalion, Apr.-Sep. 1898, RG 127; Entry for June 13, 1898, Cochrane Diary, H. C. Cochrane Papers, MCHC.

52. Entries for June 14 and 19, 1898, in Journal of the Marine Battalion, Apr.-Sep. 1898, RG 127.

53. McCawley, "The Marines at Guantanamo," 31–37; McCalla letter to CinC North Atlantic Station, June 16, 1898, Letters Received, History Section, RG 127, NARA; Sampson letter to Long, June 22, 1898, reprinted in *Appendix to the Report*, 449; Huntington letter to Bobby, July 4, 1898, in R. W. Huntington Papers, MCHC.

54. Journal of the Marine Battalion, Apr.-Sep. 1898, RG 127; McCawley, "The Marines at Guantanamo," 28, 31–40; entries for June 13–15, 1898, Cochrane Diary, H. C. Cochrane Papers, MCHC; *New York Times*, June 17, 1898.

55. Clippings "First to Fight" and "The Gallant Marines," n.d., n.p., General Clipping File, H. C. Cochrane Papers, MCHC; R. W. Stallman and E. R. Hagemann, eds., *The War Despatches of Stephen Crane*, (New York, 1964), 140–54, 171–72, and 267–74; Capt. G. F. Elliott letter to Huntington, June 18, 1898, reprinted in CMC, *Annual Report, 1898*, 29; William E. Nanscawen, Spanish-American War Survey, n.d., U.S. Military Collection, U.S. Army Military History Institute Collection, Carlisle Barracks, PA; Allan R. Millett, *Semper Fidelis: The History of the United States Marine Corps* (New York, 1981), 133–34.

56. Trask, *The War with Spain*, 172–73; Cosmas, *An Army for Empire*, 179–80.

57. Long letter to Schley, May 27, 1898, reprinted in *Appendix to the Report*, 397; Long message to Sampson, May 31, 1898, quoted in Sampson, Report of Operations of North Atlantic Fleet, August 3, 1898, reprinted in *Appendix to the Report*, 480.

58. Trask, *The War with Spain*, 175–76; Cosmas, *An Army for Empire*, 181.

59. Trask, *The War with Spain*, 182–88; Cosmas, *An Army for Empire*, 195–97. Quote is from Adm. W. T. Sampson, Report of Operations, August 3, 1898, reprinted in *Appendix to the Report*, 485.

60. Sampson is quoted from Sampson, "The Atlantic Fleet in the Spanish War," 904–5. See also Sampson letter to Long, June 22, 1898, reprinted in *Appendix to the Report*, 450–51. Although Sampson refers to the meeting of June 20 in the latter source, he does not state the objective of the Army task force once it lands. Shafter is quoted in Trask, *The War with Spain*, 204. See also Cosmas, *An Army for Empire*, 205–6.

61. Trask, *The War with Spain*, 199–205. See also Cosmas, *An Army for Empire*, 177, 205–9.

62. Cosmas, *An Army for Empire*, 209–16. See also Trask, *The War with Spain*, 225–52.

63. Messages quoted in Sampson, Report of Operations of North Atlantic Fleet, August 3, 1898, reprinted in *Appendix to the Report*, 504.

64. Chadwick letter to Cornelia Chadwick, July 4, 1898, in Doris D. Maguire, ed., *French Ensor Chadwick: Selected Letters and Papers* (Washington, DC, 1981), 194–95.

65. Trask, *The War with Spain*, 261–69.

66. Ibid., 291–93; Rear Adm. W. T. Sampson, Report of Operations of Blockading Squadron off Santiago, July 15, 1898, reprinted in *Appendix to the Report*, 609–10; Sec-Nav, *Annual Report, 1898*, 14.

67. "Minutes of a conversation between Captain Chadwick of the Navy, representing Admiral Sampson, and General Shafter," July 6, 1898, reproduced in Sampson, Report of Operations, July 15, 1898, p. 610. Chadwick in his history, however, states that Shafter had agreed to attack the Morro. French Ensor Chadwick, *The Relations of the United States and Spain: The Spanish American War*, 2 vols. (New York, 1911, reissued in 1968), 2: 208.

David Trask also says that Shafter agreed to attack the Morro, "although for unexplained reasons this aspect of the plan was not made explicit in the minutes of the meeting." Trask, *The War with Spain*, 293.

Graham Cosmas comments that from "3 July on, Shafter was engaged in his own negotiations with the Spanish commander, General Toral, looking to the surrender of the garrison. I'm not sure how thoroughly, or even whether, he kept Sampson filled in on this." Cosmas comments to author, March 1990.

68. Long, *New Navy*, 2: 152; Long letter to Sampson, July 13, 1898, in Rear Adm. W. T. Sampson, "History of Relations between Army and Navy at Santiago," August 1, 1898, reprinted in *Appendix to the Report*, 625; Trask, *The War with Spain*, 301 and 306–8.

69. Lt. Col. Robert L. Meade letter to Maj. Charles L. McCawley, March 18, 1899, Charles L. McCawley Papers, MCHC.

70. Entries for July 17–21, 1898, Cochrane Diary, Cochrane Papers, MCHC; Trask, *The War with Spain*, 350 and 353.

71. First Marine Battalion Order No. 3, June 21, 1898, Journal of the Marine Battalion, Apr.-Sep. 1898, RG 127; McCawley, "The Marines at Guantanamo," 45–48; Cochrane letter to Betsy, July 23, 1898, Cochrane Papers, MCHC.

72. A. T. Mahan, "The War on the Sea and Its Lessons," *McClures* (n.d.), 527–34, in Printed Material Folder, H. C. Taylor Papers, LC; Huntington letter to Bobby, July 29, 1898, in R. W. Huntington Papers, MCHC.

73. F. Goodrich letter to CinC North Atlantic Fleet, August 13, 1898, reprinted in *Appendix to the Report*, 301–3.

74. Ibid. McCawley, "The Marines at Guantanamo," 43–45; entry for August 13, 1898, Cochrane Diary, Cochrane Papers, MCHC.

75. CMC to SecNav, December 12, 1898, LSSN, vol. 7, pp. 84–85, RG 127, NARA.

76. Henry Clay Cochrane letter to Betsy, August 22, 1898, Cochrane Papers, MCHC; Chief, BuNav letter to CMC, August 8, 1898, Letters Received, Historical Section and CMC letter to SecNav, September 10, 1898, LSSN, vol. 7, pp. 567–68, RG 127, NARA; Ira Nelson Hollis, "The Navy in the War with Spain," *Atlantic* (November 1898): 605–16, Printed Matter Folder, Henry C. Taylor Papers, LC; *Army and Navy Journal*, September 17, 1898, 68.

Malaria and yellow fever played havoc with the Army's 5th Corps before Santiago. On July 27, 1898, more than 4,000 soldiers in the corps were in the hospital, and a few days later the death rate reached fifteen per day. Cosmas, *An Army for Empire*, 251–52.

Although Marine sanitary practices in part accounted for their low sickness rate, the Marines were fortunate that the Guantanamo sector remained dry and bred few of the mosquitos that spread yellow fever and malaria among the Army troops.

77. *Army and Navy Journal*, September 24, 1898, 95.

78. CMC, *Annual Report*, 1898, 14; *Army and Navy Journal*, August 27, 1898, 1088.

79. Capt. Littleton W. T. Waller letter to CMC, USMC, September 1, 1898, in CMC, *Annual Report*, 1898, 44–45; H. C. Taylor letter to SecNav, September 18, 1898, in Correspondence Folder, July-September 1898, H. C. Taylor Papers, LC; Capt. R. D. Evans letter to Lt. Col. R. L. Meade, August 31, 1898, Letters Received, Historical Section, RG 127, NARA; Millett, *Semper Fidelis*, 130–31; David F. Trask, *The War with Spain in 1898*, The MacMillan Wars of the United States (New York, 1981), 104, 265–66; Chadwick, *The Relations of the United States and Spain*, 2: 177; Lt. John Ellicott, USN, *Effect of the Gun Fire of the United States Vessels in the Battle of Manila Bay* (May 1, 1898), Office of Naval Intelligence, War Note No. 5, Information from Abroad (Washington, 1899).

80. Ellicott, *Effect of the Gun Fire*; Commander J, German Navy, *Sketches from the Spanish-American War*, Office of Naval Intelligence, War Notes Nos. 3 and 4, Information from Abroad (Washington, 1899); CMC, *Annual Report*, 1898; "Record of the Marines," *New York Times*, October 23, 1898, 13.

81. Hofstadter, "Manifest Destiny and the Philippines," 173–200; Leech, *In the Days of McKinley*, 238. See also H. Wayne Morgan, *William McKinley and His America* (Syra-

cuse, NY, 1963), 3, 238, 295; Campbell, *The Transformation of American Foreign Relations*, 289-90, 298, and 301; and Braisted, *The U.S. Navy in the Pacific, 1897-1909*, 21, 34-42, and 52-57.

82. Henry letter to Betsy, June 1, 1898, Cochrane Papers, MCHC; CMC letter to SecNav, December 12, 1898, LSSN, vol. 7, pp. 843-55, RG 127, NARA; Navy Dept., endorsement, March 11, 1899, File 4541 (4), General Correspondence, 1897-1915, RG 80, General Records of the Navy Department, NARA; "Marines for Cavite," *New York Times*, March 14, 1899, 1.

83. CMC letter to SecNav, November 9, 1898, LSSN, vol. 7, pp. 757-60, RG 127, NARA; SecNav, *Annual Report, 1898*, 19.

84. CMC letter to SecNav, December 12, 1898, enclosing "A Bill to Increase the Efficiency of the Marine Corps," LSSN, vol. 7, pp. 843-63, RG 127, NARA.

85. Entry for January 5, 1899, Cochrane Diary, Cochrane Papers, MCHC; U.S. Congress, House, *Congressional Record*, 55th Cong., 3d sess., January 17, 1899, 32, 720-25; "The Navy Personnel Bill," *New York Times*, January 18, 1899, 5; *Army and Navy Journal* (January 1899): 494-95.

86. U.S. Congress, House and Senate, *Congressional Record*, 55th Cong., 3d sess., February 17 and March 1, 1899, 32, 1978, 2663, and 2698. For the provisions of the law as they affected the Marine Corps, see Navy Department General Order 510, March 6, 1899, in Entry 45, Scrapbook of Navy Department Issuances, 1885-1900, Record Group 127, NARA.

87. For examples of Marine Corps officer lobbying see Henry Clay Cochrane, entries for January 21, 23-25, February 17-18, and March 3, 1899, Cochrane Diary, H. S. Cochrane Papers, MCHC. See also John A. Lejeune letter to Augustine Lejeune, February 19, 1899, Correspondence with A. Lejeune, Reel 1, John A. Lejeune Papers, LC.

88. CMC letters to SecNav, March 3 and June 7, 1899, LSSN, vol. 8, pp. 50 and 434 and SecNav letters to CMC, March 17 and 20, 1899, Letters Received, "N," RG 127, NARA; *Navy Registers*, 1899-1900; "Register of Officers, U.S. Marine Corps," in Collum, *History of the United States Marine Corps*, 430-49; *Army and Navy Journal*, March 11 and June 17, 1899, 699 and 994.

89. CMC letter to SecNav, March 4, 1899, LSSN, vol. 8, pp. 54-59 and Navy Department, "Circular for the Information of Persons Desiring to Enter the U.S. Marine Corps," n.d., Letters Received, Historical Section, RG 127, NARA.

90. Roosevelt letter to Heywood, March 2, 1899, Reel 316, Theodore Roosevelt Papers, LC; Hilary A. Herbert, "Grandfather Talks," MS, 369, Reel 1, Herbert Papers, Southern Historical Collection, University of North Carolina, Chapel Hill, N.C. See also *Navy Registers*, 1899-1900; "Register of Officers, U.S. Marine Corps," in Collum, *History of the United States Marine Corps*, 430-49.

91. Capt. C. H. Stockton letters to CMC, April 21 and 30 and May 24, 1900, Letters Received, "N," RG 127, NARA; Lt. Col. B. R. Russell letter to CMC, September 23, 1901, Letters Received, Historical Section, RG 127, NARA.

92. CMC, *Annual Report, 1899*, 13-17, and *Annual Report, 1900*, 17-28.

93. CMC letter to SecNav, May 25, 1899, vol. 8, LSSN, p. 402, RG 127, NARA; Navy General Board memo, May 29, 1915, Subj: "Review of the Naval Advanced Base," GB File 408; Proceedings of the General Board, April 17, June 27 and 29, and August 31, 1900, vol. 1, Proceedings of the General Board, 1900-1904; Adm. Dewey, President of the General Board letter to SecNav, October 6, 1900, and CMC letter to Dewey, November 22, 1900, GB File 408-2, Records of the General Board, OAB, NHD.

94. "Memorandum in Relation to the United States Marine Corps" attached to CMC letter to Representative George E. Foss, February 26, 1900, reprinted in U.S. Congress, House, Committee on Naval Affairs, *Hearings on Appropriation Bill Subjects*, 1900, 56th Cong., 1st sess., 1900.

CHAPTER 10. CONCLUSION

1. For the discussion of professional jurisdiction and its relationship to other concepts and theories of professionalism see the discussion in sections 2 and 3 of the introduction. See also Andrew Abbott, "Perspectives on Professionalism," (Paper delivered at the annual meeting of the Organization of American Historians, May 1985), 2–3, 10, 12–15, and Andrew Abbott, *The System of Professions: An Essay on the Division of Expert Labor* (Chicago, 1988), 2–3, 8–9, 18–20, 59, 69, 86–91, 318, 320–21.

2. Jack Shulimson and Graham A. Cosmas, "Teddy Roosevelt and the Corps Sea-Going Mission," *Marine Corps Gazette* (November 1981): 54–61.

3. Graham A. Cosmas and Jack Shulimson, "Continuity and Consensus: The Evolution of the Marine Advance Base Force, 1900–1922," in David H. White and John W. Gordon, eds., *Proceedings of the Citadel Conference on War and Diplomacy, 1977* (Charleston, SC, 1979), 31–36.

BIBLIOGRAPHY

BOOKS

Primary Works

Aldrich, M. Almy. *History of the United States Marine Corps*. Boston, 1875.
Ammen, Daniel. *The Old Navy and the New*. Philadelphia, 1891.
Chadwick, French Ensor. *The Relations of the United States and Spain: The Spanish American War*, 2 vols. New York, 1911, reissued in 1968.
Class of 1881, U.S. Naval Academy. *Second Annual Report*. Butler, PA, 1886.
————. *Fourth Annual Report*. Washington, DC, 1888.
————. "Fifth Annual Report." In *Annual Reports*. Annapolis, 1886–1890.
————. "Sixth Annual Report." In *Annual Reports*. Annapolis, 1886–1890.
————. *Report of 1891*. Annapolis, MD, 1891.
Collum, Richard S. *History of the United States Marine Corps*. New York, 1903.
Evans, Robley D. *A Sailor's Log: Recollections of Forty Years of Naval Life*. New York, 1901.
Fiske, Bradley, A. *From Midshipman to Rear-Admiral*. New York, 1919.
Gleaves, Albert. *The Life and Letters of Rear Admiral Stephen B. Luce*. New York, 1925.
Hamersly, Lewis R. *The Records of Living Officers of the U.S. Navy and Marine Corps*. Philadelphia, 4th ed., 1890.
Information in Regard to the United States Marine Corps. Washington, DC, 1875.
Lejeune, John A. *The Reminiscences of A Marine*. Philadelphia, 1930.
Letters from Naval Officers in Reference to the U.S. Marine Corps. Washington, DC, 1864.
Long, John D. *The New American Navy*. 2 vols. New York, 1903.
Maguire, Doris D., ed. *French Ensor Chadwick: Selected Letters and Papers*. Washington, DC, 1981.
Mahan, Alfred Thayer. *From Sail to Steam: Recollections of a Naval Life*. New York and London, 1907.
————. *The Influence of Sea Power upon History, 1660–1783*. Boston, 1890.
Michie, Peter S. *The Life and Letters of Emory Upton, Colonel of the Fourth Regiment and Brevet Major General, U.S. Army*. New York, 1885.
Morison, Elting E., ed. *The Letters of Theodore Roosevelt*. 8 vols. Cambridge, MA, 1951–54. V. 1.
Schley, Winfield S. *Forty-Five Years under the Flag*. New York, 1904.
Schofield, John M. *Forty-Six Years in the Army*. New York, 1897.

Seager, Robert, II, and Doris D. Maguire, eds. *Letters and Papers of Alfred Thayer Mahan, 1847–1914*. 2 vols. Annapolis, 1975.

Wise, Frederic M. and Meigs O. Frost. *A Marine Tells It to You*. New York, 1929.

Secondary Sources

Abbott, Andrew. *The System of Professions, An Essay on the Division of Expert Labor*. Chicago, 1988.

Abrahamson, James L. *America Arms for a New Century: The Making of a Great Military Power*. New York, 1981.

Abrahamsson, Bengt. *Military Professionalism and Political Power*. Beverly Hills, CA, 1972.

Albion, Robert G. *Makers of Naval Policy, 1798–1947*. Ed. Rowena Reed. Annapolis, 1980.

Alden, John D. *The American Steel Navy*. Annapolis, 1972.

Allison, Graham. *Essence of Decision, Explaining the Cuban Missile Crisis*. Boston, 1977.

Ambrose, Stephen E. *Duty, Honor, Country: A History of West Point*. Baltimore, 1966.

———. *Upton and the Army*. Baton Rouge, 1964.

Ambrose, Stephen E., ed. *Institutions in Modern America: Innovation in Structure and Process*. Baltimore, 1967.

Ambrose, Stephen E., and James A. Barber, eds. *The Military and American Society: Essays and Readings*, New York, 1972.

Baltzell, E. Digby. *Philadelphia Gentlemen: The Making of a National Upper Class*. Glencoe, IL, 1958.

Bates, Ralph S. *Scientific Societies in the United States*. Cambridge, MA, 1965.

Bledstein, Burton. *The Culture of Professionalism, The Middle Class and the Development of Higher Education in America*. New York, 1976.

Boulding, Kenneth E. *The Organizational Revolution: A Study in the Ethics of Economic Organization*. Chicago, 1968.

Bradford, Richard H. *The Virginius Affair*. Boulder, CO, 1980.

Braisted, William R. *The U.S. Navy in the Pacific, 1897–1909*. Austin, TX, 1958.

Campbell, Charles S. *The Transformation of American Foreign Relations, 1865–1900*. New York, 1977.

Carr-Saunders, A. P., and P. A. Wilson. *The Professions*. Oxford, 1933.

Chandler, Alfred D., Jr. *The Visible Hand: The Managerial Revolution in American Business*. Cambridge, MA, 1977.

Clinard, Outten J. *Japan's Influence on American Naval Power, 1897–1917*. Berkeley and Los Angeles, 1947.

Coffman, Edward M. *The Old Army: A Portrait of the American Army in Peacetime, 1784–1898*, New York and Oxford, 1986.

Cooling, Benjamin F. *Benjamin Franklin Tracy: Father of the Modern American Navy*. Hamden, CT, 1973.

Cooper, Jerry M. *The Army and Civil Disorder: Federal Military Intervention in Labor Disputes, 1877–1900*. Westport, CT, 1980.

Cosmas, Graham A. *An Army for Empire: The United States Army in the Spanish-American War*. Columbia, MO, 1971.

Dorwart, Jeffrey. *The Office of Naval Intelligence: The Birth of America's First Intelligence Agency*. Annapolis, 1979.

Elliott, Philip. *The Sociology of the Professions*, New York, 1972.

Foner, Jack D. *The United States Soldier between Two Wars, 1865–1898*. New York, 1970.

Freidson, Eliot. *Professional Powers*. Chicago, 1986.

Geison, Gerald L., ed. *Profession and Professional Idealogies in America*. Chapel Hill, NC, 1983.

―――. *Professions and the French State*. Philadelphia, 1985.

Goldberg, Joyce S. *The Baltimore Affair*. Lincoln, NE, 1986.

Grenville, John A. S., and George B. Young. *Politics, Strategy, and American Diplomacy: Studies in American Foreign Policy, 1873–1917*. New Haven, CT, 1966.

Hagan, Kenneth J. *American Gunboat Diplomacy*. Westport, CT, 1973.

Hall, Richard H., ed. *The Formal Organization*. New York, 1972.

Hammett, Hugh B. *Hilary Abner Herbert: A Southerner Returns to the Union*. Philadelphia, 1976.

Haskell, Thomas. *The Emergence of Professional Social Science: The American Social Science Association and the Nineteenth-Century Crisis of Authority*. Urbana, IL, 1977.

Haskell, Thomas L., ed. *The Authority of Experts*, Bloomington, IN, 1984.

Healy, David F. *The United States in Cuba, 1898–1902—Generals, Politicians, and the Search for Policy*. Madison, WI, 1963.

Heinl, Robert D. *Soldiers of the Sea: The U.S. Marine Corps, 1775–1962*. Annapolis, 1962.

Herrick, Walter R. *The American Naval Revolution*. Baton Rouge, 1966.

Hirsch, Mark D. *William C. Whitney, Modern Warwick*. New York, 1948

Hughes, Everett C. *Men and Their Work*, Glencoe, IL, 1958.

Huntington, Samuel B. *The Soldier and the State: The Theory and Politics of Civil Military Relations*. Cambridge, MA, 1957.

Israel, Jerry, ed. *Building the Organizational Society*. New York, 1972.

Janowitz, Morris. *The Military in the Political Development of New Nations: An Essay in Comparative Analysis*. Chicago, 1964.

Janowitz, Morris, and Roger W. Little. *Sociology and the Military Establishment*. 3d ed. Beverly Hills, 1974.

Johnson, Terence J. *Professions and Power*, London, 1972.

Karsten, Peter. *The Naval Aristocracy: The Golden Age of Annapolis and the Emergence of Modern American Navalism*. New York, 1972.

Karsten, Peter, ed. *Soldiers and Society: The Effects of Military Service and War on Americans*. Westport, CT, 1978.

LaFeber, Walter. *The New Empire: An Interpretation of American Expansion, 1860–1898*. Ithaca, NY, 1963.

Laqueur, Walter, and George L. Mosse, eds. *Education and Social Structure in the Twentieth Century*. New York, 1967.

Larsen, Magali Sarfatti. *The Rise of Professionalism: A Sociological Analysis*. Berkeley, 1977.

Leech, Margaret. *In the Days of McKinley*. New York, 1959.

McCullough, David G. *The Path between the Seas: The Creation of the Panama Canal, 1870–1914*. New York, 1977.

Mack, Gerstle. *The Land Divided: A History of the Panama Canal and Other Isthmian Canal Projects*. New York, 1944.

McNeill, William H. *The Pursuit of Power: Technology, Armed Force, and Society since A.D. 1000*. Chicago, 1982.

Metcalf, Clyde H. *A History of the Marine Corps*. New York, 1939.

Millerson, Geoffrey. *The Qualifying Associations: A Study in Professionalization*. London, 1964.

Millett, Allan R. *The American Political System and Civilian Control of the Military: A Historical Perspective*. Columbus, OH, 1979.

―――. *Military Professionalism and Officership in America*. Columbus, OH, 1977.

―――. *Semper Fidelis, The History of the United States Marine Corps*. New York, 1980.

Millett, Allan R., and Peter Maslowski. *For the Common Defense: A Military History of the United States of America*. New York, 1984.

Millis, Walter. *Arms and Men.* New York, 1958.

Morgan, H. Wayne. *From Hayes to McKinley: National Party Politics, 1877–1896.* Syracuse, NY, 1969.

_____. *William McKinley and His America.* Syracuse, NY, 1963.

Nalty, Bernard C. *The United States Marines in the War with Spain.* Rev. ed. Washington, DC, 1967.

Nelson, William E. *The Roots of American Bureaucracy, 1830–1900.* Cambridge, MA, 1982.

Nenninger, Timothy K. *The Leavenworth Schools and the Old Army.* Westport, CT, 1978.

Paret, Peter, ed. *Makers of Modern Strategy: From Machiavelli to the Nuclear Age.* Princeton, NJ, 1986.

Parks, E. Taylor. *Colombia and the United States, 1765–1934.* Durham, NC, 1935.

Paullin, Charles O. *Paullin's History of Naval Administration, 1775–1911.* Annapolis, 1968.

Peake, Cyrus H. *Nationalism and Education in Modern China.* New York, 1932.

Plesur, Milton. *America's Outward Thrust: Approaches to Foreign Affairs, 1865–1890.* DeKalb, IL, 1971.

Pletcher, David M. *The Awkward Years: American Foreign Relations under Garfield and Arthur.* Columbia, MO, 1962.

Preston, Richard A. *The Defence of the Undefended Border: Planning for War in North America, 1867–1939.* Montreal, 1977.

Reardon, Carol. *Soldiers and Scholars: The U.S. Army and the Uses of Military History, 1865–1920.* Lawrence, KS, 1990.

Ropp, Theodore. *War in the Modern World.* Rev. ed. New York, 1962.

Sarkesian, Sam C. *Beyond the Battlefield: The New Military Professionalism.* New York, 1981.

Schmidt, Hans. *Maverick Marine: General Smedley D. Butler and the Contradictions of American Military History.* Lexington, KY, 1987.

Schuon, Karl. *Home of the Commandants.* New and rev. ed., Quantico, VA, 1974.

Seager, Robert, II. *Alfred Thayer Mahan.* Annapolis, 1977.

Spector, Ronald H. *Admiral of the New Empire: The Life and Career of George Dewey.* Baton Rouge, 1975.

_____. *Professors of War: The Naval War College and the Development of the Naval Profession.* Newport, RI, 1977.

Sprout, Harold and Margaret. *The Rise of American Naval Power, 1776–1918.* Princeton, NJ, 1946.

Stallman, R. W., and E. R. Hagemann, eds. *The War Despatches of Stephen Crane.* New York, 1964.

Sweetman, Jack. *The U.S. Naval Academy: An Illustrated History.* Annapolis, 1979.

Trask, David F. *The War with Spain in 1898: The MacMillan Wars of the United States.* New York, 1981.

Van Alstyne, Richard W. *The Rising American Empire,* New York, 1966.

Van Creveld, Martin. *The Training of Officers: From Military Professionalism to Irrelevance.* New York, 1990.

Volmer, Howard M., and Donald L. Mills, eds. *Professionalization.* Englewood Cliffs, NJ, 1966.

Weber, Max. *The Theory of Social and Economic Organization.* Translated from the German by A. R. Henderson and Talcott Parsons. New York, 1947.

Weigley, Russell F. *The Age of Battles: The Quest for Decisive Warfare from Breitenfeld to Waterloo,* Bloomington, IN, 1991.

_____. *The American Way of War: A History of United States Military Strategy and Policy.* New York, 1973.

_____. *History of the U.S. Army.* New York, 1967.

White, Leonard D. *The Republican Era: A Study in Administrative History, 1861–1901.* New York, 1958.

Wiebe, Robert H. *The Search for Order.* New York, 1967.

Winter, Michael F. *The Culture and Control of Expertise.* New York, 1988.

ARTICLES AND ESSAYS

Primary Sources

Army and Navy Journal, 1873–1900.

Brown, Allan D. "Naval Education." *U.S. Naval Institute Proceedings* 5 (1879): 305–21.

Calkins, Carlos G., "How May the Sphere of Usefulness Be Extended in Time of Peace with Advantages to the Country and the Naval Service." *U.S. Naval Institute Proceedings* 9 (1883): 155–94.

————. "What Changes in Organization and Drill Are Necessary to Sail and Fight Effectively Our War Ships of Latest Type." *U.S. Naval Institute Proceedings* 12 (1886): 269–316.

Cochrane, H. C. "The Naval Brigade and the Marine Battalions in the Labor Strikes of 1877." Pt. 1. *United Service.* (Jan. 1879): 115–29; pt. 2, *United Service* (Oct. 1879): 617–25.

Collum, Richard S. "Our Marines in the Levant." *United Service* (Oct. 1882): 358–61.

"Colonel Charles Heywood." *United Service* (Apr. 1890): 455–56.

Forney, James. "The Marines." *United Service* (Apr. 1889): 89–95.

Foxhall, Parker, A. "Our Fleet Maneuvers in the Bay of Florida and the Navy of the Future." *U.S. Naval Institute Proceedings* 1 (Dec. 1874): 163–78.

Fullam, William F. "The Organization, Training, and Discipline of the Navy Personnel as Viewed from the Ship." *U.S. Naval Institute Proceedings,* 22 (1896): 83–116.

————. "The Systems of Naval Training and Discipline Required to Promote Efficiency and Attract Americans." *U.S. Naval Institute Proceedings* 16 (1890): 473–95.

Goodrich, C. F. "Naval Education." *U.S. Naval Institute Proceedings* 5 (1879): 323–44.

Hutchins, C. T. "The Naval Brigade, Its Organization, Equipment, and Tactics." *U.S. Naval Institute Proceedings* 13 (1887): 303–40.

Livermore, William R. "Military and Naval Maneuvers." *Journal of the Military Service Institute of the U.S.* (Dec. 1888), 411–28.

Lowry, H. B. "The United States Marine Corps Considered as a Distinct Military Organization." *Journal of the Military Service Institutes of the U.S.* (May 1895): 523–29.

Luce, Stephen B. "Naval Administration." *U.S. Naval Institute Proceedings,* 14 (1888): 561–88.

————. "Naval Training." *U.S. Naval Institute Proceedings,* 16, (1890): 367–96.

————. "Our Future Navy." *U.S. Naval Institute Proceedings,* 15 (1889): 541–52.

McAdoo, William. "Naval War College." *U.S. Naval Institute Proceedings,* 22 (1896): 429–45.

————. "Reorganization of the Personnel of the Navy." *The North American Review* (Oct. 1894): 457–66.

Mason, T. B. M. "On the Employment of Boat Guns as Light Artillery for Landing Parties." *U.S. Naval Institute Proceedings,* 5 (1879): 207–23.

Mason, Theodorus B. M. "The United States Naval Institute." *The United Service* (April 1879): 290–96.

New York Times. 1877–1900.

Niblack, A. P. "The Enlistment, Training, and Organization of Crews for Our New Ships." *U.S. Naval Institute Proceedings,* 17, no. 1 (1891): 3–49.

Porter, D. D. "Naval Education and Organization." *The United Service* (July 1879): 470–86.

Rogers, William L. "Notes on the Naval Brigade." *U.S. Naval Institute Proceedings*, 14 (1888): 57–96.

Sampson, W. T. "Outline of a Scheme for the Naval Defense of the Coast." *U.S. Naval Institute Proceedings*, 15 (1889): 170–232.

Soley, John C. "The Naval Brigade." *U.S Naval Institute Proceedings*, 6 (1880): 271–90.

Taylor, H. C. "The Fleet." *U.S. Naval Institute Proceedings*, 29 (1903): 797–807.

———. "Naval War College." *U.S. Naval Institute Proceedings*, 22 (1896): 199–208.

Todd, C. C. "The Personnel of our Ships' Companies." *The United Service* (March 1882): 257–63.

Truxton, W. T. "Reform in the Navy." *The United Service.* (July 1879): 378–82.

Wainwright, Richard. "Modern Naval Education." *The United Service* (January 1890): 11–21.

———. "Our Naval Power." *U.S. Naval Institute Proceedings*, 24 (1898): 39–87.

Wallach, Richard. "The War in the East" *U.S. Naval Institute Proceedings*, 21 (1895): 691–740.

Wilson, J. C. "Suggestions on the Reorganization of the Personnel of the Navy, Pt. II." *United Service* (July 1891): 28–40.

Secondary Sources

Barber, Bernard. "Some Problems in the Sociology of the Professions." *Daedalus.* Fall 1963, 669–88.

Becker, Howard S. "The Nature of a Profession," in Becker, *Sociological Work.* Chicago, 1970, 87–103.

Cosmas, Graham A., and Jack Shulimson. "Continuity and Consensus: The Evolution of the Marine Advance Base Force, 1900–1922." In *Proceedings of the Citadel Conference on War and Diplomacy, 1977*, ed. David H. White and John W. Gordon. Charleston, SC, 1979, 31–36

Crowl, Philip A. "Alfred Thayer Mahan: The Naval Historian." In *Makers of Modern Strategy, from Machiavelli to the Nuclear Age*, ed. Peter Paret. Princeton, NJ, 1986, 444–77.

Davis, Allen F. "The Politics of American Studies." *American Quarterly* (Sept. 1990): 353–74.

Gates, John M. "The Alleged Isolation of U.S. Army Officers in the late 19th Century." *Parameters: Journal of the U.S. Army War College* (Sept. 1980): 32–45.

———. "The 'New' Military Professionalism." *Armed Forces and Society.* (Spring 1985): 427–36.

Goode, Thomas H. "Southern Congressmen and the American Naval Revolution, 1880–98." *Alabama Historical Quarterly* (Fall and Winter 1968): 89–110.

Goode, W. J. "The Theoretical Limits of Professionalization." In *The Semi-professions and Their Organization*, by A. Etzioni. New York, 1969: 266–313.

Greenwood, Ernest. "Attributes of a Profession." *Social Work* (July 1957): 45–55.

Grenville, J. A. S. "American Naval Preparations for War with Spain, 1896–98." *Journal of American Studies* (Apr. 1968): 33–47.

Haskell, Thomas L. "Power to the Experts." *The New York Review of Books* (Oct. 13, 1977): 28–33.

Hofstadter, Richard. "Manifest Destiny and the Philippines." In *America in Crisis*, ed. Daniel Aaron. New York, 1952: 173–200.

Karsten, Peter. "Armed Progressives: The Military Reorganized for the American Century." In *Building the Organizational Society*, ed. Jerry Israel. New York, 1972: 197–232.

Millerson, Geoffrey. "Dilemmas of Professionalization." *New Society* (June 1964): 15–16.

Millett, Allan R. "Professional Military Education and Marine Officers." *Marine Corps Gazette* (Nov. 1988), 45–56.

Parsons, Talcott. "Professions." In *International Encyclopedia of the Social Sciences*, ed. David L. Sills, vol. 12. New York, 1968: 536–47.

Reisinger, H. C. "On the Isthmus, 1885." *Marine Corps Gazette* (Dec. 1928): 220–37.

Russell, William H. "The Genesis of Fleet Marine Force Doctrine: 1879–1899." *Marine Corps Gazette* (Apr.-July 1951).

Sarkesian, Sam C. "Moral and Ethical Foundations of Military Professionalism." In *Military Ethics and Professionalism: A Collection of Essays*, ed. James Brown and Michael J. Collins. Washington, D.C., 1981: 1–22.

Scott, Donald M. "Public Lecturing." In *Profession and Professional Ideologies in America*, ed. Gerald L. Geison. Chapel Hill, NC, 1983: 12–28.

Seager, Robert, II. "Ten Years before Mahan: The Unofficial Case for the New Navy, 1880–90." *The Mississippi Valley Historical Review* (June 1953): 491–512.

Shulimson, Jack. "U.S. Marines in Panama, 1885." In *Assault from the Sea, Essays on the History of Amphibious Warfare*, ed. Lt. Col. Merrill L. Bartlett, USMC (Ret.). Annapolis, 1983: 107–20.

Skelton, William B. "Professionalization in the U.S. Army Officer Corps during the Age of Jackson." *Armed Forces and Society* (Aug. 1975): 443–71.

Wicks, Daniel H. "The First Cruise of the Squadron of Evolution." *Military Affairs* (Apr. 1980): 64–69.

Wilensky, Harold L. "The Professionalization of Everyone?" *The American Journal of Sociology* (Sept. 1964): 137–58.

GOVERNMENT DOCUMENTS

Appendix to the Report of the Chief of the Bureau of Navigation. Secretary of the Navy, *Annual Report, 1898*, vol. 2.

Bainbridge-Hoff, William. *Examples, Conclusions, and Maxims of Modern Naval Tactics.* Office of Naval Intelligence. *Information from Abroad*, General Information Series. Washington, DC, 1884.

Beehler, W. H. "Naval Manoeuvres, 1887." In Office of Naval Intelligence. *Information from Abroad: Naval Reserves, Training, and Material*. General Information Series no. 7. Washington, DC, 1888, 122–78

Commandant of the Marine Corps. *Annual Reports*, 1873–1900.

Commander J., German Navy. *Sketches from the Spanish-American War*. Office of Naval Intelligence, War Notes nos. 3 and 4, Information from Abroad, Washington, DC, 1899.

Congressional Record, 1876–1900.

Ellicott, John. *Effect of the Gun Fire of the United States Vessels in the Battle of Manila Bay.* May 1, 1898, Office of Naval Intelligence, War Note no. 5. *Information from Abroad.* Washington, DC, 1899.

Gilman, Howard K. *Marines' Manual.* Washington, DC, 1885.

————. *The Naval Brigade and Operations Ashore.* Washington, DC, 1886.

Goodrich, Lt. Cdr. Casper F. *British Operations in Egypt*, Office of Naval Intelligence. *Information from Abroad.* General Information Series. Washington, DC, 1883.

Karmony, Lincoln. "Notes on Small Arms." *Information from Abroad.* Office of Naval Intelligence, General Information Series. Washington, DC, 1894, 155–74.

"The Landing of the Naval Brigade on Gardiner's Island." In Office of Naval Intelligence. *Papers on Naval Operations during the Year ending July 1885: Information from Abroad.* General Information Series no. 4. Washington, DC, 1885, 101–10.

McCalla, Bowman H. "The U.S. Naval Brigade on the Isthmus of Panama." In Office of Naval Intelligence. *Papers on Naval Operations during the Year ending July 1885: Information from Abroad.* General Information Series, no. 4. Washington, DC, 1885, 41–100.

Navy and Marine Corps Orders, 1877–1903. Library Rare Book Collection, Marine Corps Historical Section.

Navy and Marine Registers, 1876–1900.

Rogers, Charles C. "The Coast Defense Systems of Europe." Office of Naval Intelligence, General Information Series no. 1, *Information from Abroad.* Washington, DC, July 1891, 339–83.

Sears, Lt. James H., and Ens. B. W. Wells, Jr. *The Chilean Revolution of 1891.* Office of Naval Intelligence, War Series no. 4, *Information from Abroad.* Washington, DC, 1893.

Secretary of the Navy. *Annual Reports,* 1873–1900.

U.S. Congress. House. *Estimates of Appropriation.* 55th Cong., 2d sess, 1898. H. Rept. 478.

―――. *Personnel of the Navy.* 52d Cong., 2d sess., 1892. H. Misc. Doc. 38.

―――. *Proceedings at Alexandria, Egypt.* 47th Cong., 1st sess., 1882. H. Misc. Doc. 46.

―――. *Promotions in the Marine Corps.* 52d Cong., 2d sess., May 27, 1892. H. Rept. 1502.

―――. *Reorganization of Naval Personnel: H.R. 10403, with Accompanying Report.* 55th Cong., 2d sess, 1898. H. Rept. 1375.

U.S. Congress. House. Committee on Naval Affairs. *Appointments and Promotions in the Marine Corps.* 46th Cong., 3d sess., February 1881. H. Rept. 314.

―――. *Appropriations for the Naval Service.* 54th Cong., 1st sess., Mar. 24, 1896. H. Rept. 904.

―――. *General Board Hearings.* 58th Cong., 2d sess., Apr. 1904.

―――. *Hearings before House Naval Affairs Committee.* 44th Cong., 1st sess., 1876.

―――. *Hearings on Appropriation Bill Subjects, 1900.* 56th Cong., 1st sess., 1900.

―――. *Marine Corps,* 39th Cong., 2d sess., 1866. H. Rept. 22.

―――. *Personnel of the Navy.* 53d Cong., 3d sess., 1895. H. Rept. 1573.

U.S. Congress. Senate. *Organizations among Naval Officers.* 51st Cong., 1st sess., Mar. 15, 1890. S. Ex. Doc. 86.

―――. *Report of a Board upon . . . Officer Stagnation.* 53d Cong., 2d sess., Sept. 26, 1894–95. S. Misc. Doc. 98.

―――. *Statement to Accompany Bill to Reorganize and Increase the Efficiency of the Personnel of the Navy.* 53d Cong., 2d sess., Feb. 7, 1894. S. Misc. Doc. 76.

―――. *Use by United States of Military Force in Internal Affairs of Colombia.* 58th Cong., 2d sess, 1904. S. Doc. 143.

U.S. Congress. Senate. Committee on Appropriations. *Appropriation Report.* 54th Cong., 1st sess., Apr. 9, 1896. S. Rept. 652.

U.S. Congress. Senate. Committee on Naval Affairs. *Appointments and Promotions in the Marine Corps,* 46th Cong., 3d sess., January 1881, S. Rept. 762.

―――. *Appointments and Promotions in the Marine Corps,* 47th Cong., 1st sess., December 1881, S. Rept. 15.

―――. *Appropriations for the Naval Service.* 50th Cong., 2d sess., 1889. S. Rept. 2430.

―――. *To Equalize the Grades of Officers of the Marine Corps: S. Rept. 931 to Accompany Bill S. 2049.* 50th Cong., 1st sess., 1888.

Witzel, H. M., and L. Karmony. "Preliminary Notes on the Japan China War." *Information from Abroad.* Office of Naval Intelligence, General Information Series. Washington, DC, 1895, 215–34.

UNPUBLISHED WORKS

Abbott, Andrew. "Perspectives on Professionalization." Paper delivered at annual meeting of the Organization of American Historians, May 1985.

Allin, Lawrence C. "The United States Naval Institute: Intellectual Forum of the New Navy." Ph.D. dissertation, University of Maine, 1976.

Barnett, George. "Soldier and Sailor Too." Manuscript, n.d.

Bartlett, Merrill A. "Cadet Midshipman Barnett." Manuscript, n.d.

―――――. "Naval Cadet Lejeune." Manuscript, n.d.

―――――. "The Road to the Commandancy, 1890–1920." Manuscript, n.d.

Beaver, Daniel. "The American Military and the 'New' Institutional History." Paper delivered at the annual meeting of the Organization of American Historians, May 1985.

Denny, F. L. "Scrapbook." Library Rare Book Collection, Marine Corps Historical Center.

Herbert, Hilary A. "Grandfather's Talks about His Life under Two Flags." Manuscript in Hilary A. Herbert Papers, Southern Historical Collection, University of North Carolina Library, Chapel Hill, NC.

Jackson, Cmdr. R. H. "History of Advanced Base." May 15, 1913. Navy General Board Records, File 408.

McCalla, Bowman H. "Memoirs of a Naval Career." Manuscript, Navy Library, Naval Historical Center.

McCawley, Charles L. "The Marines at Guantanamo." Manuscript, n.d., in Charles L. McCawley Papers, Marine Corps Center.

Mannix, Daniel Pratt, Jr. "Hewers of Wood." Manuscript, n.d., in Daniel Pratt Mannix Papers, Marine Corps Historical Center.

Metcalf, Clyde. "The Naval Expedition to the Isthmus of Panama." Manuscript, Geographic Files, Reference Section, Marine Corps Historical Center.

Moore, Jamie W. "National Security in the American Army's Definition of Mission, 1865–1914." Manuscript, Sept. 1981. Paper read at 1982 meeting of the American Military Institute.

Nenninger, Timothy K. "The Fort Leavenworth Schools: Post Graduate Military Education and Professionalization in the U.S. Army, 1880–1920." Ph.D. dissertation, University of Wisconsin, 1974.

Reardon, Carol Ann. "The Study of Military History and the Growth of Professionalism in the U.S. Army before World War I." Ph.D. dissertation, University of Kentucky, 1987.

Remey, Charles Mason. "The Remey Family of the United States of America, 1654–1957." Typescript, 1957. Copy in Library of Congress.

―――――. "Reminiscence of Colonel William Butler Remey United States Marine Corps and Lieutenant Commander Edward Wallace Remey, United States Navy." Typescript, 1955. Copy in Library of Congress.

Sexton, Donal J. "Forging the Sword: Congress and the American Naval Renaissance, 1880–1890" Ph.D. dissertation, University of Tennessee, 1976.

Simon, Joe A. "The Life and Career of General John Archer Lejeune." MA thesis, Louisiana State University, 1967.

Spector, Ronald H. "Professors of War: The American Naval War College and the Modern American Navy." Ph.D. dissertation, Yale University, 1969.

Walkup, Capt. Homer A., JAGC, USN. "A Summary History of the Office of the Judge Advocate General of the Navy." Judge Advocate General Anniversary Ball Souvenir Program, 1980.

Wicks, Daniel H. "Dress Rehearsal: United States Intervention on the Isthmus of Panama, 1885." Manuscript.

————. "New Navy and New Empire: The Life and Times of John Grimes Walker." Ph.D. dissertation, University of California, 1979.

MANUSCRIPT AND RECORD COLLECTIONS

George Barnett Papers. Marine Corps Historical Center.

John L. Broome Papers. Marine Corps Historical Center.

William Chandler Papers. Manuscript Division, Library of Congress.

W. C. Church Papers. Manuscript Division, Library of Congress.

Henry Clay Cochrane Papers. Marine Corps Historical Center.

Department of the Navy General Records. Record Group 80.

George Dewey Papers. Manuscript Division, Library of Congress.

William F. Fullam Papers. Manuscript Division, Library of Congress.

Hilary A. Herbert Papers. Southern Historical Collection. University of North Carolina Library, Chapel Hill, NC.

Robert W. Huntington Papers. Marine Corps Historical Center.

Stephen B. Luce Papers. Manuscript Division, Library of Congress.

Charles L. McCawley Papers. Marine Corps Historical Center.

Daniel Pratt Mannix Papers. Marine Corps Historical Center.

George W. Melville Papers. Manuscript Division, Library of Congress.

William H. Moody Papers. Manuscript Division, Library of Congress.

Naval and Marine Examining Boards Proceedings, 1890–1941. Entry 62, Records of the Navy Judge Advocate General, Record Group 125.

Office of Naval Records and Library Naval Records Collection. Record Group 45.

Navy General Board Records. National Archives (formerly in the Operational Archives Branch, Naval Historical Division).

Joseph H. Pendleton Papers. Marine Corps Historical Center.

David D. Porter Papers. Manuscript Division, Library of Congress.

Remey Family Papers. Manuscript Division, Library of Congress.

Theodore Roosevelt Papers. Manuscript Division, Library of Congress.

Robert W. Shufeldt Papers. Manuscript Division, Library of Congress.

H. C. Taylor Papers. Manuscript Division, Library of Congress.

Benjamin Franklin Tracy Papers. Manuscript Division, Library of Congress.

U.S. Marine Corps Records. Record Group 127.

U.S. Naval Academy Records. Candidates for Admission, 1876–1900, Record Group 405.

U.S. Naval War College Naval Historical Foundation Collection. Miscellaneous. Manuscript Division, Library of Congress.

John G. Walker Papers. Manuscript Division, Library of Congress.

Littleton W. T. Waller Papers. Marine Corps Historical Center.

Thomas N. Wood Papers. Manuscript Division, Library of Congress.

INDEX